RICH STATE, POOR STATE

Why Some Countries Succeed and Others Fail

GREG MILLS

PENGUIN BOOKS

Rich State, Poor State

Published by Penguin Books
an imprint of Penguin Random House South Africa (Pty) Ltd
Reg. No. 1953/000441/07
The Estuaries No. 4, Oxbow Crescent, Century Avenue, Century City, 7441
PO Box 1144, Cape Town, 8000, South Africa
www.penguinrandomhouse.co.za

First published 2023
Reprinted in 2024 (twice)

3 5 7 9 10 8 6 4

Publication © Penguin Random House 2023
Text © Greg Mills 2023

All rights reserved. No part of this publication may be reproduced, stored in a retrieval system or transmitted, in any form or by any means, electronic, mechanical, photocopying, recording or otherwise, without the prior written permission of the copyright owners.

PUBLISHER: Marlene Fryer
MANAGING EDITOR: Robert Plummer
EDITOR: Bronwen Maynier
PROOFREADER: Dane Wallace
COVER DESIGNER: Ryan Africa
TYPESETTER: Monique van den Berg
INDEXER: Sanet le Roux

Set in 10.5 pt on 14 pt Minion Pro

Printed by *novus print*, a division of Novus Holdings

ISBN 978 1 77639 139 4 (print)
ISBN 978 1 77639 140 0 (ePub)

Contents

Acknowledgements vii
Abbreviations ix

Introduction: Why Leadership and Strategy Matter 1

Africa 29
    Challenges of Diversification 38
    Separating Reasons for Success and Failure 50
    Can a Liberation Movement Reform? 67

Asia 91
    Don't Be a Prisoner of the Past 98
    The Value of Policy Change 115

Europe 131
    Agents of Change 135
    Getting the Politics Right 155
    Division to Integration 172
    A Study in Leadership 191

Latin America 209
    Please Pay for Me, Argentina: The Problem with Politicians 217
    How to Set Reforms in Stone 236

North Africa and the Middle East 257
    Between Iraq and a Hard Place 274
    Have a Good Crisis 284

Conclusion: From Poor State to Rich State 297

Notes 325
Index 355

Acknowledgements

THE origins of this book can be traced back to the inception of The Brenthurst Foundation (www.thebrenthurstfoundation.org) in 2005. From the outset, the Foundation aimed to identify global best policy practice in development and to provide this information to African policy-makers to strengthen the continent's economic performance. Of course, economies don't operate in isolation from political, social and security issues, and this mission drew us inexorably into other areas of study and policy application. It also resulted in more than twenty assignments as a governmental strategic advisor over the past eighteen years in Asia and Africa, during which time many lessons have been learnt as to why things happen, and why they don't, and the art of the possible.

The benefits of being the director of the Foundation arise not just from the diverse research and travel possibilities that have been afforded, but also from the chance to meet and be educated in working with some of the world's brightest minds, in Africa and further afield.

I owe many people a debt of gratitude for this journey.

Nicky and Jonathan Oppenheimer had the idea of the Foundation and have been extraordinary supporters, through thick and thin. Professor Christopher Clapham has remained wise counsel for nearly four decades. Robin Auld, Richard Harper and Bobi Wine have provided both friendship and their musical and photographic talents to make the experience more varied and to draw a different crowd into the debates that have often accompanied the research behind this book. My colleagues at the Foundation, notably Ray Hartley, Ghairoon Hajad, Leila Jack, Mariam Cassoojee, Henry Sands and Richard Morrow, have weathered my many absences from the office and assisted beyond the call of duty. A special word of thanks to Marie-Noelle Nwokolo for her efforts, particularly with this publication. Various diplomatic missions graciously assisted in arranging meetings, including those of Lithuania, Poland, Spain, Comoros and Peru. Stephan Malherbe, Dave Kilcullen, Dickie Davis, Dianna Games, Lyal White, Hulme Scholes, David Horsey, Kate Almquist Knopf, Bugs du Toit, Rod Hagger, former presidents Olusegun Obasanjo and Ernest Bai Koroma, former Colombian minister of defence Juan Carlos Pinzón, and former prime minister Hailemariam Desalegn have all been thoughtful and stimulating – and somewhat tolerant – research and travel companions. And the Penguin Random House team not only enthusiastically responded

ACKNOWLEDGEMENTS

to the initial concept, but under the eagle eye and deft editorial touch of Bronwen Maynier also most efficiently brought the draft to publication.

The burden of all my wanderings has fallen on my family – Janet, Amelia, Beatrix and William, not forgetting Amazon, Freckles, Rover and Jester. They have selflessly never wavered in their support and have encouraged me to pursue my fieldwork and write this book. My heartfelt thanks go to them.

GJBM
JOHANNESBURG, JULY 2023

Abbreviations

ACP: African, Caribbean and Pacific
AI: artificial intelligence
ANC: African National Congress
APRA: American Popular Revolutionary Alliance
ASEAN: Association of Southeast Asian Nations
BEAC: Business and Economic Advisory Council
BSS: business services sector
BVC: Beach Village Committee
CEO: chief executive officer
CFK: Cristina Fernández de Kirchner
CIA: Central Intelligence Agency
CNC: computer numerical control
CPA: Coalition Provisional Authority
CPF: Central Provident Fund
CSP: concentrated solar power
DA: Democratic Alliance
DRC: Democratic Republic of Congo
DTC: Diamond Trading Company
EEC: European Economic Community
EPZ: export processing zone
EU: European Union
FDI: foreign direct investment
FOZ: Felipe Ortiz de Zevallos
GDP: gross domestic profit
HDB: Housing and Development Board
ICJ: International Court of Justice
ICT: information and communication technology
IDP: Integrated Development Plan
IDZ: industrial development zone
IMF: International Monetary Fund
INEC: Independent National Electoral Commission
IS: Islamic State
KDP: Kurdistan Democratic Party
KGB: Committee for State Security
KPO: knowledge process outsourcing

ABBREVIATIONS

KRG: Kurdistan Regional Government
KRI: Kurdistan Region of the Republic of Iraq
LKY: Lee Kuan Yew
MMM: Mauritian Militant Movement
MP: member of parliament
MRTA: Túpac Amaru Revolutionary Movement
NAFTA: North American Free Trade Agreement
NATO: North Atlantic Treaty Organization
NGO: non-governmental organisation
NKVD: People's Commissariat for Internal Affairs
OECD: Organisation for Economic Co-operation and Development
OMON: Special Purpose Militia Unit
PAP: People's Action Party
PiS: Law and Justice party
POUM: Workers' Party of Marxist Unification
PP: People's Party
PRASA: Passenger Rail Agency of South Africa
PRO: Republican Proposal
PSOE: Spanish Socialist Workers' Party
PUK: Patriotic Union of Kurdistan
PZL: State Aviation Works
PZPR: Polish United Workers' Party
R&D: research and development
SB: Security Service (Poland)
SEZ: special economic zone
SMMEs: small, medium and micro enterprises
SOE: state-owned enterprise
SS: Schutzstaffel
UAE: United Arab Emirates
UCR: Radical Civic Union
UIA: Argentine Industrial Union
UK: United Kingdom
UN: United Nations
URA: Urban Redevelopment Authority
US: United States
USSR: Union of Soviet Socialist Republics
VSIP: Vietnam Singapore Industrial Park

Introduction
Why Leadership and Strategy Matter

POLITICS and its corollary, a failure of leadership and strategy, explain why Africans are half as wealthy today compared to their global peers than they were at independence, why there is a persistent default to economic crisis, and why the appetite to carry out reforms never matches the rhetoric. Politics is where elites compete for power (or hold onto it) and the protection and extraction of rents and preferences. In Africa this occurs in systems where the clientelist political economy ensures the persistence of policies that address short-term popular needs over long-term reforms necessary for economic development.

Elites continue to follow this path because they can, by employing combinations of identity politics and populism, and using external support to barricade their power. They get away with it – most of the time, at least – because they are allowed to by citizens trapped in a system of government that deliberately emasculates and undermines the impact of their vote.

Politics seeps into the fabric and operations of institutions too. Bureaucracies become less a check and balance on executive power than a roadblock to getting things done, at risk of operating in narrow personal and vested interests, subject to incompetencies and job insecurities.

This helps to explain why the cost of Africa's lost economic ground is so vast – and why the upside of getting things right, or at least better, is encouragingly positive.

None of the countries in this volume had any apparent advantages at their moment of independence. So, what has made the difference between Singapore and Swaziland, or Spain and South Africa, or Mauritius and Comoros, to take a comparative African success?

The answer appears to lie not in the technocratic details of reform – since these are comparatively easy to identify and specify – but rather in the choices that leaders and their political networks make. These choices are all about politics and leadership, and the strategies adopted. There is no fixed reason why countries should not reform and recover, even though circumstances – from climate to geography – can make this more difficult. More important is the manner in which governments seek to make changes – their ability to plan, prioritise and implement; ultimately, the way in which leaders back their people.

Good leaders armed with strategic nous and moral integrity can make a difference.

INTRODUCTION

The pianist who changed history

He is old now, having turned ninety in October 2022. He walks with a stoop. But his mind is as razor-sharp as ever.

You would never think the stippled-fawn apartment block in suburban Vilnius housed a former head of state, let alone one that played such a pivotal role in the end of the Soviet empire – no armed guard, no doorplate, no flag flapping, nothing to mark the venue as extraordinary. Having rung the wrong doorbell, we were met by a friendly elderly woman who gathered her coat and boots and ushered us to the correct door. 'It happens all the time,' she laughed.

The apartment was cosy, jumbled with photographs, paintings, books and memorabilia of a long career, clutter that contrasted with the tenant's absence of nostalgia. Hinting at a lifelong pursuit, a grand piano dominated the kitchen-cum-living room.

Vytautas Landsbergis graduated from the Lithuanian State Conservatory in 1955. An author of more than thirty books, his early works focused on the subject of his PhD thesis, Lithuanian composer M.K. Čiurlionis. Landsbergis became a professor at the conservatory in 1979, where he worked until 1990 when his life took a different direction.

On 3 June 1988, a group of mostly artists and intellectuals established Lietuvos Persitvarkymo Sąjūdis (the Lithuanian Reform Movement, known simply as Sąjūdis) as the first opposition party in Soviet Lithuania. Landsbergis was elected to the steering committee and later, at their inaugural conference in October 1988, to the position of chair.

He shrugs when asked why he went into politics. 'It was a normal evolution since we were part of the developments. Freedom was a common idea, an achievable goal,' he says.[1] He is being modest. As the Cold War ended, his leadership would contribute decisively to a bold new direction for his country – and his region, placing it on a trajectory of democracy, human rights, growth and development.

On 6 August 1989, together with other representatives of Lithuania and the diaspora, he signed the Gotland Communiqué on the eponymous Swedish island. The document proclaimed that the 'vital goal' of Lithuanians worldwide was the restoration of an independent Lithuanian state. It was a goal Landsbergis was to oversee.

'We did not consider it a transfer of power from one system to another, but rather a return to our old system,' says Landsbergis, referring to the twenty-two years of independence enjoyed by the three Baltic states – Lithuania, Latvia and Estonia – from 1918 until the Soviet occupation in 1940.

As a pawn between Hitler's and Stalin's versions of totalitarianism, and adjacent to the Baltic Sea port of Königsberg, later renamed Kaliningrad, Lithuania's post-1940 history was especially bloody and violent. 'It was a court of two criminals,' Landsbergis remarks. 'Though supporters of the Soviet Union differentiated between Hitler and Stalin, with Hitler being very bad and Stalin less so, this did not change what had happened to us in 1940, which was totally illegal.'

In 1940, while Germany conducted its military campaign in Western Europe, the Soviets invaded the Baltic states and occupied and annexed Lithuania. A year later, in 1941, the Nazis successfully invaded and took over occupation. The palace on Lukiškės Square in the capital Vilnius became the headquarters of the Gestapo. Some 240 000 Lithuanians were murdered by the Nazi regime, and a further 60 000 deported as slave labourers. By the end of 1944, Lithuania was back in Soviet hands after the Nazis' defeat. After being incorporated into the Soviet system, the Baltics were subjected to 'fake elections, fake parliaments, and fake decisions', says Landsbergis. Opponents of the regime were dealt with harshly. Over 130 000 Lithuanians were deported to the Soviet Union (including Landsbergis's wife and her family, who spent eight years in a Siberian camp), some 28 000 dying in transport and 20 000 to 25 000 more in the camps. Of the 200 000 Lithuanians arrested by Soviet authorities, more than 1 000 political prisoners were murdered in the basement of what was now the NKVD (later KGB) Palace on Lukiškės Square. A further 21 500 Lithuanian partisans (resistance fighters) were killed by the Soviets.

Fifteen per cent of the Lithuanian population was effectively eliminated during the fifty years of Soviet occupation.

The goal of the resistance, according to Landsbergis, was not the break-up of the Soviet Union, and nor were they a separatist movement. 'We wanted to be free of Soviet colonialism, to be free and independent again so that we can make our own choices, not having these made by Moscow,' he explains.

The opportunity came with the changing of the Soviet guard in Moscow. Leonid Brezhnev was succeeded as general secretary of the Communist Party by Yuri Andropov in November 1982, and Andropov by Konstantin Chernenko in February 1984. The music, however, continued playing, until a year later, when Mikhail Gorbachev was elevated to the position of de facto leader of the Soviet Union, after Chernenko's death. Twenty years younger than his predecessors, Gorbachev had already spoken of the need for *perestroika* (or 'reconstruction') of the economy, having realised that the Soviet system was faltering.

Once in the top post, he introduced the idea of *glasnost*, or 'openness'. While simultaneously pursuing reforms at home, Gorbachev focused on lessening global tensions, concluding an arms limitation agreement with United States (US) president Ronald Reagan, improving ties with Beijing, and signalling to Kabul his intention to withdraw from the Soviet's disastrous foray into Afghanistan.

In July 1988, he successfully proposed the creation of a Congress of People's

Deputies of the Soviet Union, whose members (which would include Landsbergis) were to be elected in a largely free vote and who, in turn, would elect members to the Supreme Soviet, the most authoritative legislative body of the Union of Soviet Socialist Republics (USSR).

Abandoning imperialism abroad and improving democracy at home did not mean that Gorbachev wanted to undo the Soviet Union. On the contrary, his actions were designed to keep it together. But this was not Landsbergis's goal. It was just one step on a different path: not to consolidate Soviet rule but to undo it in the Baltics. 'We wanted self-determination, the right to decide what we wanted to be, human rights including the rights of the individual and the nation's rights not to be enslaved, and free elections.'

The 11th of January 1990 proved the turning point, when Gorbachev visited Vilnius to try to convince Landsbergis and others not to push for independence. From the outset, Landsbergis made the Soviet leader's status clear. 'He was welcomed as the great leader of a neighbouring country,' he chuckles.

The spark for the visit was the adoption of a resolution by the Lithuanian Congress of People's Deputies on 24 December 1989 that the occupation of the country was illegal and unlawful, though care was taken 'to make Stalin guilty, not the entire Soviet nation,' recalls Landsbergis. 'My position was to appeal then to Gorbachev to appeal our legal situation. He did not agree, but he could not deny the legal grounds.'

As author Jonathan Steele argues, Gorbachev failed to appreciate why the Baltic nations wanted independence and 'at heart he was ... a Russian imperialist',[2] a man who thought of the Soviet Union as being largely synonymous with Russia.

What was Gorbachev like to do business with? 'He was chosen for the special role of saving the Soviet Union,' says Landsbergis. 'It was bankrupted at all levels and could not survive. Reforms were thought about as the means of preserving their "essence", their borders and the legitimation of their powers in their captured territories.'

Landsbergis describes the Soviet system as one 'where the military, Politburo and the KGB retained power and influence over us. Gorbachev was not a decision-maker as was presented in the West. He was given instructions.' Landsbergis saw the last Soviet leader as a 'prisoner' of the system that promoted him and whose interests he served.

The next month, February, Sąjūdis dominated the first democratic elections in Lithuania since 1926, declaring the country independent from the USSR in March 1990.

Česlovas Juršėnas, a former speaker of the Seimas (the Lithuanian parliament) and one of 124 signatories to the Act on the Re-Establishment of the State of

Lithuania on 11 March 1990, believes that the act of breaking away was as significant as the fall of the Berlin Wall. 'Whereas Gorbachev saw it as an act of self-destruction since we had no natural resources, he had obviously received the wrong information about the depth of the feeling of Lithuanians. Even the most humble factory worker wanted to leave the Soviet Union. I had many disputes with Landsbergis, but not about whether we should be independent; rather about what would be done after it.'

A crackdown in January 1991 saw Soviet troops trying unsuccessfully to take control of key institutions in Vilnius, including the parliament, killing fourteen people and injuring hundreds. It was Lithuania's Tiananmen Square moment.

'I tried to call Gorbachev,' recalls Landsbergis of the time, 'but they said he was sleeping. I got through to [Boris] Yeltsin, and he then immediately called Gorbachev, and Yeltsin said, "Stop these atrocities."' Lithuanians still hold Gorbachev responsible for this final outrage. 'Lithuanians will not glorify Gorbachev,' declared the country's foreign minister, Gabrielius Landsbergis, Vytautas's grandson, on the last Soviet leader's death in August 2022. 'We will never forget the simple fact that his army murdered civilians to prolong his regime's occupation of our country. His soldiers fired on our unarmed protestors and crushed them under his tanks. That is how we will remember him.' Lithuania's defence minister, Arvydas Anušauskas, who in a previous life researched underground resistance to Soviet rule, went one step further, calling Gorbachev 'a criminal'.

It was not just the Soviet leader's reaction that disappointed Lithuanians. Western leaders were similarly reluctant to give support to independence movements within the USSR, walking a line between their fear of the Soviets and upholding the rights of Lithuanians and others. 'The West told us that Moscow had to give us our independence, that the key to our independence lay in Moscow. It's not unlike the situation today in Ukraine,' Landsbergis says. 'The West is supporting Ukraine but not too much. Same as they did for us.' Again, that chuckle.

'Gorbachev used to say to me personally, forget your dreams, you will never have your independence. He wanted to convey that he was the master. But he wasn't. His country was weak and disintegrating.'

And yet Landsbergis had to be cautious. 'We had to make it not about the Soviet Union, but rather about us, about the Baltic states. We did not call for the abolition of the Baltic states or of communism. We just wanted out of that business.'

Gorbachev tried to use the argument that Lithuania was divided, that part of it wanted to stay with the Soviet Union, an echo of the tactics today in Georgia, Ukraine and Moldova. 'Perhaps this was a pretext to use force. But these efforts failed. I asked Gorbachev: "Are you a continuation of Stalin?" He wanted to play a role as a reformer, but you could not reform a system in which we remained prisoners.'

While the dissolution of the Soviet Union may not have been the intention – and it was strategically wise not to seek that objective since it might have raised the stakes to unacceptable limits – it was the outcome. Freedom in the Baltics was the beginning of an expeditious end to the Soviet Union.

An abortive coup by hard-line conservatives in Moscow in August 1991 aimed at curtailing Gorbachev's restructuring provided the political opportunity for the rapid implementation of Baltic independence. Gorbachev swiftly gave way to his bitter opponent Boris Yeltsin, who suspended Communist Party rule the same month. In September the three Baltic states were admitted to the United Nations (UN), once more recognised by their peers as independent nations. 'In the event we went all the way, not for some freedoms, but for everything, total freedom,' says Landsbergis. 'Gorbachev could not be convinced. He was not a free man due to his communist education and the environment which had appointed him. It was not Gorbachev and not Yeltsin who gave us our independence, but the will of a nation striving for liberation in spite of terror, in spite of bloodshed.'

Today Lithuanians are outspoken in their support for Ukraine, and for democracy elsewhere. 'We know only too well the price of foreign domination,' reminds Asta Skaisgirytė, chief advisor to the president of Lithuania.

The overall narrative was about freedom, starting with the independence process itself and culminating in membership of the European Union (EU) and the North Atlantic Treaty Organization (NATO) in 2002. But there were unexpected, key moments along the way, including the bronze medal victory by the Lithuanian basketball team in the 1992 Barcelona Olympics. Sponsored by the American rock band Grateful Dead, and replete in tie-dye team kit featuring a slam-dunking skeleton, the Lithuanians beat the Unified Team, a joint team consisting of twelve of the fifteen former Soviet republics, 82–78. The medal result was part payback to Russia for the fifty years of occupation, by a team 'that fulfilled the dream of a nation'. Several of the star players had won gold with the Soviet team four years earlier. 'Lithuania really won that gold medal in 1988 for the USSR, but its name wasn't there. It was one more untruth that we had to fix,' recalls Landsbergis.[3]

The Soviet period was seen as an aberration, the Lithuanian passage to returning the country to its pre-war state seemingly unstoppable, but not without its challenges. 'In the Soviet Union we were considered an advanced Western, better-developed region,' recalls Andrius Kubilius, the physicist who unwittingly found himself thrust into a political role, serving as Lithuanian prime minister, twice. 'For us, however, we went from being first among our peers to last among the Western camp, from the West to the worst in one step.'

Yet the sage, steadying hand remains. Of these troubled times, when the world seems to be changing rapidly on so many fronts, demanding a continuous reassessment of risk, Landsbergis says: 'As democrats, we must believe we still have choice.' The remedy to today's seemingly increasing distance, especially among young people, from democracy lies not in an obsessive search for popularity, or in partisanship, but rather in good politics and finding the appeal of participation.

Of course, Professor Landsbergis would never, ever claim that he sank the Soviet Union. His modesty is the ultimate mark of a great man who shaped the destiny of not only his nation, but 400 million others in the Eastern bloc.

Good leaders are rare, and they have to work with institutions that don't always share their thinking. There is a premium on leadership, especially where institutions and governance are weak.

Good leaders need good institutions

'You can't share poverty' was the advice clearly given by President Hakainde Hichilema to key members of his cabinet and civil servants as we endeavoured, together, to finalise a large mining investment in Zambia in April 2022.

Hichilema had taken office with the promise of putting right the wrongs of bad policy and corruption under his predecessor, Edgar Lungu. But the end of his first year in office was fast approaching, and there was little to show for the tremendous amount of hard work that had gone into clearing up the fiscal and other messes left behind by the previous incumbent other than the possibility of sealing this multibillion-dollar investment. There was an imperative for growth; and growth required investment; and that, in turn, demanded a predictable (and preferably not hostile) policy and governance environment.

Yet for all the presidential will in the world, critical parts of his government – especially the civil service – went off and did precisely what they wanted, which in some cases was to dig their heels in and run interference on the transaction. This was not because the deal on offer was bad for Zambia; rather, it was the best reset in the investment environment in a generation, at least. It was not because there were better deals on offer; there were not, and something needed to happen to get the wheels of economic growth turning. It was not fraught with issues of governance. To the contrary, it was a deal remarkable for its shared and almost instant benefit to the whole economy, and not just the mining sector.

One can only assume that the reasons for the resistance were either to do with vested institutional interests (the bureaucratic 'Yes, Minister' phenomenon), which tend to intersect with elite rent-seeking control and vested personal financial interests within and outside the bureaucracy, or a default antagonism towards private business notable in a country with a professed socialist background. The latter was especially on display among some members of government who liked to use every occasion to give a little lecture about how the private sector was making money, effectively at the expense of their birthright. It was an attitude that explained why Zambia had struggled for so long, and why it had nationalised its copper industry back in the 1970s, a decision that had cost it some $45 billion in mining income as a result of lost investment and production (its 2020 gross domestic profit, or GDP, was $23 billion).[4] This proved a massive opportunity cost, given that simply keeping the mines open by the 1990s had incurred the government a loss of $1 million per day, a failure amplified by the relative success of Chile, which went from the same production levels as Zambia in 1972 (when the latter's mines were privatised) to ten times more by 2000, by which time Zambia was forced to privatise.

Public reaction to the proposed mining reset fell usually into two categories: silent support or angry blustering about why this was a bad deal for Zambia, with an overwhelming focus on the political rather than legal or commercial aspects. Even a transaction with obvious benefits, negotiated through a give-and-take process, was quickly politicised, with government critics feeding off Zambians' suspicion of their leaders, in part presumably because they had been so badly let down in the colonial and post-colonial eras.

The Chilean contrast to the outcome of Zambia's poor choices and management is even greater when considering the comparative success of some Middle Eastern countries, including Saudi Arabia, the Emirates, Kuwait, Qatar and Bahrain, in buying out foreign interests and then running their own oil facilities. Perhaps it is this failure that has led to the high level of open antipathy towards foreign ownership, and especially towards foreign-owned success in many African environments.

Whatever the case, the civil service filibustered, creating problems where there were none. It would take a tremendous effort to get the investment announcement heaved over the line by deadline; still, the bureaucracy, and some ministers, fought back, slowing the approvals process to a crawl. Treating one of your major foreign investors in this manner is as nonsensically short-sighted as it is churlish. Consequently, even though the deal was announced amid fanfare at the Mining Indaba in Cape Town in 2022, completion of all the related statutory actions stalled no fewer than four times. After enduring a Stalingrad-type, memo-by-memo, line-by-line process of obstruction by the bureaucrats, some of whom used every imaginable tactic to scupper a process in the country's best interests, we eventually got it done in January 2023.

On whose behalf were they acting, you may well ask?

The simple answer is that there are people who profit from change and those who do not. Although Hichilema is a reformer, there seemed to be an endless well of malign actors. Moreover, some of the people who were clearly not acting in the national interest were politically important to the composition of his government and its representivity, a factor that presumably they knew only too well. Contrary to the belief in some quarters that 'what Africa needs is a benign dictator' (forgetting the oxymoronic nature of this construction), this example illustrates that reform cannot be one man (or woman) deep. There is a need to inculcate a spirit of national service over the pursuit of personal financial interests, a spirit sorely lacking on much of the continent, it seems. There also must be clear consequences for mismanagement.

This is not an easy path for a reformer. It requires critical skills, along with the usual dose of vision and leadership. It demands holding people to task, and for everyone down the chain of command to display discipline to the goals. It's the difference between having a government with policies that are, in the words of Daron Acemoglu and James Robinson, inclusive rather than extractive.[5]

But inclusive policies are easier to define than write and action. Why do reforms stick? How must politics and economics align in this regard? How best can the political context and justification for reform be provided, thus allowing reforms in the political space and rationale to proceed? Moreover, what other factors are necessary – such as, for instance, being frank about the terms and duration of delivery, the choice and timing of reforms, and the mix of technocrats? All this seems comparatively difficult in Africa.

But it has been possible, in Africa and elsewhere, as the case studies in this book illustrate in highlighting both successes and failures.

None of these case studies – with the possible exception of Argentina – involve a situation where government enjoyed an easy inheritance. Instead, there is an overwhelming incidence of military juntas, colonial and racially exclusive regimes, difficult neighbourhoods, civil wars and occasional occupations among them. Geography is also not a fundamental determinant of economic failure or success, and neither is size, religion or culture. Smaller states have their disadvantages, but they are generally easier to govern. Rather, it is the choices made by government and its leadership, and the speed of implementation, that determine success or failure.

A million metaphoric miles from Zambia, the 'Baltic Tiger' of Estonia has many excuses for not escaping the suffocating effect of half a century of Soviet occupation. It is small (population: 1.4 million), its geography (on the border with Russia) is tricky, and it has no easily accessed natural resources.

But today Estonia is one of the leaders in e-government, and in reducing the role and footprint of government altogether. Its GDP per capita has risen threefold in the twenty-five years since 1995, to $21 421 by 2021, faster than fellow Baltics Latvia and Lithuania, themselves stellar performers by global standards.[6]

With the collapse of the Soviet Union, choosing a new model was not difficult. There was no choice. The question was how to reform, and reform quickly. Estonia was in a fortunate position – as part of the 'Soviet West' – in having a relatively sophisticated industrial and agro-industry base. But the chosen path of reform was a radical one, led by a youthful government headed by Mart Laar, the thirty-two-year-old history professor who took over as Estonia's prime minister in 1992. A fan of Margaret Thatcher, he says of that time: 'We had a whisky in the cupboard that we agreed not to drink before fulfilling three goals: get Estonia independent, get our own currency, and get the Russian troops out.'

All three were managed in short order. Even though there were 570 Soviet military sites with 35 000 personnel in Estonia, by 31 August 1994 they were gone, but not without some difficult negotiations. Amid rampant inflation, and the loss of around one-third of its GDP between 1991 and 1994, a new currency was instituted in 1992 to gain monetary control.[7] Even though international agencies advised against moving away from the rouble, this too was managed quickly. The creation of a privatisation agency followed, prices were liberalised, monopolies were curtailed, social welfare protections were installed, especially on education and pensions, VAT and a 26 per cent flat income tax were instituted, and the restitution of private property seized during the Soviet era was arranged. Where most Estonians once worked in agriculture, today nearly three-quarters are employed in services, a figure that is set to increase with the automation of most routine and physically demanding jobs in the next twenty-five years.

Although Estonia might not necessarily produce as much today as it did while under Soviet control, fixated as it was on targets and benchmarks, the quality of goods and life has improved beyond measure. It's a smarter, faster, easier, richer society – and a free one.

Around the same time that the Baltics threw off the yoke of fascist Soviet rule, South Africa underwent its own negotiated transition to freedom, from apartheid to democracy. But whereas the Baltics transitioned quickly from a state-centric to a liberal system, South Africa headed in the opposite direction, replacing one racial oligarchy with another, with the state at the centre as the means of redistribution. Aside from making a few (often politically connected) entrepreneurs exceedingly rich, further down the income totem this was effected through civil service jobs and, at the bottom, through welfare payments.

As a consequence, the civil service grew from little over one million in 1994, at the time of the country's first democratic elections, to over three million by

2020, up by 357 000 in the preceding ten years alone.[8] And by 2020, there were 18 million welfare recipients, a figure that increased during the Covid-19 pandemic to 28.3 million.[9] But this was never going to be enough, in at least two respects: the first in terms of the money that could be redistributed to meet expectations, and the second in terms of the corrosive effect on the state itself.

The result was the 'state capture' period suffered under President Jacob Zuma, who took office in 2009, which removed (or simply ignored) governance strictures in handing out contracts, a process that cost the country an estimated R500 billion ($30 billion),[10] or 25 per cent of its annual budget, little of which has to date been recovered. The Judicial Commission of Inquiry into Allegations of State Capture, Corruption and Fraud in the Public Sector (the Zondo Commission) itself cost R1 billion. Institutional erosion and then failure led to a loss of confidence in (and respect for) the state, compounding the effect. The outcomes can be seen in a collapse of basic service delivery, the poor performance of municipalities (just 41 of 257 countrywide received a clean audit in 2021, of which most were run by the opposition),[11] the problems experienced in electricity and water delivery, low levels of growth and investment and a corresponding increase in unemployment, and, most starkly, a radical increase in crime, especially violent crime. South Africa's homicide rate, for instance, fell spectacularly as the politics settled from 64 per 100 000 in 1994 to 29 per 100 000 in 2011, before steadily rising again to over 40 per 100 000 a decade later.[12] Other forms of violent crime, including robbery, rose even more steeply.

There is clearly more to the quality of life than economic growth. But irrespective of where the poverty line is set, economic growth is necessary to ensure no one lives below it. Lower inequality is an important goal, and a political concern, but GDP growth is also necessary to ensure everyone can enjoy a decent standard of living.[13]

Education offers another distressing metric: factoring in the number of dropouts, the effective pass rate of matric (Grade 12) was 51.4 per cent in 2021, and that with a pass mark requirement of just 30 per cent.[14] At the core of this weakness has been the quality of teaching. While teacher graduates fell below replacement rates, just 20 per cent of student teachers achieved more than 50 per cent for maths at school. One study found that Grade 3 teachers struggled to achieve 50 per cent in literacy and mathematics assessments designed for Grade 6 learners.[15]

Yet the education sector consistently commands one-fifth of South Africa's national budget, or 6.6 per cent of GDP, well above the global average of 4.3 per cent.[16]

Such qualitative measurements of the failure or effectiveness of the post-apartheid regime may be disputed given the skewed nature of educational services under apartheid. But on the deterioration in the provision of rail services and electricity, for instance, the metrics are clear. While some in the African National Congress (ANC) may have sought to change the entire governance system in their belief that it only delivered because of its exploitation by one race group, such analysis undermines the value of skills and training so necessary to any system of government. The apartheid inheritance was in several respects both terrible and corrosive, since it planted a seed of failure in terms of the mismatch between human resources and aspirations and fuelled an anger that has proven difficult to dispel.

The education sector has some strong competition, not least in the fate of Eskom, South Africa's electricity parastatal, once ranked in the top ten worldwide in terms of outputs and even higher in terms of efficiencies, but where the losses make state capture look like a sideshow. By the end of 2022, the cost of load-shedding to the economy since 2015, some 383 days, was estimated at R1.2 trillion (or $77 billion), nearly one-fifth of the country's annual economic output.

To turn this situation around without a change from the political party that got South Africa into this state is at best aspirational if its leaders are unwilling to recognise their role and responsibility.

There are dangers in the increasing temptation of authoritarianism, which is not a huge leap in attitude for a liberation movement steeped in communist ideology and a struggle where the ends routinely justified the means, and in a region surrounded by other similarly minded movements, from Angola through Namibia and Zimbabwe to Mozambique and Tanzania, all still firmly ensconced in power since independence. Most have operated less through outright fear and violence than more sophisticated means, a combination of mafia-like economic schemes, control of the media, and weakening of institutions, a careful mixture of 'calibrated coercion' involving the application of some fear along with the distribution of rents, intimidation and propaganda, elaborate ideological schemes and other 'loyalty rituals' from bribery to self-censorship.[17] These methods include the use of offshore banks and institutions to both protect their assets and bribe others to their cause.

Spain under General Francisco Franco offers a different set of lessons, a system of government that was a product of a bloody and brutal civil war, and at least at the outset, based more on fear than favours. But, contrary to the politically correct view that everything about Franco was bad, the reforms of the 1950s are essentially what delivered modern Spain, especially after the International Monetary Fund (IMF) was invited to assist in 1959 and the country opened up to foreign investment and tourism in the 1960s. The trick post-Franco was less to reform than to keep the reforms going in the face of leftist deviation (in a way not dissimilar to Chile's transformation from the military junta of General Augusto Pinochet to the democratic government of, first, Patricio Aylwin in 1990 and since).

The transition of power from General Franco to civilian authority was carefully managed, in part by the role of the king, Juan Carlos I of Spain, but the test came with the election of the socialist government of Felipe González in 1982. Continuity between the past and present was subsequently ensured by membership (in 1986) of the European Union (along with the retention of NATO membership), which reinforced the parameters of government policy through incentives and clear redlines of governance and fiscal transgression.

Power alone is not enough. Once in power, there is a need to act, as the Zambian anecdote illustrates, and to keep innovating to keep moving ahead.

As Singaporean prime minister Lee Hsien Loong says, the drive for competitiveness is 'a marathon without a finish line'. His country has responded to this challenge by continuously reforming, through labour-intensive manufacturing, for instance, in the 1960s, which was coupled with a government plan for housing (giving all a stake in the system) and education (enabling continuous improvement), through creating a service economy to its focus today on green growth. As British prime minister Margaret Thatcher noted about the island state: 'Talent, initiative, endeavour, risk, confidence, vigour have made Singapore an example to other nations of success – an example whose clear message is that you can't enjoy the fruits of effort without first making the effort.'

Even though Lee Kuan Yew, or 'LKY' as the first prime minister and head of the team that put Singapore on the growth path is known, had a reputation for uncompromising leadership, the administrative approach has been at least as bottom-up as top-down, where incentives have played a critical role in performance. 'This required an effective civil service,' observes Barry Desker, who has served in a variety of senior roles in business and government in Singapore, 'which has underpinned whatever has been attempted by LKY and his political colleagues, to create the conditions that allow talent to rise, properly paid and not needing to seek "extracurricular income".'

Tharman Shanmugaratnam served as deputy prime minister and minister of finance before being appointed one of two senior ministers in the Singapore cabinet in 2019. 'Building state capacity requires both quality and incentives,' he says. This system is dependent on 'selection on merit, the development of people, and rewarding performance' within 'a culture of working as a team across government'.

In setting the direction of policy, cabinet operated as a 'collective', avoiding the adoption of five-year planning documents and rather 'spending a lot of time' discussing and iterating developments in a 'model of anticipating the next opportunity'. In the process, cabinet 'didn't disagree infrequently'. But these differences were not based on a 'belief system, but rather around fundamental, practical dimensions rather than ideological questions'. And like the civil service, cabinet is assessed on performance metrics, bonuses being awarded 'in a private matter in consultation with the PM,' says Shanmugaratnam.

There are different lessons from other countries. Mexico benefitted from the external discipline of the North American Free Trade Agreement (NAFTA), and the benefits of sticking with an access agreement with a market five times wealthier than the global per capita income average, even though its social and educational provisions have been gradually diluted down to a trade agreement. Consequently, while 75 per cent of Mexico's economy falls under NAFTA rules, less than 14 per cent of workers benefit from this access, says Luis Rubio, chairman of México Evalúa, a think tank focused on public policy monitoring and evaluation, and former chairman of the Mexican Council on Foreign Relations. NAFTA worked because Mexico's survival depended on it, and the presence of foreign firms proved important not only as a source of technology, trade and employment, but also to the anti-corruption fight.

Mexico's reforms were thus enabled, at least at the start, by having a political class that provided 'top cover' to the technocrats negotiating reforms and agreements, such as NAFTA. The same applied to other notable reformers such as Poland, where President Lech Wałęsa and the Solidarity movement enabled the political context for technocrats like Leszek Balcerowicz who managed the detail of reform.

Solidarity's victory precipitated the fall of the Berlin Wall and widespread political and economic change across the Soviet-controlled Eastern bloc. Wałęsa is not exaggerating when he claims: 'By knocking the teeth out of the Soviet bear, we helped other nations win their freedom.'

Professor Balcerowicz became minister of finance in the first non-communist government in 1989. 'We all thought that Poland would persist as it was,' he reflects from the Warsaw School of Economics, where he now teaches. 'However, the basic conclusion we reached was that economic liberalisation matters for results from reform; the variable is whether the political regime allows the necessary reforms to happen. Without political liberalisation there could be no changing the economic structure.'

While the world now knows Ukraine through the prism of war with Russia following the latter's 2014 seizure of Crimea and the Donbas and the 2022 Russian invasion and obstinate Ukrainian resistance, Ukraine's performance as an independent nation since 1991 is mixed. The Soviet economic system was replaced by one of preferences to various oligarchs, more like South Africa than the Baltics and Poland. One of the few exceptional sectors was agriculture. The Orange Revolution of 2004 and the Euromaidan protests ten years later started a process of liberalisation in its ties with Russia, where Kyiv's focus increasingly shifted westwards towards Europe. Whether it will accomplish this transformation depends on the outcome of the conflict started in 2022, the realisation of its aspirations for EU and NATO membership, and the pace and depth of its domestic institutional reforms, all of which together would allow Ukraine to exhibit its undoubted inner stuffing of human talent and organisational skills so evident in its resistance to Russian aggression. Whether earlier encouragement from the EU and NATO towards Ukraine could have motivated its good governance ambitions and forestalled the Russian invasion is moot.

All this matters for Africa. The continent's countries are today vulnerable to a perfect storm of a burgeoning youthful population, insufficient infrastructure, benign donor neglect and more malign foreign interference.

This has its roots in decades of weak economic performance. Sub-Saharan Africa's share of global per capita income has halved to just 15 per cent since the heady days of independence in the early 1960s. That's not to say things have not improved. They just have not improved at the same rate as the rest of the world.

African excuses for such failure have focused, understandably from a political vantage, on external factors. Change the world, and the unfair and uneven distribution of benefits, and Africa can prosper, or so the argument goes. By this thesis, increase aid, make the world an easier place in which to do business, and Africa can change.

But from similar domestic environments and in the same world order, countries across Asia, Europe and Latin America have developed in leaps and bounds. This would suggest that Africa is poor because its leaders have chosen the wrong path, and that politics, not economics, is the principal development impediment.

Vietnam illustrates how the outside world can best assist in creating stability and improving the results of better domestic choices, both in terms of its appalling example during the Vietnam War and subsequently when Vietnam shifted from a command economy in the mid-1980s to one driven by market forces, and its people, fundamentally, by a different and more positive set of incentives.

The failure of the American military intervention was down to three basic errors. One, a belief that the war could be fought and won strategically with technology, when the battle was for hearts and minds on the ground. This points to the two other, related errors: the belief that the war was a numbers game, that by increasing the number of American troops (which grew from 56 000 'in country' in

1965 to 385 000 by the end of 1966, and peaking at 550 000 in 1969) Hanoi could be defeated, and that this could be measured, too, in terms of aid flows and projects and casualty rates; and that the struggle was thus primarily military. Instead, it was a political struggle between a feckless (and corrupt) South Vietnamese government and an inspired communist regime in the north. The more America associated with the Saigon government, the less likely was long-term success for both, given the mutual taint of association.

American failures were long excused by the argument that Washington had stumbled into the crisis with a naive sense of shared well-being rather than the quagmire being the consequence of a misguided and deliberate policy.[18] This excuse is not dissimilar to the aid argument today, that success hinges on the metrics of money and technology and speed of delivery rather than alignment with internal policy and governance forces and factors.

Vietnam's rapid and positive development transformation post-1986 is primarily, by contrast, the result of the country making a different set of economic decisions and pursuing access to global markets. It's an inside-out paradigm, where change is driven at home, rather than outside-in. Local must be viable globally, but global can't lead change locally even though it can reinforce it through incentives, as with the EU and NAFTA.

Similarly, Estonia is now richer because its leaders made the right choices. It was not effortless, and it could easily have slipped back into old Soviet habits without firm leadership. South Africa has failed, comparatively, in its task to emancipate South Africans from the development injustices of apartheid. This can be explained, as in other post-colonial situations, in a variety of ways. Both the Estonian and South African governments wanted to be different from the past they had left behind: in the Estonian case, this was the Soviet model; in the ANC's case in South Africa, it was the Western alignment chosen by the apartheid government. Throw in past allegiances, a dose of ideology and identity politics, and South Africa, instead of throwing off the yoke of statism that had served the majority so poorly, opted to double down on this version in the mistaken belief that this time it would be different, and better.

The ANC's decision was not irrational; far from it, it was a rational choice to stay in power through a path of redistribution. But the overall effect has been to discourage investment, stunt growth, disincentivise better governance and lower investment. Without investment and its corollaries of growth and trade, there is no job creation and little hope of job retention. But the rule of rent remains a powerful tool, shaping policy, governance and choices.

This is not a uniquely South African dilemma, but one shared across the African continent and other milieux.

More interesting is why countries don't change once the path they have chosen has proven harder and less lucrative than their expectations. In South Africa's case, as will be seen, the need for ongoing financial and political rents from the post-1994 model must be balanced against the costs and benefits of change. In other words, the ANC knows it must change but is uncertain whether it can afford to among constituencies critical to its political survival. There are appropriate excuses at hand for stalling, including the need for racial redress, the externalist paradigm that the outside world must change before South Africa can transform (the question of agency), and cliches about the nefarious role of monopolies, white capital and foreign interests. Such factors change the metrics of achievement and the purpose of activity, measured less by financial return to SA Inc. than the available rents and the prominence of rhetoric. And all this is compounded by a worsening ineffectiveness among the bureaucracy, since their purpose, too, is less about delivering professional service than acquiring personal rewards.

Additionally, for South Africa, aside from the obvious point that the window for reform is open only for a limited time – should the government want to use this – is the essential point about leadership and vision. It is necessary not only to describe a pathway to the future, looking a decade out hence, but for this to be informed by a sense of realism. In this, leadership has to do just that, lead and decide, rather than attempt to facilitate and mediate. There is no need to seek confrontation, but also no point in trying to avoid it all the time. There is also an imperative to plan and problem-solve, rather than simply set out promises and goals. In addition, a believable narrative involves speaking more about accomplishments – or runs on the board, to use a cricketing or baseball metaphor – and less about aims.

Similarly, in Argentina the government has got stuck because structural reforms are unpopular and leaders are short-sighted. Former minister of finance Alfonso Prat-Gay argues that the margin for manoeuvre is very small in those societies mired in high levels of poverty 'where the margin for error is correspondingly huge'. This results in 'structural reform usually occurring out of panic and desperation rather than out of hope'.

There is a need to realise, however, that political suicide will occur even if leaders don't carry out reforms, and that risking one's support base is worthy of the national interest. And there is a need to understand that overall success depends fundamentally on the success of business, and that popularity depends on the success of reforms. A blunt style of communication of the problem, and the pain of the solution, might well help. Equally, while business usually has made its own contribution to the mess, it would do well to get more transactional with government.

Even if the African model has, in the main, become about the distribution of rents, some of the answers come, too, from Africa.

From a low-income economy based around agriculture, principally sugarcane, Mauritius diversified through textiles, apparel and tourism into offshore financial and information and communication technology (ICT) sectors. Mauritius now receives as many tourists today as there are citizens, some 1.3 million. Liberalisation of the economy was carefully staggered through the creation of export processing zones (EPZs) in the 1970s. There are 21 500 offshore businesses and nearly 930 global funds domiciled in Mauritius, where the top rate of corporate and personal income tax is just 15 per cent. As a result, economic growth has averaged over 5 per cent since independence in 1968, at the same time significantly reducing inequality. Democracy has been a key part of its story, explaining why political competitiveness has driven better economic choices, and why Mauritius has prospered and not Madagascar next door, where the thirst for power has constantly been greater than the interests of the people.

The same applies to Comoros, which shares a French colonial history with Mauritius, and a similar geography and climate, but little else. The politics of Comoros, with twenty coups and attempted rebellions since independence in 1975, has proven a dramatic handicap, as has the level of external interference, from France and others.

Comoros' comparative lack of performance shows that being small is not necessarily a guarantee of success, just as China and Poland, among others, illustrate that larger states are not preordained towards development failure.

Despite being a relative giant compared to Mauritius, Morocco's reform experience of EPZs and incentives, facilitated through world-class logistics infrastructure, has been similar. Like other nations in North Africa, Rabat faced an existential moment with the Arab Spring in 2011; unlike others, the king and his government acted quickly and decisively to open up the economy, reform the political system to introduce greater accountability, and invest to stay ahead of the social turmoil experienced in Egypt and Tunisia.

Botswana has got much right, including making a fairy-tale commodity deal with the diamond-mining behemoth De Beers early on in its independence, which set it up for a regular and growing stream of revenue. It was a joint venture that worked. What has worked less well, however, are the subsequent attempts to diversify, perhaps because the government has got used to extraordinary returns for very little effort. Also, their politics, while democratic on paper, are autocratic in reality – there has been a single-party state since independence, a feature common to many southern African states, with evident effects on their policy direction and competitiveness.

The self-governing Kurdish region of Iraq has not been without its challenges since the removal of Saddam Hussein from power in 2003. Despite enormous challenges of political and economic cohesion, and a tough neighbourhood, Erbil has been able to make relatively rapid and stable progress over the last twenty years, reflecting political consensus, a large natural resource endowment and the success of ongoing attempts at diversification. But the way these resources are managed, and the corruption around them, suggests that its liberation from foreign investment and control has not been the perfect formula for success, just as in Zambia. What combination of domestic and regional politics has contributed to Kurdistan's relative poor performance, and what has to change to take it in a more positive and diversified direction?

Good leaders need good strategy

Rich State, Poor State is unabashedly focused on the relevance of these case studies and lessons for Africa, given that it is where the majority of the world's poor – and failed states – reside. The continent is also going to experience an extraordinary population increase in the next generation: a projected increase from 1.3 billion people to over 2.5 billion by 2050. The business-as-usual approach taken by donors and Africans alike is simply not going to suffice. The swell of young people, and their demands and possible anger, should create a sense of urgency. As the 2022 African Youth Survey shows, more than half of young people in Africa, aged eighteen to twenty-four, are likely to consider emigrating in the next few years, citing economic hardship and education opportunities as the top reasons. Less than one-third of those polled across fifteen countries felt their country was headed in the right direction.[19]

There is an upside to Africa's relatively weak development performance. Demographics will drive demand and direction. Europe and Asia's ageing populations combined with increasing wage expectations could result in as many as 150 million jobs being up for grabs by Africans, even with reskilling and the greying of the workforce elsewhere, and substitution by automation.[20] China's manufacturing boom grew sixfold between 2004 and 2017, for example, to $3.5 billion, or one-quarter of the world's manufacturing base. Yet real wages increased by around 10 per cent between 2005 and 2014, allowing space for cheaper wage entrants. Moreover, China is now moving from light manufacturing for export towards diversification into services and higher technology.[21]

Africa will have to position itself to gain this investment and employment, or migrants in Asia and Europe could fill these jobs. There are challenges. For one, Africa is not a low-cost environment, both in terms of wages and the costs that influence investment, such as the quality of roads and ports, the extent and reliability of electricity infrastructure, political stability, and the level of excessive bureaucracy and corruption. Encouragingly for Africa, the formula for improvement is hardly unknown, not least given Asia's recent economic transformation.

This book is thus a call for an end to business as usual by showing what is possible.

What *Rich State, Poor State* is not, however, is another examination of solely what has gone wrong and who has profited from the failures. Although an understanding of past problems is necessary to make better choices, the forensic examination of the underworld of state capture, while of journalistic (and even legal) intrigue, has limited policy utility. It also reinforces a mercantilist, zero-sum view of the world: that failure is primarily a consequence of someone else's wealth or doing. Rather, it is necessary to put politicians on the spot for the choices that are available and to hold them to account.

Nor is this book an examination solely of the technical and tactical measures that are necessary to translate high-sounding concepts and words into practical and measurable plans for action. That much is presumed.

It is a book about strategy, defined as a coherent plan of action where the ends are aligned to resources and enabled by careful prioritisation to achieve a long-term aim.

Strategy encompasses more than just technical capacity since it is an undertaking based on principles, values and rules, demanding a systematic method that includes all the attributes and sources of state power: of people, institutions and processes. Success requires a combination of all these factors.[22]

Managing complex relationships places a premium on leadership. Flexibility, dexterity and simplicity of vision are all bywords for the successful implementation of strategy.

Crucial in the leadership of strategy is providing what today are known as the 'softer' aspects, particularly when it comes to relationships. It demands a sense of timing, and the courage and ability to make tough decisions. For example, Nelson Mandela instinctively knew that South Africa could not move forward without racial reconciliation. To this end, he stared down the extremists within his party. Subsequent South African leaders have struggled to hold the line with the same determination as a rising tide of populism has returned race-based policies to political centre stage.

The centrality of people in strategy is, however, not only to do with leaders. Populations, too, have to take a long-term view in seeing development as a generational endeavour, and be encouraged to do so by their leadership in a fast-paced digital world where the need for instant gratification, and immediate answers, can trump the imperative for patience and understanding.[23]

The path from poor to rich state thus lies largely in politics, since economics is politics by other means, to misquote Prussian general Carl von Clausewitz. In Africa, democracies have tended to do much better empirically at growth and development, not least because they offer the sorts of protections that encourage diversified investments not linked to natural resource endowments.[24] While Singapore, Franco's Spain and Vietnam are included in these case studies, this is not to suggest that authoritarianism is the developmental answer for Africa. For one, whereas some Africans might once upon a time have wanted a Lee Kuan Yew, the African experience with authoritarianism has been one of brutality, wastage and corruption rather than management and efficiency. And whereas the more sophisticated version of authoritarianism à la Vladimir Putin or Venezuela's Hugo Chávez might have its attractions for those elites wanting a democratic facade with limited institutional and public scrutiny and accountability, the record shows that this version of government can encourage corruption, impunity and an unresponsive government, not to mention its cost in terms of human rights. The temptation for leadership to steer away from liberal ideals is obvious, not least since it removes the constraints on manoeuvrability and reduces levels of transparency and accountability.

Authoritarianism is thus not just about violence per se, or even whether votes count – and are counted – in domestic elections. It's about a system and purpose of government where elites profit disproportionately and have little (or no) accountability or chance of being evicted via the polls.

Little wonder that the interests of Africans, according to polling across Africa, align with democracy and openness rather than the brand of elite-centred governance promoted by Putin. More than two-thirds of Africans regularly surveyed by Afrobarometer, for instance, prefer democracy to other forms of government.[25]

Yet just six African countries were described as 'full' or 'flawed' democracies by the Economist Intelligence Unit in 2023.[26] The remainder were denoted as 'hybrid' or 'authoritarian' regimes. According to Freedom House, which categorises countries into 'free', 'partly free' and 'not free', by 2023 there were just eight 'free' countries in Africa, meaning that only 7 per cent of 1.4 billion Africans, north and south of the Sahara, live in 'free' countries. This democratic recession from a peak of twelve 'free' countries in 2003 is in line with global trends. As Freedom House noted in its 2022 report: 'The present threat to democracy is the product of 16 consecutive years of decline in global freedom. A total of 60 countries suffered declines over the past year, while only 25 improved. As of today, some 38% of the global population live in "Not Free" countries, the highest proportion since 1997. Only about 20% now live in "Free" countries.'[27]

Getting the politics right does not mean stability at any cost, including a cost in civil liberties. This may be a straw man, a tautology for leadership to justify its policies and its perpetuation, not least since it is difficult to prove the counter-factual. We don't know, for instance, if Rwanda would grow its economy faster or be more or less stable without Paul Kagame, or Russia without Vladimir Putin. The Baltics averaged a government a year in their first decade of freedom from Soviet occupation, but what they did do very well was to act decisively and boldly in setting the stage for the recovery and growth that followed for the next thirty years.

Democracy rests on the building blocks of judicial independence, the rule of law, a free media, respect for individual rights, and strong and diverse political parties to fuel policy competitiveness and ensure accountability. It also places a premium on political talents in maintaining support while carrying out difficult reforms. In those cases where expectations for change, and redistribution, are high, politicians must walk a difficult path promising one thing and delivering another. 'You should indicate left, but turn right,' observed Juan Perón of gaining power and running Argentina, though he spent most of his time attempting to turn left too with a resultant lack of forward progress. Similarly, it is said that taking power and running a country is akin to playing the violin: you pick it up with the left and play it with the right. If you attempt to play it with the left, it will make scarcely any sound at all.

Politics can easily turn out to be the problem if leaders are unwilling to use the opportunity granted them, if they are unstrategic and unfocused, or too gradualist or dithering on difficult decisions, or simply fearful about losing support on account of slim margins or of making enemies in service of principle. The clientelist nature of politics ensures policies that preserve power, while undermining any commitment to fiscal discipline and long-term structural reforms.[28]

The term 'political economy' describes the relationship between government economic policy choices and people – how the state affects the market.

Across Africa, the political economy has been described as 'rentier' – where the economy relies on extracting income from rents, usually from foreign entities, rather than developing through improving productive capacity and competitiveness. As the World Bank describes with respect to Malawi, for instance: 'Malawi's stagnation is in large part driven by a stable but low-level equilibrium, in which a small group of elites compete for power and political survival through rent seeking. The competitive-clientelist political settlement creates strong incentives for policies that can be seen to address short-term popular needs (such as agriculture subsidies, market and price distortions), while undermining the ability to credibly commit to fiscal discipline and long term reforms needed to spur productive structural transformation.'[29]

Essentially, the elite shape policy choices and practices in a manner that enriches them before all others. This can take multiple forms. For example, in terms of procurement contracts – maintenance contracts on South African power stations would be an example, or the coal contracts that drive dependency on that system of power and enrich the middlemen, many of whom have close connections with the ruling party. Another is in terms of import substitution – where high tariffs on foreign goods penalise the poor while ensuring a local elite gain uncompetitive market share. The same applies to local ownership or, in the case of South Africa, racial ownership stipulations, ensuring a politically protected class. Fixed exchange rates are another method – such as in Nigeria and Ethiopia – where the difference between the government and the market rate creates the conditions for local arbitrage, essentially enabling elites to buy at one (fixed) rate and sell at another (market) price, while at the same time reducing the competitiveness of exports. In Malawi, cited above, this takes the form of state intermediation in agriculture pricing while preventing exports, ensuring the price to the farmer is low. In one of the most egregious forms of exploitation, the produce is stored and then sold back to the farmer at a higher price later in the season when hunger bites.

The list is endless: from the engineered failure of railways to drive road transport monopolies, to fuel importers benefitting from the collapse of power grids, rents from the ownership of a resource (such as oil) and the political engineering around both the volume and distribution of aid, especially emergency humanitarian assistance, to transit charges and systems of fuel and agriculture subsidies. As Douglas Yates puts it with regard to oil: 'The rise and fall of these states is more than just another boom-and-bust cycle of resource dependency. Instead of cultivating an ethic of hard work, oil rentiers follow an easy path to quick riches, spending money which they have not earned. The more eagerly they spend their unearned oil revenues striving to reach development, the farther they recede from it.'[30]

The problem is clear. Not only does the existence of these systems hinder development progress through improving productive capacity, but it also has a negative impact on the development of open political systems. While elites are reluctant to give up their preferences, in an unhealthy development pact, the relative absence of taxation as a means of state income makes citizens less demanding and politically engaged. Perhaps the most astonishing aspect of Nigeria's abject economy is that government revenues (including from oil) are around just 6 per cent of GDP, compared to the global norm of 13.5 per cent or the developed world norm of 15.3 per cent.[31] Nigeria's rate is among the lowest in the world, virtually implying anarchy, but manages to meet the minimum required to ensure access to patrimony flowing from control over various aspects of the economy. And this is way too low to enable the state to invest in and look after the people.

This system lasts so long as there is enough patronage and power to pay off insiders – relatives, trusted friends, influential families – with contracts, cash and appointments. But as the state hollows out, and the population inexorably balloons, increasingly there is less to go around. Outsiders get angry, people flock to the cities in search of income, and the state invariably gets both more brutal and interfering as it searches for means of income and control in a tautology of destabilisation and violence.

Nigeria is Africa's largest economy, though it ranks just 133 out of 184 in terms of GDP per capita (at $2 429). This reflects low growth and a rapid increase in population, from 45 million people at independence in 1960 to 215 million sixty years later. Now four out of ten Nigerians live below the poverty line, and many – especially in the north – lack education and access to basic infrastructure, including potable water, electricity and sanitation. Most are engaged in subsistence activities, with just 17 per cent holding wage jobs.[32]

Young people under the age of thirty-five comprise 76.5 per cent of the population, yet politics is notable for low levels of youth participation and representation. There is endemic insecurity in parts, especially in the north-eastern states of Adamawa, Bauchi, Borno, Gombe, Nasarawa, Taraba and Yobe due to Boko Haram, which has produced 3.3 million internally displaced people.

It's a governance system that incentivises corruption. Take Mohammed, a young immigration officer based in Lagos. He earns $400 per month and spends $1 500 annually on his accommodation, $10 per day on food, and $1 on transport to and from work. He has to make some money on the side just to survive, let alone prosper. A few steps from his desk, at passport control, the officer taps a $10 bill on his computer keyboard. 'I need some help,' he says to me, increasingly agitated. Getting things done in such situations inevitably demands citizens having to drop a few notes to oil the otherwise creaky wheels of bureaucracy.

Altering this political economy is difficult, requiring both tough-minded leadership and a marathon effort likely over generations. For example, during the civilian administration of Olusegun Obasanjo in Nigeria, between 1999 and 2007, the economic growth rate rose to 6.6 per cent, two percentage points higher than the sub-Saharan average, helped by higher oil prices but also driven by improved governance and a strategy for debt relief. The growth rate for the decade following was 4.7 per cent, as politicians descended once more into rentier habits without a plan for recovery, reform and growth.

For all the setbacks, Nigerians are today much more aware of their democratic rights and threats. The extension of electoral and political inclusivity – in terms of youth, gender, regional voting accessibility and patterns, registration, media coverage, cyber-integrity, voting technology and voter education – is firmly on the agenda, representing a refinement of expectations and standards beyond simply holding elections *per se* free of violence. This is reflected, too, in the increasingly sophisticated agenda of international observer missions beyond purely declaring elections 'free and fair'. The Nigerian election held on 25 February 2023 was an example of both the complexity of running polls in a large country with weak institutions, and an increasingly sophisticated electorate.

This poll required the establishment of 176 846 polling stations across the country's thirty-six states (plus the Federal Capital Territory around Abuja) capable of processing 93.4 million registered voters involving 547 million ballot papers and more than one billion pieces of paper in total, with the mobilisation of 310 000 police officers and 94 000 other security officials plus 1.4 million election officials. As the chairman of the Independent National Electoral Commission (INEC), Professor Mahmood Yakubu, admitted, 'We understand the benefit of credible elections, not only in our own country in terms of peace and stability, but in terms of the ripple effect across the region.'

Nigeria has much going for it, including a dynamic media environment (with more than 100 television and nearly 200 radio stations in 2019) and a high-energy population that constantly finds ways to get around the lack of institutional capacity. 'No water, sink a borehole. No decent education, send your children to private schools. Get sick, fly out of the country. With lockdown, people are no longer cushioned from bad governance,' says Aisha Yesufu, a Nigerian human rights activist.

Not for nothing is it said that in Nigeria things 'collapse into place'.

On the flip side, the corruption, violence and vote-buying surrounding the elections and pervasive *emi lo kan* ('it's my turn now') politics, along with the dynastic and corrupt practices that go with this sentiment, are synonymous with the democratic process, while representation remains skewed in favour of vested interests. 'Democracy has been commercialised,' notes Emmanuel Njoku of Connected Development, a non-governmental organisation (NGO) promoting government accountability. Parties pay scant regard for imposed limits on spending of no more than $7 million for presidential candidates, and donations of no more than $7 000 per individual. 'Funding limits are observed more in the breach than compliance,' says Iyorchia Ayu, chairman of the People's Democratic Party, the main opposition in the 2023 election. 'If you were able to stick to them, you would not actually be able to run any elections ... No serious political party observes these limits.'[33]

There were also issues of representivity. Just 10 per cent of all candidates were women in 2023, for example, well below the global mark of just above one-quarter of all parliamentarians. While eighteen- to thirty-five-year-olds comprise more than half of total registered voters, Nigeria's past five democratic elections have been notable for low levels of youth participation as candidates. Students comprised the largest single voting bloc, with 26 million registered, almost twice the number of the second-largest constituency, farmers and fishermen, with 14.7 million. Still, the use of biometric voting (facial and fingerprint recognition) technology boosted initial confidence in the voting process.

Take Kano, Mohammed's home town and Nigeria's second-largest city after Lagos, located at the edge of the savanna and on the trans-Saharan trade route. Politically it is better known as the birthplace of two military heads of state: generals Murtala Muhammed, the military leader in 1974–75, and Sani Abacha, the last military strongman before the transition to democracy in 1999. Abacha has the dubious distinction of being involved in five of Nigeria's military coups: the 1966 'counter coup', along with those in 1975, 1983, 1985, and in 1993, the last time before democracy returned.

Kano's politics and history of sectarian rioting, plus the fear of rigging and exclusion in an environment of economic scarcity, constantly pose a threat of violence. The day before the election, three people were killed in a clash between members of the ruling All Progressives Congress and supporters of the New Nigeria People's Party presidential candidate Rabiu Kwankwaso. On the day, however, 25 February 2023, all was relatively calm, though there were other problems. The INEC turned up very late, some polling stations barely getting going just before the cut-off at 14:30, a trend across the whole country. Many of the polling units were staged in the open, the non-existent marshalling of the crowds and absence of many voting booths meaning it was, at best, chaotic. Problems of control were compounded by a lack of signage and basic facilities, including tables and chairs. Tallying was transparent but hampered by the lack of training and experience of the election officials, and a lack of lighting for those who carried on into the night.

The event was, in the words of one foreign observer, 'an extreme sport'. As I wrote at the time:

From Kano, A Warning?

Dusty, searing streets
No Naira, no luck
In classrooms, corruption means no seats
Danger, the weaving tuk-tuk

Woven agbada
In big man blue

Sweating, wheeling kuran ruwa
Make yourself part of the crew

Hanging harmattan
Please Sah, say the schoolgirls in Kumbotso
A world shaped by religion and clan
The Nigeria of 400 million tomorrow

Bald men, old combs
Promises of change
The talk of 'recovery', 'renewed hope', 'brave reforms'
A youth estranged

Staggering logistics to manage
Heroic officials hold the line
Minimise the damage
A few dead, but it will be fine

Women in black
Youth in mourning
Victory for vested interests and the kickback
But for politicians, a warning?

Samson Itodo of Yiaga Africa, the civil society group dedicated to the promotion of governance, says that there is, in this regard, a clash between the faith of Nigerians in democracy as an opportunity 'to reclaim the state, a stake heightened by the expectation that their vote will count' in a country 'polarised along ethnic and religious lines' compared to 'political actors who are still the same and playing by the same rules ... and for whom this is their only chance to seize power'.[34] Though the opposition cried foul, the election was officially won by the ruling party's Bola Tinubu, an ageing powerbroker who campaigned on a Muslim-Muslim ticket in a country divided equally between Christians and Muslims. Despite expectations to the contrary, the turnout was just 27 per cent, lower than the 2019 election of 35 per cent.

The best conclusion on the process is that people who wanted to vote eventually got to vote, the biometric system worked and only a few people died. Of greater concern was the slowing of the transmission and release of results, usually a tell-tale sign that the rig is in. It is worth asking several questions, however: At what point is the credibility of the system compromised by myriad logistical problems, and to what extent were the problems encountered in the transmission of results deliberate? And if money politics and the ability to re-engineer tallies is pervasive, convincing even, and the means of remedy weak, what are the mechanisms then available to change the political incentives to reform? Having started out as a bag carrier for Chicago drug dealers and moved on to become the 'Godfather of Lagos', Tinubu was not going to let the presidency slip from his grasp easily.

Why is it so hard to carry out economic reforms, to make changes for the better?

Politics centres on the agency of sometimes agonisingly difficult choices, and often the inertia of the grave can overcome the desire for reform. Change is possible and can have a tremendously positive effect – witness the impact of freeing up the telecom sector from government control. But when state operating systems are soaked in the vested interests and preferred methods of a predatory elite, changing them is hard and requires tough-minded leadership with a plan and a mandate to carry out reforms.

Good examples of change can also help.

Africa

LOMÉ, a city of schizophrenia.
Even down the sweeping beachfront Boulevard du Mono, where vendors cook brochettes of chicken, buck, turkey, goat and duck, and Togolese gather to party, drink ice-cold Djama and play football in the steamy heat, it is abundantly clear that the place is as poor as its $630 per capita World Bank statistic suggests. Swarms of boys hawk cigarettes neatly stacked in yellow-painted cardboard props; women sway through the traffic selling cooking pots balanced on their heads. Others do the same with plastic containers of nuts and dates, tissues and sachets of water, while taxi drivers and *zem* scooters weave in and out, peeping and yelling for rides, their occasional loud arguments punctuating the ambient hum of the traffic. Lining the route are vendors dealing in everything from second-hand football boots to electronic appliances, plants, clocks, thermoses, bags and beer.

Lomé is poor, but Togo's eight million people are out there hustling to make their lives better. Still, in the circumstances, a lot of effort is burnt in just surviving.

And yet Lomé is also synonymous with trade in more ways than one, and since trade is generally indicative of growth, why has this not filtered through and down?

Lomé's port is evidence of the promise. It made it to the Lloyd's List of top 100 busiest ports in the world in 2021.[1] With a throughput touching two million containers, up nearly 14 per cent on 2020, it is the service centre for the West African and Sahel hinterland, trucks waiting patiently in line to shuttle their cargo to Burkina Faso, Niger and Mali. In the bay, container vessels sit at anchor, sheltering from piracy in the Gulf of Guinea. A bay of stability in a sea of lawlessness, Lomé is also a preferred transhipment port for Benin and Ghana. While Lomé's port has undoubtedly improved from private sector concessioning, there is still room for improvement, ranking 349th out of 370 container ports listed on the World Bank's efficiency index.[2] This is encouragingly on an upward curve, however. Between 2020 and 2021, container transit time fell from 13.4 to 11.45 days for containers bound for Togo, and from 16.95 to 15.5 days for containers in transit.[3]

The regional role has been facilitated by a large investment in roads, many of them built by the Chinese. Togo's airport, too, has become a hub, with the basing of ASKY, the Ethiopian Airlines–run regional airline. 'We are in the centre, small and accessible,' notes Abiratou Bonfoh, one of seventeen women members of parliament (MPs) in the ninety-one-strong Togolese parliament. It takes just eight hours by road from the north to the south.

So, where is the disconnect between the efficiency of the port, the road network and the airport with the plight of Togo's people? Why is Togo an example of strategic and leadership failure?

'The problem is politics,' says one private sector port operator echoing the view of many. More specifically, it is the problem of no choice and highly regulated competitiveness. Put differently, there is no danger of the elite losing power, and until there is, change will be slow.

Togo's political history takes in all the harsh African low points and trouble spots: a bitter colonial past and even more destructive post-colonial political turbulence, where rule has been more about the interests of personality than those of the population.

From the sixteenth century for 200 years, this coastal region was known as the Slave Coast. Then, in 1884, the territory was declared a German protectorate and rechristened Togoland. After the First World War, rule was transferred to France. Shortly after independence in April 1960, prime minister Sylvanus Olympio and his Party of Togolese Unity took power. Leaders of opposition parties were arrested and their parties dissolved. In elections the following year, Olympio won 90 per cent of the vote and all fifty-one national assembly seats to become Togo's first president.

His comeuppance was swift. A coup followed in 1963 when he was assassinated by a group of soldiers under Sergeant Étienne Gnassingbé Eyadéma, a ten-year veteran of the French Army, which handed over power to a government led by opposition leader Nicolas Grunitzky, who had been barred from the 1961 election. Then, in July 1967, (now Lieutenant-Colonel) Eyadéma overthrew Grunitzky in a bloodless coup and assumed the presidency, banning activities of other political parties and relying 'on repression, patronage, and a bizarre leadership cult' to cement his rule for thirty-eight years.[4] Unquestioning support from France (especially President Jacques Chirac) didn't hurt, and neither did the allegiance of an army packed with members of Eyadéma's northern Kabye ethnic group, a 20 per cent minority in a country dominated numerically by the Ewe.

The head of a highly oppressive one-party state meting out violence to political opponents, with the lives of the elite padded by access to riches and their luxury imports protected by the CFA franc, Eyadéma fully embraced the African 'Big Man' caricature – an entourage including 1000 dancing women who sang in praise of him, and a comic book that depicted him as having powers of great strength and invulnerability, are but two examples. Following an air-crash in the presidential Dakota in 1974, in which he (untruthfully) portrayed himself as the sole survivor, Eyadéma attributed his survival to mystical powers and declared the day of the crash, 24 January, to be 'Economic Liberation Day'. He changed his first name from Étienne to Gnassingbé to mark the date and erected a monument near the crash site, featuring the great man on a plinth flanked by images of those generals who had perished in the event. Eyadéma claimed the aircraft had been sabotaged. The date of another failed assassination attempt was commemorated as the 'Feast of Victory Over Forces of Evil'.

Eyadéma garnered a remarkable 99.97 per cent of the vote in the presidential election held in 1979 and was re-elected to a third consecutive seven-year term in December 1986 (when he survived another coup attempt) with 99.5 per cent of the vote in yet another uncontested election.

By 1991, parties other than Eyadéma's Rally of the Togolese People were allowed, though the EU froze development cooperation after the president's unsurprising re-elections in 1993, 1998 and 2003. Despite a promise to step down at the end of his second elected term in 2003, Eyadéma decided to 'sacrifice himself once more', in the words of his prime minister, and the constitution was amended to let him run again. Yet the political environment remained tightly controlled, backstopped by a pliant Paris that favoured stability and reliability over the threat of impartiality and the promise of prosperity. No one, it seems, was immune. Opposition leader Gilchrist Olympio, son of the slain founding president, was ambushed and seriously wounded by soldiers on 5 May 1992.

At the time of his death in 2005, with the earlier passing of Morocco's king, Hassan II, Eyadéma was the longest-serving leader in Africa's post-colonial history. His legacy, according to those who knew him, was 'stability, peace, a sense of national pride, and a strong army'. But in the opinion of his family's inner circle, he neglected other basics: infrastructure, education and healthcare among them.

He was succeeded by his son, Faure Gnassingbé, who initially left power for two months after an outcry over the dynastic succession, but then held and won elections. More than 400 people were killed in the resulting violence, and 40 000 Togolese fled the country. The younger Gnassingbé was re-elected in 2010 and 2015, winning a fourth term in 2020. There have been no fewer than eight known coups and attempted coups since independence, fuelling an atmosphere of suspicion and obedience.

It's a great family business, Togo, involving the father, son and holy spirit, but not all the family. In 2009, even the president's half-brother was arrested on coup-plotting charges. The younger Gnassingbé has, however, uplifted the country through spending on roads in particular, in line with the logistics focus, and by prioritising education, healthcare, water management and agro-industry. It is a more competitive political environment with the president winning the 2015 election by just 59 per cent, a fraction of what his father might have once expected. But it is still one defined by identity and regional politics, especially north versus south.

There is more at stake, not least given the rise of terrorism in neighbouring countries, directly attributable, Togolese politicians maintain, to the fall of Muammar Gaddafi's regime in Libya in 2011. 'If the objective [of NATO countries] in killing Gaddafi was to protect people,' says MP Abiratou Bonfoh, 'then they have failed because more people are insecure today than before.' The growing role of Russia's Wagner Group in Mali and Burkina Faso is a consequence, she says, of the failure of Western-led efforts to stabilise the situation. 'Russia is not their first choice, but going to Russia is like taking another woman if you cannot have a baby with your wife,' Bonfoh says. 'The French don't like this, but they need also to reflect. How to manage Africa in the seventies and eighties is not the same as the 2020s.'[5]

Lomé has also given its name to the special trade relationship between the European Economic Community (or EEC, as the EU was known at the time) and the African, Caribbean and Pacific (ACP) group of countries, comprising mostly former colonies and among them some of the poorest in the world. Concluded in 1975, the Lomé Convention provided aid, trade and tariff preferences to more than sixty ACP states, allowing them to export goods duty-free to Europe based on the provision that they did not compete with European goods.

Despite the convention's provisions, the ACP failed to maintain their share of the EEC market, faring worse than other least-developing countries. In 1976, ACP exports accounted for 6.7 per cent of total European imports from outside the member states, falling to 3.7 per cent in 1992.[6] Little diversification was achieved in ACP exports. In contrast, the EEC maintained its position in ACP markets. The Lomé Convention was replaced by the Cotonou Agreement in 2000 when the World Trade Organization ruled it anti-competitive.

The Lomé Convention suggested that constraints other than simple access matter when driving development, including technology, know-how, and the bureaucratic and other frictions of running businesses in the ACP countries themselves.

Fast-forward fifty-six years from when Faure Gnassingbé's family first took power, and Togo promises 'development but not democracy'.[7] Yet the Togolese apparently are desperate for both, ignoring Gnassingbé Eyadéma's claims that democracy in Africa 'moves along at its own pace and in its own way'.[8]

Afrobarometer polls show that 72 per cent of the Togolese prefer multiparty competition to other systems. But just 37 per cent of those surveyed thought that elections enabled voters to remove non-performing leaders, and just 57 per cent thought that the last election was free and fair.[9] The Togolese know better than most what's good for them, but with a government safety net of pro-Westernism, and a tight if testy relationship with France and the West, not least because of Islamist chaos on the borders, the Togolese elite are sitting comfortably, for now.

The cost of elite behaviour, privileges and practices, shielded as they are by an absence of a vigorous democracy, has been great across Africa.

If the continent had managed nothing spectacular in terms of economic growth but had just retained its comparative global position of sixty years ago, the income of the average sub-Saharan African would have grown (in real terms) threefold from $1 135 to $3 475. Instead, the average African per capita income is today $1 597. During this time, average global wealth has leapt more than 300 per cent to $11 010, whereas Africa's has increased by just 40 per cent. Given additionally that these figures mask the rise of a wealthy African elite, the continent has fallen far behind its peers.

Africa's poor performance obscures the relatively high rates of growth enjoyed by many African countries in the 1960s, as they redistributed the benefits of decolonisation, only for this boom to fall away again in the stultification of an era of one-party and military rule and the cost of widespread social and political instability. South Africa, for example, had a fourteen-year growth run from 1960 that averaged at 5.1 per cent, Gabon eleven years from 1965 at 13.1 per cent, Côte d'Ivoire eighteen years from 1960 at 9.5 per cent, Lesotho twelve years from 1970 at 9.9 per cent, and even Tanzania at 5.7 per cent from 1961 to 1975.[10] Though a few standout African performers (including Morocco, Botswana and Mauritius) have managed steady performance throughout the post-independence period, the continent's growth record has been overwhelmingly dismal by global standards. This is particularly so among the larger African economies. While the world's income has increased threefold, South Africa's per capita income has gone up just 50 per cent in the last sixty years despite its strong performance in the 1960s and early 1970s, while Nigeria's has gone up 66 per cent to $2 429. Ethiopia has performed a little closer to the global norm, its per capita income going from $305 (in 1980) to $835, while the Democratic Republic of Congo (DRC) has managed a remarkable 60 per cent drop to just $501 in 2021. Other smaller countries with a solid natural resource inheritance have also stumbled: Zimbabwe's per capita income expanded by just 13 per cent in sixty years to $1 289, and Zambia by just 5 per cent to $1 258.

This comparison of 'what might have been' should factor in the lost potential of growth, and the relatively bountiful natural and human resource wealth of Africa. To put this differently, if Africa had increased its wealth at the rate of Vietnam, a country with a particularly difficult post-colonial inheritance, it could be touching the global per capita income average instead of being nearly seven times less, or at the rate of Chile (another mineral-rich country), nearly half the global average. If it had grown at the pace of Singapore, Africans would be twice as wealthy as the global average. And if sub-Saharan Africa had grown its economies at the rate of South Korea, its citizens would be enjoying wealth of over three times the global average.

Instead, today, the wealth of Africans is a fraction of their global peers, at under 15 per cent and falling.

The comparative performance of Africa poses many questions.

Why, for instance, has a country like the Kingdom of Lesotho, with all the relative logistics advantages of South Africa (it is totally enclosed by the republic), done so poorly, with a per capita GDP five times less than that of South Africa? More particularly, why has Lesotho been unable to transform its local textile and clothing industry from being foreign to locally owned, and to move it further up the value chain, as happened in Asia? Instead, the textile industry has remained largely Taiwanese-owned and run, even with duty- and quota-free preferences in the US and EU markets. Instead of diversifying into other areas such as electronics, Lesotho has remained stuck in clothing, with the result that its markets remain vulnerable to foreign trends and preferences, from fashion to logistics costs and production through artificial intelligence (AI). Development requires growing and diversifying all the time.

This is compounded by 'people benefitting from their actions for themselves', reflected businessman-turned-politician Sam Matekane just weeks after taking over as Lesotho's prime minister in October 2022. And yet 'people have a lot of expectations, as most people are unemployed, though they think things will change tomorrow'.[11] Welcome to politics.

Attempts to address these conditions in a strategic fashion have been inevitably trumped by a combination of short-term imperatives that have consumed time and financial resources, as well as the feeding frenzy that has marked the behaviour of the political and administrative class with few exceptions. This tendency has been compounded by the tactical myopia of external funders intent on solving today's needs and according to their own template, rather than according to longer-term, strategic factors. In the case of Lesotho, it will never break out of its low-income, low-growth trap by playing the same game better; it needs to play a different game.

And where there have been economic successes, such as in Botswana's growth from dirt tracks to diamonds, the inability of African economies to diversify away from commodities is as perplexing as it is concerning and necessary if the continent is going to be able to provide the jobs to ensure its youth have a stake in stability through prosperity, and if the continent is, in so doing, going to be able to address its mountain of poverty.

Even before Covid-19 struck in 2020, one-third of Africans – 445 million people – lived in extreme poverty (living on less than $1.90 a day), a figure that increased by thirty million two years later and which is nearly ten times the average for the rest of the world. Africa has twenty-two of the world's poorest twenty-five countries.[12]

Examples of African failures to reform and diversify abound. The strategic challenge that has led to systemic micro, tactical-level disappointments in African development rests fundamentally in the inability to break out of the colonial model of economic extraction and growth. Rather than liberating the economy of its protections, monopolies, frictions and inefficiencies, post-colonial African regimes simply replaced one elite with another, and maintained the same extractive, commodity-heavy model as their colonial forebearers. In this they were encouraged, aided and abetted by external powers and interests, who had too vested an interest in the continuation of the relationships, both inwards in terms of goods and outwards in terms of commodities, earlier established.

And as problems of slow growth, weakening governance and social instability took hold in the post-colonial era, the response was to undo constitutional bounds and tighten the reins of power, leading to repression and ever-greater violence, including military coups. The Cold War provided greater political wiggle room as countries manoeuvred in soliciting superpower patronage, though this amplified the focus on power and control rather than growth and development. As the Cold War waned, so democracy waxed as authoritarians had fewer options (and excuses), and the pressure for change and rights grew and became a concern for some outside powers – and less impeded by others. But the narrowing of ideological options and strengthening constitutionality still fell foul to the entrenched, vested interests operating in the half-light of government enterprises and boards, the bureaucracy and crony capitalist schemes. And so, African growth has not reached the heights required for its burgeoning youth, in the main because governments have not made the policy decisions or allowed the space for business to grow. Small and medium-sized businesses are the backbone of the global economy, accounting for one-third of GDP and 45 per cent of the workforce in high-income countries, and 98 per cent of employment in the Asia-Pacific region.

'SMMEs [small, medium and micro enterprises] thrive despite the government,' says Geordin Hill-Lewis, the mayor of the City of Cape Town. 'I don't think our government has ever really bothered to properly understand the constraints SMMEs face and how the state can help to get around them, even the local government. We add terrible red tape for small businesses and informal traders to comply with. Ridiculous licensing conditions, etcetera. Limitations on trading space.' The mayor has made it his business to 'strip out all that nonsense. Everyone who wants a trading space must have one. Everyone who wants to be licensed must be.'[13]

We know all this. Are there African examples of success in breaking out of these 'traps' of colonial inheritance, elite rent-seeking and low growth? What are the lessons in strategy and leadership that enable change and hinder development?

Challenges of Diversification

> 'Botswana is a poor country and at present is unable to stand on its own feet and develop its resources without assistance from its friends.'
> – Sir Seretse Khama, first president of Botswana, 6 October 1966

IMAGINE this scenario.

Visitors arrive at Gaborone's Sir Seretse Khama International Airport on one of the regular low-cost charter flights direct from Osaka, Shanghai or Manila. The airport has recently opened its second cargo hub terminal servicing western and southern Africa. Next to it is the private jet parking terminal that Botswana pioneered, a concept that others seek to emulate throughout the region. The visitors connect immediately with the hourly charter service to the swamps for a three-day stay in the internationally famous Central Kalahari Park. The park offers the freedom of vast open plains, saltpans, ancient riverbeds, sand dunes and flat bushveld to stressed city-dwellers. But there's more. Visitors can experience the culture of the San people, the indigenous inhabitants of the Kalahari. On their return to Gaborone, they are moved through the Diamond Processing Zone, where first-hand they can select a rough stone and setting, and have the final cut and polished product delivered to their holiday chalet. Or honeymooners may decide to choose their stone directly from Jwaneng, where they've spent the day on a special tour that takes them from 'mine-face to finger'. They return to their room on the outskirts of the city, where wildlife mingles with golfers on a world-renowned, Tiger Woods–designed golf course, the home to the Classic Diamond Open.

This is a vision of Botswana as an exemplar not only of sound government, but also of how to develop beyond high growth rates and ostentatious consumerism. Such a vision fortunately does not require a vivid, unrealistic imagination; it is well within the policy art of the possible.

This is a future Botswana. Or, at least, it could have been.

Botswana's success

Botswana is a remarkable development turnaround story. But it also shows how difficult it is to wean a country off its dependence on natural resources, and how difficult it is to do the next stage.

Botswana enjoyed the highest rate of per capita growth of any country in the world from the 1970s, averaging 9.6 per cent from 1970 to 1989. It did so despite minimal colonial investment in institutions and infrastructure. At independence in 1966, it was one of the world's least-developed and poorest nations, with a per capita income of just $460 (or $90 in nominal terms), with the majority dependent on subsistence agriculture, in the company of Bangladesh, Burkina Faso, Burundi, Comoros, El Salvador, Ethiopia, Equatorial Guinea, Haiti, Indonesia, Laos, Lesotho, Mali, Nepal, Niger, Rwanda, Sudan, North Yemen and Vietnam.[14] By 2015, Botswana was ranked 102nd in GDP per capita among 212 countries and territories. No fewer than twenty-seven of the bottom thirty are African, among them many of the countries highlighted above, which Botswana has managed to leave in its dust.

Amid the cranes, traffic jams, new hotels and shiny skyscrapers, Gaborone is today a far cry from nearly sixty years ago when Sir Seretse led the country to independence on 30 September 1966. Possessing then just twelve kilometres of tarred road, there was scant access to health, sanitation, water, telephones, electricity, public transportation and other services. Some 90 per cent of the population was based in rural areas. There were just twenty-two African university graduates and 100 citizens who had completed secondary education. Literacy was around one-third, the country possessing only 251 primary and nine secondary schools with fewer than 80 000 students enrolled, of which around 1 000 were at secondary level, from a population of 570 000.[15]

The country was heavily dependent on the export of beef. Manufacturing accounted for just 8 per cent of GDP in 1966, with only a fraction of the population in formal employment. An estimated 20 per cent of the adult male population worked in South Africa. Botswana depended then on British foreign aid not only to develop but also to survive.

By 2021, per capita GDP was more than South Africa's, at $6 887 (compared to $5 659),[16] with literacy at 87 per cent among a population of 2.3 million, of which 72 per cent lived in urban areas.[17] The reason for this transformation is simple. Botswana learnt quickly how to gain maximum value from its natural resources, in this case diamonds, by establishing a productive relationship with De Beers.

This achievement should not be sniffed at. The continent is awash with examples of how natural resources, absent good governance, can translate into predatory regimes and civil war. For every Botswana, a diamond-rich state, there are plenty of Central African Republics, Congos or Sierra Leones, mineral-rich but failed states. Botswana is also landlocked, and until thirty years ago it was dependent on the trade routes through apartheid South Africa, a political enemy.

What made the difference in Botswana was a good deal with a reliable partner early on, a deal that was renegotiated continuously over time.

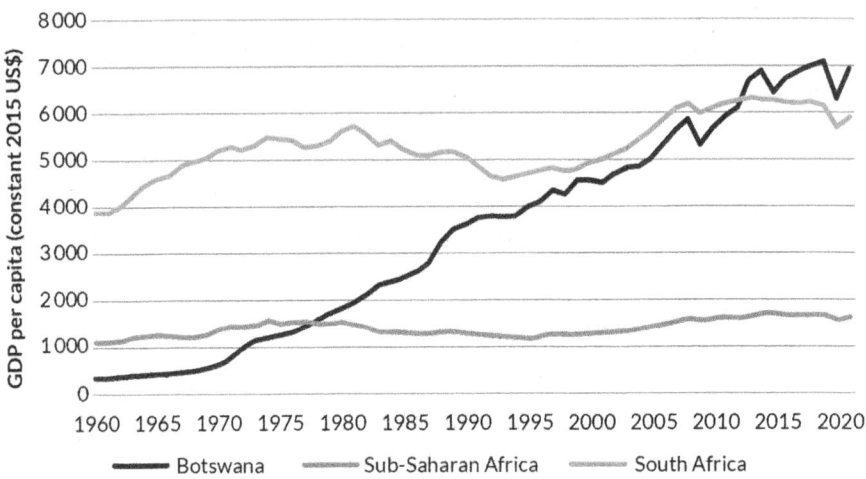

When better choices pay off: Tales of GDP per capita growth

Source: World Bank, World Development Indicators

There were other factors. A large territory – a little smaller than Ukraine, but larger than France, Spain and Kenya – combined with a high level of ethnic unity helped. Good institutions were also a key part of the success story, though what came first is questionable: good institutions or good leadership. Botswana has ranked consistently high in measures of the quality of institutions: political participation, rule of law, and control of corruption. On Transparency International's 2021 Corruption Perceptions Index, Botswana ranked 45th out of 180 countries with a score of 55/100, the third-highest performer in sub-Saharan Africa.[18] It came in at 61 out of 177 on the Heritage Foundation's 2021 Index of Economic Freedom and 91st out of 140 on the World Economic Forum's 2019 Global Competitiveness Index, seventh in all of Africa.

Like Mauritius, the other star African performer, Botswana is the only country to have been democratic continuously since independence. Botswana is considered 'free' by Freedom House and one of the most stable democracies in Africa.[19]

How Botswana did it

Botswana achieved this rapid development by following orthodox economic policies, an anomaly on a continent where, typically, 'good economics' is politically impossible. Researchers Daron Acemoglu, James Robinson and Simon Johnson suggest that good policies were chosen in Botswana because good institutions, which they refer to as institutions of private property, were in place.

They suggest that these institutions were the result of relatively inclusive pre-colonial institutions, placing constraints on political elites. The effect of British colonialism on Botswana was minimal, leaving the local institutions more or less intact. Following independence, the maintenance and strengthening of institutions of private property was in the economic interests of the elite. Botswana's subsequent wealth in diamonds meant that no group wanted to challenge the system, which created sufficient rents.

Of course, good institutions are built by mortals. This system was reinforced by several critical decisions made by the immediate post-independence leaders.[20]

Sir Seretse Khama's passing of the Mines and Minerals Act in 1967, which conferred subsoil mineral rights to the national government from the tribes, centralised the state's power. Moreover, Khama resisted 'indigenising the bureaucracy until suitably qualified citizens were available; so expatriate workers were kept, and international advisers and consultants were also used', which added to institutional strength and fabric. Similarly, the adherence to national development planning and budgeting principles, with development plans based on a six-year planning cycle, along with a consistent focus, since 1966, on economic growth, helped to consolidate this central authority.[21]

There were other advantages, not least in being situated next to a relatively functional and wealthy big power in South Africa, no matter its political system. Indeed, apartheid may, in fact, have helped to offer some advantages in donor funding. For example, between 1966 and 1994, Botswana received an annual average of $77 per capita in net official development assistance, well above the sub-Saharan average of $17.

Perhaps more than anything, four events were to shape the country's fortunes and propel it from a struggling ex-colony to a model of growth and development.

First, De Beers announced its rich diamond discovery in Orapa in 1967. Situated 240 kilometres west of Francistown, the mine became operational in 1971. Now the largest open pit mine in the world, it kickstarted the Debswana joint venture between De Beers and the government of Botswana. Originally the government acquired a 20 per cent share (excluding taxes and royalties) without having to invest any capital.

Additionally, Bamangwato Concessions Ltd (initially a joint AMAX, government of Botswana and Anglo American subsidiary) developed the Selebi-Phikwe copper-nickel deposits, which opened in 1974. While not a success financially, the mine employed 5 000 workers at its zenith.

Third, the renegotiation in 1969 of the 1910 Customs Union agreement with South Africa resulted in a greater share of revenue for Botswana, which, even by 2020, amounted to 30 per cent of government income. Exports increased almost sevenfold from 1969 to 1975, helped by a near doubling in export demand for Botswanan beef to 209 000 tonnes by 1974.

Then, in 1975, the government crucially renegotiated the original mining lease with De Beers, the 20 per cent share being upped to 50 per cent with the development of the Jwaneng diamond mine, since paid for through retained earnings. The deal, recalls Gary Ralfe, the former chief executive officer (CEO) of De Beers, 'was a very tough negotiation'. This was again renegotiated several times, to the point that the Botswanan government now retains an even greater share of pre-tax profits. Still, this remains the most important partnership, notes Ralfe, 'in the whole of the diamond world'.[22]

Addressing Botswana's failures

Diamonds account for 27 per cent of GDP and around 87 per cent of exports. Botswana's impressive success in the diamond arena has created other problems, however, problems of dependency on an industry that creates extraordinary profits and expectations. In a form of Dutch disease,[23] the diamond domination has kept the value of the Botswanan pula up, making exports of any manufactured goods challenging.

As much of the rest of the economy depends on this industry, Botswana's dependence on diamonds is almost total. This has not been lost on successive governments.

In 2005, the Brenthurst Foundation assembled a group of international specialists at the invitation of the government of Botswana to help devise a strategy for economic diversification. This was a great opportunity to work in a country that had done all the hard work already. Atypical of much of our work in Africa, this did not involve recovering from a traumatic period of collapse. The foundation of diamonds was already in place; the fortieth anniversary of independence in 2006 offered a symbolic opportunity to take this to the next level.

Out of these discussions emerged the Business and Economic Advisory Council (BEAC) to oversee the strategy we developed. Not much happened, however. In part this may have been down to not having the right people in the BEAC; in part bad timing given the temporary collapse of the diamond market in 2009; but in part something else, a feature that has continued to afflict Botswana in realising its diversification ambitions.

This occasion was not, of course, the first time that Botswana had attempted to diversify, though various efforts have consistently been costly failures.

The Financial Assistance Policy, terminated in 1999, provided labour and capital subsidies. Very few of the 3 000 operations started under this programme survive. The Citizen Entrepreneurial Development Agency policy that replaced it offered low-interest loans, along with mentoring and support programmes, but met with very limited success. High-profile attempts at industrialisation also met with limited success and occasional failure, such as the Hyundai assembly plant in Gaborone, which closed in 2000 with the loss of 1 900 jobs. With assets exceeding liabilities by R1 billion, the parastatal Botswana Development Corporation was left with losses of R135 million.[24]

Instead of creating permanent jobs, these schemes generally institutionalised inefficiencies and high operating costs, even though, to Botswana's credit, it closed them down, a rarity in the developing world given the strong political constituencies that usually quickly gather around subsidy programmes.

There has been no shortage of other attempts and institutions. The Local Procurement Programme, introduced in 1997, was aimed at enhancing the development of local entrepreneurs. A policy on SMMEs was adopted in 1998 to foster citizen entrepreneurship. The Botswana Development Corporation was created in 1970 to fund the establishment of commercially viable businesses to diversify the economy. Established in 1997, the Botswana Export Development and Investment Authority was also set up to drive economic diversification through joint ventures between local and foreign investors, as well as develop factories for use by start-up manufacturers. The Local Enterprise Authority was established under the Small Business Act of 2004 to promote and facilitate entrepreneurship and enterprise development among SMMEs. The Botswana National Productivity Centre, the Public Enterprises Evaluation and Privatisation Agency, and the Botswana Bureau of Standards, among others, were all created with similar intentions, as was the Botswana Excellence Strategy within the Office of the President. Most recently, in 2016, the government established Vision 2036 to create a blueprint for the development of Botswana.

While services have more than doubled as a share of GDP to some 66 per cent between 1980 and 2020, despite these efforts, the share of industry has fallen from 44 per cent to 28 per cent and agriculture from 13 per cent to 2 per cent.

The serial failure of institutions to successfully address diversification is puzzling, particularly given the strong sustained rate of economic growth. While the proliferation of 'fragmented, piecemeal' policies made implementation of various diversification plans difficult,[25] and the various plans lacked resources and timeframes, something else has been lacking.

Several reasons other than the effect of the strong pula stand out in explaining the failure of diversification.

Just fifty-five years old when he became president in 2008, Ian Khama, the son of Botswana's first president, Seretse Khama, has long been forthright and clear about the foundation of the country's success. 'It is based on a cultural and traditional commitment to democracy and what democracy entails,' he said in 2016. This commitment, he observed from his modest presidential office in Gaborone, 'has little to do with colonial legacy, not least since the British capital of the territory was outside [the country], in Mafikeng. Rather, it is both cultural and dependent on leadership. More than being just a good intention, or rhetoric, the commitments to democracy and good governance are now deeply ingrained.' Botswana's poverty was initially an advantage. 'Always starting from a bad situation, you can make good.'[26]

Khama, who relinquished office in 2018, says that Botswana was able to make some progress in diversifying not from mining, per se, but from diamonds. 'We put in very good legislation for prospecting – for coal, despite the question marks about harmful emissions, for gold, copper and uranium.' For example, the time taken for a mining prospecting right in Botswana is just forty days; in South Africa it is 354, explaining the relative dearth of investment in the latter.[27]

'We also focused attention on improving tourism through improving our key product, our wildlife, and its protection, and stepped up our agriculture performance, despite being a water-scarce country like Israel,' notes Khama. As a result, tourist numbers trebled to 1.8 million arrivals annually between 1994 and 2018.[28] However, tourist spending as a percentage of exports peaked at over 15 per cent in 2008 and has fallen to its 'normal' level of between 7 and 8 per cent since.[29] And despite the attention, agriculture remains a poor performer. By 2022, the sector contributed less than 5 per cent of GDP, while the country imports food to the value of 11.4 per cent of total import value, mostly from South Africa, and most of it comprising cereals (maize, wheat and rice) and sugar.[30] The Botswanan government's response in 2022 was to ban South African vegetable and fruit imports, including tomatoes, carrots, beetroot, potatoes, cabbage, lettuce, garlic, onions, ginger, turmeric, chilli peppers, butternut, watermelons, sweet peppers, green mealies and fresh herbs. This was met by an outcry from traders, given supply shortages in the water-scarce country.[31]

Certainly, while life on diamonds is not a guarantee of riches (only look elsewhere in Africa), it has proven very easy. 'When they wake up in the morning, they know they have only to work half a day since half their income is guaranteed,' a Costa Rican colleague, who was part of our original 2005 team, said of this phenomenon. 'We, on the other hand, have to work from the moment we wake up – there is no natural resource dividend.'

Khama concedes that there is a problem of apathy among his citizens, the guarantee of diamond income demotivating business to 'get out there'. As he noted in 2016, 'Occasionally we get offered opportunities, but we are laid back in leaping at them because of having diamonds. Also, there is a dependency syndrome on government since we were once so poor and have done a lot through social interventions. Many people probably get assistance who should be looking after themselves – this is a trend. The question they have always is, "What is government going to do for me?"[32]

As one measure of this effect, the size of Botswana's bureaucracy had increased from 2 000 at independence to 21 000 by 1985,[33] to 138 000 in 2015 and 155 000 in 2020,[34] representing one-third of formal sector employment. Not only is this unsustainable, but the frictions inherent in this expansion are exacerbated by access to skills, in government and in commerce. The civil service is also not seen as an institution that empowers business.

Skills are another, related impediment. While access to education is at a net enrolment high of 91 per cent, learning levels do not match up. An analysis of learning levels among Botswana's Grade 5 scholars conducted in 2017, for example, found that over 85 per cent of students could not divide, and half of students could not read a simple story.[35] More than the need for academic results is the need for a corresponding culture of entrepreneurship, which is a metaphor for the acceptance of risk and failure. The lack of the right skills, and an environment encouraging of such entrepreneurship, is why concepts such as a 'knowledge economy' remain unrealisable dreams, since Botswana lacks any comparative advantage in this regard.

The cost of diamonds has less to do with the resource curse per se than the manner in which its returns have skewed the way government in Botswana views business. The profit-to-revenue ratio of Jwaneng, for instance, is around 90 per cent. Few industries can rival this rate of return, perhaps only some in the oil business.

Given its high profits, there is a risk of government viewing all businesses in the same light, with the same level of profit expectation and government assistance. The consequence of this is that it has failed to attract anything but captive business – driven by nature or resources – as opposed to those which can go and invest anywhere, hence the focus on mining and its beneficiation, and high-end tourism.

It also explains the difficulty in attracting a polishing and cutting industry, despite Botswana's comparative advantage in the raw product. The cost of cutting in India and Vietnam – where there are a million workers in the sector – is around $10 per carat; in Israel, it's on the $20 margin, while in South Africa and Botswana it costs more than $30. Hence the rest of the world outside India having fewer than 50 000 people in this industry. Botswana cuts and polishes perhaps three-quarters of Debswana's output (by value), but still the industry only amounts to fewer than 2 000 employees across thirty factories. Added to the 9 000 employees of Debswana, including contractors, diamonds might be a revenue provider for government, but it is not a big employer, and it's difficult to see where more jobs can be added.

All this explains why attempts to look inwards and localise have been less than successful. Botswana has so far been too expensive, too bureaucratic, and too spoilt by diamonds for it to instil a mindset of competitiveness and a policy suite to match. Throw in a failure of critical, outward thinking and lack of internationalisation, and it has got stuck.

But, while diamonds have been too forgiving, they will not be around forever. Jwaneng will likely move to underground operations before 2030, and profits will come down substantially as mining costs increase. And the resource itself will only last for another generation. There will have to be a life beyond diamonds for which Botswana will need to start planning today.

Conclusion: Make hard choices and compete

Landlocked and subject to the whims of regional bureaucracy, Botswana's diversification depends on streamlining trade flows and the growth that moves with them. There has been some progress in regional infrastructure, not least in constructing the bridge at Kazungula, where Zimbabwe, Namibia, Botswana and Zambia meet. A curving one-kilometre South Korean–built bridge crosses the Zambezi from Botswana and meets, on the northern bank, a one-stop-shop border facility in Zambia housing both the Botswanan and Zambian authorities.

But this facility reminds us that expediting trade and transport is not just a function of the hardware of infrastructure, as crucial as that may be. It also requires the software of skills and institutional architecture. The new bridge is important but by itself is not enough. The roads on all sides plugging into it have to work, be free of incessant stop-and-go roadblocks and be streamlined to encourage the inward and outward flow of trade.

Getting through the Kazungula one-stop in 2022 involved a Covid-19 check, emigration check and stamp, and vehicle documentation check at the Botswanan desks. It all seemed too easy, and sadly was. Zambia's bureaucracy involved a bewildering process of Covid check and stamp, passport stamp, insurance payment (in a separate building), Interpol car clearance inspection and ATA Carnet stamp in another separate building (second time around; they were on lunch the first time), payment of the road toll ($20), carbon tax (Kw660), council fees (Kw50) and bridge toll (Kw450), and then custom stamp (also second time around, as lunch was again being served), before driving out to the gate where all documents were again taken away and inspected. Welcome to Zambia.

While Botswana is not responsible for Zambia's inefficiencies and bureaucratic peccadilloes, they reflect poorly on the other side of the river and add a premium to the cost of doing regional business.

A combination of apathy and the wrong choices explains why the airport in

Gaborone remains only fractionally employed after its opening in 1984, with less than thirty flights each day from a facility certified as a 3-Star Regional Airport. The new facility's freight usage hit a peak of just one million tonne-kilometres in 2019, compared to South Africa's high of 1 233 million tonne-kilometres in 2006.[36] Yet just a few kilometres away from the airport is De Beers Global Sightholder Sales, previously known as the Diamond Trading Company (DTC), a sorting, valuation and sales centre. The DTC was moved in 2012 from London as part of a deal struck around the renewal of the lease on the giant Jwaneng and Orapa mines. In 2021, the sales centre handled thirty-two million carats (worth $5.6 billion) of De Beers' diamond production for global distribution among sixty-five dealers known as sightholders. But while this may have created a bubble economy in accommodation, catering and local transport, the numbers are small.

A hunger for change is lacking in Botswana. Even though they have been excellent for the country, diamonds do not offer a perpetual industry. There is no constituency in Botswana to stick to the tough road to diversification and global competitiveness, rather than simply rely on its comparative advantages: what's under its soil plus its unique high-end tourist offerings in the Okavango.

Instead, Gaborone is intent on squeezing more out of diamonds. In January 2023, President Mokgweetsi Masisi warned that the diamond deal that had delivered such prosperity was under threat, and that the government could sever the relationship.[37] Addressing supporters in his home village of Moshupa, Masisi said Botswana is prepared to pull out of the long-standing arrangement with De Beers: 'We are dealing with a giant. It is the first time it has been shaken like this. We want what is ours. This is our company, we want a majority stake, and we are doing so through negotiations. If the talks become difficult, we will say, no, let everyone pack and go separate ways.' This approach risks upending a relationship that has brought prosperity to Botswana for reasons that may be more personal than they are to do with national development, not least in terms of the public breakdown of Masisi's relationship with his presidential predecessor, Ian Khama. The rationale for attacking the country's long-term investment partner is also profoundly political as a populist gesture in seeking development answers through redistribution.

But such a move also reflects Botswana's difficulties in developing and diversifying beyond one sector, and reinforces the question: Why has Africa found it comparatively so difficult, when viewed alongside Asia, for instance, to move up the value chain?

There may be several reasons.

For one, development needs an elite that wants development to happen. When the elites come from politics, or from the bureaucracy, or from the NGO and aid world, this seems to be less likely. Their knowledge and their constituencies are outside of the business sector, and sometimes these elites are deeply ideologically antithetical towards business.

This antipathy may have its roots in past exploitative experiences, and the deep-seated hostility towards outsiders, including those in business, that followed. It's not rational, of course, and more visceral than cerebral, just as those outside London harbour a baseless animosity towards a metropolitan elite. Fortunately, this prejudice is decreasingly common in Africa. In parts of the continent, it is today acceptable (and even laudable) to be described as a businessperson.

This also may relate to the nature of the pre-colonial economy. In many cases the transition to independence simply involved a transfer of benefits from one elite to another, with little change in the economic structure and absent any incentive to do so. Much of this 'business' occurred around extorting subsidies and extracting value around commodities. This helps to explain why Nigeria's post-colonial business successes did not grow from the textile sector in Kano, for example, but rather from the elite preferences around energy and market protections. Where there was a larger indigenous trading elite, such as with the Asian community in Kenya, for instance, there was more space for commercial activity, replicating the growth patterns that have occurred farther afield in East Asia and in the Gulf.

Crucially, many of the post-colonial elites not only lacked a constituency for domestic development, but their power was also based on perceptions of wealth and its redistribution – hence the 'Big Man' phenomenon, most notably portrayed by the likes of Mobutu Sese Seko, but common to many settings. For these elites, there was little apparent benefit to being anything other than extractive, not least on where their wealth ended up. While the wealth of even the most corrupt Asians usually stayed in-country, where there was a pride in development outcomes, there was apparently no such compunction in their African counterparts. Given the absence of a development imperative, there was little need to raise money for development, which explains why systems of taxation were so neglected, as were local banking institutions and capital markets.

If it's going to diversify, the first thing Botswana must do is reduce the costs of doing business to below those of its nearest and greatest competitor – South Africa. This does not demand subsidies but rather a general improvement of the competitiveness environment. This would have to encompass bandwidth costs, tax rates, and the comparative ease of doing business, from registering a business to obtaining visas, expediting the flow of traffic and repatriation of capital. To fail to differentiate itself would simply be to join its regional anchor in the plummet to the development depths.

This includes mitigating the high value of the pula, a factor that may not be in the interests of the import-hungry elite. Efforts by the BEAC to address this via the then governor of the Reserve Bank were met with stony-faced responses, since development was not, we were informed, part of the bank's mandate.

More than anything, however, success at diversification requires making growth and development the central objective of government policy, the issue that everyone in government bangs on about from morning to night, every day, week, month and year. Such a laser focus on development is, after all, what set East Asia on a different trajectory, and made it an attractive destination for investors who could have gone anywhere.

There is another aspect that Botswana lacks, which is essential to competitiveness, and that centres on politics. Nearly six decades of one-party rule risks staleness. Yes, Botswana has benefitted from stability, and there has been a regular turnover of political leadership in terms of presidents, a system of refresh that has provided a predictable methodology. Yet how to get the right balance between change and continuity remains a tension.

Some critical choices stand out: whether Botswana sticks with what it knows versus taking more risks with the policies that will produce diversification; between a growing wage bill versus capital investment, especially in logistics and power; whether it chooses to benchmark costs against the region or to protect inefficiencies; whether it seeks closer regional integration or attempts to differentiate itself through better policies and cheaper costs; and finally, whether it is to be characterised by increasing political openness or a closed shop in seeing the opposition and civil society as a threat rather than a spur for change and competitiveness.

The vision described at the outset of this chapter is not something dreamt of today, but one that was provided to the government back in 2005. It has not happened, of course, reminding us of both the missed opportunities through inertia and the need for deliberate actions by leadership to bring about long-term benefits, just as Sir Seretse Khama did following independence.

Separating Reasons for Success and Failure

'Mauritius always has stability in its favour.'
— David Coutts-Trotter, former CEO: Sun International

MAURITIUS was once a prime example of the evils of globalisation – or 'globalisation at its worst'.[38]

The dodo has become a metaphor for an outdated concept or object, hence the expression 'dead as a dodo'. It is also slang for a dim-witted person. Once endemic to Mauritius, the flightless bird was a slow-moving target for the newly arrived settlers, its one-metre height and hefty build making it an easy food source. Combined with habitat loss, alien predators and competition with newly introduced livestock, the last dodo was killed in 1681, and the species lost forever.

Luckily the island has proven to be much more resilient and adaptive.

Habitation of the island commenced at the end of the sixteenth century with the arrival of the Dutch, who infamously harvested its ebony trees using slaves imported from Madagascar. Ten years after the Dutch decamped for the Cape, the French landed in 1721. Sugarcane was planted, and the island slowly developed, even though the settlers were vulnerable to passing pirates and disease. Control passed from France to Britain with the defeat of Napoleon in 1814, though the Franco-Mauritians remained as the landowning elite, slavery only being abolished in 1835, three decades after the rest of the British empire.

To replace the slaves, half a million indentured workers were brought from India between 1849 and 1923 in what was termed a 'Great Experiment'; as a result, production and exports from the plantations grew rapidly. Political liberalisation was slow but inexorable. Under the 1886 constitution, the British governor allowed a Creole elite to join the Franco-Mauritians among the national representatives. When a new constitution extended the franchise to all literate adults in 1948, the Indian-dominated, socialist-minded Labour Party won a majority. It was opposed by the Franco-Mauritian oligarchs who feared 'Hindu hegemony'. Over time, the two opposing forces drew closer. The Labour Party became more moderate, changing its original stance on nationalisation of the sugar plantations. This decision 'was to prove a key turning point' in several respects. It helped establish the precedent of safeguarding property rights, in contrast with other African countries. It also helped reconcile the somewhat appeased Franco-Mauritians to independence.[39]

Mauritius gained its independence in March 1968 with the Labour Party's Seewoosagur Ramgoolam, who had assiduously managed a turbulent run-up, as first prime minister. Although the Mauritian Social Democratic Party, the conservative party representing the oligarchs, initially stayed away from the independence process, it soon joined a government coalition. The space to the left was filled by the Mauritian Militant Movement (MMM) led by Paul Bérenger, and which later, amid high economic growth, also entered the coalition.

Measures of success

Mauritius is a success story by almost every measure.

Its average score in the World Bank's 2018 Ease of Doing Business index was 77.54, ranking it 25th, compared to the sub-Saharan average of 50.43, or the score of its Indian Ocean neighbour Madagascar in 162nd position at 47.67. The next highest sub-Saharan country, Rwanda, was 41st. Kenya was 80th, South Africa 81st and Botswana 82nd.

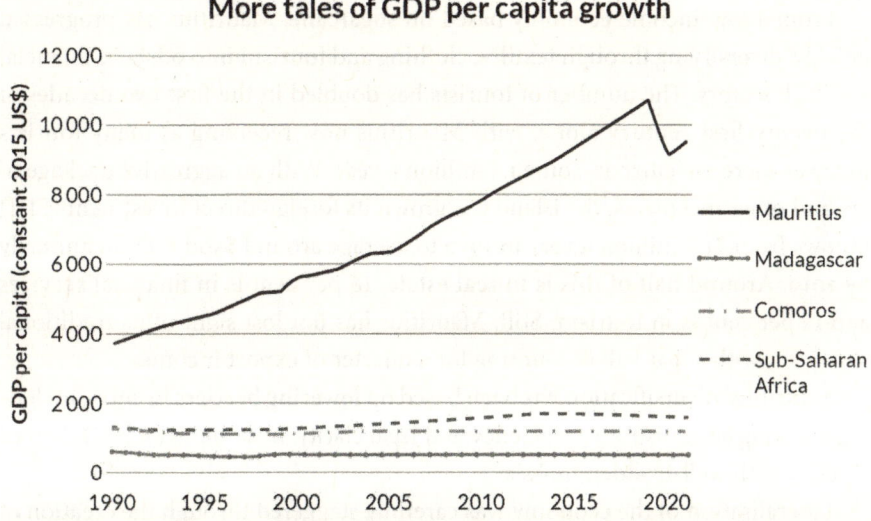

More tales of GDP per capita growth

Source: World Bank, World Development Indicators

On the Ibrahim Index of African Governance, defined as the provision of political, social and economic public goods, Mauritius topped the African rankings in 2019, scoring 77.2. Cabo Verde was second with 73.1, with Seychelles completing the top three with a score of 72.3. Mauritius' GDP per capita is $9 422, well above the 2021 sub-Saharan average ($1 612), that of Madagascar ($450), and South Africa and Botswana ($5 865 and $6 888). Only in this key regard does it rank below Seychelles, where, with a population of just 95 000, per capita GDP is over $15 000.

The average life expectancy of Mauritians in 1960 was fifty-eight; now it's seventy-four, whereas sub-Saharan Africa has gone from forty to sixty-two over the same period.

No obvious reasons for success

Yet Mauritius had no obvious advantages at independence. It was small in geography and population, lacking economies of scale. Hardly well-endowed with natural resources, it ranked as one of the most remote countries alongside those of the South Pacific islands, and moved even further off the beaten track with the opening of the Suez Canal in 1869. It possessed an ethnically diverse population, usually a factor conducive to political unrest, particularly given the history of factionalism. The dependency on a volatile monocrop in sugar highlighted all these weaknesses to the point that, in 1961, Nobel Prize–winning economist James Meade predicted a dismal future for the island given its vulnerabilities to weather and price shocks, and lack of job opportunities outside the sugar sector.

And yet Mauritius' path to prosperity is now well understood.

From a low-income economy based on sugarcane, Mauritius has progressed quickly, diversifying through textiles, clothing and tourism into offshore financial and ICT sectors. The number of tourists has doubled in the first two decades of the twenty-first century alone, with Mauritius now receiving as many tourists today as there are citizens, some 1.3 million a year. With an aggressive package of tax and other incentives, the island has grown its foreign direct investment (FDI) inflows from $1.6 million a year in 1970 to average around $500 million annually by 2019. Around half of this is in real estate, 16 per cent is in financial services and 13 per cent is in tourism. Still, Mauritius has not lost sight of its traditional strengths, with sugar still accounting for a quarter of export income.

Mauritius' diversification has been based on lowering barriers to entry, including ensuring administrative efficiency and legal clarity. In so doing, it has followed a policy path well-trodden in Asia.

Liberalisation of the economy was carefully staggered through the creation of export processing zones in the 1970s. By 2018 there were 21500 offshore businesses and nearly 930 global funds domiciled in Mauritius. During the 1990s, capital and current accounts were liberalised, contributing to an investment and employment boom. The inflow of FDI brought with it managerial skills. In the 1990s, as wages rose and Chinese investors left to pursue low-wage opportunities elsewhere, Mauritius responded with further diversification and liberalisation, particularly in the financial services sector.

As a result, economic growth has averaged over 4 per cent since independence, at the same time significantly reducing inequality. It's too easy, however, to put

Mauritius' success solely down to sandy beaches, great weather and financial incentives.

Neither was this path preordained. Despite Meade and others giving the island little hope of progress, given its geographic isolation, rapid population growth and fraught colonial history, some now put its success down to its diverse national make-up, albeit with a clear Indian majority. Yet plenty of countries in Africa have a similar ethnic tapestry, which more often than not is given as a reason for corruption or instability.

So, why Mauritius?

Making things happen

Trade was not a critical part of the story, although Mauritius was a highly protectionist economy during the 1970s and 1980s.

By the early 2000s, it ranked in the top third of countries in the Heritage Foundation's Index of Economic Freedom. By 2022, it ranked first among the countries in sub-Saharan Africa, above Cabo Verde and Botswana, and twenty-sixth overall out of 176 countries listed.[40] This transformation was not simply about openness. Mauritius pursued, as did China in following this example, a 'heterodox' trade policy through the use of export processing zones. Established in 1970, the EPZs promoted exports through tax advantages, eliminating tariffs and enabling a lower minimum wage within the zones (initially 50 per cent between EPZ and sugarcane workers, for instance). But this in and of itself was not enough; many other countries, including some in Africa, have established EPZs without similar success.

The presence of foreign expertise and technology was also not a dealmaker, since the extent of foreign ownership in Mauritius (by employment) was much lower than in East Asia, for instance (12 per cent versus 64 per cent in Malaysia). It may, in fact, have been down to the opposite factor – higher local ownership – if one compares Mauritius to Lesotho.

Surrounded entirely by South Africa, the Kingdom of Lesotho has many advantages that Mauritius does not possess. It is well integrated into South African logistics and power networks. It has an abundant labour pool. It has duty-free access to the US and European markets. But its attempts to prosper through textiles, like Mauritius, have faltered. In the early 2000s, with the creation of the African Growth and Opportunity Act by Washington, many, mostly Taiwanese textile and clothing firms set up operation in Maseru, the capital of Lesotho. In addition to duty- and quota-free access to the United States, they received preferential rental rates for their factories. Although the number of jobs rapidly increased to top 50 000, by 2022 this had come down to little more than 30 000. This decline was caused by several factors, not least the increasing cost of Basotho labour and volatility in the US market.

Unlike Mauritius, where half of the total equity of firms in the EPZs is owned by Mauritian nationals, in Lesotho local ownership is locked in single digits after three decades of clothing manufacturing. The lack of local knowledge and a small capital base does not help, but this does not explain why Lesotho has failed to diversify out of textiles, whether by foreign or local investment.

Lesotho's GDP per capita is just $1 035, 50 per cent less than the continental average and five times less than the South African mark. One-third of its 2.1 million people live in poverty. A breakdown in governance – the rule of law – alongside low growth and high inequality lends itself to violence. Lesotho has a murder rate of 41.25 per 100 000, on par with neighbouring South Africa. Mauritius' murder rate, in comparison, is 3 per 100 000.[41]

The vicious cycle of violence and poverty illustrates a deeper problem. Whatever challenges Lesotho had before, they have been amplified by sixty years of sustained population growth, during which time it has more than doubled. This would not be a problem, say, in Singapore, but this coterie has been fed into a low-skills, low-growth market. The differential in income with South Africa is illustrative of the frictional costs of doing business – in terms of bureaucracy and logistics in particular – between the two.

And most importantly, Lesotho has never had to develop its own development path replete with hard choices and ownership of its destiny. There has always been a soft, diplomatically directed option: donor funding, especially during the apartheid years, unfettered access to the European and US markets, and a share of the pooled revenue between the countries of the Southern African Customs Union, namely South Africa, Botswana, Namibia, Lesotho and Eswatini.

The endless political changes and tribulations – Lesotho has had seven elections since the reintroduction of democracy in 1993, and four coups or attempts – have made little difference to the Basotho, other than failing to provide a stable platform for growth and development. Instead, with few exceptions, they have simply offered opportunities for different factions among the elite for rent-seeking.

Mauritius shows that the comparative quality of institutions, especially property rights and the rule of law, helps to determine which countries experience good performance and which do not. Better policy makes little difference without the institutional structure and human resources to support it. This architecture has allowed Mauritius to skilfully manoeuvre and adapt its offering as markets have changed.

But where do these 'good' institutions come from? Acemoglu, Johnson and Robinson argue that a key variable is in the extent and duration of European settlement, meaning the longer the colonial period the better the institutions, the duration of which relates in turn to a suitable climate and presence of diseases.[42] Of course, the latter is dependent on growth, since higher growth leads to swamps being drained and diseases being brought under control. Yet some hostile geographies and climates have prospered, including Hong Kong, Malaysia and Singapore.

There are other factors: Mauritius has long invested heavily in quality schooling. Sir Ramgoolam boldly granted free education to all citizens. As a result, the country achieved a high rate of literacy early on by comparison to its once-colonised peers: 80 per cent in 1990 versus Kenya's 74 per cent.

Mauritius also successfully used international diplomacy to its advantage, preferring European pricing and a large quota, contrary to the African norm. Its attempts to diversify were assisted by a competitive exchange rate. Mauritius was quick to use differential tax rates to attract foreign investors, notably from jittery South Africans looking for a contingency. The combination of a flat and low income and corporate tax (just 15 per cent), no exchange control, and no corporate gains tax was a powerful incentive.

Why Mauritius made these good policy choices when so many other countries did not is partly down to good leaders. While it helped to have good leaders at independence to set the country on its path, the duration of these reforms suggests that leadership went beyond a few good men and became embedded in the entire political system. Good practices became good institutions. As Professor Deborah Bräutigam notes: 'Although the institutions put in place at the time of independence were established to solve the immediate problem of economic and political instability in an ethnically diverse land, they also created a set of norms, procedures, and constraints that continued to shape political and economic strategies and behaviour in the post-independence decades.'[43]

Why do other governments in Africa not make similar choices when examples of success abound? Or, more bluntly, why has nearby Madagascar been such an abject comparative failure?

Part of the answer may lie in Mauritius' democratic status. In 1980 it was one of two African countries considered democratic, the other being Botswana. It has maintained its democratic record since independence, notwithstanding a wobble in the early 1970s. In 2022 it was scored 86 out of 100 by Freedom House (where 100 is regarded as 'most free'), the second-highest score in Africa. By comparison, South Sudan achieved the lowest score at 1 out of 100, followed by Eritrea with 3; Cabo Verde ranked above Mauritius with 92, and the next highest after Mauritius was São Tomé and Príncipe with 84, followed by Ghana with 80, South Africa and Seychelles with 79, Kenya with 48 and Nigeria with 43.

This goes hand in hand with strong institutions, particularly a developed legal system and code that have made the foreign investment climate in Mauritius one of the best in the region. This relates to the level of investment in people, with Mauritian nationals accounting for 90 per cent of entrepreneurs in the EPZs and in the manufacturing sector.

Mauritius has also taken what it can from the past and moved on.

On the quayside of the waterfront in Port Louis is a statue of Sir Seewoosagur Ramgoolam, often referred to as *Chacha* (literally, 'uncle'), who led the independence movement. Facing him, across the road, is a statue of the ambitiously named Bertrand-François Mahé de La Bourdonnais, a central figure during the French colonial period between 1721 and 1810.

This is not surprising since Mauritian politicians are at pains to point out the importance of racial inclusion in their society, especially of the tiny (perhaps 1 per cent) French minority, which continues to wield a disproportionate economic influence.

Success is also down to a practice of consensual politics. Ideological differences have waxed and waned since the late 1960s.

Ramgoolam was the first prime minister of a coalition government of the Labour Party and the Mauritian Social Democratic Party. In 1969, Paul Bérenger founded the opposition Mauritian Militant Movement. As Bérenger, born in 1945, notes, 'we were very, very radical – sometimes called the Mauritian Marxist Movement and even,' he smiles, 'the Mauritian Military Movement'. He was among the MMM leaders held 'in political detention', as he refers to this period, for a year in 1971 after strikes led to an outbreak of violence.

Yet, by 1982, Bérenger was in a coalition government serving variously as deputy prime minister, minister of finance and foreign minister, and was prime minister from 2003 to 2005, the first Caucasian to serve as head of government of a post-independence African country.

Speaking from his study, piled high with government documents, in Vacoas-Phoenix, Bérenger says that Mauritius was 'supposed to fail rather than succeed. Things in our history and at independence were indicative of trouble ahead. Many in the private sector were against independence, and 44 per cent of the population voted against it in a referendum. There was violence in the run-up and immediately afterwards, and elections were postponed in 1969. It was the Wild West of politics.'

The reasons for success, reflects Bérenger, were, first, 'that the Labour Party, which, too, was very radical, did not go ahead and nationalise industry, even though some saw this as a betrayal, including my own party. If we had done this, we might have ended up as another Zimbabwe. The result was that the private sector stayed and diversified according to a clear deal: I [the government] will not touch your property, but the state is my part.'

Second, 'personalities were also important. The old man, Sir Seewoosagur Ramgoolam, was very special. We fought like mad but got on very well.'

And third, 'democracy has undoubtedly also played an essential part in Mauritius' success, along with the constitution, which is very strong on fundamental freedoms, separation of power and protection of private property. We have an exemplary electoral setup, with an independent electoral commissioner with the security and tenure of a judge, with their own staff, and an electoral commission chosen by the president after wide consultation ... even though we have an awful first-past-the-post, undemocratic electoral system.'

All this does not mean, Bérenger notes, that Mauritius is without problems, including 'corruption and abuses of power – though compared to other countries in Africa, we are better'. The democratic system also allows, he admits, accountability, policy innovation and self-correction.

Barlen Vyapoory, who served as vice president and then president between 2016 and 2019, agrees that the island's economic success is related to its democratic success, reminding us that 'democracy is like, as Churchill said, the worst system of government apart from all the others. We have believed in the process of democracy as the best option, and we have worked towards making everyone feel secure, through welfare and through accommodating each ethnic group's aspirations. Although the majority of people are of Indian origin, we have tried our best to live peacefully. While the white population are a small minority, they have been given all opportunity to participate.' As if to emphasise the point, Vyapoory warmly welcomed me into State House, a colonial chateau built as a fortress in 1749, and formerly the governor's residence.

'Democracy has to work hand in hand with education to be a bottom-up process,' notes Vyapoory. 'This has enabled us to capitalise on our strengths. And it has ensured political stability and security, and institutional development, which has played in our favour.'

This aspect may explain why Mauritius has succeeded and not Madagascar next door, where the thirst for power has consistently been greater than the interests of the people.

Having no army, like Costa Rica, may have helped too, certainly by comparison to the serial (successful and attempted) coups experienced by both Madagascar (five since independence in 1960) and Comoros (twenty since independence).[44] The pacifist route seems to have paid off. Security spending in Mauritius in 2000, for example, was $8 per capita, equal to 0.2 per cent of GDP, compared to the 6.7 per cent spent on education and health. Comparative statistics for other sub-Saharan countries are far higher, security averaging $9.6 per capita, or 1.5 per cent of GDP.

The lack of expropriation or taxing away of the Franco-Mauritians' sugar plantations, which both allowed them to give up political power and established the importance of property rights, had a further benefit: the inculcation of a shared system of wealth and ownership. For instance, the share of Muslims and Chinese in the senior public service rose in the first three decades after independence. None of the ethnic groups is excluded from the system. As economist Jeffrey Frankel notes, 'it is intriguing that the three African countries with the highest governance rankings (Mauritius, Seychelles and Cape Verde) are all islands that had no indigenous population'.[45]

Comoros: Where ylang-ylang should have beaten war-war

'We must count on the sea – our seas,' says Fouday Gouilame, the head of the planning section in the Comoros government. 'They are one thousand times bigger than our land. Everything depends on our national expertise. But our history weighs on our development. Unlike Mauritius, which benefits from the Indian traditions and Chinese influence, most of the time we are trying to get rid of the burdens of colonialism.'[46]

Snuggled in the Mozambique Channel, the islands making up Comoros are 1600 kilometres west of Mauritius. They share the Indian Ocean and French influence but little else. Whereas the Comoros archipelago's per capita income, at $1600, is on the African average, and its poverty at nearly one in five of the 890 000 population, the average wealth of Mauritians is nearly six times greater, and poverty is effectively zero at 0.1 per cent.

And whereas Mauritius' political history has been one of stability and improving inclusivity, for twenty years until the turn of the century Comoros was quite the opposite, a swirl of coups d'état, countercoups and external intervention, where power and wealth were elite preoccupations, and the rest were focused on survival.

The death of Colonel Bob Denard at seventy-eight in October 2007 in a Paris hospital signalled the end of at least the white mercenary's part in that era. Born in Bordeaux as Gilbert Bourgeaud, after seeing early service in Vietnam as a marine commando just as France's Indochina empire crumbled, Denard served with the police in Algeria and Morocco before spending a year in jail for his involvement in a plot to kill France's prime minister, Pierre Mendès-France. After a spell selling kitchen appliances, in 1961 he signed up to train Katangan secessionist forces in the wake of Congo's independence from Belgium the previous year.

Denard was part of a team that rescued white civilians encircled by rebels in

Stanleyville (now Kisangani) in the Congo in 1963. The raid formed the basis of the 1978 adventure film *The Wild Geese*, starring Richards Burton and Harris, and Roger Moore among others, and helped to establish Denard's fearless reputation.

Affable, tall and outwardly urbane, Denard supposedly also inspired Frederick Forsyth's novel *The Dogs of War*, the story of a small group of successful (and principled) mercenaries in West Africa. Yet, at the same time, Denard and his men acquired a well-earned reputation for brutality and a nickname to match: *les Affreux* ('the Dreadful').[47]

He next fought in Yemen, where he was badly wounded, moving at the end of the 1960s to Biafra to assist in the region's ultimately unsuccessful attempt to break away from Nigeria. During the 1970s he was active in Benin, Chad and Angola before turning his attention to Comoros where, in August 1975, he organised the first of his four coups, this one against President Ahmed Abdallah Abderemane, who had overseen independence from France less than a month earlier. Abdallah had earlier been a member of the French senate from 1959 to 1973.

Thereafter followed a stint in Rhodesia (now Zimbabwe) where, employing his friendship with the legendary sanctions buster Jack Malloch, whom he knew from Benin and Biafra, Denard organised the French-speaking (but largely ineffective) 7 Independent Company to fight for the minority government, before he returned to Comoros in 1978 with a group of Rhodesian soldiers, reinstating Abdallah and becoming head of the Presidential Guard and Comoros' de facto ruler.

Denard was widely believed to be working *with* if not *for* French intelligence, the Directorate-General for External Security, or DGSE. One former DGSE head said in Denard's defence at his final trial: 'When special services are unable to undertake certain kinds of undercover operation, they use parallel structures. This was the case of Bob Denard.' Denard himself wrote that: 'Often, I didn't exactly have a green light from the French authorities, but I went on the amber.'[48]

Denard settled in Comoros, married his sixth wife and converted to Islam, taking the name Mustapha Mahdjoub. He accumulated a small fortune, not least in working with the apartheid government in South Africa, with which he maintained good ties. As Glenn Babb, a former deputy director-general in the South African Department of Foreign Affairs notes about the era: 'The [South African] army had a listening post in the Comoros which would pick up ANC radio transmissions from northern Mozambique. Bob Denard, who was a straightforward man if a bit of a rogue, saw that there was potential in Comoros in farming, tourism and industry. If I ever had to make a presentation to the president [Abdallah], he would always say, "*Il faut en parler avec Bob*" – "We must ask Bob."

'Denard had been encouraged to intervene there by the French government given their concerns about President Ali Soilih for their rule over Mayotte, which had voted to remain French in the independence referendum,' recalls Babb. Soilih had replaced Said Mohamed Jaffar who had replaced Abdallah. Babb had been instructed by the Department of Foreign Affairs to meet Denard, who wanted funding for various development schemes. Starting in the 1980s, 'We managed to convince Sol Kerzner and Southern Sun to build a hotel there, and the department funded a hospital, chicken and maize farms, built a housing compound [taken over by the Presidential Guard], encouraged diving as an activity given its proximity to where coelacanths had been found, and even used their colours on a South African Airways plane.'[49] The listening post came about as the French government was keen to share the load of the funding for the Presidential Guard, and Denard was always on the 'lookout for a bigger budget'. Although some of the projects made a difference, others did not. The maize farm, which was aimed at finding a staple other than imported rice, ended up feeding the president's chickens.

The South African operation was supposedly secret, 'but all the Comoros, a country running on the adrenaline of gossip like most small islands, knew of it,' recalls Babb. This awareness was increased by the army medic's role in assisting the local population, and the posting of a South African consul. Denard, says Babb, 'ran the country uncontested, except for the programmes promoted by the French government, where they tried to keep their distance from their mercenary creation'.

There were tensions between Denard and Abdallah, not least over the monopoly that the president's son enjoyed on imports, especially rice. In 1989, Abdallah was assassinated in mysterious circumstances, and Denard fled the islands.

While the French issued a warrant for his arrest and sent a vessel from Mayotte for his capture, a deal was hatched between Pretoria and Paris whereby Denard secured free passage to South Africa with his archives and indemnity from prosecution for members of the Presidential Guard. After a time in South Africa, Denard returned to France to stand trial.

He was given a suspended sentence for trying to overthrow Benin's government in 1977 and acquitted of organising Abdallah's murder. In 1995, Denard returned to Comoros with a small band of men landed by rubber dinghies to once more attempt to seize power. It was one coup too many for Denard and his last action as a dog of war.

French troops were sent to restore order. Denard was arrested and prosecuted by a French court a decade later. By then he was suffering from Alzheimer's and was considered too ill to attend the trial. He was given a suspended five-year jail term, later increased on appeal to a year in jail, but he never served it due to his health. It was not the first time, Babb holds, that Denard was 'undone' by the French government even though he had done its bidding.

Whatever Denard did or didn't do, the effect of misrule on Comoros has been to ensure the inhabitants of the three independent islands of the group (Grande Comore, Mohéli and Anjouan – a fourth, Mayotte, did not vote for independence and is administered by France) remain stuck among the poorest worldwide, ranking 156th out of 191 nations on the UN's Human Development Index (Mauritius is 63rd).[50]

Despite the moniker of the 'Perfume Islands' for their cultivation of ylang-ylang essence, less than one-sixth of the land is covered with forest, the result of rapid deforestation caused mainly by firewood consumption. The twenty coups since 1975 have not only discouraged investment but also seem to have distracted successive leaders from the development purpose of power.

While Denard's passing might have signalled the end of the chapter of the white man's coups in Africa, it did not signal the end of the era of bad politics. Tourism should have offered some opportunities, like Mauritius, but the combination of political instability and declining post-apartheid South African influence, coupled with the need to import most construction materials and consumables onto the volcanic islands, mean that it has never taken off in the same way as Mauritius, Seychelles or even Madagascar, despite Comoros' scenic beauty.

Comorians are an imaginative and hard-working people despite the circumstances, though much of their labour goes to surviving rather than prospering. About one-third of national income is generated by smallholder agriculture, where 80 per cent of the labour force is employed, and yet close to 40 per cent of all imports are foodstuffs, illustrating weak markets, poor communications and the absence of an enabling environment. Remittances provide around a quarter of GDP, a source of income for 40 per cent of Comorian families, reflecting the incessant loss of young talent from the islands, but also fuelling a consumption culture.

The combination of Afro-Arab and francophone strains in the national character has proven less conducive to development, it seems, than obstructive. The love-hate relationship with France – epitomised by the Denard period and the issue of Mayotte, where an estimated 300 000 Comorians live – has shaped the psychology of understanding the responsibility for change, whether this be from within or without.

Nourdine Bourhane, who served in a multitude of senior government positions, including vice president from 2011 to 2016 and prime minister for a short spell in the late 1990s, says that the issue of culture works against Comoros in several ways. The combination of an 'Arab aristocracy' on Mayotte; the role of the French, who 'used the island character to divide and rule'; and the 'hegemony' of Grande Comore over the other two islands has ensured a lack of unity. Instead of the 'business culture of the Indian families in Mauritius', says Bourhane, Comoros is dominated by 'prestige traditions' where a culture of consumption shades that of careful investment. For example, families spend up to $150 000, mostly remittances, in the pageantry of the 'grand marriage' ceremony. Bourhane, who is Anjouan by birth, advocates increased decentralisation as the best route to better governance.

There is another, more pernicious burden to the French colonial hangover. Comorians believe not only that France is responsible for their current plight, but also that Paris is still calling the shots and that there is a conspiracy to keep them down through contracts and schemes such as the CFA franc zone. This sentiment disempowers Comorians from taking responsibility.

Comoros took its name from the Arab seafarers who referred to it as Djazair al Qamar ('Islands of the Moon'). The capital, Moroni, on Grande Comore is dominated by Mount Karthala, the world's largest active volcano, and edged by a tapestry of brilliant white and dark-grey volcanic beaches. The city is constructed in the Arab style, and men in traditional *kanzu* (long white robes) and *kofia* (skull caps) play dominoes or *bao* (a board game) in the streets. In Moroni's Volo Volo market, female vendors in brightly coloured *chiromani* (cloth wraps), their faces caked in yellow sandalwood paste, hawk freshly caught fish, fruit, spices, vegetables and much else.[51]

Such appeal aside, the problem for visitors is that there are few decent places to stay since the closure (and destruction) of Southern Sun's Le Galawa Beach Hotel on the northern fringe of the island. And although Comoros is blessed with fresh seafood, herbs and spices, there is only a handful of formal restaurants attractive to Western visitors. Anjouan is densely covered with clove trees, banana plants, ylang-ylang plantations and endless palm trees, its highlands offering a cooling escape from the tropical steam. Again, however, there are few places to stay, and the streets and beaches are filthy. The smaller island of Mohéli is still less developed, but with enormous ecotourism potential.

Situated on two of the best beaches on Grande Comore, with its access roads and infrastructure funded by the South African taxpayer, the 181-room Le Galawa was opened in the early 1990s, offering a full range of sports, entertainment, cuisine and a casino.[52] Despite subsidies, the hotel was mothballed in 2001 due to political turmoil and high costs. An attempt was made to renovate it in 2005 with another group, but the plans soon ran into red tape and the project was shelved. The hotel complex was demolished in 2007, apparently to build a new resort with Emirati financing, which never materialised. Today the virile undergrowth has reclaimed all evidence of the resort, even as the road to the nearby Lac Salé, the dramatic inland salt lake, and the accompanying resort at Maluja beach also slowly disintegrate.

The relationship with the South African government made the resort work, with the Industrial Development Corporation providing loans for Le Galawa as well as the Golden Tulip hotel in Moroni. Without this help, Comoros had to succeed – or fail – on its own merits. As the former CEO of Sun International, David Coutts-Trotter, put it: 'The biggest thing with such destinations is air access, then price, costs of booze, etc., and taxes. Even though it may not have had the best beaches, and probably not as good as Comoros, Mauritius always has stability in its favour, and its price when compared to Seychelles and Maldives.'[53]

As a consequence, while Comoros might have enjoyed 45 000 tourists in 2019, pre-Covid, tiny Seychelles had nearly ten times this number with 428 000 (among a population of just 100 000), Madagascar 486 000, Zanzibar 538 000 and Mauritius 1.4 million.[54] Of the 45 000, an estimated two-thirds were returning diaspora on holiday.

Despite its much higher visitor number, Zanzibar, another scenic Indian Ocean destination similarly renowned for its beaches, is equally poor, with an annual per capita income of just over $1 000. It lacks the excuses of transportation costs, being a ferry ride from Dar es Salaam.

If there are common threads between Comoros and Zanzibar, they can be found in the poor infrastructure, weak educational system, and absence of both planning and the means to execute. This relates to skills. The net enrolment rate for ordinary secondary education in Zanzibar, for instance, is just 44.8 per cent.[55] Only 3 per cent of Zanzibari citizens aged fifteen and older have obtained a university qualification, while 12 per cent have no education whatsoever. Local hospitality businesses prefer to recruit more literate and numerate staff from mainland Tanzania for customer-facing jobs, leaving islanders out in the cold. In Comoros, 59 per cent of the population is literate, while the primary-school completion rate is just 77 per cent (compared to the global average of 90 per cent).[56]

Both nations have great ambitions but making the connection between plans and projects has proven difficult, in part because of a mismatch between ambition and a lack of infrastructure, funding, human capacity and prioritisation, and an unwillingness to let some (money-making) preferences go. That Comoros has a paltry thirty-seven megawatts of installed electricity capacity tells its own story of investment (where Comoros has a capital-to-GDP ratio of around half the sub-Saharan average), but the low demand (of just eighteen megawatts, despite 90 per cent of the population being connected to the grid on Grande Comore) tells another of a lack of income and the high costs of diesel. There are also frequent outages given the high costs of production ($0.61 per kilowatt-hour) and high levels of subsidy ($0.21). Transportation similarly continues to add a premium to the cost of doing business. With the only deep-water port at Anjouan, most goods are transhipped from Réunion or Mombasa.[57] Comoros doesn't even feature on the World Bank's port performance index, which rates 370 container ports worldwide. Mayotte, however, is in 294th position.[58]

In 2019, President Azali Assoumani announced that he was looking to raise $4.6 billion to improve the economy according to a fresh plan – *Plan Emergence* – which would run until 2030. Assoumani is a former army commander whose first stint in power came after yet another coup in 1999, which was justified on the basis of protecting territorial integrity after government had begun negotiations with Anjouan for greater autonomy. He served as president from 2002 to 2006 and again, this time via elections, from 2016. Amid opposition criticism after he amended the constitution to enable him to remain in power until 2029 and with the suspension of EU aid due to shutting down the constitutional and anti-corruption courts, Assoumani was re-elected in April 2019 to a further five-year term.[59]

His son and advisor Nour El Fath Azali, a US-educated business graduate, says the focus must be on the implementation of *Plan Emergence* in order to exorcise the 'ghosts of the past' – the threat of coups, violence and civil war. During his father's first term, without such a vision, 'all efforts were focused just on keeping the islands together, on putting out fires'.

Assoumany Aboudou, a former minister of economy and internal affairs, heads the government agency to implement *Plan Emergence*. 'We need a cultural change of mentality, without which a plan won't work,' he observes. Or as the minister of agriculture, fisheries, the environment, tourism and handicraft Houmed Msaidie says, 'the most difficult thing about my job is to get things done'. He hankers after the era of Southern Sun and Le Galawa, 'which showed us the way'.

So, how do you turn around Comoros and Zanzibar?

The principal action is to make economic growth inclusive by opening up to capital. The common drivers of growth in both cases hinge around the 'blue' economy, in tourism, fisheries and aquaculture, and maritime trade and infrastructure. The key enablers for these sectors include, in the short term, the quality, speed and adaptability of government decision-making, and in the longer term, infrastructure and skills development. In practical terms this means focusing on the actions that don't cost money (as unattractive as that is to politicians seeking the benefits of construction rents), for example by scrapping visas, moving to a digitised paperless bureaucratic system, tidying up the plastic strewn across the islands, picking up the endless hulks of scrap vehicles, and getting government out of the business of rice importation and power provision.

Making market access cheaper would be a critical strategic driver, for business and tourism, via sea and air. The difference between visiting and refuelling in Pemba (already not the cheapest place in southern Africa) and Moroni is $60 versus $1 000. Visas for Moroni cost an additional €30, while leaving Prince Said Ibrahim International Airport involves no fewer than eleven checks and steps.

The politics must be right otherwise politicians will make bold pronouncements and state equally bold plans without any intention or means to execute them. Here Comoros, in particular, is light years away from Mauritius, while Zanzibar too, with its history of claustrophobic one-party rule since independence and fractious relations with the mainland, has its own challenges. Without a change in this aspect, politicians will not possess the incentives – and thus the will – to actually do rather than just say.

Former prime minister Nourdine Bourhane, who was charged with high treason in a case that was only resolved in 2022 after four years, believes that 'the current regime has turned the Fomboni Accords [so named after the capital of Mohéli, which delivered a political settlement in 2001] upside down. Coups and mercenaries created a trauma in our country, especially among intellectuals who do not dare speak. Instead, people take refuge in religion and in their traditions.' Fomboni established a rotating presidency, which President Assoumani was opposed to. Bourhane said that our meeting, in January 2023, was the first time in four years that anyone had engaged with him on political matters, which was 'like oxygen' according to the seventy-two-year-old.

The late Comorian president Ahmed Abdallah Abderemane was apparently a man of many witticisms, one of which was 'the tongue has no bone in it', and another 'it's all wind in the coconuts'.[60] Promises of reform are cheap – all wind in the coconuts – absent the political will to carry them out and the inherent discipline of competitive electoral politics.

Conclusion: Not such a dodo

When Meade painted his bleak picture of Mauritian economic prospects in 1961, the island had half its 2022 population. He was convinced that the country was caught in a low-economic-growth, high-population-growth Malthusian trap from which it could not escape. And yet, since independence in 1968, Mauritius has developed from a low-income, agriculturally based economy to an upper-middle income diversified economy through various phases, including the expansion of agriculture through global access, the development of EPZs and, more recently, rapidly expanding the financial, ICT and tourism sectors.

Mauritius has even managed to do well out of the unfortunate dodo, which survives on the country's coat of arms, currency and in literature. Lewis Carroll's *Alice's Adventures in Wonderland* gave the bird an image of being clumsy, tragic and destined for extinction. Hilaire Belloc included a poem about the dodo in his *Bad Child's Book of Beasts* from 1896:

The Dodo used to walk around,
And take the sun and air.
The sun yet warms his native ground –
The Dodo is not there!
The voice which used to squawk and squeak
Is now for ever dumb –
Yet may you see his bones and beak
All in the Mu-se-um.

It could not be a less apt metaphor for contemporary Mauritius, which has proven itself to be a fast learner, agile and capable of keeping one step ahead of its opposition. Inheritance, it seems, is not destiny. With all the potential ingredients of a fractious multi-ethnic society, a combination of internal and external openness, the building of institutions through practice, and leadership intent on inclusivity rather than racial exclusion have ensured prosperity.

Better choices by Zanzibar, Madagascar and Comoros, and their ability to translate plans into priorities and practice, could ensure that Mauritius is no longer the exception to the regional rule.

Can a Liberation Movement Reform?

> *'The revolution will eat its children
> I see the river of dreams run dry'*
> – Johnny Clegg

SEEDY. The word that best sums up the circumstances of many of the towns dotted around rural South Africa. The country's governance record and the patronage-driven nature of its political economy explain why.[61]

Of 257 municipalities countrywide in South Africa, just 41 received a clean audit in 2021, of which the majority were run by the opposition Democratic Alliance (DA). The auditor-general reported that 73 per cent of municipalities in the DA-run Western Cape received clean audits (22 out of 30), while municipalities in the other eight provinces mostly run by the ruling African National Congress averaged just 8 per cent (or 19 out of the 227 ruled by the party).[62]

The ANC has a lamentable record of local governance. For example, between the North West, Northern Cape and Eastern Cape provinces, just nine out of a total of ninety-three municipalities (including two metros in Buffalo City and Nelson Mandela Bay) received a clean audit. The towns and cities bear testimony to this record, their roads often badly potholed and rutted, water and sewerage systems creaking under the strain of poor maintenance frequently spilling their loads into the streets and pavements, low levels of available funding contrasting with expanding population numbers, public buildings scarred by years of neglect, and the greatest social cost of all, high and visible levels of unemployment.

In the Eastern Cape, the town hall in Makhanda, the largest town in the Makana Local Municipality, home to 150 000 people, is a case in point. The building was shrouded in darkness when we visited in November 2022, the country being on stage four loadshedding at the time. Up and down the town's High Street, one could hear the excited rattle of the generators keeping the shops on life support, a patchwork combination of banks, Pakistani-run cellphone stores, restaurants and coffee shops to service the school and university students.

Makhanda hosts Rhodes University, the Eastern Cape Division of the High Court, the South African Library for the Blind, the South African Institute for Aquatic Biodiversity (formerly the JLB Smith Institute of Ichthyology), the International Library of African Music, the Albany Museum, the Institute for the Study of English in Africa, a diocese of the Anglican Church of Southern Africa, and the base of 6 South African Infantry Battalion, an air assault unit of the South African National Defence Force.

The town was officially renamed from Grahamstown in 2018 to honour the Xhosa warrior and prophet Makhanda ka Nxele. The old and new names highlight South Africa's two very different histories since the town was founded in 1812 as a military outpost by Lieutenant-Colonel John Graham, whose task it was to make the region safe for settlement – his approach included the use of scorched-earth tactics against the local tribes. In April 1819, 10 000 Xhosa warriors, under the leadership of Makhanda, launched an attack against the 300-strong British garrison stationed in Grahamstown. When the attack failed, Makhanda surrendered and was imprisoned on Robben Island. On Christmas Day in 1819 he made his escape but drowned in the attempt.

This bitter and divisive history plays out 200 years later in the selection of priorities by local government, and its general direction and role. The governing generation after 1994 has been caricatured as those taking their 'turn to eat' or as 'captured'. But it is the system rather than the individuals that is primarily at fault. The supposed developmental state has become a patronage state, in which good and true people are a minority, and where the past is used to justify the present and the future. In this system there is little record-keeping and documentation, as a steady flow of contracts and jobs feeds the safety of union membership and personal and party bank accounts.

As one Makhanda activist put it, 'It's a carefully calibrated system in which no work happens.'

Grahamstown grew to become the second-largest city in South Africa after Cape Town in the nineteenth century. Excellent private schools were founded, as was the court, and in 1904 Rhodes University College was established with a grant from the Rhodes Trust, becoming a full university in 1951. Makhanda is also home to the oldest surviving independent newspaper in South Africa, *Grocott's Mail*, founded in 1870.

In 2022 the newspaper, now under the editorial management of the university, carried an analysis of the state of Makana's governance in light of the national municipal audit. Makana was one of twenty-five municipalities that received a disclaimer audit assessment for the third year running. This is the worst assessment a municipality can receive from the auditor-general, indicating that its financial statements have no value. 'If you are unable to do the very basic thing of showing what you have done with public funds, it demonstrates that you have no commitment to living up to your moral obligation to serve as a steward,' read the auditor-general's report. 'It shows that you have absolutely no will to drive transparency and no interest in demonstrating accountability.'

A disclaimer audit means that the municipality's finances are so poorly managed that it cannot provide evidence to support its financial statements. The auditor-general, therefore, cannot form an opinion on those statements. Yet Makana spent almost R1 million on consultants for 'asset and expenditure management'. The reason cited for hiring the consultants was 'lack of skills'.[63]

The ground-floor foyer of the town hall is lined with pictures of famous South African political figures, including Nelson Mandela, F.W. de Klerk, Albert Luthuli, Steve Biko, Helen Suzman, Mahatma Gandhi, Joe Slovo, O.R. Tambo, Walter and Albertina Sisulu, Govan Mbeki, Chris Hani, Helen Joseph and Raymond Mhlaba. 'Oom' Ray, the first premier of the Eastern Cape province after South Africa's 1994 liberation, had been sentenced with Nelson Mandela to life imprisonment during the Rivonia Trial, which he served, like Makhanda, on Robben Island for twenty-five years before being released in 1989. Each photograph carries with it a quote from the subject. That for Slovo, the once general secretary of the South African Communist Party, reads 'Revolution is the only hope for the hopeless', Hani's 'Socialism is the future', and Mhlaba's 'Dialectical materialism referred to the fact that all phenomena in the universe are subject to study and subject to change'.

We all need our heroes, and these are heroes of South Africa, those who sparked chinks of hope during apartheid's dark days. Their words of wisdom, however, reveal the role of Soviet-era ideology in shaping the country's political culture. It is a culture where democratic centralism attempts to instil discipline and manage perceptions, spinning the narrative and effectively limiting democratic choice. Allowing and institutionalising bad practices in this manner is not very helpful where a culture of impunity has taken hold and politics is used to cement patronage practices that have defined South Africa's political economy for centuries, and where identity, including language and race, has been used to preferentially access state resources.

The grandees' statements might, among others, help to explain some of the problems encountered by South Africa since 1994 in putting together a growth agenda that can deliver the aspirations of the population. For there is no doubt that South Africans are most unhappy with their lot, and increasingly so. And it is also obvious that the country finds itself in several terrible binds because of low growth and high demands. The problem is that 'dialectical materialism', 'revolution' and 'socialism' don't offer suitable, practical answers for the majority, even though as political slogans they might help those in power stay there. The same is true in other respects of ANC policy.

Between the shortage of water, the sporadic electricity – by 2023 the phenomenon of loadshedding due to undersupply had become a daily occurrence throughout the country – and the prevalence of potholes, the conditions in Makhanda are, as the audit statistics hint, hardly unique. Many of South Africa's smaller towns are locked into such a hellish reality, less a post-apartheid world of opportunity than a version of a post-apocalyptic world of grinding poverty and hopelessness. It is scarcely believable what has happened to local governance, not least in taking its cue from the national centre, and how this has so badly impacted the lives of South Africans.

Consequently, by the time South Africa entered its third decade of democratic government, its citizens increasingly despaired of the future. A poll conducted countrywide by the Brenthurst Foundation in October/November 2022 showed that 80 per cent of South Africans believed that the country was going in the wrong direction, including two-thirds of ANC supporters. Over 55 per cent cited jobs and corruption as the biggest challenges facing the country. In a version of Stockholm syndrome,[64] most South Africans continue to support the ANC, consistently twice as many as any other single political party. Until the majority of South Africans realise what the problems are, and own them, they will be unable to repair them.

This is not, however, the only bind that ties South Africa to low growth and weak governance.

The binds that tie

South Africa is a paradox. Political liberation in 1994 came ultimately with no revolution and little violence, at least by the standards of southern Africa's liberation history and contrary to the expectations and fearmongering of many. It was a smooth transition from one political order to the next. But therein lay the seeds of the subsequent development problem, summed up as the inability to grow the economy fast enough to ensure economic (rather than political) liberation.

Rather than offer a rupture with the past and ensure that the politics enabled a necessary change of economic direction, the ANC government essentially took the same basic economic formula – a form of rent-protectionism – and continued with it. As a result, inequality has remained high and stuck (South Africa has the highest recorded Gini coefficient worldwide), even though the racial make-up of the poor and rich has changed, in part through the redistribution of rents among the wealthy elite, now increasingly black. This wealth gap is widening: the top 10 per cent in South Africa earn two-thirds of national income and the bottom 50 per cent just 5.3 per cent.[65] Previously the fortune of South Africans was largely determined by their skin colour; in post-apartheid South Africa their life chances are shaped by their location and, by extension, their education and job prospects.

Location, Lokasie

Location, Location
Cries of realtors
Lokasie, Lokasie
Tears of reality

Vaalspan
Depressant for life
Plastic land
Rubbish is rife

Kids on nyaope
Burning tyres at the entrance
Goats in the street
Abattoir at the exit

Hartswater Municipality
No heart, little water
Long drops
Loud dops at the shebeen

The trains, they take
Not since apartheid
Let them eat cake
Chewing chesanyama instead

Ensure our future
Reconcile our past
Liberation
From what, to last?

Driving along South Africa's N2 highway provides a practical illustration of this imaginary dividing line, with townships largely on the landward side and expensive residential areas on the beachside. Plettenberg Bay on the Garden Route, for instance, is one of the most sought-after destinations for annual holidays by wealthy South Africans and foreigners, famed for its beaches, weather and restaurants. But the multimillion-rand homes, views and lifestyles of the polo-playing, canapé-quaffing elites are metaphoric miles away from the harsher lives and reality of the townships that service these pleasures. And it is not as if the local government is doing much to help. For the majority, it is an inaccessible monolith seemingly more interested in the maintenance of privilege than access to a different life. Finding a way out of conditions in the townships, such as the sprawling Kwanokuthula ('place of peace') to Plett's south, is that much harder.

Spatial inequities reinforce inequality of access to work and services, and limit the horizons and opportunities of inhabitants. While dearth and excess are more noticeable in the wealthier municipalities, the conditions may be even worse in the poorer ones, given the relative absence of opportunity.

The *lokasie* of Vaalspan is an example of such dystopianism. Servicing Jan Kempdorp, itself a poor agricultural town in the Northern Cape nearly 100 kilometres north of the provincial capital Kimberley, nearby formal employment opportunities are limited to the local abattoir. Drug abuse, especially of *nyaope* (also known as whoonga) brewed from cannabis, heroin and antiretrovirals, and other concoctions involving the use of lightbulbs for smoking, is endemic among younger people. A thick pale of tyre and plastic smoke hangs over Vaalspan, the township strewn with rubbish and dotted with goats, the shebeens and open fires of the *chesanyama* the centrepieces of social life. While there is piped water and electricity, there is no piped sewerage, the population dependent on pit latrines.

Life for thirty million South Africans persists in this way, thirty years after the end of apartheid.

Among the middle classes, rents find their way into the population through an expanding civil service, which has nearly trebled in size over the last thirty years. It may be larger, but it is less effective as productivity has declined. Poverty, too, has got stuck, and remains at 55 per cent of the population, according to the national poverty datum line, while a total of 13.8 million people (23 per cent) experienced food poverty in 2014.[66] By the end of 2022, redistribution through welfare payments to more than 28 million South Africans had helped to remove poverty's most bitter edges, though this remains a problem as much for the fiscus as for the economy in creating an off-ramp from this system of dependency, even though this state of being suits the ruling party.

South Africa has twice as many welfare recipients as employed, registered taxpayers. The government introduced a temporary monthly stipend of R350 ($23) in response to the Covid-19 pandemic in 2020, which was extended through to March 2023 and is likely to be extended in perpetuity. This added about 10.3 million people to the welfare net.[67] South Africa's available labour force is 40 million.

While the system of expanding public service numbers and welfare payments may have solved some short-term political problems for the ANC, it has created different longer-term economic ones, notably by stressing public finances. The percentage of debt to GDP rose steadily during the 2000s, from under 40 per cent at the turn of the century to over 70 per cent twenty years later.[69] More import-

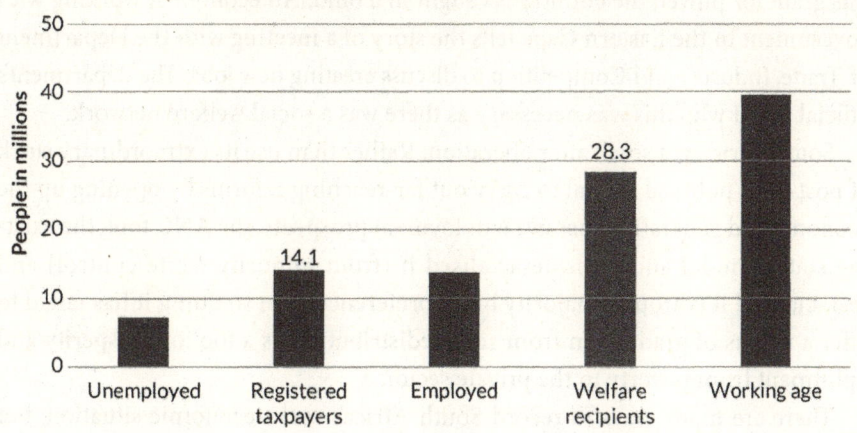

Source: Presidency, Statistics South Africa, National Treasury[68]

ant is the composition of government spending, with salaries around a third of its budget, compared to the global average of around 10 per cent.[70] After the end of apartheid in 1994, the governing ANC sought to empower millions of black people. This included giving them public sector jobs through a 'cadre deployment' system, which amounted to appointing politically loyal but often incompetent people to important technical jobs. Government spending on salaries more than tripled between 2007 and 2019, in part too because of above-inflation wage deals with the unions allied to the ANC. This practice has continued unabated, especially since the ANC government has failed to get the economy onto a growth footing.

Another aspect is the failure to graduate from this system of redistribution towards one where the private sector – whether in employment or self-employment – is vibrant and lucrative enough to reduce dependence on state handouts.

Doing the right thing for South Africa's burgeoning indigent population has thus created other problems, not least in incentivising the type of reforms and governance practices needed to empower people to graduate from government welfare. There is an urgent need to increase the number of productive taxpayers in the economy, and to reduce the amounts spent on welfare and other forms of consumption without leaving vulnerable people without protection. A quarter of South Africa's R2 trillion 2022 budget is funded from borrowings and a quarter from personal income tax. The welfare payment system amounts to 13 per cent of South Africa's annual budget.

Yet when half your population depends on this grant for survival and there are few other options available, and when the ruling party depends on maintaining this grant for power, the country is caught in a bind. An economist working with government in the Eastern Cape tells the story of a meeting with the Department of Trade, Industry and Competition to discuss creating new jobs. The department's official asked why this was necessary as there was a social welfare network.

South Africa got stuck after liberation. Rather than use its extraordinary stock of post-1994 political capital to carry out far-reaching reforms by opening up the economy and generating massive employment prospects, the ANC took the existing statist model and both deracialised it (from minority white control) and re-racialised it (through majority black preferences). In so doing it has failed to offer a means of graduation from state redistribution as a tool of prosperity and upliftment from poverty to the private sector.

There are many ways to record South Africa's socio-economic situation, but the most revealing is the extent to which South Africa is falling behind others in terms of its share of global per capita income. The chart below outlines the performance of a selection of countries under study in this volume over their first twenty-five years of liberation. This is the result of comparatively low growth in South Africa, averaging 2.4 per cent between 1994 and 2021 compared to the low- and middle-income country average of 5.2 per cent.

A comparison of the first twenty-five years of liberation

	% global per capita income at independence	% global per capita income after twenty-five years
Baltics	80.5 (1995*)	166.0 (2020)
Botswana	10.4 (1966)	55.7 (1991)
Mauritius	42.6 (1976*)	71.5 (2001)
Morocco	16.6 (1966*)	23.9 (1991)
Poland	75.4 (1990)	122.9 (2015)
Singapore	99.5 (1965)	343.0 (1990)
South Africa	66.5 (1994)	55.6 (2019)
Ukraine	49.2 (1991)	21.0 (2016)

* Data points with an asterisk (*) denote the earliest available data from independence years

In 1960, the average South African's share of global per capita GDP was 107 per cent. While it is important to note that racial inequity was deeply entrenched under apartheid policy, the *average* income nonetheless tells us that it was punching above its weight on the world stage when it came to economic performance.

Sixty years later, in 2020, the average South African's share of global GDP had plummeted to just 54 per cent of the global average. While the world moved ahead, South Africa fell back sharply.

The effects can be seen in rising unemployment and rising criminality. Both fell until the early 2000s and have risen again inexorably, as seen in the chart below, which registers unemployment and homicide rates.

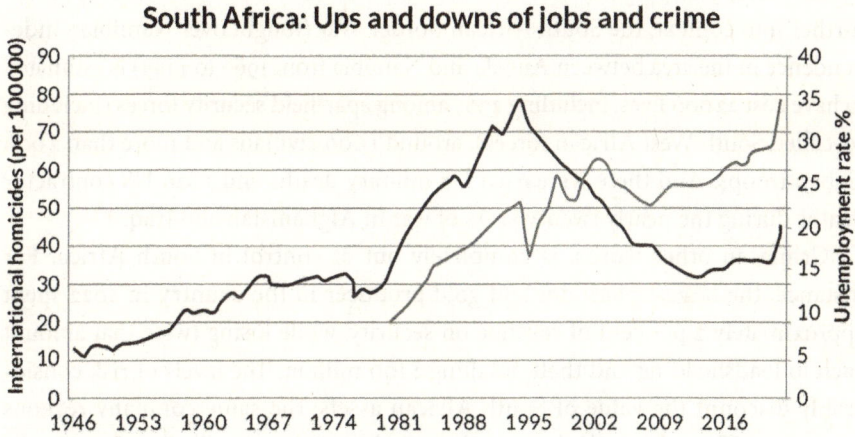

Source: Global Initiative Against Transnational Organized Crime; unemployment data from IMF DataMapper

With political conflict steadily ratcheting up from 1947 (when the murder rate was 11 per 100 000) to the early 1960s (by which time it was 30 per 100 000), it rapidly increased to nearly 80 per 100 000 by the early 1990s. From then the rate steadily declined until touching 30 per 100 000 again in 2012, after which time a combination of weak law enforcement coupled with increased vigilantism and organised crime saw a steady rise once more to over 40 murders per 100 000 by 2022.[71] In the Global Initiative Against Transnational Organized Crime's 2021 Organized Crime Index, South Africa ranked nineteenth in the world for criminality – ahead of Libya, Brazil and Russia – with high levels of all four types of organised crime: mafia-type groups, criminal networks, state-embedded actors and foreign groups.[72]

The Rhodesian Bush War, or Second Chimurenga, waged from 1964 until 1979, cost an estimated 20 000 lives, including those of some 10 000 guerrillas and 1 361 Rhodesian security force members. The level of violence, and the radicalisation and dehumanisation it produced, is viewed as being responsible for the atrocities and policies later perpetrated by Robert Mugabe, including the Gukurahundi genocide against his ethnic rivals in Matabeleland, which lasted from 1982 until 1987 and cost around 20 000 civilian lives.

To put South Africa's level of violence into perspective, police minister Bheki Cele admitted in February 2023 that 7 555 people were murdered just between October and December 2022, and 3 144 of these by firearms (the projected total for the year was 27 000 murders).[73] During the year, an average of thirty people were shot and killed each day; that's 10 950 in one year, more than were killed by the Rhodesian security forces in fifteen years of armed conflict. To put this further into context, the South African Border War (fought over Namibian independence in the area between Angola and Namibia from 1966 to 1989) is estimated to have cost 22 000 lives, including 2 365 among apartheid security forces (including so-called South West African forces), around 1 000 civilians and more than 2 000 Cuban troops. And there were 6 951 US military deaths and 7 820 US contractor deaths during the nearly twenty years of war in Afghanistan and Iraq.[74]

Crime, in other words, is completely out of control in South Africa. For instance, the largest platinum and gold producer in the country in 2022 spent approximately 2 per cent of revenue on security, while losing twice that amount each to loadshedding and theft, totalling $200 million. The levels of risk considerably discount the value of South African assets: the same company reckons 35 per cent. They also make large-scale capital investment unlikely, at least in the mining sector where recovery and profit are calculated over a generational timescale. It must be asked: If things happen for good reason and don't happen for good reason, why have the police not got a grip on crime? Is it incompetence or vested interests?

It's hard to create prosperity without stability, and hard to ensure stability without, at least, governance and a glimmer of the prospects of positive change.

The answer to the conditions that created this crisis lies in a series of poor policy decisions and a bureaucracy less and less able to implement them, de-industrialisation due to poor labour-market choices and overregulation, energy scarcity due to poorly run state enterprises and slow actions in bringing on board the private sector, cadre deployment and corruption hobbling the public service, and a reliance on a creaking infrastructure.

But there are still deeper reasons.

Essentially South Africa is reliant on an economic pie that was mostly baked in the fifty years from 1920. Real gross domestic product grew at an average yearly rate of 5.2 per cent between 1945 and 1965 and further picked up from 1966 through 1972, growing at a remarkable annual pace of almost 6 per cent.[75] Of course the benefits of this growth were disproportionately skewed in favour of the white community, but the basics of a sound economy were put in place regardless.

During this time, several key institutions were established, propelling growth. Anglo American was founded in 1917, becoming the doyen of the private sector, and dominating the Johannesburg Stock Exchange. Anglo became the majority shareholder in the De Beers diamond company in 1926, invested in Zambian copper from 1931, moved into coal in South Africa in the 1940s, and developed (ultimately) seven major mines in the Free State goldfields along with Vaal Reefs in the 1950s. In the state sector, with the creation of the Union of South Africa in 1910, all ports, harbours and railways were placed under joint control. Development, including electrification of the rail lines, continued through the next sixty years, aided by restrictive legislation on road transport. As a result, South Africa had the world's eleventh-largest rail network, with 30 400 kilometres of track, by the 1960s.

Iscor was established in 1928, following from the creation of Eskom five years earlier, the latter which grew to become one of the largest electricity utilities in the world during the 1970s and 1980s. From 1960 to 1990, Eskom increased its installed power production capacity tenfold to 40 000 megawatts to not only keep up with but also spur economic growth, opening nineteen new power stations during this time.

However, by the 1980s the country's growth had slowed due to a combination of bureaucratic statism and international isolation along with the burgeoning costs of increasingly militarised foreign and domestic policies. Between 1973 and 1994, annual growth fell to average just 2 per cent. This picked up again in a post-apartheid bounce-back to average 3.6 per cent between 1994 and 2008, but thereafter fell to just under 1 per cent until 2021 and the time of writing.

By the late 2000s, the wave of investment made in the 1960s and 1970s – that, for example, enabled Eskom to be ranked the world's best power utility in 2001 – had started to run out, exacerbated by the global financial crisis and political ruptures in the ANC. Serial state undercapitalisation was compounded by mismanagement and corruption. The failure to build new generation capacity illustrated the inability of the ANC government to implement reforms. A white paper proposing a shift to private energy production was issued in the late 1990s, but never acted on due to opposition to 'privatisation' from within the party and from its allies in the trade union movement. The result was paralysis as demand grew and supply diminished, leading, eventually, to loadshedding – blackouts designed to protect the grid from going down, but which have cost industry billions and put a cap on growth.

In some sectors – from communications and policing to education and healthcare – the state's failure could be papered over by a combination of private schools, private security and private hospitals, and the digital revolution.

Eskom eventually responded to the generation crisis by commissioning the building of Kusile and Medupi, two of the world's biggest coal-fired power plants. But, having reduced its engineering and project management capacity, it was throwing money into an environment where rents had to be paid and where skills were in short supply. Initially supposed to be completed in 2014, these power stations were not in full service eight years over schedule. Their estimated total cost of R464 billion was almost triple their initial budget. To fund these projects, as well as defaulting municipalities (a debt touching R50 billion by 2022) and the higher costs of coal, Eskom went heavily into debt.

And then there was corruption: on coal contracts and on the construction of the power plants. The Japanese firm Hitachi had to pay a fine of $19 million to settle US Securities and Exchange Commission charges that it had made 'improper payments' of $6 million to Chancellor House, the investment arm of the ANC, with which Hitachi had partnered to install boilers at the plants.

While the ratio of Eskom staff to power has remained constant, with 44 000 full-time employees for 45 000 megawatts generating capacity (on paper, 27 000 megawatts in reality) in 2020 compared to 40 000 staff for 38 000 megawatts in 1994,[76] there are reportedly 'major gaps in technical skills and knowledge'.[77] Moreover, management is no longer a stabilising force. Between 1923 and 1994, for example, Eskom had six chairmen and (from 1985) two chief executives; from 1994 to 2023 there were ten chairmen and fifteen CEOs.[78] The rot of cadre deployment and a patronage political economy driving a procurement agenda based around coal have combined to undo Eskom as a force for growth and good.

The political economy driving policy choices and action is aligned to the interests of the ruling party, which do not necessarily coincide with those of South Africa; in fact, they don't. For instance, the coal contractors and road hauliers who are reputed to pay a tithe to Luthuli House (the ANC headquarters) drive up the cost of coal. At the giant 4 100-megawatt Kendal power station, for example, the 50 000 tonnes of coal a day (or 18.4 million tonnes annually) used to fire the six boilers should be supplied directly on giant conveyors from the nearby mine. But ANC contracting stipulations demand that half of all coal be procured from preferred black economic empowerment suppliers, who are more likely to use road transport. The road haulage cost alone is three times the mine price. Replicated across South Africa's fifteen coal-fired power stations and one can only imagine the profit, especially when lower-grade coal is substituted.[79]

The pernicious nature of the political economy helps to explain why critical policy choices were not made after 1994 to better position South Africa to compete in the world, and why so little faith was placed in business. Did government resent or fear the success of business as a driving force for transformation? Or did it simply pander to vested interests within its own ranks, encouraged by the disintegration of law and order and incentivised by the political and economic rewards on offer to comrades, notably in coal and trucking, and via the trade unions?

Consequently, says Busisiwe Mavuso, the CEO of Business Leadership South Africa, 'South Africa is stuck in three key traps: low economic growth, state weakness and declining capacity, and social instability.' Yet instead of addressing the problems and creating a conducive environment in which capital can flow, 'the government does not understand the problem, so they don't understand the solution. And there are too many crooks in the ANC that outnumber those who want to see change.'[80]

This is not only the view of elites in business. Indeed, one of the problems with business in South Africa is that it has been unwilling to call out government on its failings. This may be a legacy of apartheid shame, or it may be down to straightforward rent-seeking. Business, after all, has never found a government it did not like.

While the ANC understandably prefers to lay the blame for its failings on apartheid, most voters no longer accept this argument. The poll conducted by the Brenthurst Foundation in October/November 2022 showed that, while 72.4 per cent cited unemployment, corruption and loadshedding as the country's biggest challenges, more than half of voters blame the ANC government for the problems facing South Africa, while just 8.8 per cent blame apartheid and 7.4 per cent racists.

South Africans' declining share of global wealth raises a converse question: Why has South Africa not kept pace with global growth, let alone the growth of some countries that were not blessed with the natural resource endowment and infrastructure South Africa possessed in 1994? How much richer could the country be if it had kept up with its peers in the G20 and lived up to its potential?

Living next door to Alice

Originally known as Lovedale, the small town in the Eastern Cape with a permanent population of just 15 000 was renamed Alice for Queen Victoria's daughter in 1947.

Settled by the British in 1824 as a barracks for imperial troops, it was converted in 1916 into a university for black students. The University of Fort Hare is the alma mater of the who's who of African leaders, including Nelson Mandela, Sir Seretse Khama, Lesotho's former prime minister Ntsu Mokhehle, O.R. Tambo, Roberts Sobukwe and Mugabe, and Mangosuthu Buthelezi. Given the links to the institution and the Eastern Cape, the university houses the ANC archive.

Despite this history and the political connection, Alice falls under one of the municipalities in the Eastern Cape that was on the brink of financial collapse by

2022 and was being investigated by the Directorate for Priority Crime Investigation (the Hawks) for corruption. Only four of the thirty-nine municipalities in the Eastern Cape received clean audits. In total, eleven were regarded as dysfunctional, fourteen as high risk and fourteen as low risk. Across South Africa, thirty-three municipalities were placed under administration after being declared dysfunctional due to their failure to meet their financial obligations and provide essential services. Among the six that owed the most was Raymond Mhlaba Local Municipality, whose ambit includes Fort Beaufort and Alice.

Across the Eastern Cape, the salary bill for all the municipalities exceeded the share of funding the province received from national government.[81] In the Great Kei Local Municipality within the Amathole District, for instance, the percentage of revenue acquired via local billing on rates, taxes, electricity and water, which should provide the bulk of income, has fallen to just 3 per cent of budget. The failure of the South African Post Office as a means of billing and corresponding low rates of collection, as well as high levels of indigence mean that most municipalities operate (illegally) unfunded budgets, and don't pay their bills, including for electricity and water. But that's not all.

With more than half the municipalities in the Eastern Cape being investigated for corruption, in an attempt to halt the financial mismanagement, political instability and infighting in the province, national government has been forced to take control of eight municipalities that were red-flagged by National Treasury as being on the brink of collapse and requiring urgent intervention: O.R. Tambo, Amathole and Chris Hani district municipalities, and Makana, Amahlathi, Walter Sisulu, Enoch Mgijima and Raymond Mhlaba.

In Alice, the historic railway station on MacNab Street has fallen into disrepair and is now a squat. Nature is slowly reclaiming the area surrounding the station, and the eponymous hotel opposite that once serviced passengers lies in ruins and has become an informal public drinking space. It certainly smells that way.

Instead of taking its place among South Africa's leading universities after apartheid, the University of Fort Hare has been dragged into the mire of dysfunction. Its vice chancellor, Professor Sakhela Buhlungu, was the victim of an assassination attempt in January 2023 after he spoke out against corruption at the institution. Among the issues he raised was an invoice for R15 000 for forty-eight toilet rolls (which retailed at R220).[82]

While increasing factionalism within the ANC (essentially between the Zuma and Ramaphosa groupings) has diffused the focus of government and redirected its purpose towards the distribution of rents, failing governance has in turn occurred against a backdrop of worsening economic deprivation.

The Eastern Cape's unemployment rate was 45 per cent in the fourth quarter of 2021. Although it dropped to 42.1 per cent the following year, with the expanded definition of unemployment (including those no longer looking for work) putting the actual figure at 47.1 per cent, it was still well above the national average of 32.7 per cent in the fourth quarter of 2022.[83]

More than half of the Eastern Cape's jobs are in trade and community services, the latter centring on government. Attempts to create new jobs through massive government schemes, including, for example, the port at Coega and elsewhere in the automotive sector, have been undone by several factors, not least productivity. These failures have ripple effects throughout the province but also elsewhere. For the period 2016–2021, Statistics South Africa estimated that Gauteng and the Western Cape experienced inflows of migrants of approximately 1.56 million (into a population of 16 million) and 470 657 (into 7 million) respectively.[84] This may grossly underestimate the pressure given the subsequent impact of Covid-19 and the meltdown in the Eastern Cape economy. The Western Cape, for example, is planning for a population of 8 million by 2030. This may be too low given the inflow of 100 000 migrants annually into the City of Cape Town, which has a population of 4.8 million.[85] The more the Western Cape government manages to squeeze out in terms of growth, and the greater the differential with the rest of the country, the greater the number of migrants. It's the ultimate self-licking lollipop.

Just over 100 kilometres south of Alice on the R67, Makhanda's railway station is another that is being slowly swallowed up by nature and its surrounds. The rail link to the town originated in the late 1870s. The passenger service gradually shrank: the last train ride to Port Alfred was in 1986, and in 2009 the Alice line closed. In 2000 a plaque was placed at Makhanda's New Cemetery station emphasising the importance of the railway. In little more than a decade, part of the roofing, wooden fittings, doors, windows, floors and cabling on the historic platform had been vandalised, the iron supports under the flooring removed, and the light poles cut. The goods shed, the historic post box, the plaques and the wall safe were removed, while the Garratt steam locomotive in the station's forecourt was vandalised.[86] Today the rail lines are barely discernible in the dense tangle of undergrowth, the platform alongside covered in moss and leaves, while the station silently disintegrates.

This is not uncommon. Large sections of South Africa's extensive rail network have been stripped by criminals looking to make money from scrap metal and rendered useless as a result. By 2022, only 134 of the country's 590 stations were functional and 323 had been completely vandalised, according to the state-owned Passenger Rail Agency of South Africa (PRASA). Of the country's forty train lines, twenty-one had stopped altogether; of the 2 228 kilometres of signal cables, 1 100 kilometres had been stolen; two-thirds of the 3 000 kilometres of electrified rail network were unusable; and only 800 of 40 000 coaches in its fleet were operational.[87]

This decline affects both freight and particularly passenger networks. In 1993, about 400 million tonnes of goods were transported by road, compared with 175 million tonnes by rail. By 2009, sixteen years later, road traffic had risen by 242 per cent to nearly 1.4 billion tonnes, whereas the total carried by rail had increased just 17 per cent to 205 million tonnes.[88] In 2017, rail carried 230 million tonnes of freight, but by 2021 this figure had dropped to 179 million. In 2011, PRASA handled 522 million passenger trips; in 2021/22, it managed just 17 million, representing a 97 per cent drop.[89]

De Aar, situated in the Northern Cape, with a population of around 42 000, is the second-most important railway junction in the country. It is where the Cape Town–Kimberley main line meets a line from Port Elizabeth and another from Upington and Namibia. Yet the combination of drought in an area dependent on farming and the decline of the railway have had a negative effect on the economy of this historic Karoo town. De Aar – meaning 'artery', after the underground water network – is effectively on life support.[90] Most of the rail facilities have been stripped bare, many of the station's platform roofs having been picked clean of their metal and fittings. There has been no passenger train since 2019, the porters' trollies lying idle and chained together near the entrance where passengers once thronged.

Inside the town hall, Gladwell Nkumbi, the mayor of Emthanjeni, the municipality responsible for De Aar, is preparing for a three-day session on 'the IDP' – the drafting of an Integrated Development Plan. The ANC banners, bunting and drapes are out, the smell of fresh enamel paint dominating his office. He claims that 'there is an understanding across town despite the deficit of trust in the government given the disappointments and the failure to deliver services'. He still sees De Aar as a logistics hub, not only fed by the railway, but also by its advantages in solar energy production. But he admits that things have to change to fix the railway's technical problems to reduce the endless stream of manganese trucks shuttling ore from the mines of Kuruman to the port at Coega. 'People are desperate for jobs,' he notes about the state of the economy, 'and humble to accept anything.'[91]

Yet Transnet – the parastatal that runs both freight and passenger (PRASA) services – still has 56 000 employees. In the mid-1980s, three years before the two services were split and Transnet formed out of the South African Transport Services, there were around 200 000 workers, covering ports, harbours, airports and railways, including 16 500 Railways Police. In 1947, the railways employed 170 000 of South Africa's then eleven-million-strong population, 'by far' the largest employer anywhere in Africa.[92]

Rail passenger traffic fell from an average of 49 million passengers a month in 2008 to 1.8 million in 2021. Cable theft and vandalism of stations and railway lines are some of the reasons; others relate to the role of taxi monopolies. In the Eastern Cape, all passenger trains were stopped under Covid and could not resume given the extent of cable theft. Trains were once the cheapest mode of transport. For example, a ticket in 2022 between Kariega and Gqeberha cost just R9, while the bus fee was R20 and a taxi R25.

With freight off the rails, South Africa's already congested roads are more overburdened as it becomes harder to import and export goods. South Africa has about 750 000 kilometres of roads and streets, the tenth-biggest network in the world. About 158 000 kilometres are tarred. While the inter-city networks are mostly in very good condition, by 2017 one-third of provincial tarred roads were classified as 'poor' or 'very poor', up from 26 per cent in 2013 and far above the global benchmark of 10 per cent. Of the 592 000 kilometres of gravel road, more than half was classified as 'poor' or worse. The number of commercial vehicles on South African roads has increased by between 5 and 10 per cent per year since the mid-1990s.[93]

This collapse of the rail network did not start under the ANC government. It began back in the mid-1980s when the government merged the Railways Police with the South African Police. This process 'culminated in the unchecked theft and sabotage during the 2020 lockdown'.[94] But there is little doubt that it has been hastened by ANC rule. Rail will struggle against the commercial incentive among some comrades in the ruling party to make money through road haulage contracts, not least in the supply of coal to power stations, which helps to explain why the ANC has been such a reluctant reformer on coal-fired electricity in allowing space for renewables.

Attempts to rehabilitate the railways have been controversial. In March 2014, Transnet CEO Brian Molefe announced contracts amounting to R54 billion with four international manufacturing companies to build 1 064 locomotives (465 diesel and 599 electric). Of the total, seventy would be imported complete and the rest would be built locally by Transnet Engineering in Pretoria and Durban. The first two diesel locomotives delivered to Transnet by China's state-owned CRRC Corporation were unable to operate due to technical problems. A forensic report showed that the value of the locomotive deal had been increased by at least R16 billion as a result of management intervention. Moreover, the Zondo Commission heard evidence that R122 million of R189 million paid in advisory fees had flowed to the now infamous Gupta family. Molefe and others stood trial on fraud charges in 2022.[95]

At the other end of South Africa's rail and road networks, ideological rigidity and vested institutional interests also explain the stasis in the country's increasingly dysfunctional ports, a significant obstacle to lowering trade costs. Three of the largest ports, Ngqura, Cape Town and Durban, ranked 363rd, 364th and 365th respectively (out of 370 ports reviewed) on the World Bank's 2021 Container Port Performance Index.[96] Crane productivity at the Durban container terminal is about half that of the highest-performing terminal in Africa, and around 56 per cent of the average in the same pier-type group. Cape Town, to take the example of South Africa's second-largest port, achieves around thirty container moves per ship working hour compared to the sixty to seventy in Chile and Peru. Even the port of Berbera, in tiny (and unrecognised) Somaliland, ranks higher than South Africa's ports for efficiency. Run by Dubai Ports World, Berbera sits at 184th position on the World Bank's list.[97]

South Africa's public logistics and electricity services have ceased to be a common good and have instead become feeding troughs for corrupt networks that enjoy political protection.

Surrounded by the hills of the eastern Free State at the foot of Lesotho's Maluti Mountains, the town of Ladybrand, named after the president of the Orange Free State, was established in 1867 to defend the conquered territory from the 'marauding' Basotho.

It was the site, too, of an 'anti-railway conference' in 1887, which held that railways were unnecessary, detrimental to transport riding by wagon, injurious to horse breeding, likely to entail heavy land taxes, and would encroach on property rights. Regardless, even the less-than-liberal-minded burghers realised that the day of the ox-wagon would soon be over and that they had to prepare for these changes.[98] The railway opened in 1905 and connected that same year with Maseru, less than twenty kilometres away. Ladybrand's economy grew steadily. An airport was laid out in the 1940s to fly miners into Lesotho and the town became an important hub for trade with Lesotho and the farming community of the eastern Free State.

Today, Ladybrand's businesses continue to service the Lesotho economy, many inhabitants commuting to Maseru. But its governance has lagged. The seat of the Mantsopa Local Municipality, Ladybrand's streets are a colander of potholes and patches, its once tidy if modest airport disappearing into long grass. And the trains, passenger and freight, don't run any more. The Ladybrand lesson of the old era, as for the new, is that commerce inevitably finds a way around obstructive governance, but at a discount to economic growth and commercial opportunities.

South Africa's failure to emancipate South Africans from the economic injustices of apartheid can be explained in several ways. The ANC government wanted to distinguish itself from the past, Western way of doing things. Throw in historic fealty, a dose of ideology and identity politics, plus a strong allegiance to union members and an unhealthy sense of entitlement, and South Africa veered towards a developmental state, which was an excuse for rent-seeking, rent-protectionism and statism, which, combined, facilitated redistribution and ensured low growth.

However, the glass is not entirely half-empty.

Success and failure

State institutions have been weakened and corrupted by a decade of state capture, crippling essential service delivery. The path that South Africa chose at the start may have been the only one available to it; continuing with the status quo was politically impossible, given both the rationale for change and the expectations of citizens. As wholesale redistribution would have killed the economy quickly, partial redistribution in the hope that the local economy would 'balance out', and the Third World parts meet the First World aspects, was the best hope.[99] But it did not allow for several factors. One, the world had changed by the time South African politics altered, and rent-protectionism was no longer a bet on prosperity. Two, the education system proved to be a chronic failure by failing to produce the skills needed for economic progress. Three, trade unions continued to maintain a stranglehold on political power and policy direction, cutting off many of the pathways to growth and increased employment.

One cannot understand South Africa, and its choices, without appreciating the tumult of its past. Where one might see failure, others see success.

Whereas around 63 per cent of households had access to electricity in 1995, by 2015 this figure had risen to 85 per cent.[100] The increase in water usage is similarly impressive: during the first decade of democracy (1994 to 2004), an estimated 13.4 million more people had access to basic water supply services.[101] In the first decade, too, 3.3 million low-cost homes were built.[102]

But these metrics are slightly misleading. Where targets are the provision of basic services, it does not adequately illustrate the health of the economic and governance system that enables this to occur. It neither indicates whether this is sufficient given increases in the population size – which grew from forty to sixty million between 1994 and 2022 – nor adequately explains whether enough has happened, or whether more could have happened, and whether this has simply stressed the delivery system. For example, South Africa's water system, like Eskom, is failing due to a lack of investment and skills. It was estimated that Johannesburg Water alone would require an astounding R61 billion to replace critical water infrastructure over the next decade as the city's infrastructure built in 1917 is collapsing, with 42 of Johannesburg's 128 reservoirs leaking through walls and pipes.¹⁰³ And the means of delivery for much of the increase in electrical connections is via municipalities, which account for R50 billion, or 12 per cent, of Eskom's debt in unpaid bills.

'The fundamental developmental error is that we don't have a capable state,' notes Mavuso. 'While cadre deployment happens elsewhere, we don't get the best people. Governments set countries apart. Not geography, not climate, but governance.'

Change requires making different choices, and it's never easy because there are always some who benefit from the way things are. The ruling party has managed to set up a system that is simply self-defeating for the country. Indeed, South Africa is hostage to the ANC and the system of governance it has instituted. This explains why governance failure is so commonplace. After so many years of rampant corruption, it would be naive to think that vested interests and patronage could just disappear overnight.

Conclusion: A time for difficult choices

'What do you think of Nelson Mandela?'

I was sitting in a minivan in Ukraine with Ugandan opposition leader Bobi Wine when he turned to me and asked this question. He had been watching an old television clip from 1990 in which Mandela had been questioned on his continued friendship with Libya's Colonel Muammar Gaddafi and Cuba's Fidel Castro. He had defended his loyalty to these authoritarians by saying that they and Yasser Arafat 'support our struggle to the hilt' and he had no hesitation about 'hailing their commitment' to human rights. 'Our attitude toward any country is determined by the attitude of that country to our struggle,' Mandela had said. 'One of the mistakes which some political analysts make is to think that their enemies should be our enemies.'¹⁰⁴

Bobi's question was the sort to which some South Africans, at least in my case, battle to give an honest and unambiguous answer. Having given my usual reply that Mandela was a great negotiator and reconciler, had an innate sense of timing, was exactly what South Africa needed at the time, and set us on the right democratic path by leaving after one term, Bobi's next question surprised me. 'Why did he feel the need to excuse their lack of democracy because of what they had provided in the past?' Bobi asked.

It is a good question, one that goes to the heart of the constraints in South African politics in general and its foreign policy in particular. It explains much about the expectations shaped by the past, one that weighs heavily on the country. But this path is a choice by its political leadership, who prefer to externalise South Africa's problems and solutions, and blame much on apartheid. In a way, the country is a hostage of its painful history because its leaders want it to be. The leadership is unable to see right from wrong. It's all about the struggle.

Spend your life looking in the rear-view mirror if that's the direction in which you want to head. Past ideological and fraternal allegiances and formative relationships will have an impact, but they should not entirely define a country's history and options.

Excuses are needed, given the most notable flaw in the post-apartheid government: the inability to get stuff done. There was a moment in the 1990s and early 2000s when a confluence of highly trained academics and activists worked productively in government, reflected in the higher-than-average economic growth rate of 3.73 per cent, peaking at 5.6 per cent in 2006.[105] Thereafter, growth collapsed amid the compounding effects of the global financial crisis and the accession to power of Jacob Zuma over Thabo Mbeki, from which South Africa has never recovered.

The problem is amplified by how South Africa's leaders use their political capital and their time. Much of the country's international relations is about summits or friendly meetings with dubious autocratic states that once helped the exiled ANC, it appears. At home, a lot of effort is put into managing the internal politics of the ANC, with the president famously spending one day a week at Luthuli House. And yet the solution does not lie in what Mavuso describes as 'the theatre of investment conferences and podiums'.[106] It lies in the gearing of the country to problem-solving, and to planning and implementation. The dysfunction of an overly bloated bureaucracy makes this all the more difficult.

The World Bank estimated the national cost of loadshedding to be in the order of $200 million per day, translating into $76 billion since loadshedding started in 2015, with $40 billion alone in 2022.[107] These costs include lost efficiencies, not least to communications; the failure to get off coal and into renewables (where there is funding available); the cost of emergency power generation, especially the high cost of emergency diesel generation; and lost income.

The answer to how the country got here lies in a statement by André de Ruyter shortly before he was forced out as the CEO of Eskom. 'The one good thing about the sun and wind is that it cannot be stolen, first of all. It also cannot be exported to China, beneficiated there, and then be sold back to us.'[108] An alleged attempt on De Ruyter's life in December 2022 followed, showing the 'intense battle taking place in SA', said minister of public enterprises Pravin Gordhan. This is a battle, said the minister, being fought between 'those who want SA to work and thrive, and those who want to corruptly enrich themselves'. He failed to mention, however, that those who want it to fail in this way are within the ranks of the ruling party.[109]

The principal problem with South Africa remains the politics behind the choices, and the vested interests that have come to dominate critical choices. For instance, what the government calls 'sabotage' causing the energy crisis that has bedevilled the economy is in fact a report card of cadre deployment and carelessness. This explains in part, too, why it took three years to get legislation changed to allow for private power producers to enter the grid or, to take another example, to allow concessioning on the container ports in Durban and Coega at Ngqura in the Eastern Cape.

Business provides government with something it doesn't have, but government remains reluctant to acknowledge and employ this asset, perhaps because it reminds it of its own inadequacies, or perhaps because business represents a commercial and political rival. Yet again, in this regard, South Africans are at odds with their government. The Brenthurst poll of South African voters found that three-quarters wanted the private sector to help provide key services in energy, water and rail, while fewer than 15 per cent opposed this.

As government continues to fail to live up to its expectations, there is a risk of raising the rhetoric of a populist dimension that has always been there in the extremes of post-apartheid promises.

The question for those in the private and public sectors fearing a populist path and its inevitably calamitous socio-economic and authoritarian outcome, is how to build an off-ramp from the current path to a higher-growth economy that will absorb the growing pool of unemployed. This path will have to recognise the entrepreneur and the citizen, and not the state, as the core of business.

This is difficult for South Africa to do, not for reasons of efficiency but of political power – and of leadership.

Technocratic responses will not work, because the problem is not the absence of knowledge or good ideas. These abound, as one would expect from a society with the human capital riches that drive academia and the business community. Without voters asserting their rights, governments can rule and profit and never be held accountable.

Politics and economic choices matter. As William Easterly notes, the 'technical problems of the poor (and the absence of technical solutions for those problems) are a symptom of poverty, not a cause of poverty'.[110] The evidence across Africa shows how well improvements in individual freedoms have worked historically for development, and how governance goes hand in hand with liberty, equality, values and rights. Democratic competition is a powerful force for positive change in getting the basic ideas and principles right.

Turkeys, however, don't vote for Christmas. The ANC has been incapable of turning off the tap of rent-seeking and protectionism. Even 55 per cent of its own members no longer believe in the messages of the organisation.[111] It cannot function without such practices. It remains a prisoner of its past, in this way dooming South Africa to a low-growth and high-unemployment future. The overall choice today is whether the answers to South Africa's challenges emerge from the ruling alliance, or from competitive economic and political entrepreneurs that put people and not the state at the centre of development.

How and when did things go so badly wrong? The ANC seems intent on following a path common to liberation movements, to ruin the country to protect itself and its members' interests. This is ultimately self-defeating, of course, but entails so much damage en route.

And yet, South Africa has within its own borders an example of what success looks like. The Western Cape, home to more than seven million people, enjoys a real per capita income of R90 127, more than one-fifth higher than the national average.[112] Its matric results are 5 per cent higher than the national average,[113] increasing employability. Some 15 per cent of households in the province rely on grants as their main source of income and 28 per cent of the population is unemployed, compared to the next highest province, KwaZulu-Natal, at 25 per cent and 33 per cent, or the national average of 24 per cent and 34 per cent respectively.[114] According to the General Household Survey 2021, relative to the other eight provinces, the Western Cape is ranked first for the percentage of households with access to piped or tap water (99.4 per cent), first for the percentage of households with access to improved sanitation (94.8 per cent), and first for the percentage of households whose primary source of income is from salaries (versus pensions, remittances, grants, and so on).

The success, says Premier Alan Winde, 'starts with good governance. We focused on it for years. Audit outcomes are one of the measures. Then governance becomes a habit so we can focus on service delivery. Of course, values, leadership, vision and organisational culture are all important too. But governance, no stealing, doing your job is the first key starting point.'[115] Still there is a conspiracy of silence among academics and most media about this given that the success is largely due to the party in government in the Western Cape, the opposition Democratic Alliance. Admitting the reasons for failure – in South Africa's case, the ANC and its record of governance – is a first step towards recovery, as is the acceptance of the comparative (if imperfect) successes of the DA in the Western Cape. To do otherwise is an exercise in delusion or, at least, wokeness.

Government is the business of agonising choices, but until now, the ANC's leadership has been unable or unwilling to make these.

A party that began its life fighting for equal rights is now geared to maintaining elite access to rents. Every decision is taken with a view to keeping the party's members on board. And what keeps them on board? Access to rents – along with the delights of the ministerial handbook affording perks. To conceal this greed, a charade of ideological 'purity' is maintained. So, the ANC projects itself as avowedly social democratic but is actually oligarchic. It projects itself as being on the side of the people but is actually on the side of its rent-seeking elite. And the more avaricious its leaders become, the harder they try to project themselves as fighters for a new 'more equal' world order. Policy, including special measures and states of disaster, are there to expedite 'legal' contractual rents and preferences extracted via legislative and regulatory instruments. The problem is now that the economy is faltering, and the circle for elite favours will diminish over time. But this did not stop the Zimbabwe African National Union – Patriotic Front in Zimbabwe, and it is unlikely to stop the ANC, although South Africa differs in one crucial respect: it is more urbanised. Urban voters with access to information and a hunger for change have begun to reject the ANC in favour of opposition parties. The ANC might not be able to get away with repression and rigged elections to save itself, but it might try.

Evil conspiracies by criminal masterminds à la James Bond would be far easier to fight than the all-too-frequent combination of incompetence, ignorance and leaders simply not caring about the consequences of their actions. If you're fighting Blofeld or Drax you know you will triumph when you understand 'the plan'. It is difficult to fight back – and win – when there is no evil plan, but rather a morass of venal intentions. Changing this requires less piecemeal reform than a political revolution.

South Africa is half-empty in terms of economic liberation, and half-full in terms of the liberation of political choice. It remains for government to back its people and give them half a chance. Only the voters can make them do so.

Asia

JUSTIN Lin, the former chief economist at the World Bank, reminds us that China had frequent electricity blackouts in the 1980s when its industry was taking off, and lacked adequate roads even as growth accelerated.[1] He also disputes the role of improvements to the business environment in driving success: China was ranked 93 out of 175 in the World Bank's Doing Business index in 2007, and had scarcely climbed to 89 out of 183 by 2010. The big ranking jump came much later between 2018 (78/190) and 2019 (46/190).

Lin says that China developed fast by adapting to its own set realities and discovering its comparative advantages. He highlights the difference between what China and the rest of East Asia[2] did in utilising low-tech, labour-absorptive industries and gradually moving up the value chain, and what Africa attempted in the 1960s through income substitution. The latter approach failed as it created 'white elephants' that could not compete without government subsidies.

The cost of labour – or more politely put, the relative productivity of the labour component – is an unavoidable fact in this transformation. It highlights the comparative African axiom that the continent is poor because it is expensive, and expensive because it is poor. China, like the rest of East Asia, went up the ladder because it was cheap, as illustrated by the labour rates from 1993.[3]

Labour costs per hour in manufacturing, 1993

Germany	$24.87
Netherlands	$19.83
Japan	$16.91
United States	$16.40
France	$16.26
United Kingdom	$12.37
Taiwan	$5.46
Mexico	$2.41
Poland	$1.40
Thailand	$0.71
China	$0.44

China learnt from the Mauritius example, says Lin, in creating 'enclave' conditions through export processing zones, which enabled policy changes in patches to encourage industry while 'leaving domestic institutional reforms for later'. He adds that 'you need an honest assessment of your capacity – people, skills, resources, constraints, advantages – in trying to develop. All successful countries start with what they have rather than with what they don't have.'[4]

China also had the advantage of its own enclave in Shanghai, which has been an open, modern city for the past 180 years. In this sense, Shanghai is also a microcosm of China's development. It was not sudden at all, but rather a gradual shift, a piecemeal move to liberalisation, as Lin observes. China's development was in this way a result of a long, ongoing process of modernisation.

In effect, China had its own 'free zones' well before it emulated those in Mauritius.

In 1842, following their victory in the First Opium War, the British opened a concession in Shanghai. Thereafter the city entered a period of growth and transformation. French, American and Japanese concessions soon followed that of Britain. By the 1930s, Shanghai had developed into the most important port and most modern city in Asia, as notorious for its licentious character as it was famed for its banks and business.

The world's largest banks and trading houses set up along the area on the river known as the Bund. The city was a prototype EPZ: no visas or passports were required. At its heart it was a trading emporium, a quality that Shanghai has perfected today. In the years leading up to the Second World War, Shanghai became a haven for Jews fleeing Nazi-controlled Europe, with more than 20 000 finding refuge there. This changed forever with the Japanese invasion in 1937, when foreigners evacuated or were interned. During the war, all territorial concessions were formally signed over to Chiang Kai-shek and the Kuomintang government. After the communist takeover in 1949, the city and its industry suffered, especially during Chairman Mao's Cultural Revolution, as hundreds of thousands of Shanghainese were sent to work in rural areas throughout China. The advent of Deng Xiaoping's open-door policy in the 1980s allowed its contemporary phase to take place, signalling a renaissance to the commercial Shanghai of the pre-war years.

Taking Lin's point further, when comparing Africa to other successful areas of the world, there is no obvious reason why Africa should be poor.

While East Asia may be viewed as a self-contained region epitomised by rapid economic growth and increasing prosperity, at least from the outside, there are acute internal differences, just as there are among African states. In some, there is a tradition of a centralised state and a sense of national identity, sometimes fostered by external developments. This group, which includes Vietnam, Singapore, South Korea, Taiwan, China and Japan, has tended to perform better. In the Philippines,

Malaysia, Indonesia and, at an extreme, Myanmar (Burma), there is another tradition, that of a weak state and of ethnic and religious disunity. Generally, the greater the openness to capital, trade, skills and technology, the better the performance. Those that have sought to understand what conditions business needs to invest, whether across their territories or in enclave EPZs, have prospered. Those that have invested heavily in skills, a long-term endeavour, have moved more quickly up the innovation and value chain. The more public spending (and aid) has been focused on physical infrastructure, and less on recurrent (staffing) costs, the better the outcome.

It is, of course, not easy to transplant one circumstance to another. In Singapore, Goh Chok Tong admits that his predecessor, Prime Minister Lee Kuan Yew, would have found it difficult to make his model work in Africa since 'Africa has little in the way of a middle-class, and family ties are very strong. The system has to be for change. It is not enough just to be smart.'5 Lee would likely have insisted, as he did in Singapore, to take others along with him, and to build a coterie of alliances and like-minded individuals – in short, institutional capacity.

Regardless, the catalytic role of Lee, among other regional leaders, raises the question for Africa: How might development be pursued differently by a different leadership steeped in the experiences of Asia?

No African country has suffered more than Vietnam, for instance, with its four bouts of foreign intervention, culminating in the American war, and long periods of colonialism, notably the thousand years of Chinese rule. Nearly four million Vietnamese died in the American phase alone, which brought about widespread destruction of civilian infrastructure estimated at many billions of dollars and had a seriously disruptive effect on long-term investment patterns. Quang Tri province, for example, was basically bombed flat, with most of its capital and infrastructure destroyed: only eleven of the province's 3 500 villages were left unscathed by the end of the war. The US Rolling Thunder bombing campaign of the late 1960s 'destroyed 65% of the North's oil storage capacity, 59% of its power plants, [and] 55% of its major bridges'.6

With over five million pieces of unexploded ordnance and the lingering defoliant effects of Agent Orange, much agricultural land could not be planted and harvested even once the guns had gone silent. Vietnam also benefitted – or suffered – from international aid as much as any other country, particularly Soviet military assistance. Added to its fraught past is its discontiguous geography, with a 3 260-kilometre coastline and long and high mountain ranges complicating transport, and a diverse ethnic population. Its fifty-four language groups rival other colonial creations, not least Congo (200 language groups) and Nigeria (500), famed for their fractious and arbitrary colonial composition. Vietnam also possessed an overlay of French administration (to go with the language) and the colonial introduction of Catholicism alongside its Buddhist traditions.

Vietnam now follows the same light-manufacturing labour-intensive path that others in Asia have pursued, building its own domestic entrepreneurial elite once it was given the opportunity to do so. It has had to conquer the follies of ideology along the way. For ten years after the war, Vietnam had to survive the cost of a centrally planned economy, which led to economic collapse and famine. It can lay claim to the same excuses given for Africa's low growth, and then some: its climate is unusually repressive and its neighbourhood, which includes Laos, Thailand and Cambodia, is poor, weak and unstable. It has also received a lot of aid, for all its perverse effects, managing to utilise these inflows to its national advantage. But Vietnam has demonstrated what is possible when given the opportunity. Its economy, officially termed a 'socialist-oriented market economy', took off after 1986, averaging over 6 per cent growth for the next thirty-five years.[7]

The performance of Asian countries has been remarkable over the last seventy years – starting with Japan and progressing through the four Tigers (Singapore, South Korea, Taiwan and Hong Kong) and the rest of the countries making up the Association of Southeast Asian Nations (ASEAN) region, to China. This has enabled a transformation away from poverty to growth, as is reflected in the growing share of East Asians of per capita global wealth, from around 50 per cent in 1960 to over 120 per cent sixty years later.

This history could have been vastly different if leadership had made choices shaped by their past, as the cases of Singapore and Vietnam illustrate. Both exemplify many of the steps that others seeking fast-paced development should take, and the pitfalls to be avoided, summarised as follows:

What to do	What to avoid
Listen to business	Favour elites
Ensure openness	Mistake trading for a means to develop
Instil the basics: political and macro stability	Seek silver-bullet solutions
Boost agricultural yields	Focus on land alone as the solution
Prioritise necessary infrastructure	Adopt high-debt infrastructure-led growth
Invest in education and skills	Close avenues to outside talent
Pursue growth as an inclusive agent	Ignore the environment for the next generation
Improve productivity	Fail to improve the quality of life
Attach laser-like focus to job creation	Look to the state as the solution
Act fast and decisively	Be a prisoner of your past

On the banks of the Singapore River stands a white marble statue. The inscription reads: 'On this historic site, Sir Thomas Stamford Raffles first landed in Singapore on 29th January 1819, and with genius and perception changed the destiny of Singapore from an obscure fishing village to a great seaport and modern metropolis.' With the river and skyscrapers to his back, the Asian Civilisations Museum to his right and parliament to his left, Raffles stands, arms folded, apparently gazing out to sea. This effigy is a replica of the original bronze statue unveiled on Jubilee Day on 27 June 1887. That likeness is 100 metres away in front of the Victoria Theatre and Conference Hall where it was moved on Singapore's centenary from its earlier location at the Padang, between the fields of the (emphatically once white- and male-only) Singapore Cricket Club and the (originally Eurasian) Singapore Recreation Club.

Singaporeans seldom mention history as an excuse. Dr Albert Winsemius, a Dutch economist and advisor to the Singaporean government, suggested that the new state keep the statue of its colonial founder as a 'precondition' for success. As former prime minister Lee Kuan Yew wrote, accepting this advice 'was easy ... Letting it remain would be a symbol of public acceptance of the British heritage and could have a positive effect', especially given Singapore's need for 'large-scale technical, managerial, entrepreneurial, and marketing know-how from America and Europe'.[8]

The symbolism is important. By retaining Raffles and building on the past, Singapore has shown what is achievable with better choices in little more than a generation. 'There is no point in harping on the evils of colonialism – no point at all,' said Singapore's former president S.R. Nathan in 2013. 'It's over, you're in charge now. By talking about it, injustices will not become justices. This is in our hands. Instead, get on and go ahead with the job you have to do, and put money in the pocket of your people.' He added: 'Until you solve your problems yourself, they will not be solved.'[9]

Singapore's example is the East Asian pragmatic norm.

Don't Be a Prisoner of the Past

'We had our backs to the wall. We had no money, no skills and no resources. But we had a group of leaders with a common purpose and a common vision.'
— S.R. Nathan, president of Singapore, 1999–2011

CONTEMPORARY Singapore is a metaphor for the world-class city. The city-state's skyline reflects a continuous, driving reinvention and fast-paced expansion; one year an idea, the next a Singapore Flyer, Marina Bay Sands, ArtScience Museum, forty-two million tonnes of underground oil bunkering, a S$1 billion Gardens by the Bay, and so on. 'It is because we don't want to fail,' one official reflects. 'We also have no natural resources to fall back on.' It is the epitome of globalisation, possessing the world's second-busiest container port, handling more than thirty-four million containers annually, a ship arriving or leaving every two to three minutes. Changi Airport is consistently ranked as the world's best airport,[10] handling 150 000 passengers daily and 6 700 flights weekly. Beyond logistics, Singapore is home to 121 foreign banks and 7 000 multinational companies, two-thirds of which have their Asian headquarters on the island.

Employing the benefits of its geography has always been at the heart of modern Singapore, and so has its people's industriousness. Referring to its proximity to China and its positioning in the Malay Archipelago, Sir Stamford Raffles commented that 'it is impossible to conceive of a place combining more advantages'. Or, as Lee Kuan Yew noted in 2012, 'We became a hub because of the convenience. For shipping, you have to pass Singapore, it's the southernmost point [of continental Asia] ... we were poor and we were underdeveloped, so we had to work hard.'[11]

Following its birthing in 1819 by Raffles and Major William Farquhar as a free port, which Raffles declared would be 'open to ships and vessels of every nation free of duty', the *towkays* (Chinese merchants) quickly came to dominate regional commerce.

As the British empire flourished, so did Singapore, its growth powered by trade and its role, not unlike today, as an international financial centre. The front page of the first issue of the *Straits Times* on 15 July 1845, for example, is filled with notices on shipping activity, lists of foreign goods for sale, market reports from around the world and warehouses to let.[12]

Declared a crown colony along with Malacca and Penang in 1867, by the time of its centenary in 1919, Singapore boasted modern conveniences, including telegraph and telephone connections, electricity, cars, and the world's second-largest dry dock. In 1881, Jules Verne described Singapore in his third volume of *Celebrated Travels and Travellers* as 'simply one large warehouse, to which Madras sent cotton cloth; Calcutta, opium; Sumatra, pepper; Java, arrack and spices; Manila, sugar and arrack; all forthwith dispatched to Europe, China, Siam, etc.'

With the opening of the Suez Canal in 1869, more vessels called at Singapore's deep-water harbour at Telok Blangah, the site of the contemporary container operations known as Keppel Harbour. The completion of the causeway in 1923 connecting the Malay Peninsula enabled Singapore to profit from the booming Malay mining and rubber industries, the latter driven by the advent of the motorcar. Between 1873 and 1913, Singapore's volume of trade increased eightfold, making it the second-busiest port in the world after Liverpool.[13]

Jewel of the British empire it may have been, it was a site of great hardship, of callous division, a world of European *tuans* and coolies, bumboats and *memsahibs*, two cities and societies: one driven by international finance, steam and the telegraph that enjoyed lifestyles of leisure; the other a rickshaw society, marginalised, violent, poor, disease- and drug-ridden, and for whom laws and justice did not equally apply.

While the strategic nous underlying the appropriation, utilisation and development of colonial Singapore might have represented the best of the British empire, the social and political aspects, founded in bigotry, dispossession and exploitation, illustrated the worst, and would not have been out of place in colonial Africa.

Those rickshaw pullers, often Chinese migrants, would work up to twelve-hour shifts for as little as 60 cents a day, much of which would, invariably given the levels of addiction among pullers, be spent on *chandu* (opium). The high level of opium addiction among particularly the poorer classes of Chinese migrant workers engaged in backbreaking occupations was so concerning that, in 1896, Dr Lim Boon Keng led an inquiry into the 'four social evils': gambling, alcoholism, prostitution and 'chasing the dragon' (opium smoking). By the 1860s, there were more than 50 000 Chinese in Singapore (two-thirds of the population). Tensions between the colonial authorities and Chinese immigrants occasionally flared into violence, such as the Chinese Post Office Riots of 1876 and the Verandah Riots of 1888. After the Second World War, these frustrations found voice in the rallying cry of *merdeka* ('freedom' in Malay) and the pan-Malayan independence movement.

In 1863, Singapore joined with the Federation of Malaya and others to form Malaysia. Indonesia, which opposed the formation of Malaysia, launched *Konfrontasi* ('confrontation' in Indonesian), an armed conflict fought mainly on the Indonesia–Malaysia border, but which also saw Indonesian saboteurs mounting an indiscriminate bombing campaign in Singapore – between 1963 and 1966 there were around forty bomb attacks. *Konfrontasi* aside, the Singaporean government and the Malaysian central government disagreed on many political and economic issues. Relations broke down to such an extent that, on 9 August 1965, the Malaysian parliament voted to expel Singapore from Malaysia.[14]

After its separation from Malaysia, Singapore became independent, with Lee Kuan Yew of the ruling People's Action Party (PAP) serving as its first prime minister. The tiny island of just 580 square kilometres was a fragile, poor backwater. Born amid crisis, the city-state was riven with racial, ethnic and religious sensitivities and differences, the challenges formidable. Its limited infrastructure, including the dockyards, was geared to colonial purpose and British naval presence. There were high levels of poverty and inequality, and limited literacy (just 60 per cent). Two-thirds of its then 1.6 million people lived in squalor in overcrowded slums, most without waterborne sewerage and many without employment.

Dr Goh Keng Swee, regarded as the father of Singapore's modern economy, learnt from a social survey conducted in 1952 that of the 1 814 people who lived in Upper Nanking Street, close to his own home, just three households had their own toilet, bath and kitchen. The others shared bucket toilets and open coal fires. As a result, he 'decided that his priority should be to provide jobs. And the best way to do this was to encourage capitalism and private enterprise.'[15]

Fifty years after independence, Singapore's GDP per capita stood at more than US$50 000 – over 100 times more than at independence and 25 per cent greater than that of the United Kingdom (UK), the former colonial power. Over the same period, per capita incomes in sub-Saharan Africa had multiplied just ten times to average US$1 655.

Yet fifty years earlier, it was Singapore looking to Africa for lessons on growing its economy. In 1968, recalled Kenya's former prime minister Raila Odinga, 'a team of Singaporeans came to Kenya to learn our lessons, since we were then a more developed country than they were'. Odinga reflects: 'I took a study trip to Singapore with six ministers. That was the latest in many trips taken by the Kenyan government, about which no report was ever written, and where the participants kept everything to themselves. I said that this trip had to be different, that we had to translate our findings into actions. On our return, I asked for a plan of action from each minister learning from Singapore since there was no point in reinventing the wheel. Each minister was tasked to prepare their action plan against our Vision 2030 … But after I left government [in 2013], nothing further happened.'[16] His is the experience of many an African government official.

East Asia seemed to have few advantages over Africa at the point of decolonisation. Ethnic disunity, frail institutions and limited governance outside the capital were common. Weak democracy, subsistence agriculture, fragmentary external trade linkages and acute social stratification were also typical. Both regions shared a history of commodity and colonial exploitation. In both, 'settlers' were imposed on the local populations, arousing particularly intense hostility towards foreigners.

Colonised cousins they may have been, but from this point parallels with Africa end.

Faced with few resources in meeting the aspirations of the people, Lee's team of 'founding fathers'[17] and subsequent governments relied on gathering and efficiently deploying scarce resources. Their success exactly illustrates the value of decisive domestic leadership concerned less with grand visions, governance frameworks and mobilising aid, than with the things they were themselves in control of – policy tools, tax revenue and execution.

Singapore offers an excellent learning opportunity to understand Africa's growth puzzle from an East Asian perspective. However, often the wrong lessons are taken. It is too easy to denigrate Singapore, among other East Asian examples, as authoritarian, especially given the detention of more than 800 individuals between 1963 and 1987, the ruinous libel suits against opposition leaders in the 1980s and 1990s, changes in electoral rules and boundaries, and the store of repressive legislation on a range of institutions, from labour to civil society. This has been summarised as a 'suffocating' political and cultural atmosphere.[18] On the opposite side of the spectrum, for some Africans, East Asia's development success has been used to justify authoritarianism, given that the region's economies have managed high economic growth rates without full political rights. The need for a 'strong man' in Africa is the parlance in this regard, forgetting the historical record of such strongmen, when political power has seldom if ever been used for the benefit of development. There are good reasons why African electorates have preferred democracies over the alternative of a 'benign dictatorship', not least since this style of government is oxymoronic.

There are many other aspects of Singapore's economic success that have been similarly overlooked by advocates for autocracies. These include high spending on education, bureaucratic responsiveness, attractive policy for business investment, low-wage industries, high productivity, investment in infrastructure, raised agricultural outputs as an initial spur to growth, and an overwhelming focus on competitiveness. Authoritarian it might have been, but unlike the African examples, the Singaporean government was able to transform the country from a regional trading hub to a First World economy in just one generation. And it maintained a high level of popular support.

Principles for action

While recognising historical differences, both between East Asia and Africa and between African countries, a dozen lessons from Singapore stand out for Africa:

1. **Unity of purpose:** One of the prominent features of Lee's time in office was the vision he had for Singapore and his ability to allow others, notably the private sector, to help bring it to reality. He understood that the role of government was in creating the conditions that enable growth – as opposed to being the main driver for growth – and took development decisions towards that end by investing in education, housing, infrastructure and policies that made it easier to do business in Singapore. Growth was a 'national project' behind which people could rally.
2. **Make the difficult trade-offs:** Lee knew that you cannot do everything at once, and that focus was required to succeed at anything. Success depended on setting clear targets and making the difficult decisions that allowed those targets to become a reality. Singapore's approach to land reform, while perhaps controversial, has been instrumental in the successful economic development of the city-state. The mandatory Central Provident Fund (CPF) savings scheme, promoted by Lee, has enabled the construction of housing and home ownership on a grand scale, and seemingly offers a way around the chronically low savings rate across Africa.
3. **Change the pattern of the colonial economy:** Lee quickly realised that, with Singapore's 'limited options' to survive, the country had to 'make extraordinary efforts' and, in the process, 'render obsolete our role as the *entrepôt* and middleman for the trade of the region. We had to be different,' he concluded, in order to address high unemployment and social tension. This change saw Singapore first move into low-cost manufacturing, then convert the British military facilities that closed in 1971 to civilian use, all the while attracting multinational companies to the island. Its strategy required continuous improvement and reinvention: from manufacturing through services and a digital transition, to its contemporary green economic phase. This did not mean ignoring the country's colonial past but rather using the resources available at the time to move Singapore to a future that was not defined by the structures put in place by its colonial masters.
4. **Build institutions:** While the state under Lee was undoubtedly at the helm of this transformation, additional lessons include the guiding of all actions by commercial principles, balance of power through devolution and shared responsibility among fellow 'founding fathers'. Contrary to the notion of one person running things from the centre, the reality of Lee's rule was quite different. His government, and those of his successors, involved top-quality peers, not just one

'big man'. Singapore has relied on institutions in the pursuit of development, a mindset and practice cultivated by Lee, but which has far outlived his tenure.

5. **Integrate don't isolate:** Singapore's transformation has been underpinned by a drive to globalise rather than nationalise. Whereas African countries routinely make it difficult to move goods in and out, Singapore has capitalised on its strategic geographic crossroads in gearing its policies towards openness and building a world-class logistics business. There is a zero tariff on imported goods, low tax rates (personal and corporate tax rates are capped at 20 per cent and 18 per cent respectively), a range of free-trade agreements, and vigorous trade and export promotion. Lee used his international engagements, including a sabbatical at Harvard in 1968, to understand better the ebbs and flows of world politics and economics and, importantly, to win over investors. The Singaporeans set up the Economic Development Board in 1961 specifically to provide a one-stop shop for investors and promote investment through its overseas offices. But Lee backed this up with personal commitment. Every time he visited the United States, he would arrange to meet between twenty and fifty executives to enable those CEOs who 'had not time to visit Singapore ... to see and assess the man in charge before they set up a factory there'. He was able to gauge how these investors' minds worked. 'They looked for political, economic and financial stability and sound labour relations to make sure that there would be no disruption in production that supplied their customers and subsidiaries around the world,' Lee wrote.

6. **Attract talent:** Singapore made sure that the best and brightest were in government, that they were paid properly and that they were given full support by leadership to do their job. As Lee observed, 'That we have succeeded in the last three decades does not ensure our doing so in the future. However, we stand a better chance of not failing if we abide by the basic principles that have helped us progress: social cohesion through sharing the benefits of progress, equal opportunities for all, and meritocracy, with the best man or woman for the job, especially as leaders in government.' Moreover, legitimacy through performance was central to gaining and maintaining the confidence that the island's citizens had in government and its leadership. In proving the adage that 'any country with a skills problem has an immigration problem', the importation of talent has also been a key aspect of Singapore's success. From little over one million people at independence, Singapore's population now stands at 5.6 million, including around 1.5 million expatriates, permanent residents and migrant workers. The injection of immigrants is part of a strategy to maintain GDP targets, and syncs with the need to continuously innovate and search for a competitive advantage.

7. **Invest in the infrastructure that makes growth possible**: Singapore's focus on being a welcome environment for international investment meant creating the logistical and infrastructural framework to support that investment. An endeavour is clearly seen in the Port of Singapore. As noted earlier, more than thirty-four million containers are offloaded at the port yearly, making it the world's second busiest behind Shanghai. The customs clearance time is officially under ten minutes, though in practice this is as quick as a mouse-click for 99.9 per cent of imports. Singapore's efficiency has been achieved through technology and the implementation of seemingly straightforward procedures, such as profiling customers and goods, and imposing strict penalties for transgressors. By comparison, in African ports, cargo dwell times (the time cargo spends in the port) average about twenty days. The reason for this and the failure of solutions ranging from privatisation to expanded port facilities, says the World Bank, 'is that the long dwell times are in the interest of certain public and private actors in the system'.[19]

8. **Catalyse, don't capture**: African governments like to cite Singapore as an example in the maintenance of their own parastatals and 'partystatals' (companies owned and/or run by ruling parties), both routinely notorious in crowding out private sector competition to the advantage of narrow financial and patronage interests. Again, such lessons are wide of the mark. An example of how to do this differently is in Temasek Holdings Ltd, the government-owned investment company with a portfolio value of US$403 billion (as of 31 March 2022).[20] Despite its statist origins, Temasek's strategy and role is based on commercial and capitalist rather than political rationale. This avoids the intellectual suffocation and bureaucratic inertia of nationalised entities and creates a powerful investment vehicle for Singapore.

9. **Manage labour relations**: Labour relations in Singapore have been driven by the maxim that 'it is better to have a low-paying job than no job at all', balanced by a set of laws that spelt out minimum employment conditions, placing limits on retrenchment benefits and overtime benefits. This created a cooperative environment between government, the unions and business. As Goh Chok Tong puts it, 'Singapore Inc is a metaphor for the private sector, government, and the unions all working as one.'[21] Lee realised early on that union practices were incentivising employers to become capital-intensive, investing in expensive machines rather than creating large numbers of jobs, and creating a small group of privileged and highly paid unionised workers in the process, amid a growing band of underpaid and underemployed workers. He therefore made it illegal for a union to take strike or industrial action without a secret ballot, continuously stressing the importance of wider employment over narrow pri-

vilege, and was able to decrease strikes from 153 between 1961 and 1962 to zero by 1969.

10. **Work with comparative advantages**: Lee knew Singapore's limits, which were imposed by its population, land size and natural resource base. He therefore opted for development through sectors that could take advantage of the country's strengths, particularly its geographical position. This is how the development of Singapore into a regional air hub came about. The search for comparative advantage demands not aiming too high and seeking gradual progress up the value chain of industrial progress.
11. **Don't be a cheap date; use aid well, but don't rely on it**: Despite the fad to bash aid as the explanation for all Africa's problems, East Asian countries have received comparatively large amounts of donor assistance. During the 1960s, aid per capita received by both regions was similar. Whereas some Asian countries enjoyed especially large aid flows (South Korea and Taiwan), and this has continued until recently (Vietnam), aid has not been relied on as the single source of income. East Asian countries have put aid to good use with improved governance, sound policies, effective planning and clearer, firmer local ownership of projects. Lee was adamant that his government should nurture a 'spirit of self-reliance', avoiding an 'aid-dependent mentality'. 'If we were to succeed,' he stated, 'we had to depend on ourselves.' Or as he put it to Singaporean workers: 'The world does not owe us a living. We cannot live by the begging bowl.'
12. **Do some things differently today**: A final lesson, although not straight out of Lee's playbook, is that today's challenges call for an altogether different type of growth from Singapore and, for that matter, much of East Asia. Today, we know the cost of infrastructure- and consumption-driven growth on the environment, as we see the effects of more than a century of unchecked fossil fuel use on our air quality, changing climate, and the plastic debris in our oceans and rivers. There are other pressing issues, not least inequality, decent work and human rights, that were barely recognised in Lee's day.

In looking forward, and not back, Singapore laid out a plan for transformation and implemented it. The government's response was to align the economic, social, international and legal context to the nation's needs: land, housing, jobs and investment were the priorities. To paraphrase former Ghanaian president Kwame Nkrumah, Lee's Singapore first sought not the political kingdom but the development path.

Land and housing

In 1969, Liu Thai Ker returned from his studies in Sydney and at Yale, and a stint working under the renowned architect I.M. Pei[22] to serve first as the deputy CEO and then CEO of Singapore's Housing and Development Board (HDB) for twenty years. In 1989, he moved to the Urban Redevelopment Authority (URA) as its CEO and chief planner, and in 2008 was appointed as the chairman of the Centre for Liveable Cities within the Ministry of National Development.

His career provides a unique window on Singapore's transformation: from the slums of the 1960s, by 2015, 83 per cent of the population lived in publicly supplied HDB apartments, 90 per cent owned their own homes, the rivers were clean, the island was 15 per cent larger as a result of land reclamation and, despite the population increase, green cover had increased to 47 per cent of the territory.

Liu observes that this extraordinary transition has hinged on the government's credibility among its population. And that, in turn, has depended on delivery, and 'behind that is its record of transparency, frugality and the absence of corruption'.

To support the priority of urban renewal, Lee's government enacted the Land Acquisition Act in 1966, which granted the power to acquire land quickly and at reasonable rates of compensation. This was followed by an amendment to the Foreshores Act in 1964, which enabled the government to both embark on reclamation and build the East Coast Parkway linking Changi Airport with the city centre. By 1979, 80 per cent of land belonged to the government to be sold on long-term (usually ninety-nine-year) leases to developers. 'Without land, you can't talk about planning,' says Cheng Tong Fatt, who served as permanent secretary in the Ministry of National Development in the 1970s, and later as ambassador to China.

Land acquisition was sometimes only grudgingly accepted. 'Government had a vision and knew what had to be done, even if unpopular, for the greater good of the people,' says Peter Ho, former chairman of the URA. But it was made more palatable with the payment of compensation and a promise of resettlement.

The resettlement of those living in the central business district required alternative housing, which is where the HDB came in. The transformation of housing became an early focus of the government, providing a model for future prudency and resolve. At the end of the HDB's first decade, in 1970, one-third of the population lived in public housing. In ten years it had built 120 669 units, compared to the 23 019 constructed by its predecessor, the Singapore Improvement Trust, in thirty-two years. Now apartments are funded through a combination of homeowner grants and loans, the latter both commercial and from the Central Provident Fund, a mandatory savings scheme to which employers and employees contribute (a maximum of) 16 per cent and 20 per cent of salary respectively. In 2016, CPF loans were at 2.6 per cent, repayable over thirty years. Its aim, says HDB chairman

Bobby Chin, was and remains 'to provide quality and affordable housing for Singaporeans across different stages of their lives'.[23]

Home-ownership gave the population a 'stake in their society, building a strong work ethic, a store of value to be monetised, and a sense of belonging,' emphasises Sng Cheng Keh, HDB's deputy CEO.[24] Effectively, it turned a radical discontented society into one with conservative values, suspicious of populist solutions as they now saw themselves as owners.

Jobs and investment

Singapore has been open to external advice and ideas not just on urban development, but also on wider issues of growth and development, notably with the involvement of the (unpaid) Dutch consultant Dr Albert Winsemius, who advised the government for nearly twenty-five years until the mid-1980s.[25]

Dr Winsemius was central in the early plans to expand the embryonic country's economic base. The strategy to do so first focused on heavy industry and electronics, which would provide, Dr Goh envisaged, 50 000 jobs in the first five years. Land was set aside for export industries, notably the Jurong Town Corporation complex created in 1968. Manufacturing's share of GDP increased from 20.5 per cent in 1967 to 29.5 per cent by 1980, driving the country's annual economic growth at over 12 per cent from 1966 to 1973.

While it built on Singapore's trading legacy, the openness underpinning the socio-economic transition was not preordained. Indeed, the opposition Socialist Front, formed in 1961 by left-wingers expelled from the ruling PAP, offered a more state-directed and centred alternative, 'more akin to the Communist Chinese model at the time'.[26] Despite initial suspicions of Lee's leftist political leanings, which led to some industrialists relocating to Kuala Lumpur, his administration soon gained a reputation of being honest and pragmatic. As *TIME* noted in its report of 7 November 1960, 'Lee ... soon grasped that Singapore by itself is an island emporium ill-suited to revolutionary socialism since, among other things, it lacks any major industries to nationalise. His revised economic policy: "Teaching the capitalists how to run their system".'[27] Lee could move to the centre once the left had hived off into the Socialist Front.

With full employment in 1972 came a shift from labour-intensive manufacturing to skill- and capital-intensive operations. 'We needed labour-intensive industry to suit our needs in the 1960s,' recalled Ngiam Tong Dow, who served as Dr Goh's permanent secretary, 'but you cannot compete on low labour costs alone. We asked the employers to provide the training if we provided the facilities, since you cannot train in a vacuum but rather with a job in mind.'

This required ongoing investment in training through technical schools, vocational institutions and joint government-business training centres for workers. Early emphasis was placed on mathematics, technical subjects and science, a bilingual policy insisted on the widespread use of English, and television was used early on (from 1967) as a medium for learning. With few exceptions, from 1968 all secondary-school students had to undergo a two-year course including technical studies. By 1972, Singapore's nine vocational institutes had produced more than 4000 graduates compared to just 324 in 1968.

This was not the only 'soft' aspect. Singaporeans were actively encouraged to reduce family sizes that put a strain on healthcare, education and housing. In 1966 the government established the Family Planning and Population Board and launched a national programme to encourage smaller families. The 'Stop at Two' policy was backed with financial incentives, resulting in a decline in Singapore's fertility rate from 4.7 in 1965 to 2.1 ten years later, and 1.7 by 1980. This has created a different challenge of renewal today, however.

Education

Tharman Shanmugaratnam, Singapore's former deputy prime minister, notes that in the early days, there was inevitable concern for democracy's 'guard rails'. Especially concerning were matters to do with race and religion, particularly in the light of the ethnic composition of Singapore and the failed union with Malaysia. But politics and the inevitable 'progress to more fair play' have to be matched by efficiencies in civil service delivery and, at its foundation, education. The institutionalisation of a 'performance culture' across government, support for small and medium-sized businesses, the reduction of governance 'system' costs, and the 'enhancement of openness' through free-trade agreements were all essential attributes. But the 'bedrock', he explains, was Singapore's education system.

'Education is our most important economic and social strategy,' Shanmugaratnam says. 'From the early days the paradox was that we depoliticised the substance of education, yet we took a great political interest in creating an ethos of performance and autonomy in so doing.' Singapore 'moved educators around continuously as an organising principle to enable the spread of success and isolation of failure, never permitting entrenchment in one place. Every principal moved after five to six years. This created a performance ethic in the key arena of action, the school, and not the ministry.'

From the 1990s, Singapore took the bold step of instituting a performance-based pay system. 'This was highly contentious and took more than five years to get it fully bedded in,' notes Shanmugaratnam, who doubled as the country's minister of finance. 'Moreover, the metrics are so difficult. As a result, we overnight had to

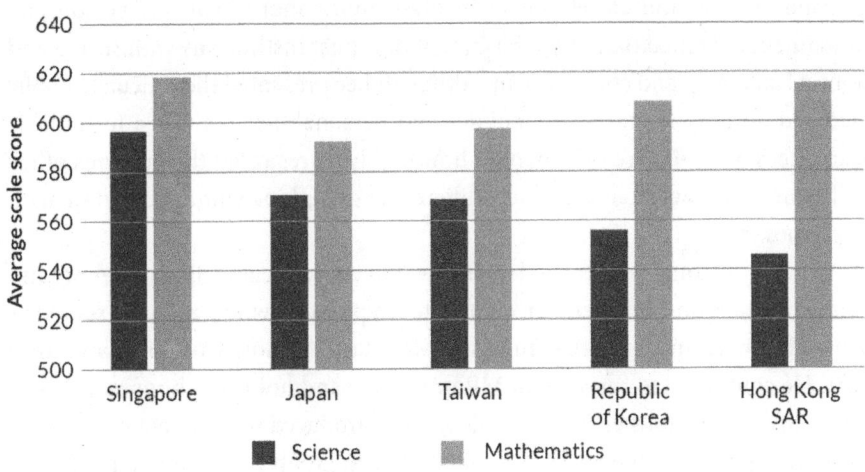

Maths and science TIMSS scores, 2015

Source: Trends in International Mathematics and Science Study (TIMSS)

make qualitative judgements. But now the culture is fully established, taking care that this is not a commercial setting, and we don't want the teachers to impress the wrong attributes.

'Education has been absolutely central to facilitating social mobility in Singapore. Our pinnacle is regarded as our public schools, not the private system. Indeed, public schooling is mandatory at the primary level. Admission is not based on the parents' means but on geography, which stems from our social housing policy which aimed to mix people up. Also, our metrics are not limited to exams alone, but rather are focused on demonstrating the individuals' abilities. We have found that this performance-based ethos motivates parents, linking parents with the teachers, motivating them.' This is also backed up by the rewards. 'We pay teachers the same as other professionals in the civil service, which keeps them highly motivated and well rewarded. Our experience at education shows that the system itself and governance counts.'

Shanmugaratnam argues that this performance ethos stems from Singapore's political system, where 'incumbents are only at an advantage if they deliver to their constituency. The People's Action Party is not entitled to rule Singapore; it depends on how we deliver.'[28]

Politics is more than power

While Singapore, like others in the region – including South Korea, China, Indonesia and Taiwan – has developed and modernised under a system of rigid political control, the image of Lee Kuan Yew as the 'Big Man' lacks sufficient nuance. Singapore's economic development involved much more than one person and fundamentally relied on the establishment of robust institutions with strong and honest leadership and commitment. Although Lee presented the articulate public face and adroitly managed the politics and personalities, his was a formidable team. Lee's memoirs are testament to how highly he regarded the opinions of his colleagues and how often there were differences of outlook within government on key issues.[29]

Goh Chok Tong, who turned eighty-two in 2023, became Singapore's second prime minister on 28 November 1990. After stepping down in 2004, he served as senior minister and as chairman of the Monetary Authority of Singapore until 2011. He continued to serve as an MP until 2020 and holds the honorary title of 'Emeritus Senior Minister'. His administration introduced several political reforms, including non-constituency and nominated MPs, group representation constituencies, parliamentary committees and an elected presidency. He led the ruling PAP to three general election victories, in 1991, 1997 and 2001, in which the party won 61 per cent, 65 per cent and 75 per cent of the vote respectively.

Goh pinpoints several lessons from Singapore's development experience. First, 'government must have the right people'. Yet, in politics, the 'character and the competency of the leadership' is seldom highlighted, he says. 'This begs the question: how do you throw up good leaders?' It is critical that leaders 'set a good example' and that they 'work for the people, not for themselves'.

Second, there is a need 'to give every citizen equal opportunities and to treat them fairly'. This meant 'ensuring that every community felt that it was part of Singapore'. Goh says that, in this regard, the island-state is 'the same as in Africa, where you have different tribes and religions, where it was difficult to bring them together'. Hence the need 'to mitigate the differences like we did, having candidates stand together'.

Third, there is a 'need to ensure that there are key leaders who can follow you – what I learnt as the term of "key man risk". Mr Lee would talk to us about what would happen if he fell under a bus or if he was on an army plane that might crash ... we could talk about key man risk as we had leaders who were not corrupt, and could leave politics, as no one had any hold on you,' Goh notes.

Producing 'the right people' is Goh's fourth essential ingredient. 'Who would want to be in politics, with its lack of privacy, especially today with social media and with all the opportunities to make money outside?' he asks. 'Yet Lee Kuan Yew would appeal to you by saying, "Do you think you can do this and make money if the PAP did not run things, if we had a dud government?" It's better to be in control of your own future. We also have built-in quality control. After three terms, MPs are expected to stand down, the same with ministers who are expected to retire at fifty-five to sixty. Otherwise, as elsewhere, you hang onto your power.'

In Goh's view, 'authoritarianism is not essential for success'. Lee sometimes said 'that if he did not have to win elections he could have done much more for Singapore. I am not sure,' Goh smiles. 'He might have become arrogant and overconfident. He would not have allowed his successors to do so.'

While Goh maintains that democracy was 'essential for our success, we had to modify the political system to suit our local situation'. He explains that since Singapore 'inherited the British Westminster system, [democracy] was a given for us. But the framework of democracy alone was insufficient for economic development as a newly independent country.' While 'democracy focused the minds of leaders on what it took to win the next election', Singapore's primary objective was 'to reduce unemployment'. Only then could they 'address what would win the hearts of the people. In our case it was housing.'

Rather than a sign of authoritarianism or a lack of democracy, Goh says that 'having one party in power [since independence] is a consequence of being able to deliver'. The former prime minister says that Lee helped Singapore to avoid entrenching power. 'He taught us always to allow ourselves to be challenged by others. To do this we needed to create an opposition within our own party.' To make space for 'genuine opposition voices', Goh's administration 'experimented by having non-constituency MPs'.

Goh cites several fierce debates within government. On the question of how to improve the system of public transport, 'one clan led by the transport minister and Lee Kuan Yew favoured the subway system', today known as the MRT, or Mass Rapid Transit system. 'Another, led by the deputy prime minister, Goh Keng Swee, favoured a bus-based system. A tremendous debate followed. Both sides engaged consultants paid for by the government, with the ministers and the consultants arguing against one another with no resolution. The subway system was going to cost S$5 billion at a time when we could hardly afford it.' In the end, Lee resolved the matter by funding the MRT through the sale of public land, 'pulling the carpet from under Goh'.

A further example is when 'Mr Lee suggested changing the voting rules to ensure that minority candidates would always be represented in parliament through the twinning of candidates.' This resulted in another intense debate 'especially in the Malay and Indian communities who were against this, and in the parliamentary select committee'. Other controversial matters included government's changing of the rate of contribution to the CPF, and the Graduate Mothers' Scheme, which 'caused a loss of votes'. The programme, formulated around Lee's eugenicist beliefs, aimed to give children of graduate mothers priority in school admission. It was reversed in 1985.

Once decisions were taken in cabinet, Goh notes, they would then go through parliament where 'in certain issues the whip was lifted'. Performance legitimacy played a part. As the eminent Singaporean academic Barry Desker has noted about the region, 'The reality is that East Asian leaders need to perform, even in an authoritarian setting, as their legitimacy and tenure is due to their successful growth performance, even in the absence of free and fair elections.'[30] While performance was, in Goh's view, 'one factor, the other is the trust that the leaders built up with the people, including the personal character of the leader in government. They had to be seen to be fair.'

This was all driven by a fear of failure and loss of control. 'For us, the thing was always "How can we win the next election?", and to do that, we needed to work out what would cause people to vote for [us].' Goh therefore refutes the depiction of Singapore as a benevolent dictatorship – 'benevolent, yes, but a dictatorship, no. I would describe our system as strict, disciplined, no-nonsense and paternalistic. Our prime minister took the view that this was a family, and we had to do what was best for Singapore. But he also took the view that he did not have to consult in the process with everyone as he had been elected.

'The key was not authoritarianism, but that we were able to win election after election as we delivered economically. The focus was always on the well-being of people, not the self-interest of the party. I notice that in other countries, once they win elections, they look after themselves.'

For Goh, the most important contribution made by Lee was the foundation of 'values of governance' that he instilled. 'Now [as a result], we have a thriving Singapore without Mr Lee. He planned for his retirement. But when I look at Africa today, most leaders hang onto power.'

Conclusion: Take the right lessons, take deliberate steps

Lee Hsien Loong, Lee Kuan Yew's eldest son and Singapore's current prime minister since 2004, paid his first official visit to South Africa in May 2023. At a press conference hosted in the Singaporean leader's honour, President Cyril Ramaphosa used the opportunity to announce an African initiative to negotiate an end to the war in Ukraine, an announcement that took the Singaporeans by surprise. While some positive discussions were held about human capital development and logistics, no time was spent on identifying the practices from which South Africa might learn. This may reflect the extent of the South African government's imagination, or its levels of arrogance, but it also illustrates that South Africa's leadership doesn't believe the developmental approach of Singapore and others is relevant to the

African context. As Mike Abel, a leading South African marketing and advertising executive, writes, 'if you look at ... what a Singapore has achieved, there is absolutely no reason, with competent leadership and smart decisions, implemented by capable people, why SA can not only recover, but succeed.'[31] That Africans fail to learn from these positive examples indubitably reflects in the paucity of development results.

Instead, as noted, often the wrong lessons – belief in the value of a benign dictator, for example – are taken by those seeking single-issue answers. Singapore's path shows that it is as wrong to extol the virtues of colonialism as it is to promote the benefits of authoritarianism. Central to the political philosophy of East Asia's first leadership generation was legitimacy through delivery – or 'performance legitimacy'.[32] As peoples' needs have shifted, however, and the first-generation leaders responsible for the heaviest aspects of repression have moved on, so too has the tone of government changed.

In this regard, altering the nature of the political economy, from the overwhelmingly commodity-dependent type of the colonial era to one that is more diversified, is critical. This means shifting to an economy run less for the elites than the population – what could be termed 'a commitment to popular welfare'. This approach can be inculcated through the establishment of a meritocracy, through skills enhancement in the short term and education in the longer term, through the adoption of a full package of reforms from infrastructure to bureaucratic red tape, and through citizens taking greater responsibility for their own destiny and holding leaders to account. Policy must be matched by government action, and fiscal measures by attention to detail on logistics. While openness is a criterion of success, the sum of measures is greater than its individual parts.

For business seeking to do well in emerging markets like Asia and Africa, a sound environment is insufficient. Sound management is also required. Businesses that have prospered have been characterised by knowledge of local markets, reflecting a long-term investment in the process.

Singapore's extraordinary transition has hinged on the government's credibility among its population and the trust emanating from that, which has forged both a sense of common identity and a unity of purpose. That, in turn, has depended on its record of delivery rather than playing politics with the past. Overall, Singapore's continuous transformation and development speaks to the importance of matching deeds with words and of careful planning. It illustrates the necessity of rooting actions in the population's principal needs – jobs and housing were the priorities in the 1960s, and better infrastructure and urban renewal in the 1970s. It has required security, achieved through local capacity and international diplomacy.

Singapore is a lesson in using the past as a springboard to the future. As Lee himself noted at the Non-Aligned Movement in Lusaka in 1970: 'The ending of colonialism does not in itself result in social and economic progress: it provides the opportunities for it.'[33]

Today, it is difficult to think of Singapore as a fragile, poor backwater. Given its turbulent beginnings, economic and social delivery – from jobs to housing – was politics by other means. While the state under Lee Kuan Yew was at the helm of this transformation, its actions were guided by commercial principles.

The pace and scale of Singapore's transition from urban slum to global city is unparalleled. Despite the common narrative of critics and wannabe autocrats that this action was down to authoritarianism, the ability to get things done has relied principally on the government's record and commitment to popular welfare. Success has also depended not on a few big or iconic infrastructure projects or even the provision of necessary funding, housing and land, even though these were all necessary aspects, but fundamentally on ensuring a complete cycle of economic growth, governance and job creation within an overarching 'can do' political framework. Singapore's growth since 1965 is testament to the importance of leveraging a crisis to create a laser-like focus on development needs, from housing to jobs, and of a willingness to take tough decisions to ensure progress and public support.

By putting the war and failed economic policies behind it, like Singapore, Vietnam, to which we now turn, has proven again the necessity for policymakers and people not to be prisoners of their past or of ideology.

The Value of Policy Change

'Now we have a problem in trying to make our power credible, and Vietnam looks like the place.' – US president John F. Kennedy, June 1961[34]

V-DAY.

Not Victory in Europe, but the moment on 30 April 1975 when Tank 390, a North Vietnamese T-59 under the command of Captain Vu Dang Toan, crashed through the gates of Saigon's presidential palace. Inside, South Vietnam's last president, General Duong Van Minh, better known as 'Big Minh', and some thirty members of his team waited to surrender to the North, ending thirty years of civil war and more than a thousand years of colonial intervention.

Vietnam was poised to transform from a war to a country. But the struggle was not over.

At the end of the 1980s, per capita income had scarcely risen. While the dust of war had settled, Vietnam was in a different battle, with a per capita GDP of just US$654 (in constant terms) in 1989.[35] This was the result of failed socialist policies that had removed any incentive to produce, leading to stagnation and shortages. Rather than the joy of peace, Vietnam experienced a dark age of doctrinaire government, collectivisation and near famine, the loss of civil liberties, isolation, wars with Cambodia and China, and endless suffering and deprivation.

Following widespread reforms initiated in 1986, average income multiplied over the ensuing three decades to $3 288 by 2019.[36]

Such dramatic change depended on lifting economic growth, which has averaged over 6 per cent since 1992. This started with a change of control in the rural areas. From ruinous collectivised farming, the country shifted to allocating long-term leases to farmers with a better productive record. But the cities have delivered even more. With more than six million people, Saigon in the south (after 1975, officially Ho Chi Minh City), for example, has experienced 9.6 per cent average growth since 2010.[37]

Vietnam before and after reform

	1984	2020
Population	58.5 million	98.2 million
GDP per capita (constant: 2015)	$577 ($6 069 world)	$3 316 ($11 019 world)
Share of global per capita GDP	9.5%	30.1%
Inflation	411%	3.2%
Life expectancy	69.9 years	75 years
Child mortality (per 1 000 live births)	44	17
Poverty	75%	3.8%
Literacy	87%	96%

Vietnam's post-liberation transformation was based on two fundamental choices.

The first was Vietnam's ability to put the past behind it, remarkable given the level of devastation wrought during the last century, including four periods of foreign intervention (Chinese, French, Japanese and American), more than three million war casualties, including two million civilians, and the retribution and communist economic folly that followed.

This went hand in hand with a process of nationalism and identification foremost as Vietnamese. Chinese rule lasted for more than 1 000 years from the invasion by the Han dynasty in the second century BC until the Vietnamese ousted their conquerors and began a southward expansion, reaching the Gulf of Siam by the mid-eighteenth century. This did not signal the end of internal discord. For nearly two centuries, contending families in the north and south feuded over control of the kings of the Le dynasty. This ended with the arrival of French missionaries in the late eighteenth century, a period that culminated in the capture of Saigon in 1859. While the area was administered by France collectively as French Indochina, the colony was made up of disparate units: Annam (in the coastal centre of contemporary Vietnam), Tonkin (to the north), Cochinchina (around Saigon and the Mekong Delta), Laos and Cambodia. While Vichy France possessed nominal control of its colony during the Second World War, effective power was transferred to Japan, which stationed 30 000 troops in the area. With first Chinese and later American support, Nguyen Tat Thanh, who took the name Ho Chi Minh ('the one who enlightens'), built up a force of guerrillas, helped by the Japanese turning on their French collaborators in March 1945. Despite French attempts to retain nominal control under a commonwealth-type arrangement in the French Union, by the time the Japanese surrendered to Chinese and British forces in September 1945, Ho's Viet Minh had already moved from their bases in the Viet Bac mountains to seize control of Tonkin and the area around Hanoi, proclaiming the independence of the Democratic Republic of Vietnam on 2 September 1945. And so was the die cast for the wars that followed, but more importantly, for the eventual unification of the Vietnamese people despite their ethnic and linguistic heterogeneity.

The second, related choice was a wholesale recognition of the importance of foreigners in this process, despite the colonial experience. One Vietnamese worker put it thus: 'We grow with foreigners.'[38]

This led to a revolution in attitude.

The War Remnants Museum in Ho Chi Minh City opened in 1975 in the former United States Information Agency building. Originally labelled the 'Exhibition House for US and Puppet Crimes', in 1990, as relations between the US and Vietnam improved, it changed to the 'Exhibition House for Crimes of War and Aggression'. It adopted the current title in 1995 when diplomatic ties were renewed and US sanctions dropped.

Since 2007, US warships have frequently visited Vietnamese ports. Today the Vietnamese military conducts regular joint exercises with its American counterpart. They have not forgotten that US forces dropped twice the tonnage of high explosives on Vietnam than the Allies did on Europe and Asia combined during the Second World War. Dioxin poisoning from Agent Orange remains a toxic legacy of a ruinous war.

But the Vietnamese are not defined by the past.

The US stake in Vietnam has grown quickly to become one of its biggest trading and investment partners despite its low starting point in the mid-1990s, a result of the US embargo and the poor health of the Vietnamese economy. US–Vietnam trade totalled $451 million in 1995.[39] Since then, it has increased well over a hundredfold to $70 billion, making the US Vietnam's single-largest trade partner.[40] Between 2010 and 2015, Vietnam was the second-fastest growing of America's top fifty export markets. US investments topped $231 billion in FDI between 1988 and 2020.[41]

The ANC's Vietnam

There was a time when the ANC was willing to take lessons from Vietnam.

In 1978, facing internal competition from the Black Consciousness Movement, the Inkatha Freedom Party and the South African Students' Movement, and with Umkhonto we Sizwe battling to make a sustained military impact, South Africa's exiled liberation movement was advised by Moscow to visit the newly unified Vietnam. There they could learn the technique of 'people's war' from military strategists like General Vo Nguyen Giap, Vietnam's 'Red Napoleon'.

A delegation, led by ANC president Oliver Tambo and including Joe Modise,

Joe Slovo, Chris Hani, Alfred Nzo, Cassius Make and Mzwai Piliso, spent two weeks in Hanoi in October 1978. Despite obvious differences between the situations in South Africa and Vietnam, not least given the scale of superpower involvement and the intensity of the respective conflicts, the ANC delegation left, as Russia's Africanist veteran Vladimir Shubin has observed, feeling 'deeply impressed by the Vietnamese methods of underground armed struggle, especially the co-ordination between illegal *en masse* activities'.[42] In the process, they learnt that a revolution 'must walk on both feet: one military, and the other political'.

Vietnam taught that, if it was to succeed in overthrowing the apartheid regime, the ANC would have to gather a broad front of international support, increase media coverage and rally local youths to build a political movement that could outlast the then South African Defence Force.

On the role of the media, a key lesson was that the Vietnam War was 'won' in Washington, not just in the trenches. General William Westmoreland, the local commander of the US forces, referred to it as 'the first war in history lost in the columns of the *New York Times*'.[43]

On their return, Slovo presented the delegation's report to a joint meeting of the ANC's National Executive Committee and Revolutionary Council in Luanda. They concluded that 'the Vietnam experience reveals certain shortcomings on our part and draws attention to areas of crucial importance which we have tended to neglect'. In Tambo's words, it also exposed the ANC as having 'fallen into a bad strategic situation, in which too much emphasis had been placed on the armed struggle, at the expense of political mobilisation, making for an impossible equation'.[44]

The Luanda meeting led to the appointment of a Politico-Military Strategy Commission, consisting of Tambo, Modise, Slovo, Thabo Mbeki, Moses Mabhida and Joe Gqabi. Tasked with 'devising an overall strategy on mass mobilisation', this commission represented the first formal review of ANC strategy since Morogoro in 1969 and culminated in the 'Green Book', what Govan Mbeki refers to as a 'highly significant document in the evolution of the ANC and the South African struggle'.[45]

The 'Green Book' enabled greater coordination of the ANC's political efforts, including the creation of a 'popular front' in the form of the United Democratic Movement, the strengthening of a propaganda wing, and a focus on the importance of international diplomatic efforts.

The ANC's visit to Vietnam represented what Howard Barrell, a former journalist who served in ANC intelligence, calls a 'Damascus moment' for Slovo and others in terms of their understanding that the armed struggle could not in itself 'regenerate' the political agenda, and that the latter needed to take precedence.[46]

The armed struggle would have to become 'secondary' to armed propaganda.[47] After their return from Vietnam, the ANC took a decided ideological turn from socialism as a matter of 'tactical caution'.[48] Far from the myth of an ANC that emerged from apartheid ideologically resolute but that subsequently compromised its 'values' in negotiations, the 'Green Book' reveals that, already in 1978, it was a pragmatic party willing to accept a negotiated settlement.

The strategic impact of the 1978 mission to Vietnam on the course of ANC and South African history cannot be overstated. It is said to have been a watershed between an exclusively militant (and likely unsuccessful) ANC and a multiracial, unified ANC. At the very least, it signified the start of the 'people's war', the point at which the ANC went beyond the armed struggle of the 1960s and 1970s in undertaking a more strategic, organised political effort.

If the ANC could learn in the past, why not now?

If the party took the same care in visiting contemporary Vietnam, it would find a country transformed, where party cadres are *au fait* with total factor productivity and institutional responsiveness, and where they don't just preach the importance of investors but act accordingly in creating space and the necessary guarantees.

For all the drawbacks of a single-party state, including widespread corruption, and the rhetorical adherence to the ubiquitous hammer and sickle and socialist banners, the thinking in Vietnam today is both liberal and pragmatic enough to realise the need for the state to relinquish its role in the economy. It is the outcome, wrote veteran journalist David Lamb, of putting 'Karl Marx and Adam Smith into an economic blender'.[49]

But it's more down to sweat than the state. The extent of Vietnam's transformation can be seen in the role of state-owned enterprises (SOEs). With privatisation – more palatably referred to as 'equitisation' – the number of SOEs fell sharply between 1990 and 2017, from 12 000 to 700.[50] Officially, this was socialism with an overriding free-market touch, but at least the veneer of state control in the economy has worn thin.

By 2020, SOEs officially employed one million (or 2 per cent) out of a total workforce of 53.6 million, having fallen from 1.5 million in 2014. Today Vietnam has 35 725 valid FDI projects with a total registered capital of over $431.5 billion.[51]

Public listings are another measure of this transition. For example, the Ho Chi Minh Stock Exchange launched in 2000 with two listed companies. Two decades later, there were 396 companies with a $148-billion market capitalisation, and another 376 on the Hanoi bourse.

The revolution is not limited to the world of finance and listings. On the ground, Vietnam is now the world's second-largest exporter of rice and coffee.

'The difference between now and then,' says Dr Le Phuoc Minh, the director of the Institute of African and Middle East Studies, part of the Vietnam Academy of Social Sciences, 'is that we have food where there was once only hunger, and the hope of becoming a middle class where previously everyone was just poor.'

Mind the Giap

General Vo Nguyen Giap, the hero of the 1954 Battle of Dien Bien Phu, is considered 'second only to Uncle Ho [Chi Minh]' in the minds of many Vietnamese. The self-taught soldier met Ho in China after the Vietnamese leader submitted an article to a newspaper Giap was editing. Asked to raise a fighting army, he set about the task with a tiny nucleus of just thirty-four guerrillas armed with flintlock weapons. The 'Grand General', the son of a rice-grower, went on to create a force that defeated the French in 1954 and the Americans who followed.[52]

Giap experienced immense hardships along the way. His first wife died in a French prison along with their infant daughter; his wife's sister was executed by a French guillotine. Following his great victory over the French at Dien Bien Phu, he spent the next sixty years living in a former French villa in Hanoi alongside what is now the Vietnam National Assembly building and just across an expansive green lawn from Ho in his stern, Soviet-style mausoleum.

'He would sit there with his commanders,' says his son Nam, pointing at a concrete table and four chairs in the back of the house, 'and they would spread out the maps and discuss the war.' Overhead is a pergola whose uprights are made from shell casings welded together. 'A hundred and fifty-five millimetre,' smiles Nam. Under the house is a bomb shelter, necessary during the various American air offensives. Just inside is a spare room that has been turned into a shrine with Giap's image, medals and two urns of sand, one from Dien Bien Phu, the other from his home province of Quang Binh, among the exhibits.

Nam spreads out maps of Dien Bien Phu in the conference room where the elfin-like Giap would host regular meetings with foreign dignitaries, his main occupation after his retirement as defence minister in 1981 and from the politburo the following year.

Without formal military training – 'he learnt from real battles,' says Nam – Giap's crucial skills were in managing the logistics and politics to sustain the war in the south. His enormous losses of troops call into question the wisdom of his military tactics yet serve to highlight the disparity of the stakes between the Vietnamese nationalists and various foreign armies. Put differently, the ends justified the means.

Dien Bien Phu, arguably the most important battle of the First Indochina War, was a testament to Giap's fortitude and ingenuity. Much to the surprise of the

French, Giap's forces were able to haul artillery pieces, many of which had been supplied by the Chinese from stock captured from the nationalist Kuomintang and in the Korean War, up and over the never-ending series of mountains and install them in burrows on the hillsides, making them virtually impervious to French counter-fire and air-strikes.

Likened by Giap to a 'rice bowl', with his forces on the mountainous rim and the French at the bottom on the plain and its hillocks, Dien Bien Phu proved indefensible, despite carefully dug French trenches and fortifications. Unlike earlier battles, where Giap squandered his forces in costly frontal attacks, he carefully amassed his troops and supplies before the battle commenced. Viet Minh artillery rained down on the French troops from the surrounding hills. After the airfield was closed, provisions and reinforcements could only be parachuted in. By the time the French realised they were in a trap and could not win, it was too late to get out.

On 7 May, the day the French surrendered, talks opened in Geneva to end colonialism in Indochina. However, liberation took a generation longer still, with the temporary division of the country along the seventeenth parallel and the creation of an analogous South Vietnamese government with American support.

Giap's diplomatic skills were also crucial in keeping open supply lines from China and the Soviet Union. At home, he organised the movement of troops and materiel down the Ho Chi Minh Trail, where thousands of porters cycled and shuffled along the border with Laos and Cambodia. 'People should not be overawed by the power of modern weapons,' Giap wrote. 'It is the value of human beings that in the end will decide victory.' And so was born his concept of 'people's war'.

During the twenty-one-year struggle that followed against the Americans and their South Vietnamese ally, Giap's star waned as that of his hard-line rival Le Duan, the general secretary of the Communist Party of Vietnam, rose. But after the disastrous cost of the Tet and Easter offensives, Giap again took military centre stage. By 1982, however, he was once more frozen out by the hierarchy, nominally a deputy prime minister in charge of science and technology and tasked with heading up a national birth-control campaign. He preferred, in his twilight years, to spend time hosting visitors and chatting about the war, as the numerous gifts in his banner-bedecked reception hall testify. Despite calls from former comrades to re-engage in politics, he avoided being drawn into criticisms of the regime.

There were differences, however. Some contend he was unreconstructed and dismissive of the market reforms made after 1986. Others say Giap was interested in retaining the South's capitalist-based system at the end of the war in April 1975 alongside the command economic model of the North, but was overruled by his colleagues, notably Le Duan. This explanation may be an excuse to retrospectively avoid personal responsibility for the economic disaster that followed unification. By the early 1980s, the country faced food shortages due to the lack of incentives for farmers to produce a surplus in a collectivised agricultural system. Inflation touched 800 per cent. There was no private sector or capital, no foreign trade outside of the state, no banking system where the treasury controlled all finances and set prices, no flow of goods even between Vietnam's sixty-three provinces, and no foreign exchange. The Soviet Union, Vietnam's main barter trade partner, also provided one-third of its budget through aid. So, when Moscow throttled back on its assistance to deal with its own internal crises during the mid-1980s, Hanoi wobbled.

More than this, there was an old, Soviet mentality. 'The mindset was most difficult of all to change,' says Vu Khoan, who served in various ministerial portfolios, as a member of the politburo and as a former deputy prime minister.[53] 'In 1957, after the Geneva agreement was signed, we carried out a socialist transformation in the north,' he recalls. 'We invited Chinese and Soviet specialists to help work out a plan. As an interpreter, I accompanied the Russian delegation. We were told,' he smiles, 'that we should calculate the requirements of cloth by multiplying the number of women by the metres required to sew a dress, never mind the colour or type of cloth.'

Doi Moi – or starve

Doi Moi, meaning 'renovation', was the name given to the economic reforms started in 1986, first in the agriculture sector. Previously all tools of production – land, capital and working assets – were collectivised and owned by the state, and peasants were paid in rice and other produce that 'the state bought at a predatory price', says Khoan. This was changed to allow farmers to keep their surplus at a market price. The flow of goods across internal borders was encouraged, and other goods were marketed based on supply and demand. Foreign trade was spurred by an end to the barter system between socialist states.

The results were staggering. With more secure property rights and market-based pricing (rice had been trading at one-tenth of the market price in 1988), households leapt at the opportunity to sell surpluses. As a result, the value of agricultural exports surged from $500 million in 1986 to $40 billion in 2018, an average annual growth rate of over 15 per cent.[54] Vietnam's coffee producers now have the highest yields in the world.[55]

A foreign investment law followed in 1987, with FDI growing steadily from $320 million in 1990 to a total stock of $177 billion in 2020.[56] At the same time,

GDP per capita leapt from just $596 in 1987 to $3 316 in 2020.[57] Vietnam's trade-to-GDP ratio is at 208 per cent, sixth in the global rankings. Between 1986 and 2020, Vietnam's economy grew at an annual average rate of 6.5 per cent, notably higher than the average for Southeast Asia (5.2 per cent) and all lower-middle-income countries (4.3 per cent).

Policy was shaped to meet growth needs, as the example of Vietnam's many successful EPZs illustrates.

From fire zones to free zones

The city of Bien Hoa, roughly thirty-two kilometres from Ho Chi Minh City in Dong Nai province, is one of the key industrial centres of Vietnam, with a multitude of industrial development zones (IDZs), factories and warehouses dominating the local economy. The nearby province of Binh Duong, however, has become the epicentre of investment in the country, by 2018 attracting 3 444 new foreign businesses from sixty-four different nations, with a total registered capital of $331 billion, and employing 450 000 out of a provincial population of 2.1 million. It is little wonder that Binh Duong's economic growth rate was at 14.5 per cent between 2011 and 2015, and that per capita income was over $5 100, 2.4 times the national average, or that Vietnam's export-to-GDP rate was 200 per cent, second worldwide only to Singapore at the time.

The Vietnam Singapore Industrial Park (VSIP), a joint venture with a Singaporean consortium headed by Temasek Holdings, is a standout facility in Binh Duong. Established less than twenty-five kilometres from Ho Chi Minh City in 1996, it encompasses several parks in the area and farther afield, with $11 billion invested by 800 tenants, providing 200 000 jobs. With more than 6 000 container trucks leaving the VSIP facilities daily, the trans-Vietnam highway, or Route 1, towards Ho Chi Minh City is a slow-moving mass of rattling heavy vehicles.

It was not always this way. In the 1960s and 1970s, Route 1 was a focus of National Liberation Front attacks on American convoys. The area around Bien Hoa especially suffered badly during and after the war, with the settlement of large numbers of refugees worsening an already severe humanitarian situation.

Bien Hoa was the site of the main US airbase. By the early 1960s, it had become a joint facility for the US and Republic of Vietnam air forces and was one of the last bases to fall to the advancing North Vietnamese troops before the collapse of the Saigon government on 30 April 1975.

The costs of conflict were massive. Just off Route 1 is a South Vietnamese army cemetery, where some 18 000 are buried, 10 000 in unmarked graves, part of the 250 000 South Vietnamese military dead. Once neglected, more attention is now being focused on the gravesite as the wounds of war heal, the change in its name from Bien Hoa Military Cemetery to Binh An People's Cemetery reflecting a change in spirit. Similarly, the US government has committed more than $200 million to the decontamination of the land around the Bien Hoa airbase from the notorious Agent Orange. For a decade from 1961, US forces sprayed 80 million litres of the defoliant over 78 000 square kilometres of southern Vietnam in an attempt to create a demilitarised zone and reduce the cover for their Vietnamese foe.

The VSIP is one of more than 320 industrial parks across the country. The first, Linh Trung, was created in 1993 within Ho Chi Minh City as a joint venture between the Vietnamese government and a Chinese state-owned company. In 2018, annual exports totalled $2.9 billion, with $1.2 billion invested. By 2020, there were over 200 companies in the various phases of Linh Trung, employing 75 000 people. It is one of seventeen IDZs in the city. The Linh Trung facilities form part of the city's EPZs, which attracted a total of $600 million in investment in 2021 and generated annual export revenue of $7 billion, which accounted for 15 per cent of the city's total export revenue, contributing some $886 million to the government budget each year and creating 281 000 jobs.

Why did these investors come to Vietnam?

'In 1993, this was a very poor place, more like a village than the city you see today,' says Linh Trung president Yang Kai Yong. Originally from Guangzhou, China, he admits that the main advantage of being in Vietnam is the comparative cost of labour.

Labour costs in the major cities (Hanoi, Da Nang and Ho Chi Minh City) average $200 per month, and some $180 in Binh Duong province, against $500 in China in comparable industries.

But it's not all about the cost of labour. 'Vietnam made a decision to open up quite early on,' Yang observes. 'Their policies have learnt from the experience of other countries. It is also a stable society, since the first thing that an investor considers is security.'

Export industries pay no VAT, corporate income tax is at 20 per cent (compared to 33 per cent in China), and there is a 10 per cent tax incentive for the first twelve years. Electricity rates are 50 per cent lower than China, though logistics efficiencies are around 20 per cent less.

Most importantly, these factors together meant that investors 'made money, which is why we stayed, and why we reinvested,' says Yang. 'Vietnam has been good for us, and its trade with China good for Vietnam.' However, given that other countries also offer low wages and incentives, something more was required. Hence the stress, still today, on making it easy to invest, with one-stop shops and a welcoming attitude being the norm. And the industrial parks did not wait on investors to knock on their doors. In 2018 alone, for example, the VSIP staged thirty seminars and promotions for potential investors around the world.

While many African countries are hung up on concerns about local procurement and value addition in such parks, often forestalling these initiatives before they even take off, the Vietnamese approach has been different. They see the principal value in growth terms, of both employment and the economy. For example, the average income to labour at the VSIP has increased sixfold over the last twenty years. As a result, by 2022, the industrial parks employed roughly four million Vietnamese from just 86 000 in the late 1990s.

It's a labour revolution, but not the one imagined by the country's revolutionaries back in 1945.

There will be challenges, of course, as Vietnam's labour costs inexorably rise, and machines become cheaper and more efficient. Investment in manufacturing is notoriously disloyal. This can be offset by increasing local content (and thus adding more value domestically) and improving productivity.

Yet even today, these parks are far from the caricature of cut-and-trim, sweatshop garment industries. On the contrary, most businesses are relatively high tech. In Linh Trung, for example, less than one-third of the 133 factories are in garments or shoes. Japanese engineering firm MiSUMi, for instance, arrived twenty years ago and now employs 3 000 computer numerical control (CNC) machine operators across three factories.

And neither are these businesses a story of the big, bad Western multinational. The vast majority, some 90 per cent, are Asian. This explains the government's concentration, too, on securing free-trade agreements with the other ASEAN member states, as well as Japan, Korea, China, the United States and the EU. Vietnam joined the World Trade Organization in 2007, a fact of which government officials are proud. They cannot get enough of globalisation in the form of capital, trade and technology.

The IDZs have been a triumph in Vietnam because government has been responsive to the needs of investors and Vietnamese workers alike. The workers, too, have reciprocated with enthusiastic alacrity. There are no magic ingredients to this success, being founded less on innovation than blood, sweat and policy. As one investor put it: 'The economy is the economy. You invest because of the conditions, not because of how you might like them to be.'

Not all easy

There are problems, of course, as the country strives for middle-income status. For one, the gulf of efficiency between domestic and foreign capital illustrates the challenge of skills and the unfavourable bureaucratic environment. Today foreigners provide 20 per cent of total capital, but account for half of GDP and 75 per cent of exports.

As the high degree of foreign investment in EPZs illustrates, foreign capital will go wherever the margins are highest and incentives are best. The longer Vietnam relies on foreign capital, the more dangerous it becomes for the country given the unfaithful nature of such investors, and the greater the imperative to strengthen domestic competitiveness.

Domestic pressures will add to this imperative, as seen in the widespread 'anti-Chinese' riots that broke out in mid-2018 after government proposed increasing leases for foreign companies in special economic zones (SEZs) from seventy to ninety-nine years.[58]

Some gains can be made through privatisation of the approximately 700 SOEs that remain under state control. As mentioned, so far around 11 000 have been 'corporatised', either through amalgamation or privatisation since *Doi Moi* began in 1986.[59]

Other ways of encouraging domestic competitiveness will include a focus on education and skills building, as well as a concerted effort to make it easier to do business for locals.

Education remains a challenge, despite widespread literacy of about 97 per cent. Under *Doi Moi*, education and training became a national priority. Yet today the entire higher-education system faces a quality crisis, linked to outdated curricula and large-scale graduate unemployment. A study by the Vietnam National University in Hanoi found that 26 per cent of graduates were unable to find a job.[60] Far from the socialist dream, the government subsidises only primary schools to 50 per cent of the total tuition cost. High enrolment rates mask low quality and high drop-out rates.[61]

Meanwhile, stimulating businesses to create jobs is critical for Vietnam's fast-urbanising population. Yet registering a business can take an average of seventeen working days.[62] No wonder then that most of the urban poor set up informal shops on sidewalks. Around 1.2 million people migrate to cities every year, where about a quarter of the workforce is now made up of informal street vendors selling traditional *pho* and *bun cha*, or the now famous Vietnamese *banh mi*, a twist on the French baguette.[63] A clean-up campaign in 2017, which failed to make even a dent in the number of vendors, resulted in the resignation of Ho Chi Minh City's District 1 deputy mayor and 'Captain Sidewalk', Doan Ngoc Hai.[64]

Despite an image of stern governance and anti-corruption values, there is a lack of democratic opacity, with Vietnam ranking 77th out of 180 countries on Transparency International's 2022 Corruption Perceptions Index and sitting among the least free countries in the world for civil and political liberties (19 out of 100) as rated by Freedom House.[65]

Politically, *Doi Moi* has ushered in a new, younger leadership and streamlined the country's more cumbersome bureaucracy, including through the one-stop shops within the industrial parks. There is a new language on corruption, at least, with officials openly admitting it is a serious problem. Vietnam is thus today a 'hybrid': an increasingly free-market economy under one-party rule, with private business operating alongside state-owned companies.[66] There is still a lack of openness in the mass media, with more than 100 people arrested in 2017 for criticising the government, protesting, or joining unsanctioned religious or civil society organisations, according to Human Rights Watch.[67] Arrests, criminal convictions, and physical assaults against journalists, bloggers and human rights activists have also continued.

In the face of the stresses produced by economic growth, including the resurfacing of development tensions between the north and the more *laissez-faire* south, the challenge to the Communist Party of Vietnam is whether it possesses the capacity to persist with economic reforms through the myriad political and administrative changes required. For free enterprise, economic activity is inimically pluralist, at least in the long run.

Yet, while per capita income is growing and consumer spending increases by about 10 per cent per year (well above the global average), concerns of governance are secondary to the question of further growth and foreign investment, at least from the perspective of government.

Services have expectedly taken an increasing share as the economy has changed. As one measure, the number of foreign tourist arrivals has risen from 2.1 million to 18 million just this century.[68]

Why this path?
The most interesting question is why Vietnam's leadership took the free-market reform path, if the route taken by others (such as Venezuela, Zimbabwe, Laos, North Korea and Myanmar) suggests they could equally have doubled down.

Vu Khoan explains it in terms of a long struggle. 'We think that communism is still the future of mankind. That objective may be very long. We are in the first phase. That is why we use the term "socialist-oriented market economy" to explain our path.' Some younger Vietnamese laugh at this comment, seeing it as an ideological fig leaf to justify past failures.

On the contrary, the answer is partly down to the numerical dominance of a 'highly aspirational' youth, with two-thirds of the population under thirty-five. They have little connection with the past and their grandparents' struggles. Their lives are defined by the world outside, even though the war continues to shape external perceptions. As one thirty-something who runs a start-up in Ho Chi Minh City put it: 'In my generation, we didn't grow up with a war. Yet the only thing that everyone I met at business school [in the UK] knew about Vietnam was the war.'

And yet, in part, the answer lies in the attitude, too, of the older generation, even those steeped in ideology. While Giap remained a committed communist, he was also a committed nationalist. One foreign ambassador expressed it optimistically thus: 'Malaysia's constraints are around race, and the governance problems this engenders. Vietnam's constraints are around ideology. It's much easier to get rid of communism than race.'

Undoubtedly, the generation that followed the 'liberators' (Giap, Ho and others) has seen a monumental improvement in living conditions. Vietnam's life expectancy improved from fifty-three in 1972 to seventy-five in 2020, while child mortality dipped from fifty-four per thousand live births to just seventeen.[69] Through an almost stubborn focus on social welfare, poverty was reduced from over 75 per cent to below 10 per cent in the same period.[70]

Now there are other things to focus on.

Giap's son, who left the army in 1994, is now in information technology, having worked in Hungary for nearly a decade. Where his father's struggle centred on unification and liberation, Nam's generation is more interested in wealth creation. To make the same sort of difference to Vietnam's fortunes, the next generation will have to be preoccupied with environmentalism – that is, if the Vietnamese are to keep their success going.

Vietnam's income aspirations (mainly through industrialisation and urbanisation) will perhaps inevitably run up against the limits imposed by land degradation (especially in the Mekong Delta) and pollution of water and air, which will sorely affect the budding tourism industry. With large, vulnerable coastal communities, climate change ought to be high on the development agenda.

What they will hopefully learn from the success of *Doi Moi* is that a healthy dose of pragmatism and flexibility and a focus on homegrown reforms are imperative. With the valour of the 'liberators' against their foreign enemies, and the grit of the 'reformers' who came after them in carving a way out of poverty, this new generation will again have to look inwards to solve their domestic political and environmental issues. It will depend, of course, on what they want to be known for.

Overall, Vietnam shows that a development trajectory is by no means the inevitable result of forces outside national control. On the contrary, it is very much within the power of political leaders. They simply require the courage to make the necessary changes that will alter the fortunes of future generations.

Conclusion: Yesterday is another country

Largely marginalised from government after 1975, Giap died in 2013, aged 102. While a tough adversary, his willingness to accept military casualties – by 1969, as many as half a million of his soldiers had perished – and mete out civilian deaths made his uncompromising style unlikely to survive a democratic or even post-independence government. Subtlety was now a more necessary strategy as Vietnam's post-war priorities shifted.

Giap's passing signalled the changing of the generational guard. The wartime leaders – the likes of Le Duan, Duong Van Minh, Nguyen Khanh, Truong Chinh, Nguyen Van Linh, Nguyen Cao Ky and Nguyen Van Thieu – have all faded away. While Giap remains a national hero, second only to Ho in public polls, by the 1990s Vietnam had moved on from his leadership, loosening the reins of state control in making room for private enterprise. Although the seventeen-member politburo and the general secretary of the Communist Party were still firmly in charge, the country was now interested in prosperity, not just revolutionary rhetoric, political independence and economic survival. You could not eat ideology or ride it to work.

Dang Tien Thanh runs a Yamaha dealership on Nguyen Thai Hoc Street in Hanoi. In 2018, he was selling fifty bikes a week, ranging from the top-of-the-range 150cc scooter at fifty million dong to the entry-level moped for less than half that amount. Yet Yamaha's market share was little more than 5 per cent of a 3.2 million annual market, the fourth-largest worldwide behind China, India and Indonesia. Hanoi had about five million motorbikes for its seven million people,[71] while Ho Chi Minh City had eight and a half million for its eight million population, with sales of 750 per day.[72]

More than 80 per cent of Vietnam's population were not born when the war ended. Their fight is for personal transport and other consumer titbits, education, jobs and overseas travel. If the first liberation struggle was against the French and the Americans, the second was in the transition through *Doi Moi* to a market economy and global integration. A third might still come, as the late David Lamb posited, in the political domain, the more likely if the Communist Party proves unresponsive to the aspirations of a globalising youth.

There are inevitable problems and countless setbacks in Vietnam's economic experience. Businesses are hampered by sleaze and the requirement for endless paperwork, referred to as 'baby permits' for an obdurate bureaucracy.[73] This has had a perverse effect in encouraging foreigners to participate in Vietnam's now nearly 400 industrial parks countrywide,[74] where the operation of one-stop shops and special customs facilities largely circumvents greedy officialdom.

Pragmatism runs deep. For all his iconic revolutionary status, Ho Chi Minh was always the pragmatist. During the Second World War, when the Viet Minh received assistance from the Office of Strategic Services, the precursor to the Central Intelligence Agency (CIA), Ho praised Washington as a champion of democracy that would help them end colonial rule. He began his independence speech on 2 September 1945 invoking Thomas Jefferson by quoting from the United States Declaration of Independence: 'We hold these truths to be self-evident, that all men are created equal, that they are endowed by their Creator with certain unalienable rights, that among these are life, liberty and the pursuit of happiness.'[75]

And as he put it in a message to the Americans in the 1960s: 'We will spread a red carpet for you to leave Vietnam. And when the war is over, you are welcome to come back because you have technology and we will need your help.' After Saigon's fall in 1975, the Viet Cong did not put up a flag over the US embassy as they did in other locations. 'We are not authorised to raise one,' said a soldier guarding the premises. 'We do not want to humiliate the Americans. They will come back.'[76]

The popular notion that Vietnam's growth success is just about incentives or cheap wages is a crude caricature of the difficult policy choices Hanoi has had to make, not least the commitment to liberal change, however bumpy and strenuous that path. Vietnam shows that, no matter how important the goal of independence, it is necessary to have a plan to meet the aspirations of those who have fought for freedom beyond statist and redistributive impulses.

Europe

PONARY, a suburb of Vilnius, the capital of Lithuania, was the site of the mass murder of around 100 000 people between 1941 and 1944, most of them Jews, Poles and Russians. In 1940, Vilnius' 70 000 Jews made up half the city's population. Only one in ten would survive the war.

More than 90 per cent of Lithuania's entire Jewish population of 260 000 was killed during the Second World War, the highest casualty rate of Jews in any nation during the Holocaust. But this episode was only the latest, if most devastating, of Lithuanian pogroms, which had earlier led to widespread migration from Lithuania, including to South Africa, the United States and, ultimately, Israel. Tensions had especially escalated when Moscow blamed Jews for the assassination of Tsar Alexander II in 1881, after which homes were plundered and many in the community killed.

The site of the Ponary massacre, including the killing and cremation pits, is commemorated by several monuments to the victims. An earlier monument set up by survivors in 1948 was later replaced by a Soviet obelisk topped with a single star and dedicated to 'Victims of Fascism'. Lithuania swallowed such cultural crudities in the following forty-five years of repressive and stultifying Soviet occupation by biding its time and then, when the political moment arose through *perestroika*, moving quickly to assert its independence and change of direction from the Soviet to the European Union.

Thirty kilometres south of Ponary is the border with Belarus in Medininkai. On 31 July 1991 it was the site of the execution-style killing of seven Lithuanian customs officials by Soviet Special Purpose Militia Unit (OMON) police, who had been sent to harass newly established border posts. During Soviet times there was no immigration checkpoint; by 2022, there were eight days of queues as relations tightened in the wake of the war in Ukraine. Lithuania, like the other Baltic states, chose to integrate with the richer markets of Europe and with peoples that shared its values. It was a good choice. By 2021, the EU members had a combined (nominal) GDP of $16.6 trillion, averaging $37 000 for their 450 million people; in comparison, the 235 million people in the countries of the rump of the former USSR in the Commonwealth of Independent States clustered around Moscow totalled $2.5 trillion, or $8 100 per person.

The lesson is clear: if you are going to integrate your economy, aim to do it with richer markets.

On paper the Baltics are small, with populations under three million, geographically isolated and vulnerable to neighbouring Russia's violent mood swings. They apparently lack the economies of scale that Africans cite as an impediment to growth – and which is why Africa sees such advantages through regional integration, even though the continent's attempts to turn such rhetoric into functional reality are less impressive. The Baltics lack, too, natural resources, and their climate can hardly be considered optimal for development, their sunshine about one-third less than the African average.

Yet all these supposed obstacles have proven conquerable. The development record of the Baltics since 1990 has been nothing short of stellar, with growth averaging 4.5 per cent per year for twenty years from 1995, the highest in the European Union.[1] They have managed a difficult legacy well – indeed, one distinguishing feature between states that succeed and those that fail is how they manage their inheritance, and to what extent they allow it to determine their future.

The EU, through its *acquis communautaire* – the evolving body of common rights and obligations that is binding on all EU member states – can offer the external discipline necessary to keep reforms on track, as well as a crutch to leadership and a guide to strategy. Given the level of domestic political resistance to its fiscal reforms, it is uncertain that Greece, for instance, would have undertaken its painful adjustment in the 2010s without European incentives and disincentives, and the attraction of a market whose citizens are on average three times wealthier than the global mean. Whether the same benefits apply to all EU members equally, however, given their vagaries in size and make-up, between those on the way 'up' and those at the 'top' of the productivity scale, for instance, is debatable. At the very least, these differences demand increasingly complex systems of institutional control at the centre of the European project.

This chapter presents case studies in European transformation and the benefits of closer regional integration around policy, involving political values and systems as much as trade integration.

Agents of Change

'Do not shed your tears for yesterday, do not fear what comes tomorrow, just in a measured, steadfast way plough your furrow – straight and narrow.'
— Knuts Skujenieks, Latvian writer and political prisoner

THE *Odessa File*, a film starring Jon Voight, focuses on the fictional adventures of a young reporter trying to track down Captain Eduard Roschmann, the *Schutzstaffel* (SS) commandant of a wartime ghetto in Riga, Latvia. Based on the Frederick Forsyth novel of the same name, and set in 1963, the reporter, Peter Miller, chances across the diary of an elderly Jewish man who has committed suicide after spotting Roschmann, whose inhumanity and crimes are detailed in the diary, alive. Miller tracks down the SS officer, infiltrating Odessa, a secret organisation formed by the SS to protect and facilitate the flight of its members to safety across the world. He confronts Roschmann, among whose crimes was the murder of a highly decorated Wehrmacht officer on the quayside of the Latvian port of Liepāja while attempting to commandeer an evacuation ship at the end of the war. Miller discloses that the murdered officer was in fact his father, at which point Roschmann goes for his gun and is shot. Odessa's secret files are then used to arrest numerous Nazi war criminals.[2]

The factual story on which Forsyth's novel is based is as intriguing, although with a different trajectory.

The real-life Roschmann – known as the 'Butcher of Riga' – was assigned to the Nazi Security Service in Latvia, which established the Riga ghetto with the aim of eliminating all Jews. On two separate days in late 1941, 25 000 Jews were marched from the ghetto and shot in the forest of Rumbula, fifteen kilometres north of Riga. Apart from the Babi Yar massacre outside Kyiv in Ukraine a few months earlier, this was the biggest single-event murder in the Holocaust before the creation of the extermination camps in 1942. Only three people who arrived at the Rumbula killing site survived the war.

Forced to flee Riga in the face of the advancing Soviet army, and having been briefly incarcerated by the Allies, in 1948 Roschmann left Germany via a ratline for Argentina, where he lived comfortably until he was identified by a man who had reportedly just watched *The Odessa File*, released in 1974, at the cinema. He fled, again, to neighbouring Paraguay, where he died in 1977.

Latvia has endured horror. During the First World War, the population decreased from 2.6 million to 1.6 million; nearly 90 000 buildings, 25 000 farms, 70 000 horses and 170 000 cattle were destroyed; and more than one-quarter of arable land was laid to waste. Industry was seized and taken to Russia.

The short-lived independence of the Baltic states established in 1918 ended in June 1940 with the Soviet invasion, itself a result of the perfidious Molotov-Ribbentrop Pact between the Soviet Union and Nazi Germany, which carved Central and Eastern Europe into two spheres of totalitarian influence, at least temporarily. The Soviet takeover, which saw Estonia lose 60 000 people, and Latvia and Lithuania about 35 000 each through deportations in just twelve months, was followed in June 1941 by German invasion and occupation, and the horrors of Rumbula:

Anything to Appease

Train thundering past
Sklee slittekety slack
A clearing to last
How did we take this track

Twenty five thousand souls
Two days of horror
Jews, Germans and Poles
Putin, hold up a mirror

A menorah reaching up
Soviet anti-fascism tablet to the left
Stones and names, swing the club
No antidote to the bereft.

Wind sighs achingly
Through the trees
Achtung Achtung
On your knees

And now we say appease
Peace for land
Anything to please
Shake, here, my hand

Approximately 94 000 Jews resided in Latvia prior to the Second World War. In 1944, when the Soviet army reoccupied the territory, only a few hundred remained. About a thousand Latvian Jewish survivors returned to Latvia from Nazi concentration camps elsewhere in Europe after the war, but like the rest of the population, they then had to survive forty-six years of Soviet occupation.[3] As war descended on Europe, Latvia entered a long, painful period of economic darkness and political repression in which over 180 000 would be killed and 136 000 deported.

Riga, once a proud trading city nicknamed 'The Paris of the Baltics', was ranked as one of the ten wealthiest metropoles in Europe in the 1930s. In the city centre, at 61 Brīvības Street, is the historic Corner House. Originally an apartment and shopping complex, which also once hosted a music school, library and pharmacy, in 1940 it was appropriated as the headquarters of the Soviet secret police, a role it continued after 1944. At least 186 political prisoners were murdered in its basement, today preserved as part of a museum to the grisly history of the Soviet Committee for State Security, better known as the KGB, in Latvia. An armed insurgency, the 'Forest Brothers', resisted Soviet rule during and after the war until, in January 1949, the Soviet Council of Ministers issued a decree 'on the expulsion and deportation' from Baltic states of 'all kulaks and their families, the families of bandits and nationalists', and others. Between 1940 and 1988, an estimated 200 000 Latvians were held by the Chief Administration of Corrective Labour Camps, an agency within the Soviet Union's Interior Ministry and better known by its sinister acronym, Gulag. Latvian businessman Aldis Rumba's father Rudolfus, a medical doctor, was one, sentenced at the end of the war to twenty-five years for treating German wounded. He survived nine and a half years before being pardoned in the post-Stalin thaw in a camp that, his son recalls, was '1 300 kilometres north of Irkutsk and suffered a 90 per cent mortality rate'. Rudolfus died in 1962 'worn out' by the experience.

With the end of the war in 1945, the Baltics did not reacquire their independence but were subsumed into the USSR. Their economies were integrated into the Soviet system of planning and development, including farming, which had provided the political base among the kulaks for the interwar independence period. As a result, whereas in 1939 Estonia had been 66 per cent rural, Latvia 65 per cent and Lithuania 77 per cent, within fifty years Estonia was 72 per cent urban, Latvia 71 per cent and Lithuania 67 per cent, together the most urbanised portion of the Soviet Union.[4] The number of collective farms grew to over 4 000 by the mid-1950s, while as many as 275 000 private farms were abandoned.

Across the Baltics, Second World War and occupation deaths have been estimated at 90 000 in Estonia, 180 000 in Latvia and 350 000 in Lithuania. Latvia lost one-third of its people in the First World War, and another 30 per cent in the second. Today Latvia's population is just shy of 1.9 million, whereas in 1914 it stood at 2.5 million. It is little wonder that both Nazi and communist parties are banned across the Baltics.

Under the Soviets, goods were in short supply and salaries low. 'It was a grey place, largely absent of colour,' recalls Raimonds Jansons, a Latvian diplomat, 'where Russian was taught twice a day, and English once a week.' By 1984, the average worker received 200 roubles per month, a factory director anywhere between 300 and 700 roubles, and a professor with a PhD some 320 roubles. A pair of boots cost as much as 100 roubles, a fine Lada motorcar between 5 000 and 7 000 roubles, and an apartment in the concrete housing cooperative blocks between 5 000 and 10 000 roubles – *if* you could find one. For the car and the apartment there was a waiting list of many years, unless one was willing to pay up to five times more on the black market. There was an active underground, or *blat*, economy.[5] 'In Soviet times,' smiles Rumba, 'to survive, it was not a question of how much money you had, but how many friends.'

'Post-war life was so grey that we, a small group of friends, began to consider how to lift our spirits,' wrote Latvian dissident Ieva Lase. 'Works by foreign authors had disappeared from the University Library and all public libraries ... Those of us who were interested in French literature decided to come together to talk, to remember what each one had read.' Lase was charged with 'bourgeois nationalism and participation in anti-Soviet meetings' and sentenced to twenty-five years in a Gulag camp.[6]

The Soviet authorities encouraged the Russification of the Baltics, with inward immigration at around 20 000 per annum, diluting the ethnic Baltic population. Lithuania's Russian population had doubled to 10 per cent between the 1930s and the 1970s, and Latvia was slightly more than one-half Latvian by 1990. At the end of the century, Estonia was about two-thirds Estonian. The percentage of native peoples in the populations of the major cities was even smaller. Yet there had been a long history of the movement of people in the region; before 1940, Riga was the largest Russian émigré centre after Paris, while Vilnius was a melting pot of nationalities, including large Polish and Jewish minorities.

Mikhail Gorbachev's *perestroika* in the Soviet Union re-triggered the Baltics' independence process. *Perestroika* had itself come about to save the USSR from economic collapse. On 23 August 1989, two million Estonians, Latvians and Lithuanians participated in a mass demonstration, forming the 'Baltic Way' human chain across the three territories. Three months later, the Lithuanian parliament adopted legislation paving the way for a future referendum on independence from the Soviet Union. Gorbachev visited Vilnius in January 1990 to try to persuade Lithuania not to secede. He was unsuccessful and, following parliamentary elections in February 1990, which resulted in a pro-independence majority, Lithuania declared independence on 11 March 1990. Estonia and Latvia swiftly followed suit. In response, the Soviets imposed an economic blockade on Lithuania, which led to energy shortages and soaring inflation. The situation deteriorated into violence in January 1991, when Soviet Armed Forces clashed with civilians, killing fourteen and injuring hundreds more. The violence against unarmed people was a wake-up call for the West and put the restoration of the Baltics' statehood firmly on Europe's agenda.

The road to freedom

'Our independence was confirmation of our difference,' says Latvia's deputy prime minister Dr Artis Pabriks. 'It reminded us of what we had lost to the Russians for fifty years. We wanted to be like the West, not like Russia, to be a country where there was a separation of powers and a reliance on our historically high levels of literacy.' Latvia placed second in Europe in the interwar years in terms of the number of university students (per inhabitants), and first for the number of female students. In terms of the number of book titles published, Latvia was second behind Denmark in Europe, with 22 868 books published (and 56 million copies printed, or 30 per inhabitant, children included) between 1919 and 1936.[7]

Independence was a profoundly political process, says Pabriks, in that 'we had to free ourselves from the influx, influence and control of the Russians'. This was made more complicated by the large numbers of Russian émigrés. Government ignored the well-meaning advice to develop a 'multicultural' political system with a bicameral parliament for Russian and Latvian speakers, 'which would have made us like Ukraine,' notes Pabriks, but also had to find ways to re-establish the national character of their societies, which had been so altered by the years of war, occupation, deportations and Russian immigration.

Just as there was a political rationale, there was a political cost to acting quickly and boldly. There was a high turnover of government in the first decade, precisely because of the radical nature of the reforms, particularly to subsidies and pensions. But, following 9/11, and membership of NATO and the EU in 2004, external institutions helped to institutionalise fears about security and internal policy discipline.

The change from a repressive regime did not lead to a loss of state control. In 2021, murders in Latvia were at three per 100 000, for example – fourteen times less than in South Africa.[8] There is effectively zero poverty (0.5 per cent compared to South Africa's 20.5 per cent), adult literacy is 100 per cent, primary-school completion at 98 per cent, and unemployment at 7.6 per cent (South Africa's unemployment rate is 44 per cent). While Lithuania had some governance continuity given that the local Communist Party had broken away from the Communist Party of the Soviet Union in December 1989, Latvia and Estonia had a complete clear-out.

Performance through fear of failure and a Russian return was one thing, but fierce competition between the Baltic states helped. 'This is why we can now get a driver's licence here in just fifteen minutes,' smiles Pabriks. In Lithuania's capital, home to 620 000 people, all services are now digitised, says the former mayor of Vilnius, Remigijus Šimašius. 'The only one you have to attend to in person is your wedding, though even with that you can register online.'

Yet these small countries had no obvious advantages in 1991, no obvious reasons for success save the determination and skills of the people within their ranks. Domestic industry was small and integrated with the Soviet market. For example, Latvia possessed some indigenous technology, in radio electronics, pharmaceuticals and the Latvija minibus, but little of this survived the post-Soviet world. The Riga Autobus Factory was a Soviet case study in central planning, of managing a plant with a lack of qualified manpower, of tensions between local and imported Soviet labour, constant supply-chain issues, poor quality control, and outdated design and technology. It went bankrupt in 1998.

And save for geography and history, these countries had very different cultural make-ups. None had been independent since 1940; consequently, none had central banks and ministries of finance, among other key national institutions, and all lacked their own defence forces and foreign policy.[9] The three had accommodated around 200 000 Soviet troops across several major naval, air force, army and missile installations during the Cold War, and yet relations with Russia were difficult. For Russians, Stalin was the saviour of the Baltics, countries which saw him as their oppressor.

Their economies were in a state of complete collapse, and they were ethnically and linguistically different, with no common language. Swedish economist Anders Åslund does point out that they had 'four favourable pre-conditions': they each possessed a strong sense of community and identity around national fronts, which won clear parliamentary majorities in the early 1990s. Their renewed independence in August 1991 was not contested and, a few weeks later, was recognised by Russian president Boris Yeltsin. And although small and vulnerable, they enjoyed friendly and wealthy neighbours in the West.

Despite the clear public mandate, it was not an easy political path. 'In 1992 already, we lost the election to the former Communist Party,' recalls former Lithuanian prime minister Andrius Kubilius, a member of the pro-independence Sąjūdis who was elected to the Seimas in the wake of independence. 'It was a message: that the time of revolution was easy, that the time of unity was over. People had expected miracles and they were not happening, and they voted out the government, just as they did in Poland in 1993.' Political instability emanated from the slower than anticipated pace of transformation. 'We thought we would be like Sweden in a couple of years,' explains Linas Kojala, director of the Eastern Europe Studies Centre in Vilnius. 'But it took until 2003 to recover to 1989 levels of prosperity.'

The saviour of the process came in the form of the EU, which, in June 1993, laid down the 'Copenhagen criteria' for eligibility for EU membership, which required a state to have institutions capable of preserving democratic governance and human rights, have a functioning market economy, and accept the obligations and intent of the EU. 'People wanted to live like other people did in Europe,' says Kubilius. 'This was helped by the fact that the West had not recognised the occupation of the Baltics. Unfortunately, Ukraine and Belarus did not get such an open-door, positive signal from the West.'

By the time of the accession in 2004, however, there were doubts about the wisdom of joining the EU. 'Before the elections, we conducted a regular opinion poll to which we added a question,' recalls Kubilius. 'We asked whether the time during the Soviet Union was better or worse. We did not publish the result in which 54 per cent said that life was not better. This was a lost generation, mostly aged between fifty and sixty, poorly educated and rural-based. It was difficult to erase the nostalgia of the past.'

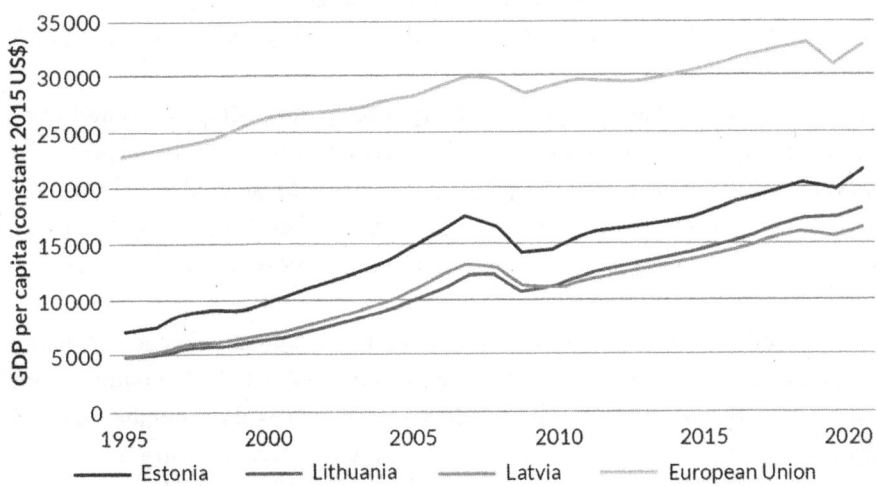

Source: World Bank, World Development Indicators

Despite a bumpy start in the conversion from a command to a free-market economy, by acting decisively and by putting the past firmly behind it, Latvia transformed from a $4 971 per capita to a $16 406 per capita economy between

1995 and 2021, Lithuania from $4 936 to $18 072, and Estonia from $7 138 to $21 421. Whatever their cultural differences, the Baltics reformed very similarly, through sharing ideas and experiences, although Estonia, now known as a leader in e-government, has tended to take the lead.

Estonia's harsh inheritance

On 10 June 2022, as Russia continued its efforts to occupy Ukraine, the Estonian foreign ministry summoned the Russian ambassador to protest the remarks made by President Vladimir Putin, comparing himself to eighteenth-century Russian tsar Peter the Great. Putin, then in his twenty-third year of power, had drawn a parallel the previous day between his and Peter's appropriation of foreign lands, including the Estonian border town of Narva.[10]

'Peter the Great waged the great northern war for twenty-one years,' Putin had declared while visiting an exhibition dedicated to the tsar in the northern city of Saint Petersburg. 'It would seem that he was at war with Sweden, he took something from them. He did not take anything from them, he returned [what was Russia's].'

In Narva, on Estonia's eastern border with Russia, the influx of Russian-speaking workers from across the eponymous river made Estonians the minority during the Soviet years, when the remnants of the city's famed baroque architecture were levelled to make way for Soviet-style apartment blocks. Various monuments to Soviet military victories still adorned the area in June 2022, the irony apparently lost on those who replaced three years of Nazi occupation with half a century of Soviet rule.

In 1990, Estonia was emerging from fifty years of Soviet-imposed state socialism. Economic conditions – and freedoms – were a far cry from those experienced at the beginning of the twentieth century, when it was considered one of the most developed regions of the Russian empire. And yet Estonia boasted twice as many workers per thousand residents and three times greater output than the Russian imperial average.

Independence in 1918 boosted this further, though Estonia remained primarily an agricultural economy, the sector accounting for more than half of output. Land reform of Russian-owned lands post-independence increased the number of small farms and output accordingly. The bulk of non-agricultural industry was in textiles, followed by metals and engineering, timber and cellulose, and construction, about half of it foreign-owned. Despite the effects of the Great Depression, the costs of food, heating, mail and transport all fell compared to the tsarist era. The development of road, rail and shipping was hastened by the outbreak of the Second World War.

Narva became part of Estonia after the Treaty of Tartu in 1920, which concluded the Estonian War of Independence. This freedom, however, lasted only until the Soviet and German invasions of 1940 and 1941 respectively. In 1944, the city was virtually destroyed by a combination of retreating German troops and a Soviet bombardment between February and March.

About a quarter of Estonians fled the country or died during the Second World War. Under the subsequent Soviet occupation, a policy of collectivisation saw mass deportations and Russification – the percentage of Estonians declined from 97 per cent of the population in 1945 to two-thirds by 1989. Much of the country was militarised and closed to public access. Living standards fell far behind those of Finland, whose capital, Helsinki, lies just eighty kilometres away across the Gulf of Finland. Ironically, it was the close integration of Estonians with Finns, culturally if not economically, that provided a model for the former's transition.

The country that emerged from the war in 1945 was completely changed. While output overall had recovered by 1950, living standards remained low. Basic goods remained in short supply. Farming suffered from the deportations and forced collectivisation. Absent mechanisation, the area under cultivation reached the level of 1940 only in the late 1970s. Pork production reached the 1940 level only after 1957, while production of beef and of poultry reached the pre-war level in 1959 and 1960 respectively. Milk production, which had recovered by the end of the 1960s, grew a little over 50 per cent over the next thirty years. While the energy sector developed fast, this was mainly to supply Saint Petersburg (then Leningrad) and later Russia's north-western region.

While the cities grew, the rural areas became depopulated. Housing stock in cities and towns increased about sevenfold during the forty-five years of Soviet rule. By the end of the occupation, the structure of the economy had completely altered. Agriculture, which had employed nearly two-thirds of the population in 1940, was left with 15 per cent of workers, while 45 per cent were employed in sectors now internationally regarded as industrial: processing, construction, energy, and so on. Half the national income came from manufacturing, a quarter from agriculture, 6 per cent from transport and communications, and 14 per cent in total from trade, catering, housing, and the like. Russians generally disproportionately took the high-paying jobs, having been specifically recruited for these roles. Nearly all exported goods went to other parts of the Soviet Union, while just 2 per cent went to the West, 2.5 per cent to Soviet satellites in Europe, and the remainder to Soviet allies in Latin America and Africa.[11]

The transformation from Soviet satellite to dynamic, digital state has been rapid and comprehensive. On the UN's 2020 E-Government Survey, which rates all 193 UN member states in terms of digital government, Estonia ranked among the top three most digitally advanced countries, together with Denmark and the Republic of Korea, recording the most significant E-Government Development Index increase from sixteenth place in 2018 to third place in 2020. In the E-Participation Index, Estonia ranked first worldwide.[12] According to the Fraser Institute, Estonia is in the first quartile in terms of economic freedom, while it ranks sixth, and third in Europe, on the Heritage Foundation's 2023 Index of Economic Freedom, which states:

> Estonia upholds all four pillars of economic freedom relatively well. An independent and efficient judicial system strongly enforces the rule of law. The debt burden remains quite low and has not undermined long-term economic competitiveness. Flexibility and openness have equipped the economy with an impressive ability to adjust to external shocks.[13]

How has this transition been possible, and how has Estonia kept it going for three decades? Its story is relevant for those smaller countries in particular contemplating radical economic reforms.

Birthing a Baltic Tiger

Following a referendum in March 1991, Estonia took advantage of Yeltsin's rise to power, declaring the restoration of independence on 20 August 1991. Four weeks later, on 17 September, Estonia was admitted to the UN, the last units of the Russian army leaving the country in 1994.

Estonia was in a relatively favourable position compared to other former Soviet republics. As part of the 'Soviet West', by the late 1980s Estonia had more foreign and joint enterprises than the other republics because of *perestroika*. Monetary reform and radical reform of ownership through privatisation and the sale of housing stock in exchange for vouchers were two key initiatives among the early reforms. In a country where two-thirds of homes were owned by the state, everything (bar the port at Tallinn and power) was privatised.

Radical reforms required radical leadership.

Mart Laar, a history professor, was just thirty-two years old when he took over as Estonia's prime minister in 1992. Amid great turmoil, his youthful government (average age thirty-five) embarked on a process of rapid economic development. A series of information panels at the entrance to Tallinn's Old Town recall the difficult choices and the painful consequences of the early reforms. Between 1989 and 1994, for instance, GDP per capita shrank by 36 per cent,[14] with a rise in unemployment from virtually zero under the Soviet model to peak (pre-global financial crisis) at 13.4 per cent in 2000.[15] By 2022, unemployment was just 5.9 per cent, better than the European average, and inequality on the median for advanced economies. As mentioned, Estonia tops the e-government rankings across the EU.

In sum, growth matters, and strong growth matters more. In the thirty years since independence, Estonia has averaged over 4 per cent economic growth annually, peaking at over 13 per cent in 1997. Constant growth has a compounding effect: as noted earlier, per capita wealth (measured in constant values) has leapt threefold in thirty years.

'We used to brand ourselves as the bridge between Russia and Europe,' says Katri Raik, the mayor of Narva, 'but now we say we are the beginning of Europe. The slogan is "Europe starts here".' But it has not been easy, 'given we have mostly Russian-speakers, who have a Russian identity, part of which is Putin. Now people speak not of being Estonian Russians, but Europeans.'

Of course, inclusion is easier when your economy is expanding.

Laar has three pieces of advice for others embarking on reform. 'You have a limited time, perhaps a year, to do radical things.' He says he learnt from Margaret Thatcher that it is important, from time to time, to 'do crazy things, to shake things up' and not pay too much attention to public opinion. Whatever one might feel about the substance of her reforms, Thatcher's leadership style never sought consensus, which she famously described as 'the process of abandoning all beliefs, principles, values, and policies in search of something in which no one believes, but to which no one objects'. Instead, she sought to lead, employing her mandate to full and uncompromising effect.

Laar's final piece of advice: to stay the course, you need to set in place rules and laws more than policy, which can be subject to leadership whim.

It was, at first, a painful process. It involved ending subsidies and protectionism, and initiating a new currency, in part to curb runaway inflation, which had reached 1100 per cent by 1992. As mentioned previously, a privatisation agency was established; prices were liberalised; monopolies were curtailed; social welfare protections were installed, especially on education and pensions; VAT and a 26 per cent flat income tax were instituted; and the restitution of private property seized during the Soviet era was arranged.

The approach, as per Laar's advice, was radical by the standards of the day. While outside actors, including the IMF, advised against moving away from the rouble, for instance, this is precisely what government did.

Siim Kallas was the central bank governor at the time. In the 1980s he worked at a savings bank 'under a detested system, which kept your hands tied, where there was no freedom of decision-making, no freedom at all. The economy was immune to people's views.'

The system of Soviet socialism was defined by the Russian term *zastoy* – 'stagnation': just enough growth to be stable but insufficient to be stable forever.

When the opportunity for reforms arrived, 'we chose to start with Ground Zero rather than take any Soviet assistance,' explains Kallas. 'We did not take even a single rifle from them. This was a good basis for radical decisions [which require] good ideas, implementation, public support and very good timing.' To enable the currency reform, 'we had to do something simple and fast' – which involved backing the new kroon with Estonian gold reserves held by the UK, the US and Denmark for safekeeping before the Second World War. 'Along with privatisation, we were able to provide a favourable climate for foreign direct investment to flow into Estonia.'

As a rule across the Baltics, government capacity for implementation lacks compared to policy ambition. 'If only we could have kept up with policy,' observes Andrius Kubilius regarding Lithuania's appetite for change, 'we would truly now be in a different country.'

This was not because of a lack of numbers in the state; to the contrary, the Baltics, like all those party to the Warsaw Pact, were stuffed full of state employees. It was more about capacity of the state. Even thirty years later there is a drive to reduce the number of state employees, improve efficiencies and reduce frictions.

While some might argue that the small populations of the Baltics have made this easier than in the bigger, more complex economies, Kallas reminds us that small size has its own complexities: 'Everyone knows each other, and there are still many opinions, and being small means fewer resources to get things done.'

Kallas's daughter, Kaja Kallas, became prime minister in 2021 as the leader of the Reform Party. She has created a reputation as the new Iron Lady of Europe with her uncompromising stance on the Russian invasion of Ukraine. In a warning to the West not to negotiate with Putin, whom she describes as a 'war criminal', she said: 'I was born under Soviet occupation. I was a generation that was living without freedom. So I am not taking it for granted and I understand its value.'[16]

Despite being under the heavy hand of state socialism for almost half a century, Estonia's performance is testament to the liberating power of the market, and what happens when people choose their fate and when government assists this process.

The shock therapy was made easier, says Estonian diplomat Riina Kionka, by the newfound political changes, Estonians being willing 'to eat potato peels since we have our freedom' as the saying of the day went. This facilitated a 'tiger's leap' in technology, straight into digitisation, with the focus on e-government and, in education, on coding and services.

The decisions made by Mart Laar and his young government in the 1990s had a big impact on where Estonia is today. Shortly after independence, Finland offered its old analogue telephone exchange for free. Laar refused this donation and decided Estonia would build its *own* digital system, aiming to leapfrog the analogue world. Laar said he knew nothing of computers but wanted the newest technology for his citizens. The internet became a symbol of democracy and freedom, Estonia being the first country to proclaim internet access as a basic human right, Wi-Fi becoming free and available ubiquitously. By 1997, 97 per cent of schools had internet; by 2020, 89 per cent of all society. By comparison, the average internet penetration in sub-Saharan Africa in 2020 was 30 per cent.[17] Estonia's capital, Tallinn, is the home of Skype and the world's first paperless parliament, the country an analogy for the intersection between innovation for problem-solving and digital engineering.

By the 2020s, Estonia's focus was on productivity growth. As the country scales the income ladder, this demands better institutions – a challenge in which it is not alone.

Baltic analogues

The shared initial goal of all the Baltics on the fall of the Berlin Wall was to secure their national independence. This stance, and their rejection of membership of the Commonwealth of Independent States, the successor to the Soviet Union, was fundamental to their economic policy, too. Independence, democracy and economic freedom went hand in hand.

Estonia pioneered the early deregulation of trade and prices and was quickly followed by Lithuania. While Estonia also abolished all foreign trade tariffs and quotas, in the process wiping out the criminal gangs of metal traders that had arrived on the scene in 1990, neither Lithuania nor Latvia went quite as far as quickly, in part because of the thriving oil transit trade from Russia through the Latvian port of Ventspils. One consequence was the domination of Latvian politics by oligarchs, illustrating the dangers of the quick entrenchment of rent-seeking interests. These interests have proven difficult to unseat.

Yet all the Baltics carried out wide-ranging macroeconomic stabilisation plans, Latvia and Lithuania following Estonia in unilaterally (without consultation with Moscow) introducing their own currency. All carried out radical fiscal cuts to achieve a balanced budget. Estonia again was the first to minimise its taxes, Lithuania later reducing Tallinn's rate of 26 per cent to 15 per cent. Rapid privatisation was matched with the restitution of private ownership of agricultural land and housing. Estonia adopted a model of privatisation through sales, while Lithuania pursued voucher privatisation, and Latvia adopted a different and slightly slower mixed process.[18]

While the Laar administration was the first, once more, to radically restructure government by laying off all government employees and inviting former employees and outsiders to apply for new jobs, the other two eventually caught up, ridding themselves of Soviet governance practices. All three rebuilt their military and security services after regaining independence.

As mentioned, Latvia was slower in ridding the system of oligarchs, who made a return to politics. 'It was a failure to permit a concentration of wealth among the oligarchs, which was a bad foundation just as in Georgia,' notes Ieva Ilves, a Latvian digital policy advisor and former first lady of Estonia. Similarly, Latvia's attempt to posture itself as a bridge between East and West was misplaced, 'since you can't build your future on partners who are criminals,' she says. A failure to remove the oligarchic tendencies has had an impact not only on corruption but also on entrepreneurship more generally, with the result that Latvia remains a major exporter of raw materials: wood products make up the largest export item.[19] The role of vested (oligarchic) interests in politics remains controversial; as the local saying goes: 'The favourite food of a Latvian is another Latvian.'

Transformation in each society had its own logic, but overall the Baltics showed that radical reforms can work, particularly if the break from the old system is both targeted and comprehensive. The most radical reformer – Estonia – has performed the best, stimulating its economic growth and improving its governance earliest. Latvia has done the worst but has still managed significant improvements over the last thirty years. 'Since many reforms were carried out in parallel, it is virtually impossible to distinguish the specific weight of each reform, but the pattern is overwhelmingly clear,' notes Åslund. The Baltic experience, with a high turnover of governments (one every year in the first decade on average), illustrates too that 'stability is overrated'. More important is the need to conduct major reform, rid governance of corruption, and avoid complacency.[20]

Break with the past

Mārtiņš Staķis, the youthful mayor of the Latvian capital Riga, started our meeting by turning off the lights. 'We are doing energy saving,' he apologised, in a nod to the war in Ukraine. But he is doing a lot more than that. He draws back the curtains in his office on the third floor of the Riga Town Hall to point out where, just across the river, a giant Soviet-era 'victory' monument was demolished only two months earlier, in August 2022. Immediately opposite his office is the slate-grey Museum of the Occupation of Latvia and next to that, a facsimile of the fourteenth-century House of the Blackheads, bombed by the Germans in 1941, razed by the Soviets in 1948 and rebuilt by public subscription in 1998.

Staķis handles a small piece of the destroyed memorial that he has kept in his office as a reminder of the event, and of the corruption and rents that permeated the Soviet system. 'I am part of the lucky generation, a golden generation, the first generation after the Soviet Union,' he says. 'When international business moved to Latvia, they did not want to deal with those who worked in the Soviet system, because of the language and because of the thinking.'

Ojārs Kehris served as Latvia's minister of economy and deputy prime minister between 1993 and 1994. He says that the most important thing was to 'destroy the old system as quickly as possible, as it could not be gradually reformed. Our challenge was, however, that the old parliament was elected to get independence, not to run the country.' They set about learning lessons from others, including and especially from the Mart Laar government in Estonia. 'You must remember that we had very little information to operate with,' explains Kehris. 'It was easier to get it from newspapers than from ministers. And we used to say in Soviet times that you only needed to read the last page of the newspapers for the truth in the sports results, as the rest of it was predictable and controlled.' It was also difficult to change the mindset from a system 'where you produced and sold at the state price rather than the price you could obtain'. In a system where everything was state-owned 'except for the vegetable market', Latvia aimed to privatise a hundred enterprises per day.

As in Estonia, Thatcher became a cult figure in Latvia, but she was not alone.

The Baltics learnt from others, and from one another. Harvard political scientist Samuel Huntington's work on political shifts was closely studied,[21] as was that of Guillermo O'Donnell, Laurence Whitehead and Philippe Schmitter on transitions from authoritarian rule.[22] 'Reading Huntington was like reading Lithuania, including our experience with the different waves or revolutions,' recalls Kubilius. In the case of Lithuania, reflects Darius Žeruolis, an advisor to Lithuanian prime minister Ingrida Šimonytė, 'we followed a "pacted" transition, which made our reforms less radical [than] in the case of Estonia'. Nevertheless, Vilnius still wanted 'to get away as fast as possible from the Soviet system, to return to Europe'. Combined with 'leadership that put the country and not politics first' and 'trust in key institutions like the EU and NATO', this helped to ensure that decisions 'were made in the interests of the long term'.

Staķis got a marketing job with an international business, 'our aim being to do everything the opposite to the Soviet Union'. The immediate goal was economic recovery, then EU and NATO membership. 'Now the biggest issue is finding out what our next goal should be,' he says. The search for a narrative, a fresh sense of purpose, is a refrain across a region that lives under the constant threat of Russian expansionism. 'We cannot afford to be average,' says Žygimantas Pavilionis, the head of Lithuania's parliamentary foreign affairs committee, 'since to survive here you have to be the best.'

The Russian military is a constant reminder of the dangers. During the Cold War, local forces were integrated within the Soviet system, which established bases across the Baltics with the specific aims of protecting Saint Petersburg's access, disrupting NATO in the Gulf of Finland, and providing – in the case of the facility at Plokstine in Lithuania, for instance – a relatively forward base for intercontinental ballistic missiles aimed at Europe. With the end of the Soviet Union, the last units withdrew from the Baltics in 1993, but the threat posed by Russia has not disappeared, necessitating a relatively high commitment to defence expenditure.

On Lithuania's south-eastern border, the town of Druskininkai opens on to the strategic territory known as the Suwałki Gap, a heavily wooded and flat 100-kilometre strip of land between Belarus, Kaliningrad, Poland and Lithuania, through which Russia accesses the Baltic Sea. Named after a Bolshevik hero and seized from Germany during the Second World War when it was known as Königsberg, Kaliningrad is a Russian enclave and home to a considerable Russian military presence, which includes nuclear weapons. The million-strong city is the birthplace of Immanuel Kant, the Enlightenment-era German philosopher whose thinking ironically set the stage for the post-war concept of an integrated Europe. Hannah Arendt, the twentieth-century German philosopher who studied totalitarianism, also grew up there. Nestled between Poland and Lithuania, Kaliningrad is today proving a site of contention between Russia and Lithuania, given the Russian invasion of Ukraine. The Suwałki Gap is regarded as the 'most dangerous place on earth'[23] and the 'soft underbelly' of NATO,[24] since it would likely be one of Russia's first targets were it to choose to go to war with NATO, a choke point to cut off the Baltic countries from their allies to the south and west. The route from Poland over the contemporary 'gap' through to Lithuania's second-largest city of Kaunas is the same way Napoleon first advanced on Russia and then, in November 1812, used to retreat from Moscow after his failed winter invasion.

This level of insecurity explains why the Baltics were among the first to provide arms to the Ukrainians in 2022 and played a key political role in stiffening European resolve. In the first six months of 2022, for example, Latvia gave 41 per cent of its military budget to Ukraine, Estonia 37 per cent and Lithuania 16.7 per cent. 'We keep telling Europe, just give them the fucking weapons,' says Artis Pabriks of this latest conflict. It also explains why they have invested money in high-tech defence, including drones. Latvia is one of the largest producers of reconnaissance drones in Europe. This sector has been built on the back of a sound education system and cheaper skills compared to other European manufacturers.

And this helps to understand why the Baltics have never looked back and have endeavoured to put as much distance as possible between the Soviet and modern eras.

Never look back

Narva's cotton mills in the sprawling Kreenholm textile plant, once the biggest in Europe employing 10 000 workers at its peak, made it the leading industrial city in Estonia. Oil shale made it a centre of electricity production. The first railway in Estonia, completed in 1870, connected Narva to Saint Petersburg, just 130 kilometres away, and to Tallinn.

But it has suffered in recent times. Mayor Katri Raik, a former minister of the interior, notes that the population has declined from 85 000 to 54 000 in the last thirty years as younger people in particular move to Tallinn or leave Estonia altogether. 'Narva needs direction, a vision built on its port, railway and electricity, but also good government, good education, good housing, good healthcare and good policy,' she says.

While the Soviets had grand plans to re-industrialise Narva, including the establishment of a uranium processing plant, these were never implemented. Instead, the plant was opened in the Baltic port of Sillamäe, just thirty kilometres away. It is a monument to Soviet achievement and its excesses, in more ways than one.

In the centre of Sillamäe, opposite the Stalinist-classicist Palace of Culture, stands a giant statue of Prometheus, the Greek god and bringer of fire, holding aloft the symbol of an atom. This Soviet work of 'art' was unveiled in 1987, a year that marked both the seventieth anniversary of the October Revolution and the fortieth anniversary of modern Sillamäe's founding, a seemingly desperate act of propaganda at a time when the writing was already on the wall for both the Sillamäe plant and the Soviet Union as a whole and the dust from the previous year's Chernobyl disaster had barely settled.

The factory's twists and turns are a metaphor for the Cold War period and Estonia's changing fortunes. A former oil shale processing plant, it was rebuilt by the Soviets between 1946 and 1948 as Kombinat No. 7 to extract uranium oxide from the locally mined shale, and later to enrich uranium from elsewhere. As such, Sillamäe was a 'closed city', officially off the map and guarded within a military perimeter, just as much of the Baltic coastline was closed to the public during the Soviet era. Until its closure in 1989, the plant produced nearly 100 000 tonnes of uranium and over 1 300 tonnes of enriched uranium, used in some 70 000 nuclear weapons.

Contemporary Sillamäe has the feeling of a Potemkin village, its facades resembling a film set given the absence of people along its broad, neoclassical avenues. While its central Lenin Avenue has changed its name to Viru Boulevard, there remains a Gagarin Avenue, after the first man in space, and Soviet motifs can still be spotted.

Kombinat No. 7 was privatised in 1997 as the 'Silmet' facility and was bought by an American firm for processing rare earths. A great tidy-up of the toxic waste left by the Soviet plant was initiated to prevent seepage into the Baltic. Cleaning up the sludge and not looking backwards is a key message from all reformers.

'Although it's important to look to the present, it's more important to look to the future, and to conceive of a place where you want to be in ten years, realising that where you end up depends on your choices today,' says Riina Kionka, a former EU ambassador to South Africa and chief foreign policy advisor to then EU Council president Donald Tusk, and who oversaw the reforms during the 1990s. 'Estonia, too, was colonised, but it's more important to own the future than to dwell in the past.'

The reasons for doing so are clear, at least on paper.

Estonia has the lowest government debt-to-GDP ratio among all EU member states. It possesses a balanced budget and free-trade regime and is seen as the champion of e-government worldwide. Its Programme for International Student Assessment scores, which examine learners in reading, mathematics and science, and what they can do with this knowledge, are among the highest in developed countries.

This has not been a process of recovery, but rather a fundamental revolution in economic affairs. Under the Soviet Union, Estonia's economy was extractive in its orientation, focused on producing what 'someone else wanted'.

'The Russians did not develop the place; rather, it was the other way round,' notes Eerik-Niiles Kross, an MP and former chief of intelligence.

This 'revolution' was assisted by the fact that Estonia 'regained' its independence from the interwar years and, through the Lutheran Church and periods of earlier foreign interventionism, understood European legal tradition. Politically, too, there was strong support for reforms across the political spectrum, reflecting the existential fear of failure with such a strong and menacing neighbour in Russia. 'We had no choice,' admits Katri Raik about Estonia's economic transformation. As someone whose parents were both geography scholars, 'you only have to look at a map' to see why, she says.

Just as West Germany did with the Stasi, Estonia sought to ensure compliance of the civil service in the wake of the Soviet occupation and the threat of divided loyalties by dismissing anyone who had worked for the KGB. Kross notes that in those countries where the security services were not properly reformed – including Russia, Belarus, Georgia and even Ukraine – 'they take it back'.

As its economy grew, Estonia became increasingly more integrated into Europe, the economy continuing its growth trajectory following eurozone membership in 2011. In 1992, the GDP was less than €1 billion, against more than €22 billion in 2017. In real terms, growth in that period was over 500 per cent.

Conclusion: From the Soviet Union to the European Union
The fact that Estonia does not have the same growth figures over the last thirty years as during the post-war period is irrelevant. Today, the country produces 78 000 metric tonnes of meat against 190 000 metric tonnes in 1989; 783 000 metric tonnes of milk compared with 1 277 000 metric tonnes; 200 million eggs against 600 million; and even less grain. However, there is more meat in the shops, the quality is better and the range of choice considerably wider.

For Estonia today is a developed country, and no longer an agricultural economy. Only 3 per cent of the workforce is employed in agriculture. Most Estonians (69 per cent) work in the tertiary sector, a figure that is certain to increase as a result of the digital revolution and the automation of all routine and physically demanding jobs in the next twenty-five years.

But the transformation is about much more than statistics. To invert Marx, quality has a quantity all its own. This is true for all the Baltics. Whatever the benefits of the Soviet system and its (dubious) production figures, most Latvians, Lithuanians and Estonians did not want to live in such a country, be it rich or poor.

The Baltics teach that patience, resilience, quickly seizing political opportunity, leadership and agency are crucial attributes in successful transitions. While the external environment was important, the Baltic governments owned their process through the anti-colonial struggle against Russia, an agency that has grown in stature because of the war in Ukraine. The radical nature of the reforms led to considerable political instability, but this was a risk that governments were ready to take. They were also clear in the direction of their reforms: less a balancing act between East and West, between Russia and Europe, than a vote to be European.

In the words of Vilnius's former mayor Remigijus Šimašius, reform was driven 'by the promise of a better life, a more just life'.

Of course, the process and the transitions were not easy or without problems. There are questions about their utility to bigger countries, where reforms are more complex. It is easier for a small country to make a sharp turn. Still, the right turn was imperative. It is easier, too, to apply for membership of the EU or NATO than to develop a spirit and practice of entrepreneurship. At the same time, you need reliable international partners, particularly in such a tough neighbourhood. Each of the Baltics, especially Lithuania and Latvia, suffers from a 'narrative problem' now that they are free and their security is guaranteed by NATO and the EU. The question is invariably 'What's next?', and the answer is a long-term period of less spectacular growth, which is unappealing to some minorities, and nostalgists in particular.

There are other, deeper social questions to be answered, not least about the complicity of the local populations in the Holocaust, and of the need to build a single purpose in divided societies. But these, too, are relevant elsewhere. As Faina Kukliansky, the leader of the Jewish community in Lithuania, asks: 'If you are responsible, you have to do something, you have to return something. You can't just say you are sorry.' During Soviet times, citizens were stuck in a constant dilemma: 'Do you go to the Communist Party to gain influence and to gain rewards but are then tainted?' asks Ojārs Kehris. 'Or do you stay out and then how do you survive in the system?' Now the dilemmas are different. Many younger Balts have left for greener pastures. In the last thirty years, nearly 700 000 mostly young Lithuanians have left, some westwards, the figure rising steeply with EU membership, and others returning to Russia. The eventual return of this diaspora with skills and capital to what is geographically the centre of Europe, and particularly the centre of European growth, is perhaps the biggest future upside for Lithuania and the other Baltics.

Overall, the reform experience in all the Baltics was fundamentally based on three key attributes, which have been essential to their success: the rule of law, responsible government and an investment in people. The key Baltic lesson for others, including those in Africa, however, is that political liberation from Nazi and then Soviet totalitarianism was not, by itself, enough. It was a first step to the next liberation, from hardship and poverty. This stage required a different way of doing things, and a government intent on creating the conditions for business to prosper. This liberation went hand in hand with local agency and ownership. As Samuel Huntington argued about political transition: 'democracies are created not by causes but by causers' – by choices and actions. The same is true for economic reform.

Getting the Politics Right

'The annihilation of this state [Poland] under favourable circumstances would mean one less Bourgeois-fascist country. What would be the harm of spreading the socialist system to a new territory and population as a result of the destruction of Poland?' – Joseph Stalin, 7 September 1939

THE Charles Bronson walrus moustache is still there, if now silver grey. Lech Wałęsa, the former president of Poland, is wearing a purple sweater bearing the phrase 'Constitution, Yes' in Polish emblazoned across the front. In his office on the second floor of the European Solidarity Centre in Gdańsk, the giant green cranes – economic giraffes – of the shipyard where he worked as an electrician loom in the window behind his desk.

This shipyard gave birth to the Solidarity trade union movement in Poland in 1980 and, in the process, was the catalyst for Eastern Europe's liberation from Soviet rule. Despite its banning and the systematic state persecution of its members, by June 1989 the movement had triumphed over the Soviet-backed Polish United Workers' Party (PZPR) in the first partially free elections after the Second World War.[25]

Outside Gate No. 2 to the Gdańsk (formerly Lenin) Shipyard, the scene of much strike action in the 1980s, is a memorial to the workers who lost their lives in the fight for democracy. Just inside the gate, the European Solidarity Centre, comprising a library, memorial and museum to the movement, was built to resemble a rusting ship under construction. Conference-goers and bands of schoolchildren are among the half a million annual visitors enjoying a cutting-edge presentation of Polish and Soviet history. Nearby is the similarly ultramodern museum to the Second World War, a detailed reminder of Poland's catastrophic twentieth century of totalitarianism, widespread destruction and dictatorship, but one which ended relatively well and has continued in that vein.

The lesson from Poland's transition from Soviet vassal to modern economy lies in the importance of getting the politics right to enable economic reform, a task that was undertaken by Wałęsa and his Solidarity colleagues effectively, as it turned out, on behalf of all the Eastern bloc.

Józef Górzyński arrived at the shipyard in July 1980 as a trainee naval engineer. 'I worked in the Fabrication Building,' he says, pointing to a tall single-storey brick structure 100 metres away. 'Wałęsa also worked there. On 14 August, less than a month after I arrived, the strike started.' Wałęsa, who had been dismissed from his job on account of his political activities, famously scaled the gate to organise the workers. The strike eventually took in a quarter of the country's workforce, paralysing an economy already hard hit by the failures and inefficiencies of a centrally planned system, including food shortages and falling production. The strike ended two weeks later with the recognition of Solidarity. But this was a false dawn of change. In December 1981, martial law was imposed by General Wojciech Jaruzelski – the man in the dark glasses – during which many of Solidarity's leaders, including Wałęsa, were detained for long periods.

When Górzyński joined, the yard employed its peak of 16 000. Forty years later it was down to around 1 500, though with several thousand more subcontractors, depending on demand. While it's a tougher business with competition from China and elsewhere, the yard has found its niche in the European market.

But there is much more to the city now. The old harbour houses a sensitively renovated waterfront, featuring top-class hotels and restaurants, and St Mary's Church, one of the largest brick churches in the world. The shipyard's distinctive skyline of cranes gives way to the glass and steel of a services economy, driven by high-tech skills, tourism and finance. The revitalisation of Gdańsk is a metaphor for Poland's transformation over the last quarter-century.

Downtown is Gdańsk Science and Technology Park. Set up in 2006 in one of the fourteen special economic zones countrywide, it houses eighty start-ups, mostly in ICT, biotechnology and energy. Inspired by visits to Silicon Valley and Seattle, this technology 'eco-system' aims to connect bright minds with the necessary capital and experience to translate good ideas into sustainable businesses. To facilitate this process, the cost of rentals is subsidised by as much as half. In 2018, for instance, Warsaw unveiled a €800-million incentive scheme for start-ups.

There are ambitious plans to turn Poland, the sixth-largest economy in the EU, into one giant SEZ. By 2018, nearly a quarter million Poles worked in the business services sector (BSS) across 1100 centres, around fifty of them with more than a thousand employees. The government has kept its eye on attracting a big slice of the knowledge process outsourcing (KPO) market, given its advantages especially of location and the widespread use of English. Poland has 1.35 million tertiary students, graduating nearly 350 000 annually, 90 per cent of whom possess proficiency in English, even though Poland's BSS operates today in forty-two languages. This is but one aspect of its internationalisation. Poland's airports serviced forty-nine million passengers in 2019, more than twice as many as Romania, the Czech Republic, Bulgaria and Hungary. The road and rail network has radically increased in three decades, with the road budget alone nearly €20 billion for 2016–18.

All this is a long way from the shadows of the bombed-out shell of post-war Gdańsk.

The effect on the standard of living of Poles in the last three decades has been staggering. The average wealth of Poles has vaulted nearly threefold (in real terms; seven in nominal amounts) in thirty years, driven by a young, well-educated workforce and policy to match. Little wonder the Polish refrain: 'We have progressed more in the last thirty years than the previous three hundred.' The transformation has been impressive, the net effect of sustained economic growth, moving the country a long way from the Poland described by P.G. Wodehouse during his Second World War internment in Toszek, to Kraków's west. 'If this is Upper Silesia, what must Lower Silesia be like?' he asked.

But it has not been an easy journey.

Embers of destruction

Poland was long a victim of bad geography.

Gdańsk's Museum of the Second World War has a copy of the Molotov–Ribbentrop non-aggression pact between Nazi Germany and the Soviet Union. Signed by the two foreign ministers on 23 August 1939, it sealed Poland's immediate fate. The Nazis used their limited access to Gdańsk (Danzig in German) as a pretext for attacking Poland on 1 September 1939. Two days later, Britain declared war on Germany, which, six years later, ended with the loss of an estimated eighty million lives globally, two-thirds of these civilians. As that war drew to a close, the port of Gdańsk saw the desperate plight of hundreds of thousands of refugees fleeing the Soviet advance.

Poland's turnaround story would be remarkable for any country, the more so for one that 'lost' one-third (an estimated 11.5 million people) of its population in the Second World War and its aftermath, including those Germans expelled (1.5 million), the annihilation of 2.9 million of the once 3.5-million-strong Jewish community, and three million additional deaths from combat, starvation and disease. No country suffered proportionately more, not Germany (7.5 million and 11 per cent) or the Soviet Union (24 million and 13 per cent).

At the start of the war on 1 September 1939, there were 1.3 million Varsovians.[26] By 1 August 1944, the start of the Warsaw Uprising, there were 900 000, with virtually all the city's Jews having been sent away to the concentration camps. By the end of the war in May 1945, there were just 1 000 left living in the city's centre. Around half the country's infrastructure and industrial capacity was destroyed in the conflict, including an estimated 85 per cent of Warsaw's Old Town.

The war hit every sector of Polish society. In the foyer of the parliament in Warsaw is a tablet with a list of more than 300 names of parliamentarians who lost their lives in the Second World War. The places of their deaths form a roll call of historical infamy: nearby Treblinka, Katyn (where Stalin's forces executed more than 20 000 Polish officers in cold blood), Sachsenhausen, Dachau, Monte Cassino in Italy (where the Polish Armed Forces in the West suffered over 4 000 casualties trying to dislodge the German defenders in a particularly bloody battle in 1944), and the centre of the horror, Auschwitz-Birkenau, just outside the historic city of Kraków, where more than a million Jews were exterminated.

The horror of the war defines the past – and, in Poland's region, sometimes the present.

Yesterday, Today[27]

Into the still air
The crunch of jackboots
Screeching, clanking railways, on time
A million souls into our midst

Never again
Is the cry
The whimper of children
On separation

History nags
'I did not speak out—Because I was not a Jew'
Principles forged, forgotten easily
Into the mists of time

It is for others
They remark
Expediency
Takes hold

Today as then
Brave men and women
No fear or favour
Remind silence is a choice

Braver still
To fight
Pricking conscience
Disturbing, fake stillness

Otherwise
'Then they came for me—and there was no one left to speak for me.'
Self-interests coalesce as
Worlds collide

The Warsaw Uprising is symbolic of this awfulness. With the Germans in full retreat from the advancing Soviets in 1944, the Polish resistance prepared for the liberation of the city. On 1 August 1944, an anti-German uprising began. On learning of the uprising, Stalin halted his forces on the outskirts of the city on the opposite bank of the Vistula. Although supplied from the air by the Allies (including a contingent of South African pilots), which kept the uprising alive for sixty-three days, eventually it collapsed with the deaths of 150 000 Poles.

German retribution was brutal. The capital was razed to the ground and every inhabitant killed or expelled on Hitler's order. The Soviets only marched into the city in January 1945.

It was an echo of the failed Warsaw Ghetto Uprising the previous year. By 1940, Warsaw's Jewish population had increased to 450 000 as refugees flocked from other areas. In November 1940, the Nazis established the Warsaw ghetto and relocated all the city's Jewish population to within its walls.[28] In April 1943, the removal of 300 000 of Warsaw's Jews from the ghetto to the Treblinka extermination camp, eighty kilometres north-east of the capital, sparked an uprising by the remnants of the community. They knew they couldn't win but they had nothing to lose. The ghetto was burnt, block by block, and a total of 13 000 Jews were killed. Today a monument in the style of a freight car with its doors open marks the *Umschlagplatz*, the railway station in the ghetto from which the Jews made their journey to Treblinka, now surrounded by Soviet-era blocks of flats. Carved with more than 3 000 Jewish forenames, it includes a chilling verse from Job: 'O earth, cover not thou my blood, And let my cry have no resting-place.'

Treblinka operated between July 1942 and October 1943 as part of the Nazis' 'Final Solution'. More Jews, as many as 900 000, were killed there than at any other Nazi extermination site apart from Auschwitz-Birkenau. Unlike Auschwitz-Birkenau, west of Kraków, there are no buildings remaining at Treblinka. With Warsaw's Jews murdered, the camp was dismantled and the ground ploughed over in an attempt to hide the evidence of the genocide.

Treblinka was exclusively a death camp. There was no other purpose in being sent there. The men, women and children were separated on arrival from Warsaw at the rail siding. They were immediately stripped, forced to walk a short distance on a cobblestone path built by prisoners to have their hair cut, and then it was just another hundred metres to the gas chambers. A small number of Jewish men were detailed to the *Sonderkommando*, the work unit forced to bury the bodies from the gas chambers in mass graves. Sometime in 1943, the bodies were exhumed and cremated on large open-air pyres, as the Nazis attempted to hide any physical evidence of their depravity. A nearby penal labour camp supplied the wood. Any remains were buried in large pits dug by giant mechanical shovels. At its peak, Treblinka processed 15 000 daily arrivals.

Today, Treblinka is surrounded by serenely beautiful fir tree forests, providing an eerie setting and scale to those murdered, the only sound the wash of wind. The site of the gas chambers is marked by a memorial and the area is covered with thousands of jagged rocks depicting the victims, some stencilled with the names of their villages: Tłuszcz, Solec nad Wisła, Końskie, Sandomierz, Mordy, Skarżysko-Kamienna...

Hitler's plan was to eliminate the Polish nation. He almost succeeded. By 1946, Poland's population had decreased from 35.1 million in 1939 to 23.9 million because of war, emigration and border revisions. Then, following the war and the liberation of Polish territories, control passed from the occupying forces of Nazi Germany to the Red Army, and from the Red Army to Polish communists represented by the Polish United Workers' Party, exchanging one uninvited totalitarian system for another. The country had to confront not only the immense physical destruction and social dislocation of the war, but also occupation by the Soviets, of whom many in society were mistrustful. While the Polish government-in-exile in London hoped that an independent Polish state would thrive as a bridge between East and West, possession and control determined Poland's fate. Between 1945 and 1947, nearly half a million Soviet soldiers were stationed in the country. All resistance was crushed. More than 150 000 Poles were imprisoned by the authorities. The introduction of a new penal code in 1946, together with the ultimately 100 000-strong Security Service (SB), the Polish equivalent of the KGB, saw tens of thousands executed for crimes ranging from economic sabotage to public provocation.

'We say the Germans wanted to kill our bodies, and the Soviets our spirit,' observes Wojciech Romejko, a Gdańsk historian. Lenin, after all, had believed that 'a man was good only insofar as he was necessary to the cause'.[29]

The Soviet plan was to maintain Poland as a bulwark against the West, a territorial centrepiece of the military alliance signed at the then Governor's Palace in the capital in May 1955, the Warsaw Pact.

Communist 'civilisation'

Warsaw's Piłsudski Square houses the surviving part of the Saxon Palace destroyed in the Second World War, along with the tomb of the unknown soldier. To one side of the square is a plaque commemorating the work of three Polish mathematicians

– Marian Rejewski, Jerzy Różycki and Henryk Zygalski – in 'first breaking the Enigma code', thus greatly assisting the Bletchley Park cryptologists and contributing to the Allied victory in 1945.

The placement of this memorial is a good metaphor for the work of the intelligence services: routinely unglamorous and tedious, occasionally interspersed by moments of fear, terror and importance. But it is also an indication of the standard of Polish education and science and the contribution its people made to the defeat of fascism.

There are many reminders of the role of education in determining economic fundamentals. At 237 metres, the Palace of Culture and Science stands out in central Warsaw. Originally known as Joseph Stalin's Palace of Culture and Science, the building was 'gifted' to the Polish people in the wake of the Second World War. Designed in the style of Moscow's Seven Sisters and completed in 1955, to the Soviets it was the epitome of Soviet excellence and brotherhood, hosting various festivals and even a concert by the Rolling Stones in 1967, the first by a major Western rock group behind the Iron Curtain. To the Poles, it is a reminder of Soviet influence over Poland, with some politicians calling for its destruction.

Yet today it houses cinemas, theatres, bookshops, restaurants, an auditorium, a large swimming pool, offices, an accredited university and two museums, the Museum of Evolution and the Museum of Technology, which details the role of Polish engineers in sectors from computing and shipping to aviation and automobiles. Occupying a wing of the nearby National Museum in Warsaw is the Museum of the Polish Army, which includes a collection of Polish aircraft. The aviation industry has a proud, hundred-year history. The first wind tunnel was constructed at the Warsaw University of Technology in 1921 and aircraft production began two years later in Poznań and Biała Podlaska.

The Warsaw Institute of Aviation was established in 1926 and was followed two years later by the creation of the state-owned State Aviation Works (PZL). In the interwar years, Poland built up its air force through the domestic manufacture of fighters and bombers, famously the PZL P.11 fighter and the PZL.37 Łoś (Elk) bomber, which featured novel wing and undercarriage designs. By 1939, the Polish aircraft industry had produced more than 4 000 planes and 1 400 gliders, as well as 3 800 aircraft engines and propellers, while training and developing 12 000 highly qualified technicians and engineers.

Aircraft production was restarted in 1949, but mostly with Soviet designs. Some 15 000 versions of the Soviet MiG-15 and MiG-17 fighter jets were produced in the early 1950s, to be replaced by the production of civilian planes by 1955. By the early 1960s, with the manufacture of Yak-12 utility aircraft, Antonov An-12 transport aircraft and Mil Mi-1 and Mi-2 light helicopters, the industry had grown to employ 29 000 workers. Poland also had a history of designing and producing trainer aircraft, including the Junak, the TS-8 Bies, TS-11 Iskra, PZL-130 Orlik, I-22 Iryda and TS-16 Grot, as well as a range of world-beating gliders. During the 1980s, the industry manufactured between 600 and 750 aircraft annually until the demise of the Soviet Union. By 2022, although local production was down to around fifty fixed-wing and rotary-wing aircraft per year, Poland had become a major component supplier to global conglomerates, including Airbus, General Electric, Raytheon Technologies, Goodrich, Lockheed Martin, AgustaWestland, Bell Textron, Pratt & Whitney and Aerotech.[30]

Today, the twenty-nine companies in the Polish aviation sector directly employ 17 900 workers in aircraft manufacturing, with nearly 100 000 jobs in related machinery and equipment manufacture. The sector turned over €1.3 billion in 2020.[31]

Life was quite different under Soviet control, when Poland moved to a communist centrally planned economy. Land reform was implemented through nationalisation without compensation of all farmlands over half a square kilometre in pre-war Polish territories and all those over one square kilometre in former German territories. Some were redistributed but most remained in the hands of the government. All enterprises with over fifty employees were also nationalised, also without compensation. Without Western assistance and given its Marxian structure, living standards remained low and debt, taken on in the 1970s, grew.

There were some positives of this era, including the rebuilding of Warsaw. So complete and systematic was the destruction that followed the uprising, and so hopeless seemed the task of rebuilding, that communist authorities even considered naming Łódź as Poland's capital. Large parts of the city, including Old Town, the city centre and the Powiśle and Wola districts, had been destroyed. Not only did returning refugees need a place to stay, and something to do, but Stalin also needed the legitimacy that reconstruction afforded. While Germany, the UK, the Netherlands, France and Italy took the decision to rebuild only select historical buildings, the reconstruction of the entire old city of Warsaw was undertaken, based on photographs, paintings and whatever other sources were available.[32]

Even so, by the 1970s, Poland was in economic and political crisis. In 1970, price increases sparked strikes on the coast, leading to violence and the removal of Władysław Gomułka, who had been leader since 1956. Despite the installation of Edward Gierek as premier, by 1976 things had worsened, with the introduction of food and fuel rationing. Queuing had become a way of life. Ration books, which had originally appeared under German occupation, became a permanent element of the urban landscape during the era of the Polish People's Republic. Soap, washing powder, meat, sugar, flour, rice, butter and even toilet paper were frequently unavailable. Mondays were designated 'meatless' to save the commodity. This was never going to solve the inefficiencies and disincentives of the system. A meat scandal in 1965 ended in the prosecution and sentencing to death of the director of the Municipal Meat Trade Company for the constant shortages. The fear of hunger, due to the malnutrition of the Second World War, carried through into the communist years. Between 1945 and 1950, the share of expenditure on food in the household budget reached 70 per cent. By the 1960s, the average Polish citizen consumed 200 kilograms of potatoes a year, about 50 kilograms of meat and 5 kilograms of fish. By 1980, the share of meat had gone up to 75 kilograms.[33] The intake of meat in post-communist Poland has fallen with the availability of other, inexpensive dietary options.[34]

The cars exhibited at the Museum of Technology were out of the reach of most Poles. In the 1950s, despite its basic technology, the price of the entry-level Syrena, known as 'the sock' because of the cloud of exhaust fumes it produced, was the equivalent of fifty salaries; the more expensive Warszawa (based on the Soviet GAZ-M20 Pobeda, and already obsolete by the time it hit production) was more than eighty salaries.

Poles became jaded by promises of change according to government plans. As Leopold Tyrmand wrote in 1972 in his essay 'Communist Civilisation':

> In communism, a plan is neither a word nor a term; it is a spell. The idea of the plan, as perceived by the classics, was to provide for the source of victory and success of the implemented solution, a magic formula opening the Sesame of the common happiness and joy of the humankind, a key to the utopia obliged to transform into a tangible paradise on earth, by the means of the plan.[35]

By the mid-1970s, the pegged foreign exchange rate had worsened economic distortions. The main determinant of economic status – and of access to goods – became access to hard currency. Little wonder that the ruling party, the PZPR, grew to three million members. As it did, development and growth slowed, with investment in economic infrastructure and technology falling behind Western Europe. By 1980, there were more than 1.7 million on the waiting list for a basic, prefabricated apartment.

The black market was thriving in the face of shortages. Hoarding and under-the-counter trading were as commonplace as empty shelves. Queue 'lists' were created to maintain order, and delivery standards reflected the person's age and type of work performed. 'A queue is as much a symbol of communism as the hammer and sickle,' observed Tyrmand. 'Nobody invented capitalism. It came with life which by some is referred to as the human history on earth. Socialism on the other hand was invented by men sitting at the desk. No wonder it constantly comes in conflict with life.'

Hundreds of thousands of Poles left the country to settle elsewhere, including some in Africa, notably in northern and South Africa. As the government, however grudgingly, accepted the need to liberalise the economy, it required the legitimacy of the opposition to do so. The idea of retaining a socialist Poland in this way collapsed amid the economic and social upheavals of the 1980s.

Solidarity with each other

Solidarity was created in August 1980, the first independent trade union recognised by the state inside the Iron Curtain. In December 1981, martial law was imposed, forcing the union underground. By the end of the decade, however, roundtable talks between the government and the opposition led to the first democratic elections in Poland in nearly forty years.

Solidarity's leader, Lech Wałęsa, who received the Nobel Peace Prize in 1983, was elected president of Poland in 1990. After 1990, Poland's economy quickly stabilised, growing at an annual average of 3.6 per cent for the past thirty years. Following its membership of the EU in 2004, it has enjoyed the highest rate of growth among the twenty-seven EU member states and ranks in the top twenty-five largest economies in the world.

The per capita income of Poles rose from $1 720 in 1990 to $15 720 by 2020, or from 40 per cent to 143 per cent of global GDP. 'I am most proud of the fact that I was able to achieve the transition from the bad, Putin-like era to the new brave one,' says Wałęsa.

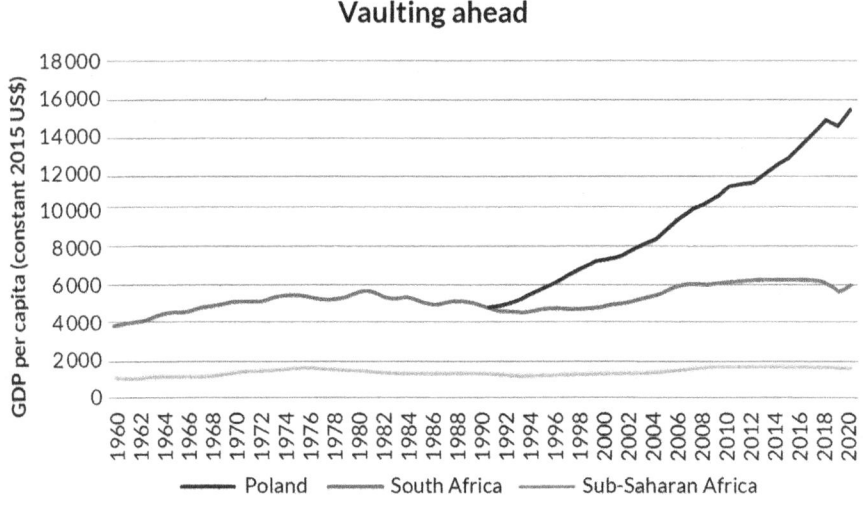

Vaulting ahead

Source: World Bank, World Development Indicators

But this spectacular transition has not been without pain, the long-term effects of which are still being felt in Polish politics.

'Solutions at the time were so different, that to get across from one era to another, I had to destroy a lot in order to be able to create something new,' reflects Wałęsa. 'The Soviet Union was importing 70 per cent of Polish exports. We had dissolved the Soviet Union and we lost that market. Which country could survive such a shock? It's very easy to go from capitalism to communism; you just have to redistribute and give it to others. It is easy to make a fish soup out of an aquarium. But the other way round, from communism to capitalism, you have to create a fishpond out of a soup.' It has not been easy, he says, 'but we are succeeding'.

Change was not only painful but also placed a premium on speed and decisiveness.

Armed with an MBA from St John's University in New York and a doctorate from the Central School of Planning and Statistics in Warsaw, Leszek Balcerowicz had gone from working at the Institute of Marxism-Leninism to Solidarity by the early 1980s. By 1988, he was a forty-one-year-old economics professor 'with a hobby of economic reform'. In 1989, he became deputy prime minister and minister of finance in the first non-communist government. Widely credited for steering the free-market reforms that set Poland on its path to success, he has since served as chairman of the National Bank of Poland.

'When I was asked by the prime minister in 1989 to take over the reform project, I was on my way to take over a visiting post in the UK,' Professor Balcerowicz recalls. He assembled a team of ten people, which enabled him to 'take a radical and risky approach'.

His team took over 'the commanding heights' of the economy, starting the project in September 1989 amid hyperinflation and falling production. With a deadline of 1 January 1990, they produced a ten-step plan 'which sought to answer two basic questions: What are your targets, and what is your model? The first was clear. We had been diverging from the West for years. We needed to catch up. That could only happen through faster economic growth, and that demanded open markets, moderate taxation and private investment. To do this, we needed to be very fast and move on a broad front.'

Balcerowicz and his team realised that they could use the political moment to their advantage. 'We also relied on psychology, never believing that *Homo Sovieticus* would not change, and that incentives could work.' In a form of 'shock therapy', prices of consumer goods were freed, state-sector wages were frozen, the złoty was made convertible and state-owned enterprises were sold via a voucher system. 'We had to innovate with vouchers since we lacked the developed capital markets,' notes Balcerowicz.

He reflects now that he would change some things faster, such as the inherited welfare system. 'We should also have done a flat tax quicker.' He reminds us that 'the speed of change in Poland in the 1980s and 1990s was very fast – that we had to learn on the job. The politics were that reforms were easier.'

There are several criticisms of Balcerowicz's 'cold turkey' approach,[36] notably that the reforms constituted 'shock without therapy'. Not all prices were liberalised, however, while social transfers remained, and the rate of privatisation was both slow and transparent. The impact on wages was shocking, in that they were around one-quarter lower in 1990 than the previous year, though against 1988 this was less than 8 per cent. While some argue that economic policy was 'excessively liberal', pensions went up relative to the average wage by 65 per cent in 1990 and to an annual average of over 70 per cent in the period 1992–94, while the number of old age and disability pensioners of all kinds rose from about 7 million in 1989 to about 9.5 million ten years later. The privatisation of large companies was usually through public auctions and slower than assumed. Poland benefitted more from the creation of brand-new private companies, explaining 'one of the paradoxes of the Polish transformation, namely fast privatisation of the economy despite slow privatisation of companies'.[37]

Finally, for those who believe that transformation after 1990 destroyed a large part of Polish industry, while this was true in 1990/91, twenty-five years later industrial output was 2.5 times higher than in 1989, and about 3.7 times higher than in 1991. Moreover, the extraction of raw materials (which had grown under the communists, particularly coal mining, which grew from 145 million tonnes in 1971 to 200 million tonnes within the decade) shrank while the production and export of processed goods, including high-tech goods, grew many times over.

Whatever the Monday morning quarterbacking, Poland 'enjoyed the best period in our history because, for the first time, we began to adapt the Western model of competitive elections, the rule of law, and market economics,' argues Balcerowicz. 'This has resulted in us converging with the West for the first time in our history.'

Paradoxically, Poland's political shift rightwards in the second and third decades of the twenty-first century has been, in part, a reaction to its tremendous contemporary period of prosperity – a result of a combination of factors, including the extent of the 'left-behinds' in the rural areas who have not benefitted as much from Poland's successful insertion in global value chains, perceived threats to nationalist cultural identity from global influences, and a lack of trust in democracy stemming from the wiretapping scandal that engulfed the centrist Civic Platform in 2014 and propelled a right-wing coalition, led by political party Law and Justice (PiS), to power.[38]

Consequently, says Balcerowicz, Poland's policies have become 'gradually anti-growth', with the renationalisation of banks and a growing state sector. Redistribution – through an expanded welfare payments system and 'rewards for politicians in lucrative posts' – has become the preferred method of ensuring support.

Politics as a reform variable

Janusz Waluś has become something of a cult figure on the extremes of Polish politics. Born in the southern town of Zakopane in 1953, he immigrated to South Africa in the 1980s, where he became active in far-right politics. Waluś shot and killed Chris Hani, the leader of the South African Communist Party, in April 1993, bringing the country to the precipice of a race war. Sentenced to death, later commuted to life imprisonment, Waluś was released from prison in December 2022. Football fans wear his image on T-shirts, scarves and banners, and parliamentarians have staged campaigns for his return to Poland.

The far-right in Poland is a significant political force. In 2019, for instance, the right-wing coalition earned nearly 7 per cent of the total vote. This support reflects the polarisation of Polish politics this century.

Since taking power in 2015, PiS has enacted numerous measures to increase political influence over institutions of state, including highly controversial judicial reform bills allowing executive authority over judicial appointments (which have forced about 40 per cent of incumbent Supreme Court justices into retirement), a law on restrictions on public gatherings, and another to create an agency to centralise control over public and EU funding for NGOs. As a result, in December 2017, the European Commission launched proceedings against Poland under Article 7.1 of the Treaty of Lisbon, citing the judicial reforms as a 'clear risk of a serious breach of the rule of law in Poland'.[39]

Solidarity

As answer to a prayer
A slogan of hope
Freedom in the air
Citizens and state, a microscope

Clanking steel
In Lenin's factory
Two choices they feel
Levers so unsatisfactory

The men behind dark glasses
Shady past
Stolen futures
Surely, it could not last

The beginning of the Soviet end
A fresh start
To others hope may extend
Horses before the cart

A man in a Bronson whiskers
A gate at which they picket
Solidarity, resisters
For Poland, just the ticket

Stocznia Gdańska, a dream
Worlds again collide
A victory for self-esteem
To us, a guide

Zofia Romaszewska has worked as a senior advisor to Poland's president Andrzej Duda. An early member of the Workers' Defence Committee – a forerunner of Solidarity set up to defend workers' rights – in the 1970s, she believes that the root of the political instability and rightward drift is in the deviation from Solidarity's original goals. 'The remnants of elites from the old [communist] time have remained in control, of the economy, the media and the judiciary,' she says. 'They are now challenged by those who feel they were deceived by this change. The roots of the ruling Law and Justice party is a descendant of Solidarity, moving on issues to the national interest.' She cites the Family 500+ programme to incentivise larger families as one example of positive change. Another concerns changes to the composition of the National Council of the Judiciary, given that 'the judiciary previously operated in the pocket of the elites,' Romaszewska claims.

These views were backed by Kornel Morawiecki, the father of Mateusz Morawiecki and the senior marshal of the Sejm, the lower house of Poland's bicameral parliament. A physicist by training, Kornel was the founder and leader of Fighting Solidarity, ostensibly the militant wing of the Solidarity movement that refused any dealings with the communists and aimed for a revolution. 'Today there is a basic division between the poor and those who have something, between those who have to endure unemployment and those who have enjoyed success,' he said shortly before his death from pancreatic cancer in 2019. 'We are, like in

Africa, divided into these two tribes – those more or less fortunate. Those who have been sidelined now have a voice in government.'

Like others around the ruling party, both Romaszewska and the senior Morawiecki express disquiet over the link between finances and democracy. 'Money has a disproportionate influence in politics,' says Andrzej Łupina, Poland's former ambassador to Algeria and subsequent head of the Polish-African Chamber of Commerce. This camp views the EU as interfering in Poland's social policy preferences and is increasingly vocal over the role of foreign companies, which it sees as 'depriving' Poles of their wealth.

Yet few politicians have clear thoughts on how to resolve the crisis they've identified. They are happy being members of the EU, given the benefits, but are unhappy about the rules of the club they joined. Having your cake and eating it comes immediately to mind.

Conclusion: A man and some lessons

Despite the absence of a state until 1918, the horror of the Second World War when it lost 85 per cent of its capital and one-third of its population, and the trauma of the Soviet era, Poland recovered.

The domestic political career of Lech Wałęsa, the man who headed up this extraordinary period of change, however, quickly disintegrated. His five-year government had seven prime ministers, eventually losing the 1995 election to a candidate from the post-Soviet camp. 'His government was unstable,' says Dr Killion Munyama, a Zambian-born economist and former Polish MP, 'which is to be expected perhaps from a broad-based movement like Solidarity.'

Wałęsa was eventually wiped out in the 2000 election, receiving just 1 per cent of the vote. 'He was like [Nelson] Mandela for Poland,' says Łukasz Jasina, spokesperson for the Ministry of Foreign Affairs and formerly an analyst at the Polish Institute of International Affairs. 'He remains a hero to us, after [Pope] John Paul II, Chopin and Copernicus. He played a very important revolutionary role and was a symbol of divine intervention.' (Ninety-five per cent of the population is Catholic.) Wałęsa, whose father had been interned in a German concentration camp, lived through hardship and struggle, progressing with little formal education from the village to the factory floor. He put Poland on the map, although he was 'more cherished abroad than in Poland, where his reputation is definitely not helped by the controversy over his state role as a spy in the early 1970s for the SB security police,' says Jasina. 'But the majority remember him for the good that he did and forgive him, but want him in the past.'

Balcerowicz, who worked closely with him, notes that 'Wałęsa's style was certainly worse than his substance. He got a lot done.' Now, like his former boss, the professor cautions against 'backsliding' on democracy and its benefits. 'We have to realise that things don't simply fall like manna from heaven, [they] only stay with hard work [and] should never be taken for granted. To do this, we need to frighten those who seek to backslide as much as they want to frighten us.'

Whatever its challenges, Poland has become a normal country, and quickly. This is evident in Wałęsa still having a voice, and there being intense competition across the political spectrum. It is little wonder that more than 80 per cent of Poles say they are satisfied with their lives, compared to 50 per cent in 1990.[40] In so doing, Poland has proven three things. First, it is possible to overcome bad geography. The method has in part been down to an iron will, sound economic policy decisions and high levels of education. Second, no matter how traumatic and devastating, history is not necessarily destiny. And third, democracy is not just about the ends, even though it provides the tools to ensure the rule of law, efficient government, fairness, freedoms, rights, sound governance and development. How inclusive choices are made is as important. The words of Pope John Paul II, illuminated at the European Solidarity Centre in Gdańsk, have relevance in this regard: 'To look into the eyes of the other person and to see in them hope and anxieties of brother or sister, is to discover the idea of solidarity.'

Poland's success, as with that of the Czech and Slovak republics, the Baltics and other former Warsaw Pact countries, reminds us, too, of the failure of the alternative. 'If there was not the success of Poland in the 1990s, there would be no [concept of] nation-building today,' observes Piotr Łukasiewicz, a former colonel of the Polish Armed Forces and later ambassador to Afghanistan. 'Poland is testament to change being possible when the system changes.' This is quite a different outcome from the one Vladimir Putin presumably had in mind when he said that the collapse of the Soviet empire 'was the greatest geopolitical catastrophe of the century'.[41]

Just 250 kilometres from the Polish-Ukrainian border in the city of Kraków is the site of the former *Deutsche Emailwarenfabrik* (German Enamelware Factory). During the Second World War, its proprietor, Nazi Party member Oskar Schindler, managed to save the lives of 1 200 Jewish workers. His metamorphosis from privileged opportunistic businessman to courageous humanitarian was immortalised in the Academy Award–winning film *Schindler's List*. Today the old administrative building hosts a museum. A plaque at the entrance is inscribed with words from the Talmud, the book of Jewish law: 'Whoever saves one life, saves the world entire.' It is an expression of the practice more than the rhetorical universality of human rights, of which all leaders should take heed in their approach to crises, both inside and outside their borders.

The rust-coloured, sheet-metal walls of the European Solidarity Centre are intended to evoke the hulls of the ships built at the Gdańsk Shipyard, but it is a living museum.

At the entrance is a photographic exhibition of Belarusian activists who have been detained, harassed, imprisoned and murdered by the regime of President Alexander Lukashenko, a close ally of Vladimir Putin. An estimated 300 people have disappeared since Lukashenko came to power in 1994, a tally that includes political opponents such as former minister of the interior Yury Zakharenko (disappeared on 7 May 1999), deputy chairman of the Supreme Soviet of Belarus Viktor Gonchar (disappeared on 16 September 1999) and businessman Anatoly Krasovsky, a close friend of Gonchar who financed the opposition movement (the two men disappeared together). There are at least 1 497 political prisoners in Belarus, a country led by a master authoritarian democrat, whose style has been replicated in Venezuela, Nicaragua and a host of African countries.

Poland is a cautionary tale of the perils of such authoritarianism. And for those who might like to turn the clock back to the glory of the socialist Cold War era, it is a reminder that there was then – and is now – another, better way.

Division to Integration

'A civil war is not a war but a sickness. The enemy is within. One fights almost against oneself.'
 – Antoine de Saint-Exupéry, quoted in Antony Beevor's *The Battle for Spain*

'The cause of Spain is not solely the cause of the Spaniards, but the cause of all progressive and advanced humanity.'   – Joseph Stalin, October 1936

'My years in Africa live within me with indescribable force. There was born the possibility of rescuing a great Spain. There was founded the idea which today redeems us. Without Africa, I can scarcely explain myself to myself, nor can I explain myself properly to my comrades in arms.'
 – Generalissimo Francisco Franco, December 1938

Forty minutes by train north-west of Madrid is the Valle de los Caídos, or Valley of the Fallen, erected to commemorate the Spanish Civil War, fought between 1936 and 1939.[42]

Work on the site commenced in 1940. Construction, in part using prison labour, took over eighteen years. Rooted in a genre of fascist classicism in the Sierra de Guadarrama mountains, the memorial is crowned by a 150-metre-high Christian cross, the tallest in the world, visible from over thirty kilometres away. Generalissimo Francisco Franco, the leader of the Nationalist faction that won the war, claimed that the monument was meant to be a 'national act of atonement' and reconciliation, though in his death it has served as a reminder of the bitter division and cost of a conflict that claimed as many as 350 000 lives (some say 500 000). The remains of an estimated 40 000 people lie beneath the valley floor, including some victims of Franco's rule.

The valley contains both Nationalist and Republican graves, but the dedication on the site reads '*Caídos por Dios y por España*' (Fallen for God and for Spain), the motto of the Francoist faction.

The war divided Spain, but also the world. It was viewed as a clash between dictatorship and republican democracy, between fascism and individual freedom, state centralism and regional autonomy, or, alternatively, civilisation and communism. It was the soft curtain-raiser of the Second World War. Germany and Italy, on the side of Franco's Nationalists, used it as a testing ground for new doctrine and military equipment. Mussolini deployed 76 000 Italian troops. The German Condor Legion numbered 17 000 aircrew and artillerymen. Hitler personally ordered his Luftwaffe to fly Franco's Army of Africa to the mainland to prevent Nationalist collapse and then to ensure its ultimate victory.

On the Republican side, loyal to the left-leaning Popular Front government of the Second Spanish Republic, around 3 800 Soviet specialists, aircrew and officers, along with an extensive contingent of agents of the feared People's Commissariat for Internal Affairs (NKVD), served in the theatre. The Soviet Union saw the war in Spain as an opportunity to spread ideology and ultimately purge its own ranks. Just as NKVD agents were used to deal with left-wing opponents of the communists in Republican-held areas, including anarchists and members of the Workers' Party of Marxist Unification (POUM), many soviet officials themselves became victims of Stalin's purges during and after the Spanish Civil War. As Italy and Germany supplied Franco's forces, the Soviets became the main suppliers of military aid to the Republicans, though Moscow expected to be paid in gold. During the war, two-thirds of Spain's gold reserves, approximately $500 million, were shipped to the Soviet Union.[43] Solidarity came at a price.

The war also mobilised wider support, including the more than 35 000 who served in the Republican International Brigades drawn from sixty-five countries.[44] A disproportionate number of those who travelled to Spain to lend the Republicans support were Jewish – most came from working-class backgrounds and lacked any formal military experience, some were unemployed or refugees, and many were sent by their local communist parties on orders from Moscow. While all may not have been communist, they were all anti-fascist.

Among the foreign volunteers were an extraordinary cast of characters, some flamboyant, others downright evil. They included the generals Emilio Kléber (aka Manfred Stern) and Pál Lukács (aka Máté Zalka aka Béla Frankl), the former dying after fifteen years in Stalin's Gulag, and the latter succumbing on the battlefield; the British NKVD spy David Crook; Clementine Churchill's nephew Esmond Romilly, whose aircraft later went missing over the Ruhr in 1941; a young American teacher named Robert Merriman, who commanded the Abraham Lincoln Battalion; the future West German chancellor, twenty-two-year-old Willy Brandt; and Erich Mielke, who served as an officer in the political police of the Spanish Republican Armed Forces and later as long-time head of the East German Stasi.[45]

There were other notables in the wings. Kim Philby, the legendary Soviet spy in Britain's MI6, worked as a journalist for *The Times* in Spain, during which time he started supplying intelligence to both the Soviets and the British. Jawaharlal Nehru, who would become the first prime minister of independent India, also visited Spain during the war and threw his support behind the government.

Others in the Republican ranks included prominent writers, artists and intellectuals. *Guernica*, Pablo Picasso's painting of the German bombing of the eponymous Spanish village (now in Madrid's Museo Reina Sofía); Robert Capa's searing photograph *Death of a Loyalist Soldier*; Ernest Hemingway's *For Whom the Bell Tolls*; and George Orwell's memoir *Homage to Catalonia* were among their many outputs and outpourings. Propaganda was a key aspect of the struggle, and remains so today, as was the use of deception. 'It is very difficult to write accurately about the Spanish War,' wrote Orwell in *Homage to Catalonia*, 'because of the lack of non-propagandist documents.'

Through these artistic and literary prisms, the war is seen as one between right and wrong, democrats versus dictatorship. The reality was, however, more complex. The two sides contained all manner of bedfellows, the Nationalists comprising royalist Carlists and Alfonsists, Falangists (fascists by another name, led by José Antonio Primo de Rivera, son of the former dictator), the Catholic Church along with other traditionalists and conservatives, and a part of the armed forces. The Republicans were made up of anarchists, communists, liberals and socialists, along with Basque and Catalan separatists, at times a confusing and incompatible cocktail of radicalism and local nationalism.

It was a war of 'two Spains', and it did not just begin in 1936. There was a long run-up – nearly 130 years, in fact, from the time of the collapse of the old monarchy in 1808 when King Carlos IV was forced to abdicate in favour of Joseph Bonaparte, Napoleon's brother. It sparked a people's rebellion against French occupation in Madrid, as portrayed by Goya in his paintings *El dos de mayo de 1808* and *El tres de mayo de 1808*, which hang in the city's Prado Museum.

Not only did these events place the military at the centre of politics, but the country suffered numerous convulsions. It lost its empire in Latin America and decoupled from the nineteenth-century variant of the Industrial Revolution. Its occupation by the French seeded a liberalism against the traditional order, with Spain adopting its first, liberal constitution – one of the earliest codified constitutions in the world – in 1812. The following year, after experiencing serious setbacks on many fronts, Napoleon agreed to restore Carlos IV's son, Ferdinand VII, to the throne. Ferdinand promptly abolished the constitution in favour of autocracy. On his death in 1833, the First Carlist War over succession to the throne and the nature of the Spanish monarchy began. During this civil war, which lasted seven years, violent anticlericalism emerged, religious orders were closed and, in the disentailments between 1835 and 1837, church property and lands were seized and sold off by the government.

In 1868, Queen Isabella II was overthrown in a military coup known as the 'Glorious Revolution', creating the short-lived First Spanish Republic and sparking religious and regional conflicts. The Third Carlist War (1872–76) followed between no fewer than three claimants to the throne, resolved in favour of Isabella's son, Alfonso XII. The king died in 1885, his wife Maria Christina being three months pregnant with his son and heir, Alfonso XIII. During these years of transition, Spain engaged in incessant and costly foreign military wars. In 1898, they lost Cuba, the Philippines, Guam and Puerto Rico after being defeated by the United States in the Spanish–American War. Closer to home, the colonial wars in Morocco were bloody and sapping affairs, Spain's Vietnam. And yet, even though the military had diminished in stature and size by this time, it was seen by some as the ultimate upholder of constitutional order.

Civil strife went hand in hand with deep-seated social and economic problems and inequalities, especially in the countryside, where, as Hugh Thomas notes in *The Spanish Civil War*, the impoverished were vulnerable to 'the brutality of the landlord's agent and the civil guards, the mercenary slyness of the village shopkeeper and the patronising interference of the priest'.[46] Even tenant farmers had few legal protections. By the twentieth century, Spain was a highly unequal place, both in societal and regional terms, with, for example, 45 per cent of the merchant fleet coming from the Basque Country to the north, which attracted a third of total Spanish investment, much of it in its great steel and iron works.

In a report to the foreign secretary, Lord Curzon, in 1920, the British ambassador to Spain, Sir Esmé Howard, noted the effect of political corruption in rendering Spain's parliamentary system 'bankrupt', writing:

> If I had to paint an impressionist painting of Spain in 1920, for which accurate and detailed drawing was not required, it would be an easier task. I could then take a large canvas and produce a stage in a state of chaotic welter on which various politicians would prominently figure pulling strings in different directions and to no purpose across a background of strikes, bombs and outrages, and apparent general discontent, of committees of military officers springing suddenly into the foreground and retiring as suddenly into obscurity for no apparent reason, of railway companies carrying on systematic sabotage against themselves in order to force the country and Government into raising rates, of banks and profiteers indulging in wild speculations in foreign exchanges, undermining all the advantages the country obtained by her policy of neutrality throughout the war, of regionalism in an extreme form increasing in certain provinces and extreme centralisation clinging to straws of hope in maintaining itself, of governments coming and going without serious programmes of reform, and, above this turmoil, of King Alfonso the only stable element apparently in it all, serenely trying now this expedient, now that, to carry on

against great odds until some sane, wise and strong man should emerge on the stage to put all these tragi-comedians into their right places and allow the play to proceed to the benefit and content of the public in the house.[47]

His observations led the Foreign Office's assistant secretary, Gerald Villiers, to conclude that 'a dose of *fascismo* would do Spain a world of good'.

By the turn of the twentieth century, life expectancy was around thirty-five years, the same as five centuries earlier, causing nearly 3 per cent of the population to emigrate in the first decade.[48] Two-thirds were illiterate. Industry and mining provided less than one-fifth of the available jobs, while agriculture, the backbone of the economy and of exports, was characterised by extreme inequality, hence the saying that 'one half of Spain eats but does not work, while the other half works but does not eat'. As historian Antony Beevor observes, 'the peasants and the king must have seemed like foreigners to each other in their own country'.[49]

Insurrections were commonplace in the early twentieth century, against the Church and the military, and for regional independence and class struggle. The military dictatorship of Miguel Primo de Rivera from 1923, after five years of virtual civil war in Barcelona, provided some respite. But not for long. General Primo de Rivera was expelled in 1930. The following year saw the dethronement of King Alfonso XIII and the proclamation of the Second Spanish Republic (popularly known as *la niña bonita* – 'the pretty girl') on 14 April 1931. Yet these actions and the victory at the polls of the left in June 1931 'proved unable to create a democratic habit powerful enough to satisfy the aspirations of either the working, or the old governing, classes, while the new rulers themselves mortally angered the latter, when not strong enough as well as not radical enough to please the former'.[50]

A rightist coup in 1932, led by General José Sanjurjo (*El León del Rif* – 'The Lion of the Rif'), collapsed. Sanjurjo ultimately perished when the plane on which he was flying to Spain in 1936, to take charge of the Nationalists after a second coup, crashed. On being warned that the aircraft was overloaded, he had responded: 'I need to wear proper clothes as the new *caudillo* of Spain.' The 1932 attempt was presented in Marxist terms as a counter-revolutionary action financed by an oligarchy of landowners. In 1934, a workers' insurrection in Asturias followed a leftist reversal at the 1933 polls, but it was quickly suppressed. In February 1936, a narrow election victory of the leftist (or Republican) Popular Front ushered in another progressive but again weak and divided government. As Thomas summarises: 'The five and a quarter years between April 1931 and July 1936 were thus a time when two sides were taking shape in Spain powerful enough to prevent each other from winning immediately, if swords should be drawn.'

To add to the trouble, the Great Depression had hit Spain hard, with export levels in 1935 about a quarter of the 1930 figure, and unemployment and wages both rising. A large measure of self-government in Catalonia and the Basque Country did not help the confusion. The first Republican cabinets were characterised by economic turmoil and escalating political violence.

By July 1936, Spain was a state in upheaval, marked by social and political schisms. When, in July, the Spanish army garrison in Melilla in North Africa rose up against the government, so began the civil war. It was the culmination of 130 years of struggles and tensions between the Church and the liberals, the landowners and the working classes, the centrists and the separatists. What the rebels conceived as a quick *pronunciamiento*, a relatively bloodless coup, took eventually three years, as workers and large segments of the army, not to mention international supporters, got behind the elected government.

Neither side was squeaky clean. Some historians calculate as many as 100 000 opponents were executed by the Nationalists, and around 55 000 were killed by the Republicans, including some 7 000 priests, monks and nuns of the 115 000 clergy countrywide. As many as 20 000 churches were destroyed in the process. While 130 000 military personnel were killed in action (or executed) on both sides, civilian deaths from the war and its aftermath numbered perhaps twice as much, including from malnutrition and sickness.

Over time, Franco, who had been smuggled into Spain with British help,[51] emerged as the leader among the Nationalist ranks. Although he declared the war over on 1 April 1939, three days after his forces entered Madrid, it took more than a decade for a semblance of social and economic stability to return, albeit in a suspended state of totalitarianism.

The 'miracle' and shock therapy of the Franco years

By 1945, despite Franco (with some further British encouragement) staying out of the Second World War, Spain was in terrible shape, with much of its infrastructure destroyed, foreign reserves all but wiped out, and per capita income among its twenty-five million people around one-third less than the European average.

The problem at this point was not the civil war, and the chaos that had produced it, but rather the manner and speed in which Spain was able to deal with what novelist Stefan Zweig described as the 'after war'.[52]

Franco's regime was at war with itself (research indicates at least 35 000 government executions of political opponents took place post-1945), and because of its authoritarian character and fascist history, it was isolated with few options internationally. Unlike other neutral European states, it was excluded from the Marshall Plan and was not even a member of the United Nations.

These were consequently the *años del hambre* ('years of hunger').

It took until the early 1950s for pre-civil war industrial production levels to be restored, though Spain remained hampered by a corrupt and creaking bureaucracy and the piecemeal nature of its reforms, manifest in a high trade and budget deficit, and inflation.

The first major change came in the 1950s with the warming of relations – driven by Cold War expediency – with the Eisenhower administration. As odious as Franco's regime might have been, none of the Western democracies wanted another civil war in Spain, which is what the Soviets would have preferred.[53] Franco's support during these years came from Argentina under General Juan Perón, with the signing of trade agreements in 1946 and 1947; from the Holy See, with the negotiation and signing of a new Concordat in August 1953; and from the United States, under the Pact of Madrid to establish US military bases on Spanish soil, signed in September 1953.

The American military facilities were established in exchange for $1 billion in aid during the decade, trade agreements and improved international ties. Spain was admitted to the UN in 1955, the Organisation for Economic Co-operation and Development (OECD) in 1958, and the World Bank and IMF in 1959. A move away from Falangist influence simultaneously occurred as technocrats increasingly featured in government and Franco cleaned house of the more extreme martial and ideological elements.

Still, some shock therapy was necessary.

The foundation of the 'Spanish miracle' of the 1960s was seeded by Franco turning to a group of liberal economists, initially based on the Catholic Opus Dei organisation, later to form into a committee on economic affairs and the Office of Economic Coordination and Planning under the prime minister. Tax reform followed together with curbs on government spending. Even though Europe took nearly two-thirds of Spanish exports, and supplied one-third, without the prospect of European membership (which Franco had dismissed regardless as a 'fantasy' given that the 'old nations' of Europe had personalities 'which cannot be erased'[54]), in June 1959 Spain unveiled the IMF-supported Stabilization Plan, which adopted measures to further restrict inflation and spending while attracting foreign investment and liberalising trade. While initially painful, leading to a drop in employment and emigration of more than half a million Spaniards, foreign investment quickly grew. Coupled with an openness to foreign tourism, Spain's growth and incomes accelerated, increasing nearly fourfold between 1959 and 1975, the second-fastest economic growth rate after Japan during this period.

Things changed fast. While there were fewer than 70 000 cars on Madrid's roads in 1960, ten years later this had increased to half a million, while life expectancy went from sixty-two in 1950 to seventy-three in 1975 – and was at eighty-four by 2019.

These were the *años del desarrollo* ('years of development'). During the last period of Franco's rule (1959–75), Spain's economy grew at an annual average of 6.7 per cent,⁵⁵ driven by both reforms and improving internationalisation.

In 1965, the number of tourists arriving in Spain was fourteen million. By the end of the decade, this figure had grown to more than twenty million a year. Spain's annual tourist numbers are now ninety million, second only to neighbouring France, and twice the size of the Spanish population. With foreigners, 'Franco's Spain found itself being subverted more by new values from without than by the old ideologies within.'⁵⁶

A combination of IMF aid, commercial loans and remittances provided the capital base for this transformation. From 1959 there was only one direction for the country, even though openness remained 'incompatible to many in the Franco regime and the elites', says Román Escolano, who served as Spain's minister of economy, industry and competitiveness in 2018.⁵⁷ Even by 1975, foreign firms represented nearly one-eighth of the total invested in Spain's top industries, with agreements with the US particularly providing access to technology, markets and skills, as well as capital. Still, there were restrictions on foreign access to the Spanish market, hence a reliance on state-owned companies in shipping and vehicle manufacturing.

Franco's death in 1975 and the drafting of a new constitution and the restoration of the monarchy and democracy not only marked a change of political direction, and increased freedoms, but also offered new economic options. It was the end of Spanish exceptionalism.

The end of exceptionalism

Franco may have (perhaps apocryphally) said, 'Just do as I do: stay out of politics.' Yet this *caudillo* proved a shrewd manager of international politics. In the same vein, the Spanish Civil War, while immensely costly, paled against the probable cost of involvement in the Second World War. The soft opening may have proved, in this way, a narrow escape.

Yet, while Franco's rightist regime might not always have been wrong in economic terms and may also have created a long-term platform for economic growth, its options were constrained by Spain's closed political system. This particularly applied to the advantages of closer integration with its European family. But the repression of the Franco years did something else, as Beevor notes, in creating 'a terrible claustrophobia, exceeded only by the harshness of living conditions imposed by the regime'. The autarky of the early Franco years and the centralisation of state control created a 'deadening form' of government, comparable to Soviet satellites during the Cold War, in which 'the degree of corruption and waste was perhaps equalled only by [dictator Nicolae] Ceaușescu's Romania'.[58]

Growth without freedom might be possible – not least through improvements in productivity – but it is seldom particularly innovative or ultimately sustainable.

National exceptionalism usually brings with it political autarky. Franco's political philosophy remained exceptionalist until the end, not least in a European context. His death enabled Spain to end its era of expectant exceptionalism. It was not special, no longer possessed an empire, and no longer had to make binary choices between a monarchy or a republic, democracy or dictatorship, church or state.

Franco's death gave the younger reformists oxygen, their rise and role reflecting shifting demographic patterns in Spanish society. The baby boom of the 1950s and 1960s meant that, by the start of the 1970s, 28 per cent of the Spanish population was under the age of fourteen.[59] By 2020, this figure had halved. Population numbers went up from thirty million in 1960 to peak (so far) at forty-seven million by 2010.[60]

Thirty-seven-year-old king Juan Carlos I took the throne on 22 November 1975, two days after Franco's death. Eight months later, he appointed Adolfo Suárez, a forty-three-year-old former Franco apparatchik, as prime minister. Franco's National Movement was abolished, while political parties, trade unions and strikes were legalised. Elections held in June 1977 were won by Suárez's centrist Democratic Centre Union. A new constitution in 1978 made Spain a parliamentary monarchy with no official religion. Contraceptives, homosexuality and divorce were all legalised. A general amnesty was granted, freeing political prisoners and permitting exiles to return, while allowing immunity for crimes committed during the civil war and in Francoist Spain.

In the economy, Franco's death was followed by an immediate period of instability, caused in part by the concentration on the political transition and in part by the increase in oil prices. Spain was dependent on imports for around three-quarters of its energy. It was into an environment of increased unemployment (at 16 per cent) and a widening budget and current account deficit that the Spanish Socialist Workers' Party (PSOE), headed by Felipe González, a young lawyer from Seville, took office in late 1982. Drawn from a generation that had resisted the Franco regime in the 1970s, he was to be prime minister for fourteen years. With a clear parliamentary majority, González's government was able to undertake unpopular austerity measures, including widespread retrenchments and the closure of unprofitable SOEs. At the same time, his government expanded universal and free education provision, including tertiary; partly legalised abortion despite opposition from the Church; and streamlined and extended the social security system.

The metaphor of taking power and running a country being akin to playing a violin – you pick it up with the left and play it with the right – is apt for post-Franco Spain.

Gabriel Elorriaga has been a member of Spain's Congress of Deputies since 2004, representing the centre-right People's Party (PP). Before public office, he served as deputy director of the Cabinet of the President. He says that the election of González was the 'moment of consolidation of the transition. Everyone wanted to know how it would turn out. Would there be a coup? In the end, González became a European social democrat, more social liberal than socialist.'

González's vice president, Alfonso Guerra, reflects that while 'there were certainly some serious social (labour) conflicts caused by the necessary "industrial reconversion", the electorate fully trusted the government out of their commitment to a historical change after four decades without democracy'. Their continued support, he argues, was down to government's continuous engagement through public meetings, press conferences and the media.[61]

González played 'an absolutely crucial role', says Pablo Hernández, the governor of the Bank of Spain. 'He came from fighting the dictatorship as a radical leftist; he wins the elections and from the very beginning he behaves cautiously.'[62] For example, contrary to expectations and the position of many in his party, González took Spain's NATO membership to a referendum in 1986, which came out overwhelmingly in support of continued involvement.

As prime minister, González set a standard of moderation, ensuring long-term stability within defined European parameters. As a general lesson from this and subsequent periods, notes Ricardo Martínez Rico, a former deputy minister of finance, 'if you don't introduce your key reforms in the first year of your term as government, you are lost. It builds political capital. And some reforms were easier for the socialists – such as labour market reforms.' The ideological variance between political parties is moderated by their continued commitment to European norms. Europe is a tool of external policy and governance discipline.

While unemployment rose initially from 16 per cent to peak at 24 per cent in 1994, the PSOE was able to improve labour market flexibility and attract new foreign investment. Growth in incomes improved from an annual low of 0.2 per cent to average 3.3 per cent during the González years of socialist government. The big driver for change was in Spain's external position, when it joined the European Economic Community in January 1986, along with its earlier membership of NATO in May 1982. Its international standing was bolstered by its hosting of the Summer Olympics in Barcelona and the World Expo in Seville in 1992.

Disaffection with PSOE sleaze saw the left give way to the centre-right PP, led by José María Aznar, in 1996. The reforms initiated by González were continued, however, with greater focus on liberalisation, deregulation and privatisation. Unemployment continued to fall while property prices rose. For twenty years until the global financial crisis, Spain led growth in Europe, and saw falling inequality and rising gender equality in the economy, too. The Aznar period averaged 3.6 per cent in per capita growth, though this fell dramatically after the 2008 financial crisis, only recovering through considerable European funding, especially in the banking sector.

Subsequent socialist and conservative governments have followed much the same recipe as their forebearers. Of course, different political parties have different emphases. 'Socialists have proven better marketers; conservatives the better managers,' says Martínez Rico by way of example. But the formula has remained the same, based on a 'balance of the need for reform and for stability of the macroeconomic variables: of fiscal rectitude, social investment, and an open economy.'[63]

Spain's transformation post-1975 towards an inclusive society was made possible by increasing revenues out of which greater investments could be made in infrastructure, education and health. Such investments 'were especially critical in convincing people that democratic systems could deliver,' argues Josep Piqué, another former minister in Aznar's government.[64]

In this, the political elite has been aided and abetted by five hidden aspects.[65]

First, the civil service has provided a degree of continuity. Civil service posts are held for life: bureaucrats, professors, judges and doctors, among others, can even take leave to run for public office and return much later to the same post. 'Socialist governments are full of university professors,' notes historian Giles Tremlett. 'Right-wing ones are full of civil service types.' Aznar was a tax inspector. Mariano Rajoy, who served as prime minister from 2011 until 2018, was a property registrar. All share and understand the culture of state employees. This may make them better at shaping policies that a civil service can actually deliver.

A second aspect is in the 'inertia of fear' instilled by the Franco years, both in terms of accepting the early reforms that enabled democracy, and in driving the direction of change towards pluralism. That the army backed the reforms, and that it decided to decouple from politics and 'recouple' with society, ensured they would stay the course. While Spain has not been free of corruption, the inheritance of the Franco years helped, too, in this regard, where the tax authorities, police and army were respected and 'worked'.

Third, the preference of both leftist and rightist governments for nationalised industry (for opposite reasons) helped to engender a culture of inclusive (not extractive) wealth. The irony, of course, is that Spanish democratic governments, whether of the left or right, promptly privatised.

Fourth, Spain entered democracy in 1975 with a relatively large middle class, ensuring a degree of continuity and stability in government, no matter the ruling party's stated political stripes. Thus, even without the parameters of European membership, there were constraints on how far the governments could go without breaking this trust.

Fifth and finally, internally, most agree that the monarchy has provided a constant, acceptable and mostly uncontroversial thread of stability, especially crucial in making the early transition to democracy; externally, Spain's European orientation has enjoyed widespread consensus across society.

New international anchors

'Stronger institutions are key to understanding the story of Spain coming from a developing country with a dictatorship to a developed country with a democracy,' says Josep Piqué. But the question remains: What builds stronger institutions? What makes them inclusive and not extractive in their orientation? These questions are relevant for Africa, more relevant than Spain's rich and long history might at first glance suggest.

Spain might have once possessed an empire that spanned the world, but it was effectively a developing country in 1975. Its political liberation came a decade and a half after most African countries achieved their independence.

The last African country to be liberated, South Africa, achieved its own transition from authoritarianism nineteen years after Spain. Of course, there were differences in inheritance compared to Spain, not least in the nature of the neighbourhood. But there were also similarities, including the extent of international isolation, highly polarised societies with a traumatic past, apparently deeply held ideological differences, and a history of inequality.

The differences between the two countries today can be explained by the choices made post-liberation.

Since then, the two countries have gone off on different trajectories, reflecting their different choices. In their first twenty-five years of liberation, as shown in the graph below, Spain's GDP per capita grew from $12 621 in 1975 to $27 268 in 2000. South Africa's grew from $6 173 in 1994 to $8 179 in 2019.[66]

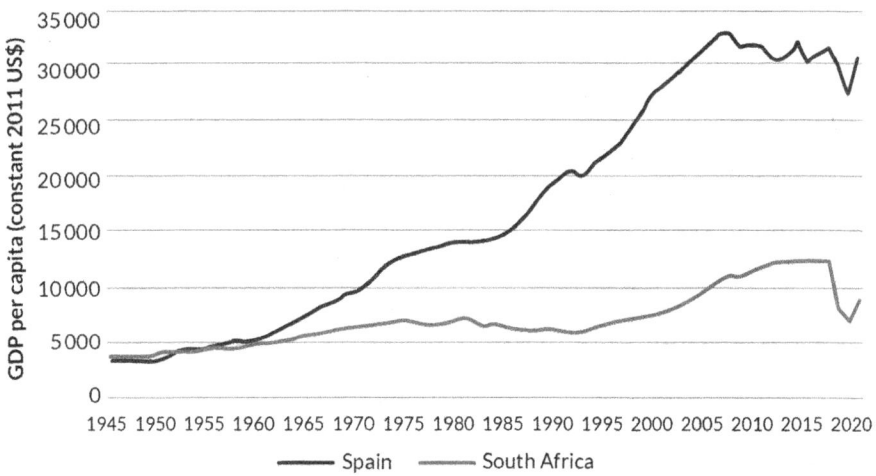

Source: World Bank, World Development Indicators

The same digression is true for Argentina, to take a different regional example. Argentina's per capita income, which was $7 362 in 1960 (Spain's was $6 215), increased through many setbacks and cycles to $12 391 by 2021, by that point less than half the Spanish figure.[67] Like Africans, Argentinians have progressively got poorer by the standards of global wealth, as the next graph illustrates.

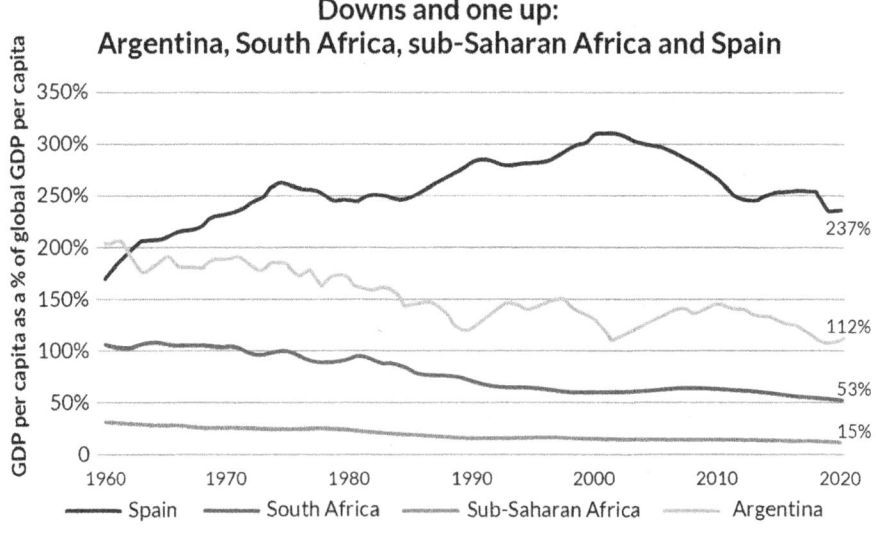

Source: World Bank, World Development Indicators

The difference, says Román Escolano, is that Argentina has been locked into a perennial 'circulating' damnation of hyperinflation, collapse and reform, where the political system 'goes in circles around Peronism'.

Spain's transition post-Franco was built on a perception that there was no alternative, viable model to swallowing the European formula.

Europe became what Ricardo Martínez Rico refers to as the 'anchor for our reforms'. Perhaps as might be expected of a country with a rich global history, despite the autarky of the twentieth century, internationalisation across different administrations has been key to Spain's success.

EU membership enabled Spain to invest heavily (and transparently) in infrastructure, especially its roads, railways and airports, while modernising its economic base and keeping pace with the rate of European growth (and narrowing the income gap with other member states). Its European orientation was further reinforced by its founding membership of the euro in 2002, which carried great political and institutional benefit.

It was easy for the population to buy into European identity, not least since the benefits were obvious. 'In the 1970s, Madrid was like Bogotá or Lima,' notes Escolano. 'By the 2000s, it was like Amsterdam.'[68] European identity was seen, he says, as 'spectacularly popular', a common feature of politics, even in the lunatic fringe.

Not only did Europe offer clear and 'irreversible' advantages, rules and parameters, but it also provided Madrid with an excuse of the 'Brussels made us do it' variety, not least since EU decisions are often considered more reasonable than state ones. 'Like Mexico and NAFTA, the EU is very demanding, but if you consider reforms as being critical to success, then this is very necessary,' says Martínez Rico.

There are other advantages to this openness, not least the interests redeveloped in Latin America. During the 1990s and 2000s, Spanish firms were very active in establishing partnerships and scooping up privatisation opportunities in Latin America. Since then, the flows of capital and talent have shifted to be as much inwards as outwards.

In the hundred years until 1950, approximately 3.5 million Spaniards went to Latin America, driven by poverty at home and attracted by opportunity. As Spain's own population changes and ages, today the flows are in reverse. Incessant problems in Latin American economies – notably Argentina and Venezuela – have driven up emigration.[69] At the start of 2022, there were an estimated 1.8 million Latin American immigrants in Spain, with Colombians, Argentinians, Bolivians and Peruvians representing the main groups.[70] About 20 per cent of Madrid's population of 3.5 million were born in Latin America, though the figure may be higher given that about a quarter of Latin American migration to Spain may be illegal.[71]

The Latin American community has easily integrated given the high level of cultural coincidence.

Spain is short of labour despite having one of the highest unemployment rates in the EU, touching 13 per cent at the start of 2022. Spaniards apparently prefer not to take menial work as labourers or waiters. These shortages are projected to worsen as Spain's population declines from forty-seven million to thirty-three million by 2100.[72]

The immigrant profile has also changed with rich Mexicans, Colombians and Venezuelans among those seeking 'golden visas' to stay in Spain. Such visas, and a two-year period of residency for citizenship (as opposed to the usual ten), are issued in return for investing €500 000 in property.[73] As Gabriel Elorriaga puts it, this aspect of globalisation has been 'like Spain winning the lottery'.[74]

Translating this experience for others

The general conclusions about Spain's transition from poverty to prosperity and dictatorship to democracy centre on the importance of institutions in building a functional and inclusive model, where the differences between the parties are marginal to the extent that they affect the standard of living. Indeed, it is estimated that the differences between the conservatives and socialists amount to a gap of just 5 per cent in terms of the state's economic share. Most are of the view that state-building must be an organic and ongoing process, where unity and trust are by-products of democracy and essential to sustainable success, and where policies need to aim to improve social cohesion and productivity. In this, functional politics depends on maintaining relations as adversaries, not enemies, and institutional effectiveness is, as highlighted above, imperative.

The presence of institutionalised freedoms – of association, media and expression – parliamentary oversight and an independent judiciary are all crucial to creating a secure and safe environment conducive to realising the potential of individuals. Of course, consensus on these issues, while necessary to build a democracy that can compete on equal terms internationally, is not in and of itself enough. It has to be matched by policy, and that has to be measured by delivery for an inclusive mindset.

The key lessons of Spain for developing countries lie in foreign policy and its developmental impact.

The first lesson is for outsiders. The prevailing political mood for many in Britain in the 1930s was that dictatorships were not necessarily a bad thing, especially for foreigners.[75] Hence Franco's relatively sympathetic reception both during and after the Second World War. The same outlook – as expressed in the 'benign dictator' thesis – is present in contemporary corners of Africa, despite the overwhelming preference of Africans for democracy, and the comparatively poor record of authoritarians in delivering sustained economic results.

A second lesson is the need for insiders to use foreign affairs to national development advantage, rather than employing it as a tool to attempt to change the world.

Franco saw Europe (and indeed much of the world) as a threat, which his followers described in terms of a 'democratic-masonic-communist conspiracy' in which a supranational Europe was the thin end of a socialist wedge, explaining his government's autarkic and mercantilist worldview. Despite this, in 1962, the Spanish government formally applied to the EEC to request negotiations for an association agreement with the potential of becoming full integration in due time. These negotiations went on for eight years, until the signature of a preferential trade agreement (much along the lines signed earlier with Morocco and Tunisia) in June 1970.

Over time, as Spain's fortunes changed within Europe, and it shifted from being a sick dependant to fellow traveller, Madrid was able to play a greater role in deepening integration and resolving difficult issues, including the unification of the two Germanys. The more Spain invested in the European project, the more it was able to extract from the process in different ways.

This approach hinges, however, on seeing the world as an opportunity rather than a threat, and on gearing foreign policy to achievable domestic needs, focused less on grand theories of political conspiracy and wizardry than on an honest assessment of realities.

At a regional level, this requires clear benefits to membership, legally binding and irreversible commitments, and institutional effectiveness. Spain illustrates the value of regional integration – though with the caveat that regional association carries costs as well as benefits. It is important, too, for the leader of the process 'not to be the old colonial power, given the levels of resentment,' observes Román Escolano (or the United States, in Latin America, for much the same reason, which explains resistance to the so-called Washington Consensus programmes of economic stabilisation and reform).

This is far from what the Southern Common Market, known by the Spanish acronym Mercosur, provides for Latin America, for example. As an intergovernmental rather than a supranational organisation, and absent both the trust and integration of Europe, it lacks the attraction. 'Argentinians don't want to be Brazilians, and vice versa,' says Escolano. 'They don't trust each other.'

All this (and more) demands a commitment to all aspects of openness. For example, Africa, and especially South Africa, is a mass exporter of capital and talent, somewhat like Latin America. That is a choice on the part of the government as least as much as it is a choice for those leaving. Addressing the reasons for the departure of capital and skills is more essential than pleading for their return.

A last pointer: it is critical not to mythologise and demonise the past, since that prevents subsequent governments from taking the best out of them, while leaving the worst aspects behind. In this regard, there were two distinct periods to Franco's regime, as Gabriel Elorriaga suggests: that before 1953, which was characterised by political repression and relatively low growth (of 'just' 2.9 per cent), and that after 1953 and the start of international opening, where growth averaged over 6 per cent and political liberalisation occurred steadily if slowly. This explains why many of the same economic basics have been maintained.

In the same way, it is difficult to compare South Africa of the 1980s with South Africa of the 1950s; to reject these differences would be to commit national economic suicide. Adolfo Suárez, a leading member of the Francoist government, was appointed to steer the country to democracy, just as F.W. de Klerk was in South Africa. Madrid's airport was renamed in 2014 to honour Suárez.

In a contemporary world, Spain's experience also suggests that foreign policy should be geared less to vague goals about changing the world, than directed at changing national fortunes based on deepening political, trade, capital and security integration.

Conclusion: Challenges come and change, but never go

The Basque town of Guernica nestles in a green valley, its surrounding forested hills capped by mist even in August. Its peace belies a terrible history: the first use of strategic 'area' bombing against a civilian population. On 26 April 1937, the German Condor Legion attacked Guernica, causing (officially) 1 654 deaths and destroying much of the town of 6 000 inhabitants. As Franco's northern campaign took hold, denying the Republicans access to local economic riches and supply lines to France, the region's towns became famous sites of battle and sacrifice: Oviedo, Pamplona, Burgos, Bilbao, Santander and Irun among them.

Guernica might live on in infamy because of Picasso's eponymous painting, but it pales in comparison to what followed in Europe within a decade. In Hamburg, for instance, 40 000 lost their lives in a single Allied air raid on Germany in July 1943, while the American strike on Tokyo on 10 March 1945 resulted in 100 000 casualties, greater than even the atomic bombs dropped on Hiroshima (80 000) and Nagasaki (40 000) that August.

And yet the Spanish Civil War continues to capture the popular, romantic imagination in a way, for instance, the Greek Civil War of the late 1940s has not. Foreign correspondents remain beguiled and seduced by its struggles. 'The architects of Spain's new democracy resolved to look squarely ahead, granting amnesty to those liable for crimes dating back decades,' wrote one journalist for *TIME*. 'But for millions of Spaniards the past never relinquished its grip.'[76]

'History to the defeated may say Alas but cannot help or pardon,' wrote W.H. Auden of Spain in 1937. And yet, the Spanish Civil War is one of the few cases where the losers come out better than the victors. This may be down to the talents of the authors, it may be down to a moral case to be made about the vicissitudes of various (or least worst) versions of totalitarianism, and it links to Franco's political ideology in a Europe to be engulfed shortly by total war in the defence against fascism.

Robert Hale Merriman is synonymous with the heroic anti-fascist struggle. According to his wife, Merriman was convinced that defeating the fascists in Spain and then Germany would prevent a second world war. Born in California, the son of a lumberjack and a friend of the physicist J. Robert Oppenheimer, Merriman was a doctoral student in economics at the University of California, Berkeley, before heading off to Moscow on a scholarship, fascinated by Marxism–Leninism. Upon his return to Berkeley, with some rudimentary university military training, he was made captain and chosen to lead the Abraham Lincoln Battalion of the International Brigades in Spain. He first saw action at the Battle of Jarama south-east of Madrid in February 1937, where the Republicans managed to stop Franco's advance, which aimed to sever the Madrid–Valencia road and cut off the capital to the south and east. The Lincolns suffered appalling casualties at Jarama and in their next actions in Brunete (in July 1937) and in Teruel, where Merriman was captured by Nationalist forces and executed on 2 April 1938.

The world moves on. Today Jarama is known for its motor-racing circuit, which hosted the Spanish Grand Prix nine times between 1968 and 1981, to the north of the 1937 battlefield. Even so, now, more than three generations after the end of the war, the so-called Pact of Forgetting – the political decision by both leftist and rightist parties of Spain to avoid directly confronting the legacy of Francoism after Franco's death – has partly unravelled.

Franco was buried in 1975 in the Valle de los Caídos, his remains lodged in a massive transept at the end of a long granite crypt, located directly beneath the giant cross outside. Following a lengthy legal battle, with the country divided on political grounds and against his family's wishes, his remains were exhumed in 2019 on the basis that he had no place in the memorial since he had not fallen in the war. They were reinterred at the obscure Mingorrubio Cemetery north-west of Madrid. Franco's hand-picked successor, Admiral-General Luis Carrero Blanco, rests nearby. He was killed in a car bomb in Madrid in December 1973 just six months after being appointed by Franco as prime minister.

It is estimated that one in five of the 35 000 volunteers in the International Brigades became, in Hemingway's words, 'part of the earth of Spain', in what today is seen as a noble and tragically idealistic struggle. And yet the cultivation of extremes of fear and hatred stripped their opponents – on the left and right – of their humanity, transforming them from Nationalists into traitors, fuelling the widespread atrocities and deep wounds synonymous with the Spanish Civil War.[77]

The pact to forget was broken – or rebalanced – by the Historical Memory Law of 2007, which formally condemns repressions of the Franco regime and gives rights to victims of the civil war. This demonstrated that the wounds remained open, or at least that there was political advantage in their reopening.

Homage to Catalonia, Orwell's personal account of his experiences as a volunteer for the Republicans in the war, was published in 1938. Unlike other foreign leftists, Orwell and his wife did not join the International Brigades but instead enlisted in the POUM. His book records the drudgery of the daily life of a soldier and his disenchantment with political infighting among the left and the culture of totalitarianism. Orwell and his circle, which included Willy Brandt, were the subjects of a later surveillance operation by Stalin's secret police.

Amid the rearward glances, Spain faces different contemporary political challenges, not least in the fragmentation of the two main parties, with populist poles at either end of the spectrum, and a resultant stalemated parliament. As Josep Piqué, who served consecutively as minister of industry and energy, foreign affairs, and science and technology between 1996 and 2003, notes in this context: 'We need to educate new generations about our old history; otherwise they could forget our starting point and forget about democracy as a value and how freedoms have been won, and forget how democracy has enemies inside and outside.'

Franco's Spain was not wrong or bad because it was rightist. It was wrong because it was authoritarian. While his victory ended the chaos of 130 years, and thus proved (whatever the contemporary revisionism) popular, not least because of his growth record, this was at the cost of human liberties. It also proved to have limits in what it could achieve in terms of economic progress, because of its political character.

Herein lies the most important lesson of all. 'The Spain of today has nothing to do with the Spain of the 1970s,' reflects Piqué. Or, as Felipe González puts it: 'We have to decide whether we want to be sons of democracy, or grandsons of Franco.' Spain's success lies fundamentally in its economic continuity and constant reform, and its political break with the past. In stark contrast to the conditions that produced the civil war, and the shocking effects of Franco's regime, Spain's great strength has rested in its unity, gradualism and social cohesion.

A Study in Leadership

'The fight is here; I need ammunition, not a ride.'
– Ukrainian president Volodymyr Zelenskyy, 25 February 2022

'Modern Ukraine was entirely and fully created by Russia.'
– Russian president Vladimir Putin, 21 February 2022

ON paper, Ukraine should have had no chance militarily against Russia. As Moscow obviously calculated, it should have capitulated quickly, its fleeing leadership making way for a more pliant, Russian-selected alternative in Kyiv. A population of 44 million against 144 million; an active-duty military of 250 000 (with 900 000 reserves) against one million (with two million in reserve); a nuclear arsenal of zero versus nearly 6 000 warheads; a landmass of 600 000 square kilometres compared to 17 million square kilometres; a GDP of $155 billion versus $1.5 trillion.

Clearly, military capability – like governance – comprises much more than power in statistics. It relies on the inner strengths of motivation, training, ability to integrate and use technology, strategy, logistics, leadership, and tactics. While international assistance has undoubtedly helped the Ukrainians defend their territory against the larger invader, it is how these weapons have been used and how hard the Ukrainians have fought with them that has made the difference.

In many respects, Ukraine's is a much better army because it has learnt how to use its local and foreign assets well. It has had to adapt quickly in the face of fighting for its immediate survival in its own territory. It has cultivated and harnessed international assistance, knowing exactly what it needs and what it wants to do with this help, in stark contrast to most countries that receive aid by simply playing the 'helpless' card. And it has used the time since 2014 – when Vladimir Putin tried to teach Kyiv a lesson following the February 2014 Maidan Revolution that evicted pro-Russian Ukrainian president Viktor Yanukovych from office, by invading and seizing chunks of the east and the Crimean Peninsula – to get this formula right.

Ukraine's performance has been driven by an existentialist imperative. But its long-term success, including whether it can develop from an exclusive to an inclusive economy and sustain itself in a hostile region, will depend on its ability to carry out institutional reform and transform its political economy. This fight against corruption and for competition as a driver of success has lessons for others, particularly those states transforming from one economic system to another and those, too, emerging from conflict.

Leadership matters

This war is personal.

In May 2022, the walk up the hill to the Presidential Office in central Kyiv from Maidan Square was lined with black-and-white photographs of soldiers who had lost their lives in defence of Ukraine since the Russian invasion began on Thursday 24 February 2022. The landings on the grand marble staircase in the governor's offices in Lviv were similarly dotted with pictures of the families of servicemen and women who had died defending their territory. If you missed these and similar photographic collages elsewhere in Kyiv and its satellite suburbs, you could not miss the thousands of 'Czech hedgehogs' (static anti-tank barricades); military and police checkpoints; sandbagged bunkers, shopfronts and metro stations; and burnt-out tanks and other detritus of war lining the Russian route into Kyiv.

They're a sombre reminder of the human cost of war and the pain and suffering of those dealing with the aftermath.

On the Ukrainian side, President Volodymyr Oleksandrovych Zelenskyy has epitomised Ukrainian resistance to Russian aggression. He represents a deep well of patriotism derived from thousands of years of history and today swelled by Russia's actions. There is not one Ukrainian, no matter their political persuasion, that is unaffected, whether they be refugees from Kharkiv or Mariupol, which have been devastated under Russian bombardment, or citizens of Kyiv, Odesa, Kherson or Lviv, cities that have become globally familiar because of the war. Tears and anger are close to the surface. Twenty-three-year-old Tanya is a guide at the Holodomor-Genocide Museum in the capital. A French and English university graduate, she is originally from a town close to Odesa, where her mother and brother still live. 'I am sad,' she says in response to the lack of sympathy expressed internationally to Ukraine's plight, before correcting herself, choking back the tears, 'I am angry. Again, they don't remember Ukraine,' she says, referring to the *Holodomor*, or Great Famine, a man-made famine engineered by Stalin in Soviet Ukraine from 1932 to 1933 that killed more than 10 per cent of the population. Oleksandr Feldman is, he emphasises, a 'Jewish-Ukrainian' businessman-turned-MP who started an ecopark for breeding endangered species in his native Kharkiv. Tears roll down his cheeks as he describes how a hundred animals were indiscriminately killed in the Russian advance.

Ukrainians see this as just the latest in a centuries-old attempt to subjugate their culture, language and independence. 'There is no doubt, Putin's ambition was to get Ukraine under a Russian flag, based on his conviction that there was no such thing as Ukrainian and no such people as Ukrainians,' says Dr Hryhoriy Nemyria of the Foreign Relations Committee in the Verkhovna Rada (Ukrainian parliament). For Russia and Vladimir Putin, this is a war to return Ukraine to a Soviet colony, something 'Ukrainians will never allow to happen,' says former prime minister Yulia Tymoshenko.[78]

The invasion of Ukraine – in 2014 as in 2022 – was justified by Moscow in terms of the protection of the Russian nation and its interests, as an assertion of Russia's historical role and as a reminder of the deep, cultural ties between the two countries. 'I said that Russians and Ukrainians were one people, a single whole,' said Putin in 2020, apparently intent on bringing an increasingly westward-looking Ukraine back into Russia's sphere of influence.[79]

While this should not excuse Putin's behaviour, and Russia's rape of Ukraine, it does help explain it.

The Russian president had become increasingly preoccupied with Ukraine and obsessed with putting right the collapse of the Soviet Union, an event that he described as one of the greatest disasters of modern history, thereby disregarding Ukraine as an independent country and Ukrainians as a separate people.

When Putin justified the invasion in February 2022, it was the West, he said, that had created the 'fundamental threats' to Russia that prompted him to attack Ukraine, and it was the West, which he caricatured as an 'empire of lies', that Russia would seek to humble in the ensuing war. After the Cold War, they 'tried to crush us, beat us down and finish us off,' he said of the West. 'We remember that and will never forget it.'[80] It was no coincidence that the 2022 invasion was launched the day after Defender of the Fatherland Day in Russia, and in the centenary of the founding of the Soviet Union.

And yet history cuts both ways. Ukraine's memory of the Soviet Union is far from warm and fuzzy. A peasant revolt across Ukraine against the Bolsheviks, which began in 1917 and was put down in 1921, caused Stalin to fear the power of the combination of Ukrainian nationalism and its peasantry. Both therefore had to be destroyed. Stalin also needed Ukrainian grain to feed Russian workers and the Red Army.[81] It is estimated that as many as ten million Ukrainians died in two engineered famines. The first, in 1921/22, the result of food confiscation, cost half a million lives; the second, the *Holodomor* (meaning 'death by starvation'), ten years later, killed anywhere between four and ten million.

The National Museum of the Holodomor-Genocide in Kyiv offers insight into Ukraine's sense of identity and cause for independence. A hauntingly simple statue of a young girl holding a stalk of wheat surrounded by twelve milling wheels is a stark reminder of the cost of the Russia-dominated Soviet Union's arrogance and the depth of Ukrainian passion in the current fight. Some historians say the *Holodomor* was carried out by Stalin to eliminate the Ukrainian independence movement. Others contend it was because of a poor crop due to the inefficiencies of Soviet collectivisation. All agree that the consequences were disastrous. And, either way, it is an indication of the depth of emotion behind today's war. With thousands of civilians killed since February 2022, destruction wrought countrywide, and evidence of widespread atrocities, there was no going back.

Ukraine has historically exhibited a powerful sense of its own national identity.

Kyiv was the centre of the Kievan Rus', the first East Slavic state founded in the ninth century, for 400 years until the Mongol invasions of the thirteenth century. Ukraine again formed an independent state in the mid-seventeenth century, and there was a resurgence of Ukrainian national self-assertiveness in the nineteenth century. A sense of nationalism was prominent during both the formative period of the Soviet Union and the Second World War. It re-emerged once more in the 1950s until a crackdown by the Soviet authorities. Mikhail Gorbachev's *perestroika* allowed the political space for another re-emergence of Ukrainian nationalism, fuelled by the 1986 Chernobyl nuclear disaster, the celebration of the Millennium of Christianity in Ukraine in 1988, and the eventual implosion of the socialist Eastern bloc. 'Nationalism has now become an intense driving force in the Ukrainian political debate, as it is in some other Soviet Republics,' noted academic and later High Court judge Matthew Palmer in the *Yale Journal of International Law* in 1991. 'It springs from a deeply felt, historically rooted desire that Ukrainians should govern Ukraine.'[82]

Colonial attitudes towards Ukraine have been constant throughout history, as Yale historian Timothy Snyder reminds us in terms of the aim of Nazi rule:

> As you will all know, the American Frontier Empire was built largely by slave labour. As we don't always remember, it was precisely that model of frontier colonialism of a frontier empire built by slave labour that was admired by Adolf Hitler. When Adolf Hitler spoke about the United States it was generally, before the war at least, with admiration. And it was a question for Hitler who will the racial inferiors be, who will the slaves be in the German eastern empire? And the answer that he gave, both in *Mein Kampf* and in the second book and in practice in the invasion of 1941, the answer was 'the Ukrainians'. The Ukrainians were to be at the centre of the project of colonisation and enslavement. The Ukrainians were to be treated as Afrikaner or as Neger. This word was very often used, as those of you who read German documents from the war will know. By analogy with the United States the idea was to create a slavery driven exterminatory colonial regime in Eastern Europe [and] the centre was going to be Ukraine.[83]

Nearly four centuries of Russian imperialism came to an end in 1991 with Ukraine's independence. But Ukraine's comparative fighting performance is founded in a sense of cultural identity and unity forged over centuries and not decades, notes Serhiy Leshchenko, an advisor to Zelenskyy's chief of staff. 'Ukraine was created centuries earlier than Russia,' he says. 'It has a different culture, different church and political culture. It respects human rights and minorities. It is a democracy, with six presidents since 1991. And ask any Ukrainian, and they identify as anything now but Russian.' One measure of the difference, he smiles, is that 'Ukraine is perhaps the only place where soldiers pay bribes to join the army if they are not accepted.'

This explains why, 'for us, for Ukrainians, there is only one option, to fight – or cease to exist,' says Ivanna Klympush-Tsintsadze, an MP and the former deputy prime minister for European integration. 'Russia denies the very fact that we exist, that we have our own language, our rights, and our territorial integrity.'

The war between Ukraine and Russia also encompasses a battle of ideas, between Western liberalism that promotes individual human rights and a 'hybrid' model that stresses collective over individual rights, the latter most aptly depicted by China.

A battle of ideas

As Polish-American journalist and historian Anne Applebaum argues, Putin's actions are driven by his aim to make democracy fail, and not just in Ukraine. While she says that the Russian leader is less a nationalist than an 'imperial nostalgist', she believes his motives for crushing Ukraine stem from his experiences in Dresden in East Germany, where he endured the fall of the Berlin Wall in November 1989. 'For KGB operatives, this was not a time of rejoicing, but rather a lesson about the nature of street movements and the power of rhetoric: democratic rhetoric, anti-authoritarian rhetoric, anti-totalitarian rhetoric.'[84] In this way, this is not Russia's war but Putin's, a war thus as personal as it is geo-political.

To keep such dangerous ideas from spreading, Russia had to 'maintain careful control over the life of the nation,' writes Applebaum. 'Markets cannot be genuinely open; elections cannot be unpredictable; dissent must be carefully "managed" through legal pressure, public propaganda, and, if necessary, targeted violence.'

In 1917, the year of the Bolshevik Revolution, President Woodrow Wilson spoke of 'making the world safe for democracy'. A little over a hundred years later, Putin and Chinese president Xi Jinping seemed determined to make the world safe for autocracy. 'Both Putin and Xi have also made it clear they believe that America's ultimate goal is to overthrow the Russian and Chinese governments, and that local pro-democracy forces are America's Trojan horse,' writes journalist Gideon Rachman.[85]

Such a worldview may well encourage and accelerate democratic regression and feed authoritarianism elsewhere, including across the African continent, with long-term negative consequences for human rights and human development. While elites might be pleased at the prospect of reducing domestic political competition, this new world order (through disorder in large measure) is unlikely to be in Africa's overall interest given the clear longstanding empirical correlation on the continent between democratic standards and developmental outcomes.

Still, Putin's model is attractive to these elites.

It offers the prospect of rapid wealth accumulation for a select few (with the 'big man' at the top of the billionaire pile, as with Putin) and of never losing power without legal limits to personal authority and state control over all checks and balances, including the media. This is foreign to Western countries, no matter the personal appeal to some leaders. Imagine, as Applebaum notes, 'an American president who controlled not only the executive branch – including the FBI, CIA, and NSA – but also Congress and the judiciary; *The New York Times*, *The Wall Street Journal*, *The Dallas Morning News*, and all of the other newspapers; and all major businesses, including Exxon, Apple, Google, and General Motors.'

In response to their own insecurity, 'instead of democracy,' writes Applebaum, Putin and his ilk 'promote autocracy; instead of unity, they try constantly to create division; instead of open societies, they promote xenophobia. Instead of letting people hope for something better, they promote nihilism and cynicism.'

Hence the decision to again invade Ukraine, to collapse its democracy and its economy, strain Western institutions to breaking point, and support authoritarians elsewhere from Syria to Sudan, all the while shrinking American influence. To parody Francis Fukuyama's line on the end of the Cold War, it's the return of history. But it's a history that is being rewritten at great risk and at huge cost. For those sympathetic to the Russian view, it presumes that once Ukraine's mooted membership of NATO is dealt with to Russia's satisfaction, Putin's imperial ambition will be slaked.

Ukrainians have answered the question about their preference for democracy clearly, not just in resisting a Russian candidate in the 2004 Orange Revolution, and again in ejecting Yanukovych from office in 2014, but also in their support for President Zelenskyy's path. His public approval rating was at 94 per cent three months into the war, up from the 73 per cent majority he earned in the 2019 election.[86]

But, as is well known, democracy – like military power – is more than an election or any other indicator of popular support. Rather it involves a system of values and trust, the ability of the state to provide services, and a political economy that shapes economic options for its citizens.

Former president Viktor Yushchenko embodies the difficult choices made by Ukraine to get it this far along the reform path. He faced down Moscow's man, then prime minister Yanukovych, in the 2004 election. Following widespread electoral fraud in favour of Yanukovych, the Supreme Court of Ukraine called for an election run-off, which Yushchenko won to become the third president of Ukraine. During the campaign, Yushchenko survived an assassination attempt when he was poisoned with dioxin. As a consequence, he suffered severe facial disfigurement.

'In the autumn of 2004, the Ukrainian nation aspired to achieve its full-fledged independence, similar to the concept of "returning home",' Yushchenko recalls. 'Back then, Putin and Yanukovych thought that Ukraine could be treated like Belarus and could not leave the Russian fold. But I disagreed.' His fight was not, as now, against Russians, but rather against Russian influence and Russian corruption, and 'our slavery in Russia's greatest colony'. 'We had two divergent views, between Ukraine's path to Europe, which we had aspired to for more than a century, and remaining within the Russian fold, the *Russkiy mir*.' Yushchenko's Ukraine chose then the European path, a choice that is now clearer than ever in its benefits.

Yulia Tymoshenko, who served as prime minister under Yushchenko, says that Ukraine's struggle for independence over hundreds of years has been a 'sacred fight for our people'. So far the only woman to serve as prime minister of Ukraine, Tymoshenko finished second in the 2010 presidential election, losing to Yanukovych by 3.5 percentage points. Shortly after the election, she faced state prosecution for what were seen as politically motivated charges and was imprisoned, though she was later cleared by the Supreme Court of Ukraine following the Maidan Revolution that saw off Yanukovych in February 2014. She ran in the 2014 presidential election but again finished second, this time to Petro Poroshenko.

'The period of seventy years in the Soviet Union was a period of colonisation, when Russia tried to eliminate our national identity, to hijack our cultural identity,' says Tymoshenko today. The Orange Revolution, of which she was among the leadership, was 'just the beginning'. Now, she adds, 'while we were always considered a country divided in the East and West, six months of war eliminated this.' Elected to parliament in 2019, she leads her party, Batkivshchyna, which is strongly committed to Ukrainian membership of both the EU and NATO. Although in opposition, she observes that since the Russian invasion, 'we don't have an opposition. We are in unity.' This 'spirit', she notes, is a key reason, along with the strength of Ukraine's army, why, even though 'the war is in Ukraine, the blood is being expended by the Russians'. International assistance is another key dimension to the country's survival, she adds. Or, as her deputy Hryhoriy Nemyria puts it, 'Ukrainians are on the frontline; but we are all at war.'

This crossroads, between looking to the past association with Russia for answers and looking westwards to Europe and the future, is relevant to the manner in which Ukraine addresses its systemic challenges beyond just survival as an independent state, but as one focused on prosperity and social inclusion.

Longer-term challenges

'WORLD HELP US' reads the hand-painted sign on the sandbagged statues on Kyiv's Saint Michael's Square, fronting Ukraine's Ministry of Foreign Affairs and an exhibit of destroyed Russian military equipment. Underneath the plea are the details of the contributions of various nations and the costs of the war. It further offers 'military recruiting for all ages, genders and skill levels (to none)' for $1 200, or 40 000 hryvnia, per month.

Global support has been critical in taking the fight to Russia, but the victim card will only get Ukraine so far. In the longer term, this is a domestic struggle about democratic choices and the rule of law, about what kind of country Ukraine wants to be. Any plan to stabilise Ukraine beyond the physical war with Russia has to be rooted in the understanding that external support is fickle (just ask any Afghan) and has to tackle the highly extractive (read, corrupt) environment that has plagued Ukraine's governance, an oligopolistic structure of crony capitalism known locally as *oligarkhiya*. A failure to fight a war on this scourge, after the Russian episode is over, will only lead to further crises and missed opportunity (again, just ask any Afghan). The fight against Russia is the immediate battle; Ukraine's fight to build a just society and economy is a much longer and, in many respects, more difficult affair.

Ukraine inherited a command economy after the dissolution of the Soviet Union, one in which decisions involving production, investment, pricing and incomes are determined centrally by government. As elsewhere in the USSR, there was an emphasis on heavy industry, military and mining, rather than on producing consumer goods such as motorcars.[87]

The Ukrainian-made ZAZ Zaporozhets was meant to be the people's car, like the Beetle of West Germany or East Germany's Trabant. Between 1960 and 1994, 3.4 million Zaporozhets of various model were produced in Ukraine, the only Soviet republic outside Russia to manufacture cars. *Zaporozhets* translates into 'a Cossack of the Zaporozhian Sich', although the appearance and quality of the rear-wheel-drive supermini, with its rear air-cooled engine, lent itself to several nicknames, including *horbatyi* (hunchback), *ushastyi* (big-eared), *zapor* (constipation) and *mylnitsa* (soapbox).

ZAZ was not the only manufacturer. Several firms, including KrAZ and LuAZ, produced trucks, trolley buses and light-utility vehicles. However, with the end of the protections of the Soviet Union, aggravated by asset stripping and a lack of investment in design and technology, the bottom fell out of Ukraine's motor industry.

By 2017, the plant that made Zaporozhets produced only 1 600 cars annually, around 1 per cent of its capacity. Production has moved over to European, Korean and Chinese brands, and especially into parts manufacture. Today, western Ukraine is an integral part of Europe's vehicle industry. Nearly every car made in Germany, for example, is made with parts from Ukraine.

Most sectors faced a similar crisis at the end of the Cold War, which further necessitated the collapse of the Soviet Union. Between 1990 and 1995, industrial output along with real GDP fell by more than half, the economy contracting annually between 9.7 per cent and 22.7 per cent from 1991 to 1996, amid hyperinflation touching 10 000 per cent, high budget deficits and hardships. Approximately half of Ukrainian households lived on less than $5.50 per day, and life expectancy declined by five years.

Economic growth did not resume until 2000. By then, industrial output was at 70 per cent of pre-1990 figures, though GDP remained stuck at little over 50 per cent.[88] As elsewhere, the period of recovery has been connected to the rate of growth.

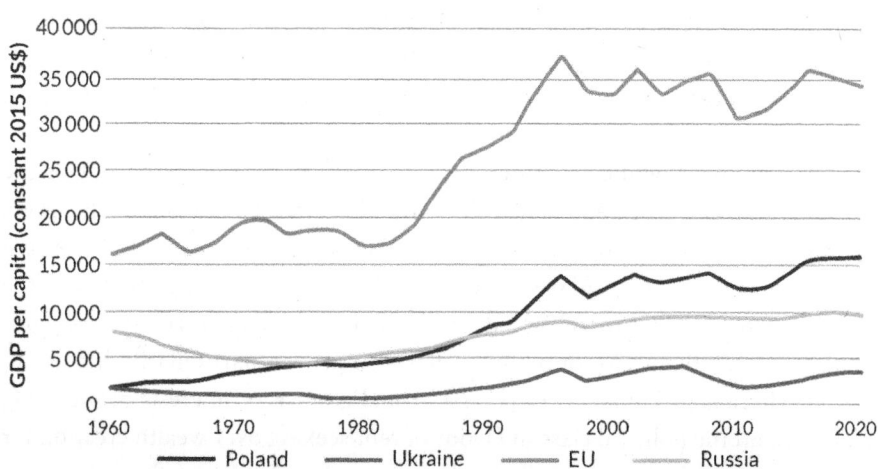

Source: World Bank, World Development Indicators

As the largest wholly European country and the fifth-largest European nation by population, it might have been expected that Ukraine would become a full member of the European and Euro-Atlantic communities via the EU, the OECD and NATO. Yet Ukraine has been a perennial underachiever, 'thanks to its geopolitical situation, historical burdens, and the mistakes made in institutional development and policy,' writes economist Pekka Sutela, formerly of the Carnegie Endowment for International Peace.[89]

The Soviet growth model relied on legacy industries dependent on cheap energy resources, commodity exports, and trade exclusively with states of the Soviet Union and the Eastern bloc. By 1990, this model obviously could not deliver the aspirations of Ukrainians. Yet the country's growth, dependent on an unsustainable mix of cheap gas from Russia and foreign borrowing, has failed to redress the economic devastation caused by the inevitable transformation of the 1990s. With an annual growth rate of just 3 per cent – what Ukraine has averaged since 1990 – it will take about fifty years to reach the current levels of income of Poland and almost a hundred years to reach the levels of Germany. This explains Ukraine's desire to join the EU, and the westward gaze of its citizens.

The path to realising its potential lies in improving foreign competition and investment. To do that, however, Ukraine must clean up an economy built on a false foundation: cheap gas from Russia. In 2008, for example, the price paid by Ukraine for gas was still less than half of that paid by Western European countries. To clean up its economy, Ukraine must address the basics of institutions and the politics that drive administration and policy. Power structures and networks inherited from the Soviet economy persist and have proven resilient to change. Francis Fukuyama uses Ukraine as one example of how regime change from an authoritarian to a democratic government will not lead to success without 'a long, costly, laborious, and difficult process of institution building'.[90] These institutional structures, as part of the process of moving away from injustice and corruption, are necessary to help secure private wealth and investment.

As mentioned, while Ukraine's politics might have progressed out of the Soviet system, its economic system has not. This system grew out of the crony capitalism established in the wake of the Soviet collapse, where Soviet-era apparatchiks gained control over state assets. 'It is the underlying obstacle to the development of fully functioning democratic institutions and rule of law,' concludes one Chatham House report. It has also proven particularly difficult to dislodge because its practice 'rests on a firm alignment of interests between big business and the political class in favour of rent seeking over wealth creation for the public good'. It has also created a class of beneficiaries across the state sector. This is particularly the case in the banking, energy, transport, media and healthcare sectors. Because of the extent of these vested interests, the system has proven resistant to political reforms.[91]

As in Russia, the rise of the Ukrainian oligarchs was connected to the processes of privatisation of state-owned assets after the collapse of the Soviet Union. Political connections and access to initial investment capital assisted a small number to seize control of former public assets. Consequently, by 2021 the top 100 wealthiest businesspeople in Ukraine controlled assets of around $44.5 billion, according to Forbes, little under one-third of Ukraine's GDP.

The concentration of wealth and power in the economy has been matched by concerns over the overwhelming focus of power in the executive at the core of this network of interests, with competitive party politics providing a facade of legitimacy to what has been a corrupt governance system.[92] When corruption and political access, rather than drivers of efficiency, investment and competition, become the principal reasons for economic success, the system becomes a cost to overall growth and a drag on welfare. Ukraine's ranking on Transparency International's Corruption Perceptions Index tells this story.

Ukraine ranked 116th out of 180 in 2022, when nearly one-quarter of the population said that they had paid a bribe for public services in the last twelve months.[93] Similarly, the Heritage Foundation's 2022 Index of Economic Freedom ranked Ukraine 130th out of 177, placing it 44th out of 45 countries in the Europe region, above only Belarus (Russia was 113th, one place behind South Africa). While Ukraine has recorded an impressive six-point overall gain in economic freedom since 2017, it is still in the middle ranks of the 'mostly unfree' countries, and its overall score is below the regional and world averages.[94] On governance, Ukraine was 81st out of 137 on the World Economic Forum's Global Competitiveness Index for 2018, with notable challenges in inflation, corruption, tax competitiveness and policy instability.[95]

The World Bank's Worldwide Governance Indicators project reports aggregate and individual governance indicators for over 200 countries and territories over the period from 1996 to 2021, for six dimensions of governance: voice and accountability, political stability and absence of violence/terrorism, government effectiveness, regulatory quality, rule of law, and control of corruption.[96] In each of these areas, apart from political stability, there has been steady improvement in Ukraine's scores since 2011, though from an admittedly low base.

Pavlo Sheremeta, Ukraine's former minister of economic development and trade, says that 'before the war, there were many challenges in Ukraine, the most important of which is that the economy was still unfree.' As a consequence of 'the communist heritage, we lack free entrepreneurship and competitive markets. But the core problem,' he smiles, 'is that the teachers who are teaching me are still teaching today.'

Sheremeta says it is therefore imperative that, once the war is over, Zelenskyy look past the deep well of patriotism that he has filled and confront the governance challenges that have long bedevilled post-Soviet Ukraine. This includes dismantling the 'closed' oligarchic system, which will require 'liberal decisions' on the restrictive labour code (instituted in 1971), the tax regime and privatisation, the latter 'which would help business relocation'. Currently, 'the only talk is about how to extract more financing from entrepreneurs,' he laments.

Sheremeta fears that, on the one hand, the war with Russia is making Ukraine 'complacent'. On the other hand, post-war Ukrainian society is likely to 'be much less tolerant than before,' he says. His hope is that this will lead to a process of reform that will be assisted by European integration 'requiring conditionalities'.[97]

Examples of reform

While the economy has failed to reform, other sectors have succeeded. Agriculture stands out among Ukraine's sector transformations of the last three decades, and not just because of its legendary rich soil. The relative absence of the main financial services groups and a focus on land reform has limited the ambitions of some of the influential oligarchs, who have sought riches elsewhere, in mining and services.

Ukraine is one of the largest global suppliers of sunflower oil, corn and wheat, its exports comprising 46 per cent of all sunflower oil, 12 per cent of all corn and 9 per cent of all wheat exports in the world. Its record-breaking grain harvest in 2021 produced 107 million tonnes of commodities. By 2022, 50 million tonnes of agricultural products were exported on average from Ukraine annually, peaking at 65 million tonnes, to more than 400 million people worldwide.[98]

Its economic significance lies in crop production, which accounts for around two-thirds of all production. But it's the rate of growth that has been most spectacular, often papering over other deficiencies in the Ukrainian economy in the process.

Agriculture accounts for about 10 per cent of Ukraine's GDP, a rate several times higher than other major European producers. It possesses the second-largest acreage of farmland in Europe (after Russia), with a total of 41.5 million hectares of agricultural land (about 70 per cent of the total area of the country), of which arable land accounts for over 32 million hectares.

In 2000, Ukraine produced 23.8 million tonnes of grain.[99] In 2013, this figure rose to 63 million tonnes. The value of Ukraine's agricultural and food exports increased from $4.3 billion in 2005 to $17.9 billion in 2012, and $28 billion in 2021. Between 2005 and 2012 alone, the export of food and agricultural products increased by 315 per cent, the sector accounting, pre-war, for 41 per cent of Ukraine's total exports.[100]

Its international markets are astounding. Pre-war, Lebanon was dependent on Ukraine for nearly 80 per cent of its wheat supply, Pakistan for 46 per cent, Libya 44 per cent, Tunisia 42 per cent, Ethiopia 26 per cent, Egypt and Indonesia for around 25 per cent, and Turkey for 18 per cent. China got more than half its corn from Ukraine, while Turkey got a third. The twenty-seven member states of the EU received nearly two-thirds of their sunflower oil supplies from Ukraine, China 59 per cent and India 75 per cent.

An increase in investment led to an increase in yields, although these remained below the levels of market leaders. Ukrainian maize yields, for example, went up from 2.5 tonnes per hectare in 1999 to 3.8 tonnes per hectare by 2002 (when the European average was 9.1); sunflowers from 0.9 to 1.2 (1.6); wheat from 2.3 to 3.0 (5.8); and milk from 2.36 kilograms per cow to 2.82 kilograms per cow (6.1). By 2021, Ukrainian maize and wheat yields were at 7.9 tonnes per hectare and 4.5 tonnes per hectare respectively.[101]

Part of the reason lies in the benefits of a favourable climate and good-quality soil. Highly fertile chernozem (or black soil) covers half the country. In the absence of land reform and given the prohibition on the sale of land to private owners, the growth of the agricultural sector has rested on improvements in productivity along with a concentration of production within very large agricultural holdings, known locally as agroholdings, characterised by large-scale intensive farming. The top 100 holdings control over 30 per cent of all the land (6.7 million hectares) farmed by the nearly 50 000 agricultural companies.[102] There are as many as four million unregistered small farms cultivating the remainder, though their rates of production are much lower given a lack of access to state subsidies or bank finance.

Absent the involvement of the oligarchs, the grain-producing sector followed a more natural, free-market-like development course, where stronger farmers started renting more and more land from their neighbours to become substantial-sized farmers. 'With the very high yield potential plus double cropping, you do not need more than 500 hectares for a farming business to start doing well and expand by investing in the latest technology available,' notes one African farming specialist with knowledge of the Ukrainian market. 'A critical mass of these farmers will also excite service and equipment providers, which is necessary in the development process of such an industry.' This environment, coupled with the presence of foreign investors, ensured that Ukrainian agriculture took off.

In 2017, the IMF signalled that ending the moratorium on the sale of agricultural land would be conditional for its financial support. Faced with a popular backlash against concentrated ownership of land, including by foreign entities, the government was forced to retreat. It ultimately proposed a version of the law that favoured the interests of the operators of small farms (up to 100 hectares) over the biggest companies. This was signed into law by President Zelenskyy.

The sale of this land is expected to lead to further consolidation and improvements in yields, as the management of multiple leaseholds by the larger conglomerates has proven costly and time-consuming. This is not the only change required, says Gennadiy Chyzhykov, president of the Ukrainian Chamber of Commerce. The increase in transportation costs because of the war with Russia, where land routes are three times more expensive than those via sea, has focused attention on the need to beneficiate and produce higher-value goods, thus reducing the transportation-cost component as a percentage of the sale price.

The war may yet have one positive effect: any slowdown of reforms aimed at dealing with monopolies, reducing the influence of oligarchs, reducing corruption and improving business conditions is likely to be strongly criticised by the majority of Ukrainians who, not least as a consequence of the war and the sacrifices made, will expect something better and different.

The inner stuffings

The military operation in September 2022 around Kharkiv, Ukraine's second-largest city, located in the north-east of the country (pre-war population 1.4 million), demonstrates just how smart the Ukrainians have become in their fight against the Russian invaders.

Ukraine's success in pushing back Russian forces in the region of Kharkiv was down, in simple terms, to a feint carried out in the southern city of Kherson (which was taken by Russian forces in the early days of the conflict to guard the supply routes to Crimea) through building up forces and pressuring the Russians amassing on the western bank of the Dnieper River. The Ukrainians' intentions were carefully telegraphed in the build-up of materiel and troops, and soon became a media focus, leading the Russians to believe that the attack would come from that direction.

Then, unexpectedly and despite a numerical disadvantage, the Ukrainians attacked the areas around Kharkiv, rapidly 'de-occupying' in less than a week an estimated 8 000 square kilometres. The US-supplied, satellite-guided High Mobility Artillery Rocket System, a light long-range multiple rocket launcher, was a critical new tool, enabling pinpoint targeting of Russian logistics, command and control, arms depots, and convoys. It quickly became a running joke that the Russian army was not just big, but long. Similarly, the fitting of US-supplied high-speed anti-radiation missiles on Ukraine's Soviet-designed MiG-29 fighter jets helped neutralise the Russian air threat, a can-do solution displaying both technological ingenuity and adaptability. The same attitude was needed when the Russian attacks shifted, in response, to targeting critical infrastructure with drones, with devastating consequences for the electricity grid in the winter months.

But the tools of war are not simply hard power and kinetic, nor are they new and entirely foreign. The battle of information and narratives has been at least as important in justifying and gathering support for the Ukrainian cause. This has had strategic impacts. For instance, pressure from the media played a big part in the relief of Odesa and the freeing of flows of Ukrainian grain.

The success of these and other ploys – both military and media – have relied on a Russian leadership unaccustomed to fighting a battle against an enemy that thought hard and fought back.

Indeed, a key lesson from the conflict is that leadership matters.

Ukraine has mobilised every asset to get through this existential crisis. President Zelenskyy's brand of leadership and language has set a Churchillian tone from the outset. But capability is evident through the ranks, as much bottom-up as top-down, and reliant on the inner stuffings of success, of education, space for entrepreneurship, the integration of technology and access to markets.

Zelenskyy's political rise is life imitating art. Although he received a degree in law from the Kyiv National Economic University, he followed his passion into acting, starring in the television show *Servant of the People*, in which he played the role of the president of Ukraine.

Zelenskyy has come to embody the fighting spirit of Ukrainians. He is the master of public relations, capable of turning a narrative on its head, as epitomised by his powerful observation to the US Congress: 'Your money is not charity. It is an investment in the global security and democracy that we handle in the most responsible way.' It's the difference between a man in combat fatigues walking the streets with his guests, engaging with his people, and a wooden Putin, seated alone at the end of a long table, maintaining a safe distance from his own advisors, never mind the rabble. Zelenskyy's personality and messaging have deliberately targeted issues that the Russians have sought to exploit, such as the 'black hole' narrative put out by Russia about the dire fate of assistance, particularly weapons, provided to Ukraine.

As the advisor to the head of the Office of the President of Ukraine, Mykhailo Podolyak, notes, the country has projected an image based on 'its internal core strength, its rapid transformation, sincerity, and its ability to understand and manage complexity'. 'Leadership allows us to have a global role and to be the subject,' he says.[103]

Zelenskyy's leadership has been enabled, too, by a high tempo of engagements, by often referencing his Jewish heritage (thus negating the supposed neo-Nazi commentary led by Putin), and by his ability to connect and tap into the swell of

Ukrainian nationalism. In a positive tautology, the more effective he has become at channelling his messages, the more united Ukraine has proven after the Russian invasion.[104] In the process, he has turned around plummeting personal rankings, jumping from just 27 per cent in December 2021 to 84 per cent twelve months later.

This does not mean Zelenskyy is without his failings. For one, members of Ukraine's parliament have signalled their increasing frustration at being overlooked, even though political differences have been swallowed in the national interest. Oversight has fallen away, with consequences, as various corruption scandals in 2022 illustrated. Several MPs have voiced criticism about how the overcentralisation of power contrasts with the need for Ukraine to develop and strengthen its institutions in line with convergence to European standards and membership. Similarly, members of civil society, including some church leaders, are upset by the president's lack of consultation. And there have been errors of judgement in foreign policy, not least in his eagerness to engage with some of the African continent's authoritarians, such as Uganda's Yoweri Museveni, undercutting his appeal to a majority of Africans who align with democratic values.

In defeat, to paraphrase Churchill's words on Field Marshal Bernard Law Montgomery, Zelenskyy has proven unbeatable. In victory, Ukraine will have to construct the governance checks and balances to ensure that he, like any other leader, does not prove to be unbearable.

Conclusion: Stopping the buck

Putin underestimated the Ukrainian will to fight and Zelenskyy's ability to lead.

This illustrates the danger of losing touch with public sentiment. Perhaps such estrangement is an inevitable consequence of being locked in the past, and in historic struggles and destiny, but it also reflects the absence of democracy – and the lack of legitimacy, sensitivity and sensibility that inevitably flows from this.

This is a warning for leaders beyond Russia. As they lose touch, governments invariably pick populist shortcuts: redistributive economics, diplomatic methods aimed at remaking the world based on historical imagination, the development of narratives inflating past glories, control of sources of power and information, and increasing alignment with like-minded authoritarians. As journalist Zoya Sheftalovich asks: 'How long will Russians continue buying into this war – a war they know Putin started, despite what their TVs might be telling them? How long will they watch videos of Ukrainian soldiers telling Russian warships to go fuck themselves in their common tongue?'[105]

The same can be asked of those Africans who buy into the rhetoric of national liberation struggles, despite the obvious failings of their governments.

In this way, Ukraine represents a clash between two political world views and systems. One is committed to liberal democracy and the expansion, however imperfect and sporadic, of open systems of government and economic interaction, the other to authoritarianism and an economy built on oligopolistic access and preferences. As was written during a visit in June 2023:

The Paradox of Choice

Moskvitch & Mercedes
Analogue and digital
Dictators and democracy
No choice, non-committal

Tatras and Teslas
Soviet and liberal
Do as he says
Literal, please not figural

Chaikas & apparatchiks
More equal than others
No right to pick
Bosses not brothers

Starvation and invasion
Tools of the dictator
Abrasion never suasion
A horrible miscalculation

Soldiers in the street
Revellers side by side
A nation back on its feet
No place now to hide

Stoicism and nationalism
Unintended by Vlad
Recognition and integration
Things going from good to bad

Destroy to liberate
But just one catch
The people have a vote
Putin's mismatch

'Today, Ukraine is at a crossroads: despite impressive success in some sectors, the foundations of the emerging new economy are still fragile, and the old economy is still having a strong negative effect on growth,' wrote the World Bank in 2019. The mismatch between these two aspects has resulted in a large outflow of skills, particularly (even pre-war) to Poland, where nearly two million Ukrainians work. 'Incentives to accumulate capital and to attract foreign investment continue to be affected by the influence of vested interests on the economy that undermine the effectiveness of Ukraine's economic institutions,' noted the World Bank.[106]

The war offers a view of where Ukraine, with the right will, might go in the future. The two paths at the crossroads exhibit, says Pavlo Sheremeta, 'the difference between Ukraine's future and Russia's past'. It is a future defined by closer ties with Europe with all its economic opportunities and governance norms, and Russia's rearward view of security through might. Before the war, political instability left little space for reforms.

Now the old balancing act between access to cheap Russian commodities and European markets has been upended. War has changed that equation. There is no going back. 'We have a guarantee of the reforms [after the war],' maintains Gennadiy Chyzhykov. 'On 23 June 2022, we became a candidate member of the European Union. We have done 70 per cent of what is required for membership already. This is how we will go forward.'

While the Orange Revolution raised hopes, it delivered less. Plans for change – such as the more than 100 proposals produced by the 2005 Blue Ribbon Commission, a body sponsored by the United Nations Development Programme – did not result in material change in laws and institutions, according to the World Bank's assessment.[107] The Maidan Revolution ten years later, which signalled the desire for greater Ukrainian autonomy in booting out Russia's pick in President Viktor Yanukovych, also failed to instil the deep economic reforms required over multiple election cycles. The break with the past in 2022 represents another opportunity for a governance reset.

In this way, the buck starts and stops with Ukrainians.

Latin America

MAHAMADOU Issoufou, the former president of Niger, says that Africa can ill-afford 'African elections' – what he describes as rigged events leading to 'banana republics', which will encourage instability and coups. Equally, says the president who stepped down after two terms in 2021 in accordance with the constitution, Africa must avoid what he calls the 'Southamericanisation' and 'tropicalisation' of its politics, where coups become the norm.¹

The number of African military coups averaged four a year between 1960 and 2000. This fell to two per year during the first two decades of the twenty-first century but rose again suddenly in 2021 when six coups or attempted coups were recorded, with successful putsches in Chad, Mali, Guinea and Sudan and failed takeovers in Niger and, again, Sudan. Two successful coup attempts in Burkina Faso followed in 2022. It was starting to look like the bad old coup days of the 1970s.

As Issoufou reminds us, the same was true of Latin American politics up until the 1980s. Between 1900 and 2006, there were 162 successful coups in Latin America, defined as 'a successful attempt to overthrow the president by a group of state officials, typically executed by a part or the entire armed forces'. There were around sixty further unsuccessful attempts. The peak decade of these events was the 1930s.²

Very few of these occurred in the last fifty years, proving, among other factors, that non-competitive regimes foment coups in the absence of constitutional alternatives, and vice versa, and that coups tend to spawn coups once that boundary has been broken.³ There is now a new blight: the advent of populist authoritarians, such as Hugo Chávez in Venezuela, Daniel Ortega in Nicaragua and Nayib Bukele in El Salvador. They represent a new version of an earlier tradition of politicians emphasising 'the people', including past presidents Getúlio Vargas in Brazil, Juan Domingo Perón in Argentina and José María Velasco Ibarra in Ecuador.

This is not only a left-wing phenomenon: Carlos Menem in Argentina, Fernando Collor de Mello in Brazil and Alberto Fujimori in Peru were all elected on populist tickets in the 1990s but implemented conservative economic policies once in power. Similarly, there have been right-wing populists, notably Jair Bolsonaro in Brazil, in power for four years until 2022.

The Latin American strongman remains prominent in the region's politics, though no longer only in military uniform. This is down in part to the legacy of military rule, which is associated with economic failure, along with the learnings of civilian politicians, the international environment and the improving professionalisation of militaries.[4] While Latin America has seen the rise of authoritarians in Venezuela, Nicaragua and Haiti, it remains the most democratic region outside of North America and western Europe, with some of the world's strongest democracies in Uruguay, Costa Rica and Chile, even though conditions in some others (including Mexico and Brazil) have deteriorated. In the Economist Intelligence Unit's 2022 Democracy Index, Latin America's overall score of 5.79 was well above the global norm of 5.29 and that of sub-Saharan Africa at 4.14.[5] Even the new wave of populist leaders – or at least most of them – have left office via competitive elections, including Bolsonaro (if reluctantly) in Brazil, Rafael Correa in Ecuador, Evo Morales in Bolivia (though amid controversy after he attempted to stay on via a fourth term) and Cristina Fernández de Kirchner, or 'CFK' as she is known, in Argentina.

Populism – like authoritarianism – seems to feed off high levels of social and economic inequality. Latin America vies with Africa as the world's most unequal region. But inequality has been falling markedly since 2000, the result of increased growth and improved governance, a greater role for women in the economy, and reduced poverty, among other reasons. Yet social protests continue, and populists return after periods out of power. Rebellion against authoritarianism plays a role in some cases, as does corruption among governing elites, with social media as an efficient facilitator.

The question why social unrest – and the political instability that goes with it – remains a routine feature of Latin American political life, including in relatively prosperous countries like Colombia, Chile and Argentina, is intriguing, not least because of the role of 'incomplete transitions' and increasing pressure on the middle class.[6]

In an echo with Africa, wealth inequality has a racial hue, related to historical factors. The first is in the subjugation of indigenous peoples by Spanish and Portuguese colonialists. While the Inca empire was in trouble before the Spanish arrived, the diseases (especially smallpox) brought by the newcomers all but wiped out the local population. In modern-day Peru, the centrepiece of the Inca empire, the population decreased from ten million to just 600 000 within a century.

The second is a result of the slave trade. From the 1500s to 1866, Europeans enslaved over ten million people. Only a fraction (around half a million) ended up in North America, the rest being destined for Latin America and the Caribbean. Torn from contemporary Angola, Mozambique, Guinea, Sudan and Congo, the majority, as many as six million, ended up in Brazil, where they were herded together in squalid *senzala* (slave quarters) and forced to do back-breaking work on sugarcane plantations. While most countries in South America banned slavery between 1816 and 1831, it was not until 1888 that slavery was finally outlawed in Brazil. Freedom seldom brought justice, however, with more than 800 000 formerly enslaved people flooding Brazilian cities in search of work and housing. These divisions persist. A 2019 study in Brazil showed that white workers had an average income nearly 76 per cent higher than black and brown people, a difference that has remained stable over recent years. Black and brown people, who represent 56 per cent of the Brazilian population, have the worst indicators of income, housing conditions, education, and access to goods and services, in addition to being more subject to violence and underrepresentation in management positions. In 2014, the richest 10 per cent of people in Latin America had amassed 71 per cent of the region's wealth.[7]

One face of Mexico represents this crisis of death, excess, weak governance and corresponding insecurity.

According to the Global Initiative Against Transnational Organized Crime, in 2022 Mexico ranked fourth out of 193 countries in terms of criminality, behind only Myanmar (third), Colombia (second), and the DRC (first).[8] By 2021, over 100 000 people had been killed in Mexico during the first three years of President Andrés Manuel López Obrador's administration. There are several reasons for this, not least the sophistication of organised crime groups and their fragmentation and growth following earlier 'wars on drugs', endemic corruption, and a poor-performing police force reflecting years of underinvestment.

And yet, today Mexico is the only large developing economy that competes with China in manufacturing. It attracted $11.9 billion in FDI during the first quarter of 2021, the highest level recorded since Mexico began tracking FDI in 1999.[9] The reason for this is a combination of labour productivity and free trade – in this case, the North American Free Trade Agreement concluded in 1994 between Mexico, Canada and the United States.

'If you calculate exports per capita from Mexico, we are almost twice as large as China, given our success in penetrating the US market,' notes Jaime Serra Puche, the Mexican lead in the negotiation and implementation of NAFTA.

This is contrary to the stereotype portrayed by series such as *Narcos* or the likes of Donald Trump, who proposed building a wall to control the influx of migrants flooding north over America's border. In the mid-1990s, the Mexican ambassador to South Africa was distraught over a television advert for a particular brand of corn chip, which portrayed an indolent *campesino* under a sombrero speaking in an accent that would make even Eli Wallach's character in *The Good, the Bad and the Ugly* blush.

Even allowing for a little nationalistic prickliness and a lack of a sense of humour, the erstwhile diplomat had a point. More than thirty years earlier, in 1965, his government had instigated a border industrialisation programme that transformed the country's job market and export profile by exploiting the comparative advantage of abundant cheap labour through 'quick and dirty' assembly and export. As part of the scheme, low-cost manufacturing plants owned by corporations in the United States were set up in Mexico, usually near the border. Known as *maquiladoras* or simply *maquilas*, these factories allowed companies to capitalise on the less-expensive labour force in Mexico and receive the benefits of doing business in the United States. Subsequently, through pioneering policy thinking and action, Mexico has proven that manufacturing does not have to be a race to the bottom of the cheap wage pile.[10]

Mexico's processes of change over the last quarter century illustrate many parallels with Africa, all of the good, the bad and the ugly: the centrality of education and research, the role of unions and labour stability in development and investment decisions, the use of innovative methods to improve industrial competitiveness and ensure transformation from a low-wage to higher-value economy, the security dimension, the critical role of trade openness over industrial policy in development, and the importance of getting the politics right.

The Gulf of Mexico oil bonanza in the 1970s seemed initially to offer an answer to the country's development needs, though as Mexico moved inexorably from a conservative to a more aggressive fiscal and monetary policy, bust followed an oil-fuelled boom. By the mid-1980s, the *maquilas* had already become the largest source of Mexico's foreign exchange and employment. Then, following the implementation of NAFTA on 1 January 1994, the number of these factories soared.

The rise has been spectacular. United States goods imports from Mexico totalled $388 billion in 2019, up more than eightfold since 1993, the year before NAFTA came into force. The US imports mostly manufactured goods from Mexico – automobiles and television screens – while Mexican imports from the US, up nearly sixfold to $290 billion by 2019, centre on agricultural goods and petroleum. It is estimated that US imports support 1.2 million jobs in Mexico, which had become the United States' second-largest goods export market by 2019. The US accounts for over 70 per cent of Mexican exports.[11]

The flow of goods north is staggering. By 2015, for example, 46 000 semi-trailer trucks drove the three hours between Monterrey, Mexico's third-largest city in the state of Nuevo León, and the US border every day. There were no fewer than 143 industrial parks in the state hosting 740 companies,[12] many of them big global names such as Accenture, American Express, Brembo, Bridgestone, British

American Tobacco, Caterpillar, General Electric, Hershey, Home Depot, Infosys, John Deere, Johnson Controls, Smiths Instruments, Kraft, LG, Lenovo, Lowe's, Mars, Navistar, PepsiCo and Whirlpool, among others.

Nuevo León's success is not unique. To take another example, Mexico produced 3.99 million cars in 2019, representing 3.8 per cent of GDP, making it the sixth-largest producer worldwide. Despite representing a decrease of 2 per cent in production numbers over 2018, Mexico still ranked ahead of car manufacturing giants South Korea (3.95 million) and Brazil (2.9 million) in seventh and eighth place respectively.[13] Reflecting over $48 billion in FDI, production almost doubled between 2010 and 2019, most of this for export to the United States.[14]

Yet, in some critical circles, Mexico's factories have become synonymous with poor working conditions, gender discrimination and low wages – in a word, sweatshops. Such critics say these industries represent the consequences of a 'race to the bottom' in labour costs. There will, of course, always be businesses that try to cut corners on decent working conditions, in Mexico as elsewhere, and in manufacturing as in all sectors. Certainly, the *maquilas* have faced increasing competition on labour costs from new entrants, including Malaysia, Vietnam, India, Pakistan and especially China.

Luis de la Calle, another NAFTA negotiator in the early nineties, reminds us that in the wake of the debt crisis in the late 1980s, Mexico had to decide how to use its situation in a way that could improve its competitiveness and productivity. The idea of a trade agreement was first proposed by Ronald Reagan in 1980 and then again by Mexico in January 1990.

'This is more difficult in democratic societies, and development is never a linear process, but rather uneven,' admits De la Calle. 'But when people say that NAFTA has not impacted Mexico, or not enough, if you are in certain regions or in certain sectors, your life has been completely transformed.' Change also 'takes time. In the first twenty years of NAFTA, productivity grew very little, an example of efforts not properly rewarded. But by 2019 productivity was growing in most sectors.'

The caricature two decades ago of a snoozing *campesino*, tequila bottle in hand while doing some horizontal PT, was clearly out of kilter even then with the nation's development and policy trajectory. For all Mexico's challenges, the more modern caricature of a government presiding apathetically over endemic violence and *maquila* sweatshops is similarly out of sync with the contemporary Mexican economy. And NAFTA, for all the harbingers of doom regarding free trade and the noisy advocates of protectionism, has externalised discipline on other areas of government policy and been a source of skills and technological, infrastructural and logistical improvement.

Other Latin American examples similarly shake the stereotype and highlight the importance of sound, strategic-minded leadership and external relations, and of the need to get the politics right.

Please Pay for Me, Argentina: The Problem with Politicians

'In politics, in open societies, you have to be a good story-teller.'
— Ricardo López Murphy, Argentine economist and politician

'Don't cry for me, Argentina,' sings Madonna from the balcony of the Casa Rosada in Buenos Aires to the chanting crowd in the Plaza de Mayo below. The movie is *Evita*, based on Andrew Lloyd Webber's 1978 musical of the same name, in which Madonna plays Eva Perón, Argentina's idolised first lady and the second wife of President Juan Domingo Perón. 'The truth is, I never left you,' she reassures her people. Eva is pleading with the public to believe that she did not invite her fame and fortune, even though to many it may have seemed that this was her objective in manipulating her husband into climbing the ladder to power.

Politics thrives on its idols and demons, especially in Argentina.

María Eva Duarte was a poor girl from the provinces. After coming to the capital to seek fame, she married Perón, the former military officer and one-time coup leader who would rule Argentina for cumulatively more than a decade. The balcony scene filmed at the Casa Rosada presidential palace was a dramatised version of a mass gathering on the nearby July 9 Avenue in 1951, where Eva declined the invitation to run for vice president. She explained that her only ambition was to support her husband in bringing the 'hopes and dreams of the people to the president' and to turn these into 'glorious reality'.

By capturing the imagination of Argentinians, Eva helped to cement the legend of Perón and his eponymous political ideology.

Between 1946 and 2019, Peronist candidates won ten of the thirteen presidential elections in which they were allowed to participate, encompassing the periods of Juan Perón and his third wife Isabel (1946–55 and 1974–76), and more recently, the presidencies of Néstor Kirchner and his wife Cristina Fernández de Kirchner (2003–07 and 2007–15 respectively). Additionally, presidents Héctor Cámpora (1973), Carlos Menem (1989–99) and Eduardo Duhalde (2002–03) are all considered Peronists, despite their varying ideological tendencies. After a short interregnum in the government of Mauricio Macri between 2015 and 2019, the Peronists came back with President Alberto Fernández and his vice president, the seemingly indefatigable CFK.

By encompassing fascist, liberal and left-wing regimes, Peronism is less of an ideology than a political platform. It is akin to a 'restaurant chain where each venue has a different theme,' says opposition strategist Franco Moccia, head of the Pensar Foundation, an opposition coalition think tank. In the words of law professor Emilio Cárdenas, who served as Menem's ambassador to the United Nations, Peronism is an 'empty capsule' that can 'be filled with virtually any ideology that you want, especially if you disguise yourself as a Christian. You can be Peronist and Marxist, or a military government and Peronist. It tempts politicians continuously.'[15]

And while Peronism, which mixes elements of nationalism, statism and labourism with populism, has proven robust as a political formula to gain power in Argentina, it has proven less effective as a system of governance to run the economy. As one measure of its economic impact, the IMF has overseen twenty-one bailouts to Argentina, including one that ended the 2002 default and the world body's largest-ever rescue in 2018. And yet this external tool of discipline has seemingly had little long-term positive impact, unlike, for example, the role of NAFTA in Mexico's development or the EU in the transformation of Europe. Despite a surfeit of natural and human resources, Argentina has maintained a boom-and-bust logic of overspending, fuelling the reckless printing of money, rampant inflation and forex crises.

Before the First World War, Argentina ranked firmly in the world's top ten largest economies. The decline since then has been costly, especially to the poor. Per capita income in Argentina between 1975 and 1990, for example, fell by 1.5 per cent per annum, while the world rate expanded at 1.6 per cent.[16] According to a 2023 study by the Catholic University of Argentina, 43.1 per cent of the population, or seventeen million people, live below the poverty line, a figure the university's researchers calculate would rise to 50 per cent without state welfare, which, in a vicious cycle, cements the fiscal policies that ensure poverty of opportunity.[17]

The job of Argentina's reformers is difficult given entrenched vested interests. For one, there are clear constituencies for the economic practices of the Peronists, including the subsidies that make up a significant proportion of government spending under their watch, and which remain the ultimate cause of the large fiscal deficits that produce the fiscal circumstances demanding regular bailouts. Essentially, Argentina lives beyond its means. As Menem's former finance minister Domingo Cavallo notes, this has political implications, too, in feeding 'the scepticism of the economic agents about the viability of a speedy process of reforms and successful stabilisation'.[18]

For example, even though Cristina Fernández de Kirchner's administration left things in a parlous state for President Macri to manage his way out of, he had only a four-year mandate to do so. Government coffers were empty, inflation was close to 25 per cent and CFK had kept in place subsidies that drained the budget. Consequently, reform became a task that Macri ultimately did not prove up to, and which the balance of power in Congress did not allow. Even though his initial plan seemed to be making headway, Macri lost both his reform track and then the 2019 election in a landslide, garnering just 40.3 per cent to his rival Fernández's 48.2 per cent. Argentina swiftly returned to Peronism, continuing the pattern of short-lived attempts at reform that has been the norm since the end of military rule in 1983.

After Menem came to power in 1989 amid hyperinflation, Cavallo instituted a convertibility plan pegging the peso to the dollar one-to-one to end inflation and instil certainty. Like the plan Macri would attempt decades later, this seemed to work initially. Menem and Cavallo simultaneously implemented market reforms, which included the privatisation of 200 state enterprises, including the emblematic state oil concern YPF, rail companies, several banks and the national airline. The previously mandatory national pension system was opened to choice by permitting private pension schemes, essentially seeding the creation of Argentine capital markets, and export taxes on commodities were slashed.

The results were impressive. In the first five years, GDP grew by about a third, fixed investment and productivity doubled, and poverty halved. Most importantly, convertibility brought inflation right down. But the reform impetus foundered on personalities and politics. Tensions between Menem and Cavallo saw the finance minister resign in 1996. This event, along with the hangover from the Mexican peso crisis of 1994–95, resulted in growing unemployment and worsening crime. Cavallo was recalled by Menem's successor, President Fernando de la Rúa, in March 2001 to try to restore order and confidence after two years of recession and capital flight. Attempts to stem the flow of cash forced the government's collapse at the end of 2001. Convertibility was scrapped, the peso swiftly devaluing and inflation rising once more.

In the same way, Macri's promise of change, and of a new and sustainable direction for the economy, did not happen. The big deficits that the government ran needed a constant funnel of foreign money to fund them, demanding high interest rates. This, in turn, pushed up the value of the peso, requiring more dollars to be borrowed to fund the deficit.

Macri's fundamental problem was that he attempted a series of gradualist responses to a situation that demanded boldness. As Kenneth Rogoff, a former chief economist at the IMF and now professor of economics at Harvard University, notes: 'Argentina made a lot of mistakes. The general principle their programme violated was that when markets overshoot, policy has to overshoot. They didn't do that – they tried a policy of gradualism.'[19]

But there were other problems. Besides some technical errors in the reform process itself, Macri failed to win the elections – his was a political failure to create common cause at the centre, an inability to sell policies of which a large section of the electorate was sceptical, including his return of Argentina to the IMF. Fundamentally, Argentina's tendency towards crisis and 'serial defaulting is a consequence of terrible macro-economic problems, which are problems of politics,' says Moccia.

Even though Argentina has maintained civilian governments for forty years, stages regular and largely peaceful elections, and has no racial, religious or tribal divisions, its social history has been marked by frictions corresponding to the economic situation and 'a persistent tendency for Argentines to identify themselves primarily in opposition to others': federalists versus unitarians, civilisation versus barbarity, radicals versus conservatives, Peronists versus anti-Peronists. As analyst Jill Hedges notes, Juan Perón's maxim 'If I define, I exclude' provided the basis of 'an amorphous and ideologically vacuous political platform that has eluded a precise definition for fifty years, thus distorting the country's entire political spectrum'.[20]

Much of the blame for this seems to lie with the Peronists, but a permanent departure from this Argentine model of self-destruction has proven difficult. Why is this the case when the economic logic appears to point to the need for political change? What has made Argentina seemingly impervious to reform?

The promises of Peronism

Argentina had long suffered from political and social divisions that Peronism was able to reconcile and, in the process, metamorphose into a political philosophy.

From early on in Argentina's political history, the *porteños* (residents of Buenos Aires) saw the rules for them as being different, with the result that while the American system of government has 'been described as a form of "centralising federalism", the Argentina formula has been viewed as a sort of "federalising centralism"', argues Hedges, with Buenos Aires at the apex of imports and exports, the hub for the railways, and the centre of government power and authority, the latter driven by key events, not least the professionalisation of the national army. While the figure of the gaucho (the brave, unruly horseman) was popular in defining Argentine character as strong, honest and silent, in reality it was the wealthy, landed elite who called the shots and governed according to their interests. Technology helped – particularly the advent of refrigerated shipping, making frozen beef exports possible and fuelling the 'Golden Age' of the late nineteenth century.

By 1914, 80 per cent of Argentina's exports were agricultural products, 85 per cent of which was shipped to Europe, and not all of it meat. Grain and oilseed exports increased exponentially, from a total of some 17 000 tonnes in 1880 to over one million tonnes a decade later; by 1910, Argentina was second only to the US in wheat exports.

Politics during this time was less about contests of ideology than 'a machine oiled by patronage and dedicated to retaining power'.[21] The general rise of agriculture boosted the resources available to the government and the attractiveness of landownership for newer members of the political elite. In other words, the state became an increasingly attractive prize because the increase in its resources spelt an increase in patronage and political power.

This also drove immigration, which in turn changed the nature of Argentine politics, from its focus on land to conditions in the urban areas. The population of Buenos Aires rose from around 180 000 in 1869 to over 1.5 million by 1914. But as wealthy families abandoned the inner city around the Casa Rosada for the richer suburbs such as Recoleta, the original centre became dominated by *conventillos* (tenements) for poor, usually immigrant families. Conditions around the *conventillos* contrasted with the improvements in the wealthier areas, where the resemblance to Paris began to take root, with British-financed trams, gas and electricity offering increasingly modern services to those that could afford them.[22]

From the declaration of independence in 1816, the first four decades of Argentine state-building were rocky. Then, from 1852 until 1930, a liberal government took over, though one with oligarchic tendencies, the outcome of elections being controlled in the interests of landowners. This encouraged the creation of new unions and political parties, including the Radical Civic Union (UCR), representing the middle class.

From 1930 until 1983, politics was dominated by the role of the military. In September 1930, the elected president Hipólito Yrigoyen was ousted by a right-wing-led coup, giving way to a three-party regime that controlled the government until 1943. This coup came in the wake of the instability of the Great Depression, which saw a 70 per cent fall in traditional commodity prices, compounding the legacy of the First World War, which saw a deep cut in GDP and bottlenecks in production as links with the outside world were broken.

Still, by the end of the Second World War, Argentina had enjoyed a higher rate of growth and lower inflation than the United States for more than half a century, ran low deficits, maintained a traditional monetary system, and possessed an institutional make-up akin to a developed country of the time. Argentina was one of the most successful emerging economies, benefitting from a bounty of natural resources and the human capital of rapid immigration. After the war, however, this soon gave way to a more populist political economy, characterised by international isolation, state intervention, high import duties, export taxes, rent-seeking, high inflation, falling productivity (including in agriculture), and the weakening of democratic institutions – tendencies that were amplified by episodic military governments.

A second coup, the Revolution of '43, signalled a change that has since shaped Argentine politics and economics whatever the regime, civilian or military. This takeover, led by the army, supported the Axis powers and modelled the new government after Italian dictator Benito Mussolini's fascist regime. Among the leaders of the military junta was Colonel Juan Perón, who oversaw the Secretariat of Labour and Social Security. Perón set about trying to improve the living and working conditions of workers, including by giving labour unions both support and government positions. Jailed briefly by opponents within the armed forces, he took power in democratic elections in June 1946. As president, he continued where the junta had left off with a 'corporatist' strategy, focused on drawing the political and working classes closer together through mobilisation of the unions, and adopting a radical import substitution industrialisation and economically redistributive policy to create social peace and a firm political constituency.

Aided by the charismatic Eva, his regime delivered economic growth and improvements in living and working conditions while universalising suffrage and nationalising the Central Bank, electricity and gas, urban transport, railroads, and the telephone. This political tendency towards redistribution lives today in Argentine politics and has fuelled expectations impossible to support in terms of investment and growth.

After Eva's death from cancer in 1952, Perón was ousted in 1955 in yet another coup. Further coups followed in 1962 and 1966, interspersed with periods of military government. Perón regained power in 1973 but died a year later, passing control to his third wife, Isabel, who was toppled by another military coup, in 1976. The populism of Perón was perpetuated through all these regimes. As journalist Rosendo Fraga observes, 'Peronism is all of a party, movement, culture, ideology and doctrine, the extreme manifestation of a general phenomenon in Argentina of weak institutions and strong personalities, where power is more important than ideology.'[23] Or, as Franco Moccia puts it, 'The only common feature among Peronists is that they want to win.'[24]

Perón suggested that, in the game of seizing and exercising power, 'You should indicate left, but turn right.' This lesson has been only partly applied in the five decades that Peronism has endured since his death, though the Justicialist Party (previously called the Peronist Party after its founder) has retained its hegemony. Peronists have put the elimination of poverty at the centre of their rhetoric. Some have criticised their methods as fascist; certainly, they have not been in the spirit of democracy, but this is not surprising given the origins of Perón's views.

In 1939, the future president was assigned to study mountain warfare in Mussolini's Italy. He returned to Argentina in 1941 with the idea that liberal democracy and capitalism, like communism, did not work, and that another way – *la tercera posición* (the third position) – had to be found, a version of Mussolini's state corporatism and nationalism. This idea had a receptive audience in Argentina, and not just among the working class, as the period between 1930 and 1945 had created a vested interest in protectionism. As Ricardo López Murphy, a former minister of defence and of economy and labour in Fernando de la Rúa's government, puts it, 'Argentina replaced the invisible hand of the state with the heavy finger of Peronism.'

Peronism drew from an ideological cocktail of 'Keynesian policies and [the dependency theory of Raúl] Prebisch, of the need for state interventionism in industry to offset the belief that while the cost of commodities fell, the price of manufactured goods would rise,' says López Murphy. The reality, however, has since proven inverse to this theory, although this structuralist argument has informed a generation of economists and political leaders in Argentina and farther afield, in part because there is a vested interest by an elite made up of politicians, unions and businesses that prefers a protectionist, if expensive, local market. This is borne out by a growth comparison with the four Asian Tigers (Singapore, Taiwan, Hong Kong and South Korea), who followed an export-led strategy.

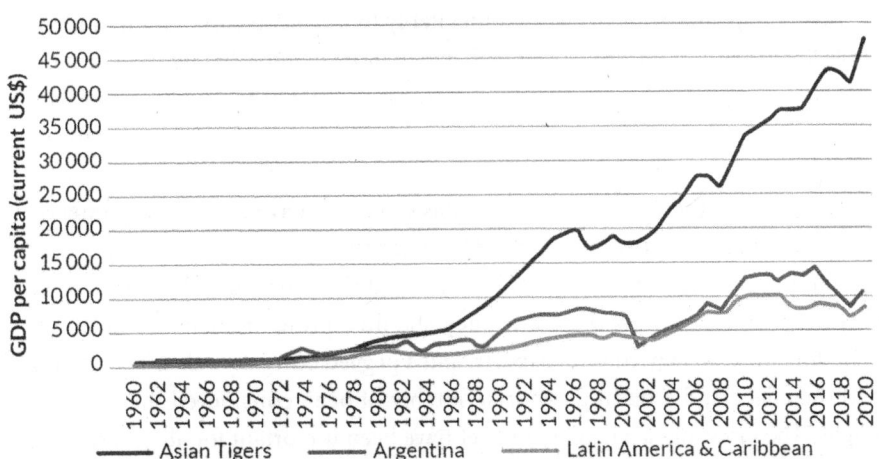

Source: Taiwan data from Economic Forecast Section, Department of Statistics, Directorate General of Budget, Accounting & Statistics; all others from World Bank, World Development Indicators

Peronism represents a system of government in which there are a multitude of beneficiaries, not least the business sector, making money in an environment of 'assisted capitalism' – protected by laws and procedures, critical of the administration while moving their money offshore across the River Plate to Uruguay to avoid taxes.

For this and other reasons, undoing statism is never easy.

The battle of the dinner plate

Not only did Peronism advocate interventionism, protectionism and high levels of state spending, but these policies also ensured the political support of the masses through subsidies and preferences. For example, to ensure his 1946 election victory, Perón persuaded the de facto president to nationalise the Central Bank and extend Christmas bonuses. While politically expedient, such spendthrift redistribution has served repeatedly to destroy capital accumulation, baulking the inevitable reality of internal budget constraints and the underpinnings of global competitiveness.

In the process, Argentina has proven that you can do very badly despite a huge natural resource advantage in agriculture, oil and mining. It is a vast but empty land, the world's eighth largest, with a population of just forty-six million. India, the world's seventh-largest country by area, has a population twenty-eight times greater.

Argentina's policies have served to make the poor more and not less dependent on the state. 'It is said that Peronism wants poverty to continue so that they continue to manage these people,' observed former president Fernando de la Rúa.

Living beyond its means has led inevitably to a rapid accumulation of foreign debt, the growth of an unfavourable balance of payments, an increase in monetary supply, galloping inflation and a decrease in foreign reserves – all of which have ended in political tears. Regardless, such populism has been a feature of virtually every Argentine government since Perón, except for those of Macri and De la Rúa. Even the various military juntas since 1955 have had strongly interventionist, even populist instincts shaped by Peronism.

The policy fare, in the process, has included the usual subsidies for the poor, exchange controls to promote currency stability, protectionism, a raft of taxes including those on agricultural exports, and a pegged currency value. The latter has had the effect of dissuading exports, notably of beef, considered the Argentine staple. 'The price and availability of beef have been important for all governments,' notes Miguel Pertino, a cattle farmer and consultant. 'By keeping beef exports low, either through limiting quotas or currency values, the government has kept the price low and its people happy.'[25] Beef exports have historically been around

10 per cent of production, rising by the 2020s to 25 per cent, most of it destined for China and Japan.

Attempts at overall strategic reform have foundered on an all-too-easy reversion to short-term populist politics and free spending.

Take Carlos Menem, president of Argentina from 1989 to 1999. From March 1989 to March 1990, inflation reached a staggering 170 per cent per month, 11 000 per cent annually.[26] The liberal government of Raúl Alfonsín, which had taken over from the junta in 1983, had proven unable to deal with the economic meltdown caused by the persistent Argentine disease of excessive international borrowing, an unsustainably high deficit and unchecked public spending. The rapid devaluation of the Argentine austral and hyperinflation caused the outgoing president to transfer power to Menem, the winner of the 1989 election, five months earlier than scheduled.

Alfonsín had tried to increase taxes and decrease spending with the support of the World Bank. While Menem never campaigned on a reform strategy, he soon woke up to the cost of stagflation and hyperinflation. This gave rise to what Domingo Cavallo calls the 'Latin American consensus of the 1990s' – distinct from the much-derided Washington Consensus. The problem for Argentina was that it had 'capitalism without markets and socialism without plans,' says Cavallo.[27] The root of this was uncontrolled fiscal spending, which in turn lay in political promises and expectations. When government proves unable to fund its spending through tax and is unable to raise more debt, Cavallo notes, printing money is a 'subtle way to collect a kind of tax that does not need approval by the legislature – the inflation tax'. This effectively imposes a tax on savings and wages, the most short-sighted and self-defeating tax of all.

A Peronist aberration?

Menem, who died in 2021 aged ninety-one, was an intuitive rather than an intellectual politician, a great observer with the common sense and charisma to realise that things needed to change and the ability to get the message across.[28] Cavallo argues that Menem's powers of observation about world events transformed Argentina from an inward-facing economy to one that looked outwards.

Forced to abandon Peronist orthodoxy in favour of a fiscally conservative, market-orientated economic policy, Menem brought in Cavallo as minister of economy in 1991. With this authority and the president providing political flavour and top cover, Cavallo was able to put into practice a plan for stability and growth that would steer Argentina onto a new growth path. The core of it was the convertibility of the peso (the austral was done away with in 1991) to the US dollar, but it was based on a philosophy that 'the entire private sector of the economy accepted the rules of the market while the public sector accepted the rules of planning and budgeting,' recalls Cavallo. It included the liberalisation of trade, a reduction of public expenditure, simplification of the tax system, and international agreements to restructure the country's burgeoning debt.

Drawing on the liberalisation experience of Chile and the monetary reforms of Bolivia, the Convertibility Law created a new monetary system that fixed the exchange rate at one Argentine peso per US dollar and was fully backed by foreign reserves. This enabled, and was in turn boosted by, widespread privatisations and a fall in public expenditure from 25 per cent in 1990 to 20 per cent by 1993, and resulted in an increase in production and a fall in inflation to low single digits. Export performance, for example, grew to rival that of Chile and was nearly 30 per cent greater than Brazil's.

Menem's younger brother, Eduardo, served as a senator from 1983 to 2005, including three years as the senate president. He says that, apart from the period where his brother was in power, 'the actions of Peronism were not orthodox, but commonly of a populist character'. 'Until he privatised state services, we could wait for a phone line for up to ten years, and television was restricted at the end of the Alfonsín government to six hours per day because of electricity shortages,' says Eduardo. 'We needed to change Argentina's profile and transform with investment from abroad.'

The difference between the Menem/Cavallo period and what went before and has come after is in the attempt to fix the problem through policy reform rather than simply refinancing. Unfortunately, the period proved a temporary aberration from Argentina's systemic chaos. After Cavallo resigned as finance minister in July 1996, things started to unravel. Rather than allowing the peso to float, his successor retained the parity convertibility with the dollar. The reason for this was political. The race between Menem and his rival for the leadership of the Justicialist Party, Eduardo Duhalde, had intensified. Any dollar depreciation of the peso would have lessened provincial expenditures, which both wanted to use as a means of financial support for their candidacy. Coupled with the Asian financial crisis of 1997/98 and the devaluation of the Brazilian real a year later, the stage was set for a traumatic devaluation.

Fernando de la Rúa, from the oxymoronically liberal Radical Civic Union, took office in December 1999 in an increasingly stressed environment. Amid a chaotic devaluation of the peso, he was out after two years, to be replaced within two weeks by Duhalde. Attempts to structure an international bailout and implement an austerity plan fell foul of widespread public protests, themselves the consequence of a combination of politics and naked self-interest. As Cavallo, who came in briefly once more as economy minister in the midst of the chaos, puts it:

'Duhalde ... and Ignacio de Mendiguren, then head of the UIA [the Argentine Industrial Union, an organisation that represents Argentine industrialists], realised that an institutional coup would give them the opportunity to wipe out all debts, public and private, held at home and abroad' with the ideological cover of ridding the country of 'neo-liberalism'.

Onto the Kirchners

The Duhalde and later Kirchner administrations quickly reverted to statist, more traditionally Peronist policies,[29] with Cristina Fernández de Kirchner proving more radical than her husband, in the process coining the term 'Kirchnerism'.

Inspired by Hugo Chávez's twenty-first-century socialism in Venezuela, CFK 'expanded the arbitrary interventions in markets, the nationalisation of companies, imposed widespread price and exchange controls and ... did not solve any of the disequilibria created by Duhalde's and her husband's governments,' says Cavallo.[30] Axel Kicillof, her minister of economy and later mayor of Buenos Aires, infamously asserted that it was now possible to centrally manage the economy Soviet-style because of the development of technology and spreadsheets such as Microsoft Excel.[31] This reveals many things, not least a misunderstanding of the nature of market forces in his belief that the cost of production determines final prices. The problem is never whether sufficient computing power is at our disposal and whether we therefore have enough information; rather, it has to do with the impossibility of successfully creating a centrally planned market.

The strict monetary policy of the early Menem/Cavallo period, which ensured stability, integration with the global economy and growth, was quickly left behind. The 'pesofication' of Argentina's debt by Duhalde, and the rapid slide in its value from parity with the dollar to four-to-one, reduced domestic debt to a quarter of its value but also did the same to dollar-based savings, in the process redistributing wealth from savers to debtors and impoverishing the middle class while doing little to affect volumes of foreign debt.

The Peronists honed an entrenched system of patronage and control at a strategic level through their relationship with the unions and through local intermediaries called *punteros*. This infected formal government departments, too. Cavallo talks about the 'mafias' that ran the postal services 'and had created a virtual parallel customs and migration service to help criminal activities'.[32] As a result, observed economist Sergio Berensztein, the unions 'owned one-third of the healthcare budget, at around 11 per cent of the national budget. This is not transparent, and a strong incentive not to fix the system which was designed around the needs of the 1970s.'[33]

Even though the power of unions around the world has been slipping for several decades, in Argentina they remain a potent political force, with nearly 28 per cent of workers unionised, the highest level in Latin America, compared to 16 per cent in Brazil and Chile, and 12 per cent in Mexico. Even highly unionised South Africa is at 23 per cent.[34] The truck drivers' union, with more than 200 000 members, and the construction workers' union are considered especially powerful. Yet one survey found that 80.9 per cent of citizens believed that trade unions were the most corrupt institutions in the country, higher than businesses (77.5 per cent), the courts (74.8 per cent), the media (67.4 per cent) and Congress (64.5 per cent).[35]

In this environment, public contracts become a source of funding for the ruling party and some politicians. Roberto Lavagna, the minister of economy, resigned from Néstor Kirchner's government in 2005, denouncing what he termed the 'construction companies' friends of government club'.

Martín Redrado, who served as the Kirchners' Central Bank head, sums up the challenge faced by successive administrations: 'Argentina is a country of weak institutions, where democracy is unable to work properly in terms of providing checks and balances.' As one measure, Argentina sits at 94 out of 180 (down from 85 in 2018) on Transparency International's 2022 Corruption Perceptions Index, with nearly half the country thinking that corruption had increased in the previous twelve months.[36]

'The problem with this model is that the number of those working and producing is 2.5 times smaller than those who are not,' says Ricardo López Murphy, defined, in his terms, as the civil service (which doubled to four million in the first twenty years of the twenty-first century), pensioners (again doubled to ten million), students, the unemployed and the youth. The government introduced the Universal Child Allowance, a cash transfer programme for parents who are unemployed or in the informal economy, in 2009 as a means of combatting poverty. But this came with a cost and a burden. The proportion of public employees reached nearly 10 per cent of the population in 2015. 'Another way of looking at this is that eight million Argentinians are paying for twenty million,' says López Murphy.

With the combination of personal and other taxes amounting to an effective 45 per cent, and corporate tax at 35 per cent, Argentina under the Kirchners was an expensive environment. 'Swedish tax rates for a Zimbabwean system,' remarks López Murphy. Still, whatever their policy follies, the Kirchners initially avoided a total economic collapse because of the natural resource boom and the legacy of the stability brought about by the Menem years. Néstor Kirchner's administration managed a fiscal surplus artificially created through a moratorium on debt repayments and a bonanza in agricultural exports.

The price paid for soy, for example, increased from $140 per tonne to $600 per tonne, the latter representing a 300 per cent profit, during their term of office.

This was largely due to outputs and efficiencies boosted by investments made by the private sector in agricultural methods and seed and planting technology, especially during the Menem years. This windfall provided additional income through a controversial export tax introduced by Duhalde, offering a means to build political power at the centre since these taxes were not automatically shared with the provinces. While these agricultural resources were not state-owned, they were the difference between failure and survival for the Argentine regime. 'The problem with Argentina is that the agriculture sector brings in over $30 billion a year in exports, and this essentially bails out the government and its failings,' says Hendrik Jordaan, a sector specialist based in Córdoba.[37]

The farmers possess political leverage but have used it only sparingly. In March 2008, the government introduced a new taxation system for agricultural exports, with rates fluctuating with international prices. This would have raised levies on soybean exports, for example, from 35 per cent to 44 per cent. The farmers staged national demonstrations including road blockages, marched on the Casa Rosada and slowed exports. Forced to send the proposal to Congress because of the protests, CFK called on farmers to act 'as part of a country, not as owners of a country'. After a senate vote went against the proposal, in July that year, the government revoked the resolution.

Undoing statism is never easy

Buenos Aires mayor Mauricio Macri entered this environment on 10 December 2015 after winning 51.34 per cent of the vote in his defeat of Peronist candidate Daniel Scioli in the first presidential run-off in Argentine history. A civil engineer and president of the Boca Juniors football club, Macri became the first democratically elected, non-Radical and non-Peronist president since 1916. In 2005, he had created the centre-right Republican Proposal (PRO) party and formed the *Cambiemos* (Let's Change), a political coalition composed of the PRO, the UCR and the Civic Coalition.

Macri campaigned on three key messages: zero poverty, a war against the narcos, and reuniting Argentinians. Like Perón's anti-Americanism and Carlos Menem's about-turn in relations with the US and Britain, Macri fastened his recovery strategy onto an external dimension – in his case, in leading the criticism and isolation of Nicolás Maduro's Chavista government in Venezuela. But he also had to close on critical domestic reforms.

Such reforms had to focus on keeping inflation under control by tightening expenditure, including cutting back subsidies, while simultaneously balancing the need to stimulate domestic production through government spending. All of this required shrewd political timing and management. As Eduardo Menem observed at the time of his election, Macri's chances of pulling this off depended on the extent of his 'political savvy'. It also depended on his ability to change the overall political mindset and expectations of Argentinians.

Alfonso Prat-Gay, who served as Central Bank governor under Duhalde, was Macri's minister of economy for the first year of his government. He recalls that five immediate priorities were achieved in the first six months: removing capital controls, fixing the legal issues with creditors on Argentina's outstanding debt and interest payments, gaining access to the market, revamping the national statistics service, and creating a tax amnesty. This tax initiative successfully doubled declared assets. The government managed to settle on an external debt 'sentence', and in April 2016 they launched a 'jumbo' bond of $17.5 billion.

But thereafter things started to go wrong, despite Macri's gains in the 2017 mid-term elections. CFK convinced non-Kirchnerist Peronists to assemble a coalition to contest the October 2019 election. She nominated Alberto Fernández, who had previously criticised her style, as the presidential candidate, a tacit acceptance that she recognised the faults of her administration. Her election strategy was successful. Macri lost to Fernández, who became president with CFK as his deputy.[38]

Understanding reformist loss

The Argentine electoral system runs on two rounds: a primary, where candidates who gain 1.5 per cent or higher of the vote advance to the next round, the general election. In 2019, Fernández finished top of the primaries with 47.8 per cent of the vote, while Macri trailed with 31.8 per cent. This was not unlike the situation in 2015, when Macri received 28.6 per cent to his rival's 36.7 per cent, though he was able to turn it around to win the election after a second-round run-off.

Macri obtained 40.3 per cent in losing the 2019 election, enough to prevent the Peronists obtaining the majority by which they could have changed the rules of Argentina's democracy, but not enough to win. As such, Macri became the first incumbent president in Argentine history to be defeated in a re-election bid. Several theses have been advanced to explain this.

The first is rooted in a belief that Latin American social protests are driven by widening inequality. In the case of Argentina, this suggests that Macri's reforms worsened inequality. However, the statistics do not bear this out. While inequality remains highest in Latin America as a region, overall it has been declining for the past twenty years, including in Argentina, despite social media–facilitated impressions to the contrary.[39]

A second, more sophisticated thesis considers the impact of the rise and fall of commodity prices, with the result that the decade from 2003 saw a decline in poverty and a growth in the middle class. With the end of the commodity boom in 2012 and the compounding contagion of the 2008 global financial crisis, social reaction to the slow-down in the pace of inequality reduction and middle-class growth resulted in protests across Latin America. Macri's poor showing at the polls could be seen as a result of this economic downturn and the social tensions that emanated from it.

Yet this understates the mistakes made by Macri, not least his backsliding on fiscal reforms, opening of capital markets and political misjudgements.

A third, related explanation is that, while CFK managed to assemble a coherent coalition, Macri lost his audience and misstepped on one of the few things that Argentinians could agree on: their dislike of the IMF. 'Macri was not able to convey, deliver and convince the political system and the public at large of the benefit of these reforms,' reflects Prat-Gay. 'It worked for a while, and then it didn't, and then he made the worst possible idea, of bringing in the Fund. Macri oversaw the IMF's biggest-ever bailout in 2018 for over \$50 billion.'[40]

There was a fundamental problem with the environment into which this funding was inserted. Macri had not only gone soft on fiscal reforms, but had also removed the restraining caps placed by Prat-Gay on the capital account. The latter led to an inflow of hot money and an outflow of capital, creating extreme market volatility. Rather than tackle tough reforms, Macri preferred to finance the fiscal deficit with debt.

A fourth explanation is that the government fell into the age-old Argentine trap of enjoying short-lived economic booms rather than finding longer-term continuity because structural reforms are unpopular and leaders are short-sighted. The margin for manoeuvre is very small in those societies mired in high levels of poverty 'where the margin for error is correspondingly huge,' argues Prat-Gay. This results in 'structural reform usually occurring out of panic and desperation rather than out of hope'.[41]

'Macri did too little, too late and too slowly,' summarises Jordaan. 'Perhaps if he had done so, there would have been chaos; the country could have been ungovernable.' In Macri's defence, he only controlled one-fifth of the senate and one-third of the chamber of deputies when in government, which impeded his reform agenda.

A fifth thesis concerns the unsuitability of Macri's re-election campaign and the traditional party system. He needed to work more on the middle who prefer the security of Peronism to the uncertainty of a halting reform agenda. Macri's former chief of staff, Marcos Peña, likens this group 'to a teenager going dark and saying to his parents, "You are not listening to me," when he fails to get through to them.'

The administration was torn between reaching out to moderate Peronists and a more combative 'our way or the highway' strategy, the latter winning the day and, in the process, dangerously increasing CFK's profile and popularity. Prat-Gay observes that the antidote to this world of endless trade-offs, between what is good politically and economically in the short term and the need for longer-term structural reform, is 'strong institutions and political dialogue'.

As the 'champion of populism, if not in the region but the world, after Perón, Argentina has shown that you will need dialogue with the opposition because they will eventually take your place,' observes Prat-Gay. It has also shown the need to build 'good, independent institutions and regimes, especially an independent and balanced judiciary,' he notes. 'Without this you have the cultural broth for authoritarianism or populism.' The responsiveness of government to demand-side factors from the population rather than a supply-side agenda from political parties also helps to shape both government's popularity and own agenda.

Until now, the political elite have not successfully sustained a reformist agenda since the growth and development it promises is slow to create, and the pain of reforms is high post-populism. The reformists inevitably pay the cost of the disaster of populism, which should encourage rapid action within a limited window of opportunity. While Argentina has several advantages in this regard over Venezuela, for example, including relatively intact institutions, a free press and an independent judiciary, bringing Argentinians together and educating them on the necessity of continuous reform is more difficult. 'The challenge for reformist parties is to produce a narrative that not only stands for cutting costs but is [also] able to project a convincing argument for a better future if we make these changes,' notes Franco Moccia.[42] As the opposition party strategist puts it: 'Talk not of the desert, but of the promised land.'

Conclusion: Make the people part of something

Argentina has its helping of legends, in sport as in politics. One of the national heroes is race-car driver Juan Manuel Fangio, who won five Formula One World Championship titles in the 1950s, probably the most dangerous era of the sport. He got his big break in Europe with the intervention of President Juan Perón, turning heads in a Ferrari purchased with the support of the Argentine government and repainted in the national colours: blue with a yellow engine cover. The front of the car was unusual for that era, emblazoned with the decals of YPF, the national oil company.

YPF remains a tool of nationalism. In 2012, in response to her failed fiscal austerity programme, CFK proposed the renationalisation of YPF, blaming the majority shareholder, Spanish company Repsol, for the energy trade deficit. The bill was passed by Congress, consolidating the earlier enforced sale of YPF shares by Repsol to a Kirchner loyalist. The stink of corruption wafted steadily through the corridors of power.

The fourth Kirchnerist government stepped straight into chaos with a new declaration of debt default, the reintroduction of exchange controls, and a suspension of the IMF programme negotiated by Macri just as the Covid-19 pandemic required additional spending and foretold reduced tax revenue. The primary fiscal deficit that in 2019 had been reduced to less than 1 per cent of GDP increased to 4 per cent of GDP in 2021, and then to over 5 per cent in 2023, financed by printing pesos. Inflation accelerated and poverty increased. It was, says one banker, 'government with a credit card'.

It was also déjà vu.

Macri had the opportunity to reset this perennial crisis. Instead, he left office and the country with little more than an extra $70 billion of debt. Consequently, Argentina has continued to go around in a circle of populist overpromising, overspending, collapse and restructuring. All the actors in this drama – Perón, Menem, Macri and the Kirchners, among others – deserve their share of the blame for the serial failure to reform. But there are risks in idolising and demonising the political actors. Rather, we need to understand the system that delivers political upheaval and policy stasis.

While she may have dialled down her more ostentatious personal tastes once her husband assumed the presidency, Eva Perón liked her Cartier jewels and Paris couture, especially the stylish *tailleur* fashions of Christian Dior. And while she endeavoured to bolster her husband's image, she used the opportunity to rewrite her own legend, too. In 1947, she was featured in a cover story for *TIME* magazine: 'Between two worlds, an Argentine rainbow'. It was the first and, to date, only time in the periodical's history that a South American first lady appeared on its cover. The story, however, mentioned that she had been born out of wedlock. In retaliation, the magazine was banned from Argentina for several months.

Eva died on 26 July 1952. An outpouring of national grief followed her death. Mourners queued for hours over two weeks to see her body lying in state. Despite never holding political office, she was afforded a state funeral attended by nearly three million people in the streets of Buenos Aires. Seventy years later, in December 2022, Vice President Cristina Fernández de Kirchner was convicted of corruption, sentenced to six years in prison and handed a lifetime ban from holding public office, although she has temporary immunity due to her role in government and has stated her intention to appeal the verdict.

The first elected female president of Argentina, CFK identifies as a Peronist and progressive. But, like Eva before her, her personal style is less poverty-conscious. Despite her professed 'pink-tide' views, she has similarly expensive sartorial tastes. 'I've always got dressed up, caked on the make-up,' she said in an interview before taking over the presidency in 2007. 'Would I have to dress like I was poor in order to be a good political leader?'[43]

Even Macri wanted some of the Peronist fairy dust. As mayor of Buenos Aires, he was responsible for erecting the first statue of Juan Perón in the city, unveiled on 8 October 2015 to mark the 120th anniversary of the statesman's birth. The five-metre-tall bronze monument depicts Perón characteristically holding up his arms in greeting. Situated in the Plaza Presidente Juan Domingo Perón, it is close to the Casa Rosada and the headquarters of the General Confederation of Labour, hinting at Perón's link between politics and labour unions. It is also close to the Plaza de Mayo, where Perón was the target of an air attack during the 1955 attempted coup, which killed over 300 people.

And so, Perón's legacy lives on, even for anti-Peronist candidates like Macri. 'Some people use the title "Peronist" to manipulate people, I am not one of those,' Macri told the crowd at the statue's unveiling. 'I want to encourage Peronists to come together, and work for the dream that is Argentina. So many people are suffering. Peronism is not arrogance or pride. Peronism is social justice, fighting for equality, and against poverty in Argentina.'[44]

Latin American elites have a long history of cynically managing their positions of privilege. The old social contract rested on an oligarchy benefitting from higher prices, avoiding taxes, and circumventing weak state systems by privatising education, healthcare, pensions and transport. This 'inequality of opportunity preserved by an oligarchic social contract' is no longer a formula for stability and growth.[45]

All people want to be part of a story. In contemporary politics, the main subject is no longer the candidate but rather the voter. With social media and digital communications, power has shifted to the individual at the expense of traditional political party–based infrastructure. The old messaging that everything will be better in ten years with the necessary reforms no longer suffices. This is especially so in those societies heavily dependent on welfare transfers (via the state through cash or employment, or via remittances) or where the informal economy (and therefore a low regulation, low/no tax setting) dominates. These environments inevitably place a premium less on ideology than problem-solving, and on values rather than promises.

To make it in contemporary politics, political actors require more empathy. They can no longer expect the people to have faith in the system to deliver change. Politicians must connect with people, provide explanations, and make figures and policies meaningful. There is a need to think long term but act with short-term gains in mind. This requires support systems for politicians that are aligned to modern demands. 'We have the same support systems for presidents today that were around with JFK sixty years ago,' says Marcos Peña. There is a premium today on personal relations and emotional intelligence rather than simple technical capacity. Argentina's lesson is that politics and politicians must learn to ask and answer the right set of questions.

There is a fundamental clash to be reconciled in this respect.

A bottom-up approach of putting the people first is at odds with the narcissistic 'saviour' image of politics and many politicians. In an era of social media where power is no longer vertical and hidden but public and horizontal, a more authentic conversation is required. The conditions in Argentina on the cusp of the 2023 general election illustrated the challenges facing politicians: inflation at 120 per cent per annum, foreign reserves all but depleted with no visible sources of credit in sight, a 12 per cent fiscal and quasi-fiscal deficit, and increasing social pressures, particularly among the youth, some 60 per cent of whom live in poverty. In general terms, turning the tide requires quick, bold action to sequence reforms carefully, and to focus both on reducing expenditure and pumping up growth. More specifically, a recovery and reform plan for Argentina will have to unify the exchange rate, bring inflation under control, implement labour market reforms, cut subsidies and government jobs, and facilitate the rapid expansion of the key growth sectors of mining, agriculture, tourism, and oil and gas. As in the early 1990s, it will be a rollercoaster ride, but there is no other way out of Argentina's populist-induced trap.

'It is the role of public policy to create the conditions for investment, focusing on the stabilisation of the economy,' says Luciano Laspina, a PRO member of Congress. And it's the role of politicians to tell the story to the electorate in a manner that captures their imagination and offers a way out of their plight. Ultimately, the success of economic policy is in politicians' best interests.

How to Set Reforms in Stone

'Everything is done halfway in Peru, and that is why everything goes wrong.'
— Mario Vargas Llosa, *The Time of the Hero* (1963)

On 17 December 1996, fourteen Túpac Amaru Revolutionary Movement (MRTA) terrorists, disguised as waiters and caterers, slipped into the home of the Japanese ambassador to Peru, Morihisa Aoki, taking hostage hundreds of diplomats, government and military officials, and business executives at a celebration marking Emperor Akihito's sixty-third birthday.[46] The MRTA, whose stated intent was its pursuit of an ideological blend of Peruvian nationalism and Marxism, demanded the release of 300 imprisoned comrades and a revision of the government's neoliberal free-market reforms.

While most foreigners were permitted to leave the chancellery in the first week, the remaining dignitaries were only freed on 22 April 1997, 126 days later, in a raid codenamed *Chavín de Huántar* and led by commandos of the Peruvian Armed Forces. It was the end of Túpac Amaru, which took its name from the last indigenous leader of the Incas, as an effective military force, though controversy dogged the government of President Alberto Fujimori in the aftermath when it was revealed that several insurgents had been summarily executed by the soldiers.

Four and a half years earlier, the Peruvian Armed Forces had captured Abimael Guzmán, the university lecturer-turned-leader of the Maoist rebel movement Shining Path (*Sendero Luminoso*), a splinter of the Peruvian Communist Party and the MRTA's opposition. Guzmán's goal was to overthrow the government through terrorism and guerrilla warfare. With support from intellectuals and appealing to marginalised groups in the slums and among peasant communities in the mountainous areas, Shining Path grew into a serious threat with around 3 000 armed members by 1990. Their war with the state resulted in the death or disappearance of at least 40 000 people, mostly in the central Andes, and hindered normal economic and social activity. Fujimori's government responded decisively and with force.

On 12 September 1992, members of the Peruvian police force's Special Intelligence Group captured Guzmán and several other Shining Path leaders in an apartment above a ballet studio in the suburbs of the capital, Lima. Intelligence operatives had been monitoring the suspected safe house, and a routine inspection of the garbage revealed empty tubes of a cream used to treat psoriasis, a skin condition that Guzmán was known to have. After his arrest and prosecution, it was only a matter of time before the remainder of the leadership was mopped up. His successor, Óscar Ramírez, was arrested five years later, after which time the *Sendero Luminoso* lost its shine.

The government's crackdown on counterterrorism prevented the MRTA from taking full advantage of Shining Path's decline. The Japanese embassy hostage crisis was their last major action. By passing a new constitution in 1993 and defeating the insurgents, Fujimori seeded the Peruvian economic turnaround that has since defined the Andean nation's growth trajectory.

Peru has enjoyed one of the region's fastest-growing economies, averaging 5.9 per cent during the first fifteen years of the 2000s. Its GDP per capita (measured in constant values) doubled to $6 440 in the first twenty years of the twenty-first century. This was against an earlier history of economic stasis. Between 1960 and 1992, the wealth of citizens had shrunk in real terms to just $2 600.

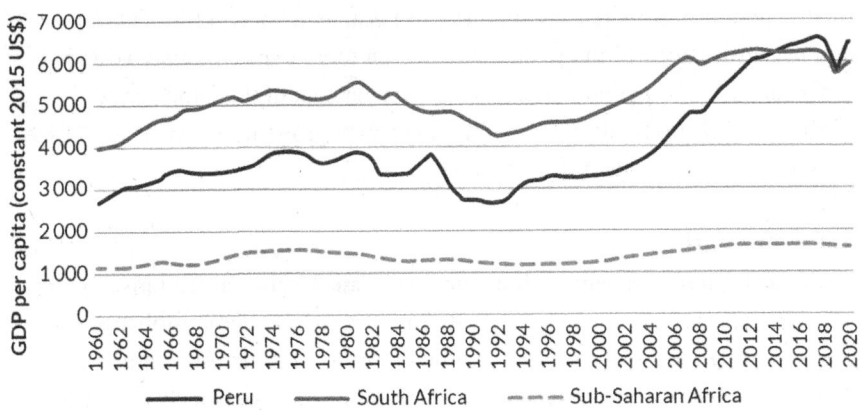

An Andean ascent

Source: World Bank, World Development Indicators

The drivers of export growth have been mining, tourism and agriculture. In 2021, Peru's largest exports comprised copper ore, zinc and gold, with a value of $25 billion, having grown fivefold in thirty years. Similarly, agricultural goods, just $220 million in 1990, touched $10 billion in 2021. The number of foreign travellers nearly quadrupled between 2003 and 2019, from 1.3 million to 4.3 million.

This impressive growth is down to several factors, including rapid urbanisation 'and the export revolution, which has driven a change in opportunity including educational standards,' says Lima-based nutrition expert Dr Claudio Lanata. 'Today, there is a mismatch between the power of economic growth through our exports and the corruption and lack of capacity of the executive arm of government,' he notes.

Indeed, political instability has persisted and with it – or because of it – challenges of governance, especially corruption. Seven presidents came and went in just six years from 2016 (including three in five days in 2020), with three different Congresses governing the country. Under the presidency of Pedro Castillo, elected in 2021 and removed from office the following year, state capacity weakened with more than eighty ministerial changes during his year in office, even though this turnover offered a means to ensure payoffs and paybacks.

While the politics have gone off-road, the economy has motored on regardless, even though problems remain. Around 80 per cent of Peruvians work in the informal sector, a figure that is increasing despite solid economic growth. Many of the rural poor survive from subsistence agriculture, often living in *adobe* (mudbrick) or tin houses lacking electricity and indoor plumbing, while the urban poor congregate in *pueblos jóvenes* (shanty towns), picking up work on the margins. Around one-third of Lima's eleven million inhabitants live in these 'new towns', most without sewerage or electricity, including as many as one million Venezuelan refugees. Still, the poor are an increasing minority in Peru, which has seen a fall in poverty from over two-thirds of the population in 1989 to 20 per cent thirty years later.[47] This is supported by malnutrition halving to 13 per cent in the same period.[48]

The thesis of this book is that politics matters to growth. In Peru, it would seem that economics is delinked from politics. Or is it?

The shiny path

Peru's most famous novelist is the Nobel laureate Mario Vargas Llosa, who ran unsuccessfully for president in 1990. In *The Time of the Hero*, published in 1963 and set among the cadets at Lima's Leoncio Prado Military Academy, which he attended as a teenager, Vargas Llosa writes: 'You can't make facts fit the rules, it is the other way round. The rules have to be adopted to fit the facts.'

President Alberto Fujimori established new rules for the economic turnaround even though Peru's political frailties have deep roots. Their origins in the struggle leading to Peruvian independence from Spain set the stage for perennial contest between a Europhile (and Church-backed) elite and the majority *indigenismo*, interspersed with periods of military rule.

When Europeans arrived in the New World in the sixteenth century, they brought development, disease and practiced dispossession. The Incas, who rose from the Peruvian highlands around 1438 to conquer most of South America, had based their empire in Cusco in modern-day Peru. After prevailing for just 100 years, they fell to a combination of internal division (the brothers Huáscar and Atahualpa, one based in Cusco, the other in Quito, fought over the throne), Spanish guns, smallpox and an influenza epidemic. At the time of the Spanish conquest in 1532, the Incas were estimated at twelve million; a century later, their number had fallen to 600 000.

In 1535, the conquistador Francisco Pizarro founded the capital of Lima, although decades of turmoil ensued. Assassinated by a fellow colonialist in 1541, his remains now rest in the Cathedral of Lima, which borders Plaza Mayor, the bustling main square where he proclaimed the city and on which sits the Government Palace, City Hall, the Union Club, the Archbishop's Palace and the Casa Riva-Agüero, the latter a museum.

An Inca insurgency also lingered, with the last Inca leader, Túpac Amaru II, captured in 1572. With rival conquistador factions jostling to take control of the country's rich mineral deposits, including guano used for fertiliser, by the early 1800s, rebellion was stirring. After leading the liberation of Argentina and Chile from Spain, Argentine general José de San Martín entered Lima and proclaimed Peru's independence on 28 July 1821. On 26 and 27 July 1822, San Martín met with Simón Bolívar, who had freed Venezuela, Colombia and Ecuador, in the port city of Guayaquil (today part of Ecuador) to discuss the future of Peru and South America in general. The two could not come to an agreement. Ill, disillusioned and politically isolated, San Martín promptly resigned from his offices and went into exile. Bolívar continued to Peru. After two decisive battles at Junín and Ayacucho in 1824, the Spanish eventually surrendered control in 1826. By then upper Peru had been separated, creating the Republic of Bolivia. Further conflict with Bolivia and Chile between 1879 and 1883, in part motivated by a tussle for control of potassium nitrate deposits in the Tarapacá region to the south, led to the loss of more Peruvian territory.

Coups and military dictatorships characterised Peru's government for most of the twentieth century. From the end of the Second World War until 1965, the high prices of agricultural exports, mainly cotton and sugar, American-led investment in mining, and rapid urbanisation and industrialisation drove an economic boom. Between 1940 and 1960, the percentage of urban dwellers doubled to 20 per cent of an overall population of ten million. Sixty years later, Peru's population was thirty-four million and the urban share 78.5 per cent.

In 1963, Fernando Belaúnde was elected president with strong middle-class support but was overthrown in a left-wing military coup led by General Juan Velasco in 1968. True to the ideological form of the 1960s and the theory of 'import substitution industrialisation' advocated by the UN Economic Commission for Latin America and the Caribbean, among others, under the military Peru closed itself to the world in the belief that this would drive domestic demand and the growth of industries. Accompanied by the nationalisation of strategic sectors; the creation of new SOEs, price and foreign exchange controls; protectionism; and the expropriation of newspapers, radio and television companies, this period instead saw a flight of foreign capital.[49] The military also re-armed with Soviet weaponry, heavily indebting the country in the process.

Peru was to learn, slowly and painfully, that whereas state-owned companies can mask inefficiencies effectively through taxpayer subsidies rather than revenues, the same rules do not apply to private businesses, which would, in these circumstances, simply go bankrupt. It is a lesson that the left in Peru has continuously sought to forget.

Velasco's agrarian reform caused a surge in urban inflows as people deserted the rural economy, inevitably creating slums. His policies had other costly legacies. In 1974, twenty-year-old Hugo Chávez and around one dozen fellow cadets and soldiers travelled to Ayacucho in Peru to celebrate the 150th anniversary of the decisive battle that secured the country's independence. Celebrated as the end of the Spanish–American wars of independence, the battle between the 'patriots', led by Bolívar's lieutenant Antonio José de Sucre, and the royalist soldiers that fought to preserve the Spanish monarchy took place between the towns of Huamanga and Quinua. Bolívar renamed the former Ayacucho, after citizens began calling the area *Ayakuchu* on seeing so many casualties on the battlefield. *Aya* means 'death' or 'soul' and *k'uchu* means 'corner' in Quechua. Shining Path used Ayacucho, located in one of the poorest areas in the highlands of south-central Peru, as its base for operations against the Peruvian government and staged an assault on the Ayacucho prison in 1982. In December 2022, the Peruvian Army fired on protestors in Ayacucho demonstrating against the removal of President Pedro Castillo from office, resulting in ten dead and sixty-one injured.

At the 150th anniversary celebration, Chávez and the others were greeted by Velasco, who presented them each with an edition of his 1973 publication *La revolución peruana* (*The Peruvian Revolution*). Chávez reportedly studied its contents and carried it on his person until losing it in his 1992 failed coup. As president, Chávez ordered the printing of millions of copies of Venezuela's constitution in the format of miniature blue booklets in tribute to Velasco's gift.[50]

Velasco was himself overthrown in a coup in 1975, the military returning the country to civilian rule in 1980 and giving Belaúnde a second bite at office. Though he returned ownership of media companies, neither state presence in the economy nor price and exchange controls were relaxed, the effect of which was compounded by the devastating El Niño of 1982–83. Belaúnde was followed by the first term of Alan García (1985–90) and his American Popular Revolutionary Alliance (APRA). The thirty-six-year-old's version of socialism, influenced by the thinking of a council of Argentine advisors, included the attempted nationalisation of the banking sector and the imposition of limits on repaying foreign debt, producing an economic meltdown and fuelling social discord and rising violence. Termed 'macro-economic populism',[51] the 'pro-poor' economic policies of García's first term resulted in hyperinflation and a 25 per cent drop in GDP in 1988–89. Poverty in Lima alone increased from 17 per cent in 1985 to 54 per cent by 1990. Per capita consumption fell by 50 per cent on average and by more than 60 per cent among the poorest of the poor.[52]

The 1980s became known as the 'Lost Decade', even though in reality the decline spanned three decades of poor governance and policies, beginning in the early 1960s. Only a change in economic model sparked by the next administration could bring about a resurgence. 'This society is collapsing, without a doubt,' said Peruvian economist Hernando de Soto in an interview in February 1991. 'There is no respect for the state, the parliament, the laws, the judicial system, not even the traffic lights. Nothing works here. But the problems here are so entrenched that you have to have a collapse before you can implement fundamental changes in the political system.'[53]

By the late 1980s, inflation had reached 7 650 per cent. Faced with the unwelcome prospect of another military intervention, in a run-off with the liberal writer Mario Vargas Llosa in the 1990 election, Peruvians shifted their support to Alberto Fujimori, a university professor and son of a gardener, who ran under the banner of Change 90, the right-wing political party he founded. During the campaign, Fujimori, whose parents were Japanese immigrants, was affectionately nicknamed *El Chino*, 'the Chinaman'. He won much support from the poor, who had been frightened by Vargas Llosa's IMF-backed neoliberal austerity proposals. Effectively, a vote for Fujimori was to a large extent a vote against the shock stabilisation plan that Vargas Llosa proposed to implement.

After less than a month in government, however, Fujimori was convinced – both by domestic advisors and prominent members of the international financial community, primarily the Americans and the Japanese – that he had to implement an orthodox shock programme to stabilise inflation and generate revenue. 'He was invited to Japan before the inauguration as the only Japanese-descended head of state outside Japan,' recalls the writer and economist Felipe Ortiz de Zevallos, better known as FOZ. 'He was even invited to an audience with the emperor. In Japan, he was told, to his surprise, that if he followed the stabilisation reform advice of the IMF, he would get Tokyo's full support; if not, he could count on no support.' At this point, in an about-turn of his pre-election position, Fujimori opted for an orthodox approach, and appointed Juan Carlos Hurtado Miller as minister of economy and prime minister.

FOZ wrote Hurtado Miller's speech, which was delivered on 8 August 1990, just ten days after Fujimori's inauguration. It became known as the 'May God help us' speech, the words used by the prime minister when he finished outlining the effects of the price changes. 'So, a can of evaporated milk that cost 120 000 intis on the street today will cost 330 000 intis as of tomorrow,' he announced on live television. 'A kilo of white sugar that was available for 150 000 intis will cost 300 000 intis starting tomorrow. The baguette that cost 9 000 intis this afternoon will cost 25 000 intis starting tomorrow.'

'Fujimori asked the IMF for support for this shock treatment,' recalls FOZ. 'I wrote the speech for the prime minister in which he raised gas prices by thirty-three times. At the time, the US vice president Dan Quayle was visiting Peru, and invited me for lunch, and asked me what we were going to do. I told him a very orthodox policy and a thirty-three-times rise in gas prices. He said at 33 per cent he wondered if he should leave the country that evening. I said no, it's thirty-three times, not per cent.'

Lourdes Flores Nano is a Peruvian lawyer and politician who ran unsuccessfully for the presidency in the 2001 and 2006 elections. She was the first woman to be a major contender for president in the history of Peru, a country where women only gained the vote in the mid-1950s. She served in Congress from 1992 until 2005, becoming the leader of the parliamentary opposition to the Fujimori regime in 1995.

'By the 1990s, the country was in a terrible state,' she says of Fujimori's inheritance. 'García, who knew nothing about the economy, had irresponsibly attacked the Central Bank. He did everything on the list of things that should not be done.' Peru, moreover, was in the grips of a violent insurgency. The economic turbulence created by the García administration exacerbated social tensions and contributed in great part to the rise of Shining Path and the emergence of the MRTA. Just half a block from where we sit is the site of the most devastating Shining Path bomb attack. On 16 July 1992, two trucks, each packed with 1 000 kilograms of explosives, were detonated on Tarata Street in the Lima suburb of Miraflores, killing twenty-five and wounding hundreds more. It signalled the start of a week-long terrorist campaign that caused forty deaths and shut down much of the capital.

Fujimori's shock programme was more extreme than even the most orthodox IMF economist was recommending at the time and quickly became known as 'Fujishock'. And yet, says Flores Nano, his reforms were accepted 'because of the size and extent of the crisis, and because Fujimori, even though he was unprepared, was not Vargas Llosa, who was seen as European and more distant, even though he would have made an excellent president.' Fujimori also had a common touch, at least at the start. There was a perception that, unlike Vargas Llosa, he was much more a man of the people. 'He had campaigned in a poncho and toured the rural areas in a small car canvassing support. He had a popular identity and the support of the armed forces, and he was a workaholic,' notes Flores Nano.

The accidental reformer

'By 1989, we had all the ingredients of a failed state,' says Diego Macera, the director of the Peruvian Institute of Economics. 'Peru was besieged by terrorism and on the brink of collapse. The country had hit rock bottom – in the absence of war, there are few comparable examples of economic catastrophe.' Fujimori wasted no time and used the crisis to good effect, his imperative being to put a stop to hyperinflation. The methods of doing so and delivering growth set up Peru for the next generation, despite his subsequent political machinations and those of his successors.

Fujimori essentially adopted the policies outlined by both Vargas Llosa and the military in their *Plan Verde* ('Green Plan'), which had been drafted by the Peruvian Armed Forces in 1989 in preparation for a coup to overthrow García. Fujimori's raft of reforms included devaluing the currency by more than 400 per cent, raising the prices of basic goods, lowering tariffs (from an average of 80 per cent to 15 per cent), eliminating government subsidies and reducing government employment, implementing price controls, unifying the exchange rate, privatising companies previously nationalised, treating domestic and foreign investors in the same manner, and lifting import restrictions. In all, more than 250 measures were adopted to transform the economy from a closed to an open market. 'It was like an atomic bomb had hit the city,' says Macera. Electricity, fuel and water prices rose dramatically, although poverty relief funds were also established and the minimum wage was raised.

FOZ says today that these measures, and particularly the dramatic increase in prices, have served as a 'vaccine' against further temptation on the fiscal deficit. 'We don't want to go back there,' he notes. It also got the pain over relatively quickly. In 1994, the Peruvian economy grew at a rate of 13 per cent, the fastest worldwide, triggering a long-term growth cycle that has continued for thirty years.

But there was a Dr Fujimori and Mr Hyde dimension to his policy and political pathology. García's APRA and Vargas Llosa's Democratic Front were in control of Congress, in Fujimori's view hindering reform and the fight against Shining Path. Believing, correctly as it turned out, that he had more support from the electorate than Congress, in April 1992 Fujimori carried out a 'self-coup', using the military to shut down Congress unconstitutionally. This set the stage for the remainder of his rule, increasingly characterised by a schizophrenia of economic reforms contrasting with political intolerance and heavy-handedness, including the deterioration of relations with Ecuador, the extrajudicial nature of the counter-insurgency campaign at home, and his ultimately calamitous decision to attempt a third term in office in the 2000 election (despite the constitution limiting a presidency to two terms).

Seeking to legitimise his new position, Fujimori called elections for a Democratic Constitutional Congress, to serve as a legislature and constituent assembly. Unsurprisingly, given the Democratic Front's earlier dissolution and with García now in exile in Colombia, Fujimori's supporters won a majority of the seats and drafted a new constitution in 1993. In a referendum the following year, Fujimori's self-coup and the 1993 constitution were approved by a margin of less than 5 per cent. This constitution remains in place thirty years later and contains basic principles of economic activity, including Central Reserve Bank independence, preventing the bank from funding government, clear limits and controls on public sector economic participation, free markets, the removal of foreign exchange controls, equal treatment of foreign and domestic investors, restrictions on the creation of any new SOEs, and respect for contracts.

With Peru reintegrated into the global economic system, it began to attract foreign investment, which increased steadily during the 1990s and into the 2000s from $40 million in 1990 to peak at over $14 billion in 2014. During the 1980s, the average annual FDI inflow was just $26 million. Between 1990 and 2021, it was $4.2 billion.[54] The sell-off of parastatals improved services, notably the delivery of local telephony. Privatisation also drew in foreign investment in mining and energy extraction, including new copper, gold and zinc mines, and the Camisea gas project.

By the end of the first decade, Peru's international currency reserves had been built up from zero at the end of García's term in 1989 to almost $10 billion. By 2023, they were over $70 billion. Fujimori also left a smaller state bureaucracy, a technically minded administration, a large number of new schools countrywide, improved roads and highways, and an upgraded communications infrastructure, all the while reducing government expenses. These improvements led to the revival of tourism, agro-exports, industries and fisheries.

'Even though there was corruption and he was authoritarian, Fujimori achieved three critical things: he defeated terrorism, changed the mood of the economy, and solved critical international problems,' observes Flores Nano. 'And he was able to achieve continuity for his reform. And he never got to do the second stage, in reforming the state, education, healthcare and all the inefficiencies of government.'

Fujimori is disliked by the left not only because he broke with the pattern of statism of the preceding twenty years, but also because he took away the one place where they could create jobs – in the state sector – through privatisation and constitutionally embargoing the creation of any new SOEs. Ismael Benavides, a banker by profession, served in ministerial positions in fisheries, agriculture and finance in various governments, including the second García administration. He says that 'the left never forgave Fujimori for pushing them out of government on which they lived, capturing Shining Path, and changing the constitution. They have since tried to liquidate any vestiges of Fujimorism, but they could never change the constitution, which is the cornerstone of the stable economy we have now.'

While the left prefers the narrative that, like Augusto Pinochet in neighbouring Chile, Fujimori created a constitution under an undemocratic system, these were very different processes. Whatever went before and came after the 1995 election that saw Fujimori re-elected in a first-round victory over the former UN secretary-general Javier Pérez de Cuéllar, the constitution of 1993 was achieved by political consensus. And since *El Chino*, the country has not had any further structural reforms, 'the building blocks remaining the same, which were essentially Fujimori's reforms,' says Diego Macera. 'There was enough momentum to keep things moving forward.'

Vale un Perú

'We had not developed a major mine in Peru for twenty-four years until the opening of Cuajone in 1992 and Yanacocha the following year,' says Roque Benavides, the president of Buenaventura, a Peruvian mining firm. 'Things changed dramatically with Fujimori, his stabilisation allowing for exploration and his economic reforms for investment.'

Today, Peru is the world's second-largest producer of copper, zinc and silver; third in tin; and seventh (first in Latin America) in gold. Mining accounts for nearly two-thirds of the country's exports. Copper ($17.5 billion in export value), gold ($9.2 billion), zinc ($2.5 billion) and molybdenum ($930 million) led in an overall sector export value of $60 billion in 2022 (in 1990, exports were just $200 million).[55]

Gold and silver drew the Spanish to Peru in the first instance, the colonists coining the phrase *vale un Perú* ('worth a Peru') to describe the depths of the country's riches. Today the phrase denotes any matter of great value. Commercial mining began in the late 1800s, with significant American-led investment in the 1950s.

According to the United States Geological Survey, Peru has 21 per cent of the world's silver reserves, 13 per cent of its zinc, 11 per cent of its copper, 8 per cent of its lead, 5 per cent of its gold and 2.3 per cent of its tin. Between 1996 and 2019, investment in mining projects totalled $71 billion, while employment increased over this period to more than 70 000 direct (and 450 000 indirect) beneficiaries. Growth of the sector is driven by mineral prices, and Peru's growth by mining.

According to one study, a 19 per cent increase in the price of copper, for example, would produce an increase in Peru's GDP of 1.28 per cent.[56]

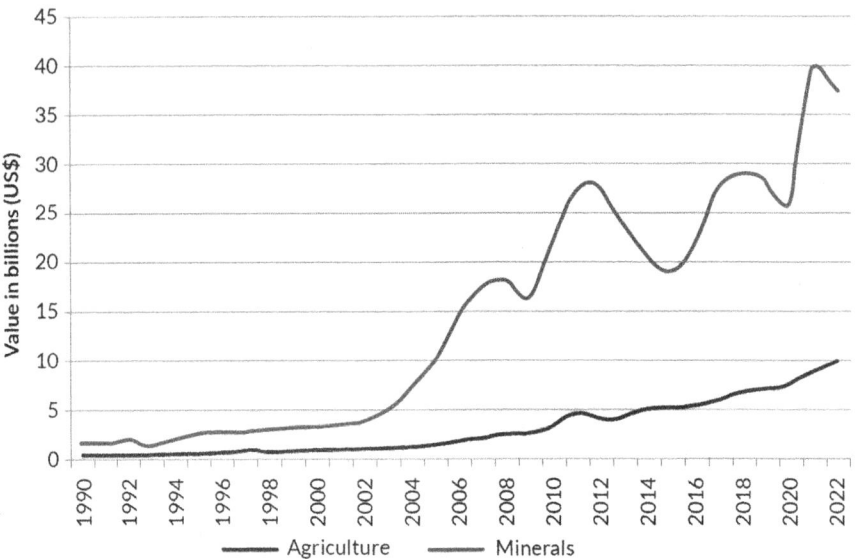

Peruvian mineral and agricultural exports

Source: Central Reserve Bank of Peru

Again, it was Fujimori who implemented several reforms allowing for growth in this sector. The Land Law of 1995 granted mining corporations the right to use land for their operations in exchange for monetary compensation to the landowners while simplifying licensing procedures. Government instituted a new tax regime that exempted mining corporations from taxation and royalties until recouping their capital investment, while also removing restrictions on capital remittances. Along with the broader aspects of market reform – such as the reduction of tariffs on imports, the removal of export taxes, the liberalisation of the capital market and the privatisation of state firms – the environment is set for a major increase in mining investment and production.

With fewer major copper discoveries and an overall decline in grades worldwide, set against increasing urbanisation and the green energy transition, copper demand is expected to rise along with interest in new sources of the metal. Yet just 0.3 per cent of Peru's total territory and an estimated 1 per cent of its reserves have so far been exploited.

With a world-class mineral potential, what is holding miners back from investing in Peru?

For one, there are concerns about relations with local communities.

'When I was prime minister, the principal problem was social conflict within the mining sector,' says Juan Jiménez, a human rights lawyer who served under President Ollanta Humala from July 2012 to October 2013. 'Before, there had been much abuse by industry of the conditions and the communities. But much has now changed, with strict regulations and more responsible companies.'

The problems persist, however. One recent example was the closure of Chinese-owned MMG's Las Bambas copper mine in February 2023 due to political unrest resulting from the removal from office of President Pedro Castillo in December 2022. By the time production was halted, the mine, which supplies 2 per cent of the world's copper, had already lost 30 per cent of its production capacity.[57] The previous owners, Xstrata, had to build a new town for the local community at a cost of over $1 billion, as well as supply cars to homeowners. Yet only around one-third of the community chose to move, the remainder staying in the town of Challhuahuacho, strategically positioned at the valley entrance to the mine. This gives the locals leverage when making demands. Between 2016 and 2023, for example, the mine's operations had been blockaded for over 500 days.

Other investors have had to deal with similar expectations, the demands of the local communities complicated by vested interests in illegal mining operations. In October 2021, Glencore's Antapaccay copper mine was forced to halt the execution of its Coroccohuayco copper and gold project when local communities staged protests, saying the mine would pollute their fresh water. In January 2023, Antapaccay suspended operations after anti-government protestors set fire to company vehicles and attacked the area around the workers' housing. Similarly, the preference of the Chinese owner of Las Bambas to truck the copper concentrate out on an unpaved road, causing pollution, is cited as a catalyst for the instability that ensued there.

'These frictions reflect the inefficiency of the state in distributing the wealth from taxes,' says Roque Benavides. Half of all tax income and all royalties accrue to the twenty-five regional governments, which have scant governance capability. 'People react not against the state, but against the companies,' he notes. Part of the reason for this is the role of the mining companies themselves, which are seen as the 'face' of governance because they drive road development and electrification in rural areas. 'But we also have shareholders, not just stakeholders, and first we have to be efficient to make profits, without which there is no business,' Benavides says of the mining companies.

According to José Carlos Saavedra, chief economist of APOYO Consultoria, a consulting firm and think tank based in Lima, surveys of local communities show that if the price of copper increases, for example, there is greater likelihood of conflict as the prospect of extractive rents increases. Additionally, the chances of conflict are reduced if local authorities invest more. Perhaps the most interesting finding of these surveys is that a key driver of conflict is the behaviour of mineworkers themselves. If they behave badly, including upsetting local social dynamics by causing higher prices and encouraging prostitution, there is likely to be more conflict.

Luis Carlos Rodrigo is a partner in a Lima-based law firm specialising in mining transactions and arbitration. 'You have big, responsible and technically advanced mining companies bringing government to rural areas,' he says. 'This creates levels of inequality between rural areas based on their proximity to these mining companies, bringing a state where there is no state.' This is the first challenge. The second is that local governments are often overwhelmed and easily corrupted by the pickings. 'For example, the village of San Marcos, near Antamina [one of the largest copper and zinc mines in the world], in 1997 had a budget of $5 000 for the whole year. After the mine was developed, it had a budget of $80 million. Of the six mayors since, one has been killed and three are in prison,' says Rodrigo. 'On the Camisea gas project, a small nearby town, Echarate, received $1 billion in royalties over the last fifteen years. The mayor went and spent half of this on the largest swimming pool in South America and a giant marketplace, yet the people in the town lack sewerage and potable water in their homes.'

A government decentralisation drive launched by President Alejandro Toledo in 2002 transformed the structures of government without the governance capacity to backfill. 'Toledo started a regionalisation programme that did not work with twenty-five regions and 2 000 mayors,' says FOZ.

Another constraint is in the capital of the mining companies themselves, not just financially, but also in terms of the human resources needed to carry out and deliver these complex projects successfully. This, in turn, is influenced by risk, in fiscal (tax) terms and by stability, which is linked to levels of unrest. 'Mines are expected to be a mixture of eighteenth-century community, the local government and a twenty-first-century company,' FOZ observes drily.

It is fundamentally difficult to get government to focus on resources that invariably have a ten- to fifteen-year lead time from concept through exploration, feasibility and environmental studies to commencing operations. And where corruption abounds, it is infinitely more lucrative to pursue short-term infrastructure projects that offer politicians lower-hanging fruit free from the scrutiny of global and corporate governance initiatives and niceties.

Despite these complications, mining has expanded exponentially, even though much more could come with better government. And it is not the only sector that is growing.

The world's pantry

Peru's geography and topography are unusual. A narrow strip of desert along the cold waters of the Pacific ramps up into the Andes and a jungle plain beyond, creating a bone-dry climate on the coast but with irrigation from the mountains above. The Incas were quick to seize on this 'Pacific greenhouse' 500 years ago, planting potatoes, tomatoes, beans, corn, peanuts, squash, avocados and cocoa, among others.

Guillermo van Oordt, a past president of the Association of Agricultural Producers Guild of Peru, highlights several advantages of farming in Peru: 'The country is close to the equator, providing more hours of stronger sunshine, allowing high yields and quality.' It also 'hardly ever rains, and there are seldom storms or strong winds. Water is supplied by the fifty-two rivers which flow off the Andes.' A further advantage lies in geographically distinct valley-based agricultural schemes, which 'limits the prospect for the spread of disease'. In addition, 'mild winters and Peru's location in the southern hemisphere offer all-year-round and counter-seasonal advantages for northern hemisphere markets.'

Yet these conditions by themselves are not enough if government is unhelpful.

Juan Velasco's Agrarian Reform Law of 1969 did away with the haciendas (large estates) on which agricultural production was previously concentrated. Under new stipulations, no coastal (crop) farm was to be larger than 150 hectares,[58] and there were to be no absentee farmers. For the decade from June 1969, more than 15 000 estates and nine million hectares of land were expropriated, being awarded in turn to 370 000 beneficiaries from co-operatives to individuals. Without technical support, however, most could not succeed, and the small size of individual land plots made commercial farming difficult. This was undone by Fujimori's agrarian reform of the 1990s, which transformed the relationship between private producers and government in three fundamental ways, notes Van Oordt.

The first was in allowing labour flexibility. Rather than forcing year-long permanent employment, the agricultural sector was permitted to employ temporary labour at the same daily rates that they would enjoy in permanent employment. The second was a 50 per cent reduction in tax payable, providing this money was reinvested in the business. The third was the establishment of free-trade agreements with all of Peru's major trading partners. The smooth application of phytosanitary standards was also key to the package of reforms.

Peru began exporting from the Viru Valley in the northern coastal region of La Libertad in the 1950s. Today, the country has around two million hectares under cultivation, of which 10 per cent drives exports. It is a world export leader in asparagus, avocados, blueberries, grapes, mandarins and pomegranates.

With 22 000 hectares under intensive cultivation, Peru exports fresh, jarred and frozen asparagus to more than seventy countries. As one measure, by 2016, Peru supplied 14 per cent of the Asian market. But blueberries are today Peru's largest agricultural export by value. The country produced 280 000 tonnes of blueberries in 2021/22 (of 1.3 million tonnes globally), of which 220 000 tonnes were exported, most destined for rich US, Chinese and European markets. By comparison, the largest African producer is South Africa with 26 000 tonnes, of which 21 000 were exported, mostly to the EU (to which Peru exports 70 000 tonnes annually).

According to South African producers, the Peruvians' biggest competitive advantages are scale and, feeding that, logistics. The comparative efficiency of Peruvian ports (ranked halfway up the World Bank's index, with South Africa's ports clustered at the bottom), amplifies the benefits of a shorter journey for producers (10 500 kilometres from Peru to Antwerp, compared to 13 000 kilometres from Cape Town to Antwerp), whatever the quality and cost of production. The concessioning of Peru's ports to private operators, including Lima's port of Callao to Maersk and Dubai Ports World, through which 60 per cent of all trade flows, has significantly improved efficiencies.

The success with blueberries is just part of Peru's booming agricultural sector. According to the International Trade Administration, Peruvian agricultural exports increased from $645 million in 2000 to an estimated $9.2 billion by 2021.[59]

Traditional products have not been neglected in this agricultural revolution. Peru produced some 220 000 tonnes of wheat and over 33 000 tonnes of cheese in 2021, while it is the largest exporter worldwide of organic bananas, the fifth largest in table grapes and fourth in mangoes.[60] Overall, the agricultural sector contributed the most to poverty reduction. Nearly half of workers in the sector are women, and future plans include major irrigation projects that will incorporate a further 440 000 hectares into commercial agriculture.

Agricultural success does not just lie in cheap labour. It demands knowledge of markets, capital, technology and logistics. In any case, labour is certainly not cheaper than the African equivalent, the average daily wage on the haciendas and in the packhouses being $20, well above the national minimum monthly wage of $266. Peru has successfully integrated rural ways with global standards. Its packhouses use the most modern, laser-driven sorting and sizing machinery to ensure that the right products reach the correct markets at a standard and price that is acceptable.

And yet, problems in politics persist.

AIDS or cancer?

While Fujimori's economic reforms were making huge strides, politically he lost the plot.

In September 2000, a video was released showing Fujimori's head of intelligence, controversial former army captain Vladimiro Montesinos, bribing a congressman. It was the tip of the iceberg. The scandal caused Fujimori's ten-year presidency to spiral out of control. The president, who had won a third term in May 2000, resigned that November during a state visit to Asia, seeking exile in Japan. He was charged in absentia for a number of crimes related to corruption and human rights abuses, but Japan refused Peru's repeated extradition requests. In 2005, apparently plotting a return to Peruvian politics, Fujimori was arrested while on a trip to Chile and extradited in 2007. He was tried in Peru and imprisoned.

In 2006, Alan García ascended to the presidency once more, although his second term was considerably more measured and moderate than his first. Between 2006 and 2011, Peru grew its economy at an average of 6.8 per cent, the fastest rate in Latin America. The poverty rate declined from close to 60 per cent in 2000 to just over 20 per cent in 2015 as trade with the US and China expanded.

Despite the blemish on the family record, Fujimori's daughter Keiko was elected to Congress in a landslide in 2006 and ran for president in 2011, losing in a tight run-off to former army officer Ollanta Humala. 'AIDS or cancer' was the way in which Nobel laureate Mario Vargas Llosa described the choice between the two candidates.[61]

In 2021, left-leaning Pedro Castillo was voted in, promising a government intent on beating racism, classism and homophobia. He didn't mention corruption, for good reason.

Castillo's rise to power was in part the product of an identity ticket, a wannabe populist who played the radical and ethnic card for what it was worth, appealing to both the *indígena* (those of indigenous descent) and the *caviares* (the comfort-seeking socialists). Born to a peasant family and one of nine children, Castillo had a tough upbringing, working as a labourer to fund his studies. He became a primary-school teacher and unionist, gaining prominence in a national teachers' strike in 2017. His moment came with the opportunity to be the presidential candidate for the Free Peru party led by a Cuban-educated former governor, Vladimir Cerrón.

Peru is a bicultural society. One half of the population speaks Spanish, adheres to Spanish traditions, and comprises whites (estimated at less than 15 per cent of the population) and *mestizos* (people of mixed indigenous and European heritage). The other half are *indígena*, most of whom inhabit rural areas in the Andes, work in agriculture and speak Quechua (and Spanish), though a minority speak Aymara. That there is a racial dimension to poverty in Peru is undeniable; what is equally certain is that populist attempts at redistribution that invite corruption are economically and socially destructive if politically tempting.

Castillo, like Fujimori before him, faced an array of powerful forces, including political and business leaders. Accused by Congress of corruption, especially after his chief of staff was found with $20 000 in his office's bathroom, Castillo survived two impeachment attempts before falling to a third in December 2022.

There are two redeeming features to Peru's 'Big Man' politics. The first is in political accountability. Alberto Fujimori (1990–2000) went to jail in 2007, initially for six years, for ordering an illegal search. In 2009, he was sentenced to an additional twenty-five years for crimes against humanity, being found guilty of murder, bodily harm and two incidences of kidnapping.

Alan García (1985–90; 2006–11), who failed in another political comeback attempt in 2016, killed himself in 2019 as officers prepared to arrest him on corruption charges. Former president Alejandro Toledo (2001–06) was also accused of corruption and was extradited to Peru in April 2023 to stand trial. Ollanta Humala (2011–16) and his successor, Pedro Pablo Kuczynski (2016–18), have been under investigation for receiving bribes in the same Odebrecht construction scandal that snared García and Toledo. Martín Vizcarra (2018–20) was ousted by Congress following reports that he had received bribes as a regional governor.

On 7 December 2022, Castillo announced that he was dissolving the 130-seat Congress and replacing it with an 'exceptional emergency government', as well as declaring a nationwide state of emergency. The president said the move was aimed at 're-establishing the rule of law and democracy'. This self-coup – known in Latin America as an *autogolpe*, by which the head of government, usually having come to power through legal means, tries to stay in power through illegal means – preceded the third impeachment vote in Congress to remove Castillo from office. Between 1946 and 2022, around 148 *autogolpes* have taken place worldwide. In Latin America, recent attempts include Fujimori's 1992 dissolution of Congress, Guatemalan president Jorge Serrano Elías's ultimately unsuccessful attempt in 1993, and Bolivian president Evo Morales's failed bid in 2019, when he tried to claim, in contradiction to international observers, that he had won a controversial fourth term and subsequently fled the country.

Castillo was ultimately detained while allegedly attempting to flee the country and was being held in preventive custody, pending investigation, in the same prison as Fujimori and Toledo.

The second redeeming feature in Peruvian politics is the independence of key institutions, notably the Central Reserve Bank, which has been able to maintain the line on monetary policy, enabling currency stability and keeping up confidence and trust – aspects lacking in Argentina.

Julio Velarde has been the governor of the Central Reserve Bank of Peru since

2006. A former professor of economics at Universidad del Pacífico, Velarde served successively as manager in the Bank of Industry, as economic advisor to the minister of industry and as financial manager of the Central Mortgage Bank of Peru. In 1990, he was appointed member of the board of governors of the Central Reserve Bank and advisor to the minister of finance. In 2003 he was named executive president of the Latin American Reserve Fund, a post he held until 2006, when he took up the position of Central Reserve Bank governor.

Many influential Peruvians regard Velarde as the personification of stability and economic prudency, an epithet he laughingly shrugs off. 'Economic reforms have managed to protect macro-stability,' he says. 'After hyperinflation, people wanted low inflation and would accept horrible measures in the process.' While the Central Reserve Bank has a stability rather than a growth mandate, 'this is not incompatible with growth, as you need stability for growth'. 'Macroeconomic fundamentals are the most important thing. You cannot substitute the fundamentals by talking,' he says, in a mild rebuke of his political colleagues. Furthermore, he notes that 'corruption' and 'childish' political behaviour have caused volatility and that, as a consequence, 'there is a need to change the rules'.

Resetting politics

Fujimori's reform momentum continued under governments that were not that different ideologically – that is, right-of-centre but with a left-of-centre narrative. The leftist Castillo is the only real exception. Toledo, for instance, furthered the Fujimori reforms by opening international trade, reforming the public pension system, and signing free-trade agreements with the US, the EU and China. With a reputation to restore after his disastrous first term, García proved very pro-investment, as his growth record shows.

But thirty years on from Fujimori, the politics have veered away from alignment with the economy. This started during Toledo's time, with what political analyst Augusto Townsend describes as 'the populist bombs thrown from Congress', which were deflected by a highly technocratic finance ministry and the Central Reserve Bank. While previously the business community found common ground with politics, they have grown more estranged. The international context – such as the 2008 global financial crisis, the Covid-19 pandemic and the related mining price downturn – has also played a role. At the same time, the press, a defence mechanism against extremism, has come under increasing attack by populists. New political funding laws have aimed to prevent private funding for political parties, even though some maintain cosy relationships with drug traffickers, illegal loggers and mining interests. 'Most politicians operated as criminal organisations, not in the business of representing voters, but trying to game the system,' notes Townsend. One measure of this is that no elected president since Fujimori has departed office without a major criminal and/or legal investigation hanging over them, often leading to incarceration.

In this environment, identity politics trumps ideas on the political battlefield. 'In Peru it has become very easy to put out and sell a populist narrative that the wealthy, Spanish elite is bribing their way to continued privilege,' says Townsend. And the lack of connection to the common voter is amplified by growing informality within the economy, where 70 per cent of the workforce operates outside the formal system, and just 5 per cent pay income tax. People have preferred to opt out, free from government interference.

Furthermore, the political terrain is highly fragmented, with eighteen parties and candidates contesting the 2021 election in a ballotage system in which the best two go through to a second round. In the absence of party primaries, however, the division of the vote at the centre, for instance, can lead to the election of the extremes. In the first round of the 2021 election, Castillo managed only 16 per cent, but because the centre-right voters divided their share of the vote between three major candidates, he got through. The second-round choice was between left-wing Castillo and far-right Keiko Fujimori, both polarising choices. In Congress, Castillo's party won only 37 of the 130 seats. A Marxist–Leninist president and a centre-right Congress were never going to work well together.

Even though the protection built into the 1993 constitution has so far prevented its change (such an act would require an eighty-seven-vote majority), the system has become increasingly dysfunctional. In sum, the checks and balances that existed before have started 'flaking', in Townsend's words, 'with a disproportionate influence on the country'.

A final concern about Peru's democratic trajectory relates to its international partnerships, especially given the prominence of China as the major off-taker of its fishmeal (in which Peru is the largest exporter worldwide) and minerals, as well as a major investor in the latter.

The instinctive response to this environment has been to create fresh laws, including those that prevent the re-election of public officials. There have also been proposals to establish a bicameral legislature and to hold mid-term elections. As in Africa, there is also support for a *caudillo* or strongman to 'get the job done', though in Latin America as elsewhere this has tended to be even worse than the civilian, democratic alternative.

The answer is less likely an exclusively institutional one than an integral one, with the development of a better system of politicians – that is, both the hardware of government and its institutions, and the software of better raw material. This means improved selection processes, preparation and training, media competitiveness, and the breaking of special interests between political patrons and political parties. There is no magic bullet, but rather a longer process of encouraging a better class of competitor to pitch as politicians.

Conclusion: The chicken and the avocado

Lima's crushing traffic is as much a product of reform and success as it is of failure. Plans by García to build an overhead railway got as far as building the uprights and a small section of track before he left office in 1989, running out of fiscal growth and, consequently, finances. It remained a monument to failed ambition for twenty years, paralysed by accusations of bribery and corruption, before the first stretch of thirty-five kilometres was finally completed in 2011, after García's second term.

Peru is touted as a land of contrasts, of jungle and desert, high mountains and endless beaches, grey sands and green valleys, rich and poor, urban and rural, rich urban and poor urban, rich rural and poor rural, agrarian and services-based, modern and ancient, immigrant and indigenous, extractive and inclusive, and where the air is gaspingly thin and where it is thick and plentiful. There are some areas where the contrasts are less discernible, between what is legal and illegal, right and wrong, between that which is private and public, fair and corrupt. It is a country where existence can be crushingly hard and even unfair, and yet exceptionally rewarding and breathtakingly beautiful.

Some lessons remain constant. Under various presidents, military and civilian, Peru learnt a tough reform lesson: modern economies depend on investment. 'Without investment there is no growth,' former prime minister Juan Jiménez reminds us. There is a need also to protect key institutions, such as the Central Reserve Bank, which have endured despite political shenanigans.

Which came first? Political change, if not stability, preceded the economic reforms that have endured for thirty years, even while the politics has degenerated. Despite its difficult social, economic and political history, Peru has made great strides, leaving similarly endowed African countries in its wake.

'*Gallina vieja da buen caldo*' as the local saying goes. 'The old chicken makes the best soup.' The chicken in this instance is the 1993 constitution, which has kept the country on its reform track, whatever the left's attempts to change it. This has birthed myriad opportunities in mining and agriculture, from blueberries to the avocado.

Vargas Llosa might complain that everything is done halfway in Peru, but the economic reforms of the 1990s were not. Whatever the political upsets, and whatever the economic premium they have extracted, they were well done and have endured.

North Africa and the Middle East

'ALL the old paintings on the tombs/ They do the sand dance, don't you know/ If they move too quick (oh whey oh)/ They're falling down like a domino,' sang the all-girl Bangles in 'Walk Like an Egyptian'.

And fall like dominoes in the Arab Spring they did.

On 17 December 2010, Mohamed Bouazizi, a poor flower-seller in Sidi Bouzid in the centre of Tunisia, set himself alight after a run-in with police over his alleged refusal to pay a bribe. His death two weeks later triggered angry protests, leading to the toppling of long-time president Zine El Abidine Ben Ali, the first leader to go in what seemed then to be a heady Spring.

Reminiscent less of the 1968 Prague Spring than the suddenness of the collapse of the Soviet bloc in Eastern Europe's 1989 'Autumn of Nations', Ben Ali fled to Saudi Arabia on 14 January 2011 in the face of mounting protests. Within the month, Egyptian president Hosni Mubarak had resigned as protestors occupied Cairo's Tahrir Square and clashed with the army and police. The arrest and torture of teenagers who had painted anti-government slogans on a school wall in the southern city of Deraa in March 2011 sparked a civil uprising in Syria that eventually led to bloody civil war. Following a controversial international humanitarian 'responsibility to protect' intervention, Muammar Gaddafi was overthrown in Libya in August 2011 and killed by militants near Sirte on 20 October. In November 2011, Yemeni president Ali Abdullah Saleh signed a power transfer deal in exchange for immunity from prosecution.

The Arab Spring was approaching its democratic climax, but all too soon it cooled into autumn. Since then, the cause of democracy has gone backwards across much of North Africa and the Middle East, though there has been a second wave in Lebanon and Algeria, the latter emerging with its own transition from a military-backed gerontocracy to something that accords better to a population whose average age is just twenty-seven.

Libya has effectively divided into two regions – west and east – as it was some 3 000 years ago under the Phoenicians and Greeks in Tripolitania and Cyrenaica respectively. Neighbouring Tunisia has not only failed to consolidate its democratic gains under President Kais Saied, who came to power in 2019 and who, two years later, sacked the prime minister, suspended parliament and pushed through a constitution enshrining his one-man rule, but it has also not yet restored the economy to the levels of prosperity enjoyed under Ben Ali, who died in exile in 2019, the penultimate surviving leader deposed in the Arab Spring. Egypt's Hosni

Mubarak died in February 2020. Yemen, like Syria, remains locked in a bloody civil war.

A quarter of the region's twenty countries rank among the bottom twenty in the Economist Intelligence Unit's 2023 Democracy Index, with only one, Israel, ranking in the top half as a 'flawed democracy'. The region's democracy score of 3.34 is well below the global average (5.29) and that of sub-Saharan Africa (4.14). As Mohamed ElBaradei, the Egyptian opposition leader and Nobel Peace Prize winner, has written: 'Democracy isn't like instant coffee. It needs an enabling environment and a hospitable culture to flourish and grow. A history of colonialism, followed by decades of authoritarianism, meant that this environment was absent in the Arab world.'[1]

Egypt, the regional giant, has gone through a cycle of civilian government following elections in 2012 won by the Muslim Brotherhood, the removal of its leader Mohamed Morsi from the presidency by the armed forces a year later, and the installation of the head of the Supreme Court as interim president before the election of Field Marshal Abdel Fattah el-Sisi, a former minister of defence and director of military intelligence, in 2014 with 96 per cent of the vote.

The 25 January Revolution in Tahrir Square to force Mubarak's resignation was largely middle class, driven by social media and middle-class values, tastes and aspirations, and led, ironically, by the beneficiaries of the system that had fuelled the political crisis. Symbolically, Google executive Wael Ghonim was a prominent organiser,[2] the digital link explaining why Egyptian activists sometimes refer to the period as the 'Internet Revolution' or 'Revolution 2.0'.[3] While 'bread, freedom and social justice' was among the most popular chants, there were other ambitions among the protestors. The middle class wanted to take Egypt to the next level, to create democratic politics, to have an 'opposition which contests policy and creates options and legitimacy for government actions,' said one journalist at the time of Tahrir Square. The revolution 'showed that we are not Chinese: growth without democracy is not enough, especially where you have an internationalised middle class. And we are not India: democracy without growth won't work in Egypt.'[4]

Among this middle class, there was anger at how Egypt's ruling elite, in particular Mubarak's National Democratic Party, his family and his coterie, had profited financially. Egypt's longest-serving ruler since Muhammad Ali Pasha (1805–48), Mubarak simply carried on despite declining health and growing public resistance, cracking down on any opposition and displaying in the process a remarkable, pharaonic degree of political contempt and personal egotism.

In their zeal to overthrow Mubarak, the January protestors unknowingly played into the hands of the military, the most powerful institution in Egypt and long seen as the institutional backbone to social order. Recognising Mubarak's loosening grip and intent on protecting its interests against political contamination and a pending transfer of power to his son, Gamal, who had no personal martial pedigree, the military allowed the protests to run their course in removing the president. In successive regimes led by Gamal Abdel Nasser (1954–70), Anwar Sadat (1970–81) and Mubarak (1981–2011), the gravitas afforded its leadership during war and its possession of 'the key levers of power' made the military the 'only institution able to effect change by force'. As such, the armed forces enjoy a 'detached, exceptional status' and are seen as the ultimate guardians of the secular, modern state.[5]

But this is only part of the picture. The 1952 revolution that overthrew the Egyptian monarchy and established the modern Republic of Egypt was carried out by a group of army officers led by General Mohamed Naguib and Colonel Gamal Abdel Nasser, who served as Egypt's first and second presidents respectively. The two abolished the multiparty system and established 'a state where the armed institutions are above any other, including the elected ones'.[6] The government's resultant absence of legitimacy and lack of a common touch was complicated by a legacy, introduced by the military under Nasser, of socialist bureaucratic inertia, vested business interests and corruption on a grand scale. The privilege of power afforded to the armed forces both maintained and enabled an empire of business interests, benefitting from 'preferential customs and exchange rates, tax exemption, land ownership and confiscation rights ... and an army of almost-free labourers' in the form of conscripted soldiers.[7] Though no official figures have ever been released, the military is said to control around 40 per cent of the economy in sectors as diverse as real estate, fuel stations, cigarettes and cement – for some, crowding out the private sector, but for others, a pillar of the establishment without whom, as one international civil servant put it in the wake of the Morsi regime, 'things would not work as well'.[8]

Egypt's population increased from twenty-eight million in 1961 to 109 million by 2021. The population of the capital Cairo alone rose from just three million to over twenty in the same period. Like the rest of North Africa, youth unemployment has steadily risen as population numbers have surged.

Under the proto-military government of Mubarak, a combination of a lack of democracy and economic opportunity divided society into the careless elite and the burgeoning, itinerant underclass, occupying two different worlds: one chic, secular and relatively comfortable, catered for and protected by the state system, where children are privately educated and take their meals at Western-style food emporia; the other ramshackle and desperate, where social needs and aspirations are met by Islamic groups, if at all, and where children rote-learn madrasa-style while chewing subsidised bread. Chief among these in the Mubarak era was the Muslim Brotherhood, an organisation founded in 1928; its political ambitions long and its reputation strong due to its relatively sophisticated service to Egypt's neglected underclass.

The two worlds are the difference between life on the man-made island of Zamalek, encircled by the Nile, with its swish shops, apartments, Edwardian mansions and cypress tree–lined avenues, and life in the old working-class neighbourhood of Imbaba, located on the mainland, northwest of the island, where those in the shantytown of Western Munira live on the edge. While roughly the same size as Zamalek (twenty-one square kilometres), Munira's population density is ten times higher, at 50 000 people per square kilometre – in thumbnail terms, more than four people per room. Unlike the comforts across the river, in the 1980s, Munira lacked schools, hospitals, public transportation and even sewerage.[9] It is little wonder that an Islamic leader, Shaikh Jabir, was able to take over the area for three years, collecting taxes and implementing a strict code of Islamic morality. 'Extremism is grown on a good soil, and a combination of injustice, poverty and insecurity is just such a soil,' reflects one Egyptian journalist.[10]

Close to one-third of Egyptians live below the poverty line, while the World Bank estimated in 2019 that 'some 60% of Egypt's population is either poor or vulnerable'.[11] While some of those Egyptians at the bottom of the social pyramid may have shared the democratic aspirations of their middle-class Tahrir Square compatriots, many had a different goal in mind. A more radical, Islamist government offered a more sympathetic alternative to those locked in the slums, with a basic education but few employable skills and even fewer job opportunities, especially for the youth (three-quarters of the country's unemployed are between fifteen and twenty-nine years old).

For a moment, the 2011 revolution brought these two worlds together, and indifference finally met indigence. But the different motives in this congregation soon became violently evident in protests in June 2013, which led to El-Sisi's taking power from Morsi in a military coup the following month. 'The Muslim Brotherhood was the most ready of all the civilian parties, but they were stupid, Egypt proving too big for them,' reflects Mohamed Anwar Esmat Sadat, the nephew of former president Anwar Sadat and leader of the Reform and Development Party.

El-Sisi's rise was a reversion to the practice before 2011 when the republic's presidents – Naguib, Nasser, Sadat and Mubarak – all enjoyed professional military backgrounds, given the armed forces' role in the 1952 revolution. Some even maintain that the 2011 revolution was a setup by the military to remove President Mubarak from power and prevent his son from taking over. It was also scarcely a clear-cut struggle between autocratic and democratic forces. Morsi was hardly a democrat-in-waiting. By quickly usurping state power, he wasted little time positioning himself as what ElBaradei described as 'Egypt's new pharaoh'.[12]

The return of the 'generals' indicated that, at least for the Egyptian elite, radicalism was not an option. And muddling through was not either, explaining El-Sisi's subsequent set of bold economic reforms. Civil service, monetary and fiscal restructuring saw pre-Covid growth spurt to over 5 per cent. Tied to a 2016 $12-billion IMF deal, some previous no-go areas went under the knife, including the Byzantine 6.5-million-strong civil service (excluding the 1.5 million in the military), which, he said, could be pruned to just one million, and the privatisation of more than 200 state-owned enterprises. This comprised more than 22 per cent of Egypt's workforce, in contrast with around 13 per cent in Turkey. The economic size of the public sector in Egypt was estimated at over 30 per cent in 2017, two to three times the average in leading emerging economies.[13]

The need for policy boldness is a salutary reminder of its absence during the previous authoritarian government of Mubarak.[14] Between 1988 and 2018, for example, Egypt's real GDP per capita barely doubled, reaching $2 407, less than half the metric for other emerging markets, while the benefits of that growth were unevenly shared, as the difference between Zamalek and Munira illustrate.

In part this is down to the growth model pursued. Whereas high-growth emerging economies, especially in East Asia, have prospered through opening up to capital, trade, technology and talent, Egypt has kept its economy closed, in part because of the state sector's resistance to change to retain its privileges and the rents it can extract from tourism, domestic industries, hydrocarbons, worker remittances, trade through the Suez Canal, and aid.

And for all the corrective discipline of the IMF, it's still not clear if outsiders can help much. Aid did little to encourage Mubarak down a reform path after all, despite his regime receiving an estimated $133 billion in cumulative foreign aid and military assistance. And longevity is not always helpful either. Mubarak was in power for three decades, becoming increasingly part of the problem, not the solution.

As one insider who preferred anonymity put it, the Mubarak era was akin to a car with four wheels: 'the economy, one of them, was being attended to; the social and political wheels were being neglected; the security wheel was overinflated. Like the Nasser and Sadat periods, there were three eras to Mubarak. The 1950s Nasser was pragmatic; the 1960s version was the Arab socialist; and that after 1967, the defeated Nasser. With Sadat, you had the man of war until 1973. Then the man of peace. And then, after the bread riots of January 1977, the man of chaos,' a period culminating in his assassination on 6 October 1981, the anniversary of his greatest victory (the Egyptian crossing of the Suez Canal to seize the Bar Lev Line from

Israel) eight years earlier. 'With Mubarak, his thirty years were, first, about learning and experimenting until the first Gulf War, when he adopted a regional leadership role. After a while, he increasingly came to delegate more authority to his son and others and was not fully in control.' While Mubarak had a pro-growth agenda and pursued financial sector reform, he wrongly assumed that trickle-down growth 'would be enough' and thus lacked specific pro-poor interventions.[15]

Despite the early period of bounce-back growth, El-Sisi's reform plans quickly ran into trouble. To fund infrastructure expenditure along with an increase in the military budget, foreign debt more than tripled between June 2013 and March 2022 to over $140 billion, raising the external debt-to-GDP ratio from 15 per cent to more than 35 per cent, around a third of which was owed to multilateral institutions. By 2023, Egypt was the second-largest IMF creditor after Argentina. With the currency now floating – a condition of the original IMF loan (with two more following by 2023) – the Egyptian pound fell by 400 per cent in the six years from 2016, driving up inflation. The prices of bread and other basic foodstuffs became unaffordable to millions of vulnerable Egyptians.[16]

The government has come under criticism for spending on megaprojects, including transportation infrastructure, a new city near El Alamein and a new administrative capital seventy kilometres east of Cairo, set against urgent needs in education and healthcare. Loans, including substantial inflows from Gulf states, have been used not to improve the conditions for doing business, critics argue, but to protect the revenue and assets of the armed forces, including financing major projects in which the military could earn significant money, and to expand the military budget for an ambitious renewal programme. This has contrasted with the implementation of austerity measures – including cuts to subsidies on fuel and electricity – to try to balance government finances. While the social wheel has been kept inflated to an extent by Egypt's flagship social protection programme, known as Takaful and Karama (Solidarity and Dignity), inflation is rising faster than its benefits.

While the involvement of the military in the economy offers a short-term remedy to problems of implementation, it poses a challenge for long-term reform and growth, not least by stunting private sector competition and foreign investment. Yet there is no incentive to reform the military out of its role in masquerading as a government and, in the words of journalist Hafsa Halawa, 'milking the country's wealth for themselves'.[17]

President El-Sisi's image adorns the walls of the Egyptian Military Academy in Heliopolis, Cairo, where he received his education. Unsurprisingly, he has fallen back on the institution that delivered him to power, relying on the military to implement his reforms and in so doing take an even greater stake in managing the civilian economy than during Mubarak's time. In the process, the military has effectively replaced the government in awarding contracts, managing the infrastructure programme and providing affordable goods. It also reflects a mistrust of the business sector.

'Egypt has since 1952 been a one-man show, sometimes tougher, sometimes softer, and without effective institutions, including the judiciary and parliament, which balance and check power,' says Sadat. 'So, everything is run by the president and his close circle.' The dangers in such an approach are manifold. 'We need to send a positive message to our friends and partners that Egypt is stable and safe, and the president alone does not decide everything and is the number one leader and number one economist.' Throw in a dollop of fear and intimidation, including the retirement or arrest of military rivals, and there is an unhealthy lack of open debate and competition of ideas.

There are other dangers in running such a 'deep state' to compensate for government weakness, or perceptions of business sector reliability, not least that it 'further weakens and marginalises' the very agencies it looks to support, racking up problems for the future and overlooking the structural issues in the economy. These centre on 'low productivity, low investment in all sectors except for energy and real estate, and low value-added, especially in technology-dependent sectors'.[18] 'The model is wrong,' says a local economist. 'It's like Dubai, all about big towers and big projects to impress the neighbourhood. Yet the infrastructure which is required is more on the tech side, in the digital economy, in human capital and in the green economy.' And, as Sadat notes, 'private business and foreign investors cannot also compete against the military [to run businesses], which have exceptions and don't pay customs duties or taxes.' To this he might add the advantages of cheap, conscripted labour and free land.

The drive west from the great port city of Alexandria along the newly built seven-lane highway to El-Sisi's New Alamein (inaugurated in 2018) is lined by over a hundred kilometres of apartment and office blocks, peaking at the city's distinctive towers, a stone's throw from the original town of El Alamein. Evidently most of these buildings, new and old, are unoccupied, the business premises to support them lying empty, the fading window signage hinting at past ambition. The coastal resort names come regularly – Lazorde Bay, Marassi Golf Resort, Marseilia Land, Marina this and Marina that – many little more than an impressive gate and a series of partially completed complexes. In between this freshly poured concrete landscape is the site of two key battles of the Second World War, a history quickly being overtaken by the future.

Old Alamein, New Alamein

A dusty railway station
Now a famous name
On which history hinged
El Alamein

When the battle
For Britain, was at its height
Mussolini's imperial mettle
Took to Egypt the fight

So began, urged that chief
The Desert War
Rommel to the Italian relief
Raging up and down Gazala's shore

A last line of defence
A site of attack
Alamein where the forces would condense
No turning back

Rommel's stretched lines
Denying by bluff and guile
Hidden by a Devil's Garden of mines
Aimed for the Nile

Wellington's lesson
They came on in the same old way
Choked by the Qattara Depression
Led by Monty, he of the fancy beret

After Alamein said Winston
Never a defeat
So the war's outcome was written
No more retreat

Eighty years past
First-hand memories fade
The laws of desert combat
Of logistics and mass are victories made

The sweetness of the bougainvillea
The courage of young men

The flower of the Commonwealth, Greece, Poland, Italy, Germany, France, and India
Fighting for kith and ken

All soldiers
Dug in the hard desert limestone
A world on their shoulders
There 16 240 rest, another 49 000 unknown

First World War battle
Fought with Second World War equipment
Now the Third World has problems to tackle
Once azure horizon indignant

The battlefield enveloped
A headstone for paradise
Egypt to be developed
The ultimate price?

The lesson from El-Sisi's contemporary record is that reform is complex and involves getting more than one thing right, in this case big infrastructure.

Egypt is a cautionary tale too of the gulf between the enthusiasm of investment bankers and the people on the ground, and the difference between growth and debt. One investment bank called Egypt the 'most attractive reform story'[19] in the Middle East, Africa and Eastern Europe as investors flooded in after 2018. By 2023, the government had allocated nearly two-thirds of its budget to pay the interest, loans and instalments on its debt.

The underlying question, however, is what are the incentives for the military regime to do the right thing? The institution is unlikely to want to reform itself out of a job entirely, given the depth of its commercial tentacles. It may eventually have no option, not least since democracies have historically performed better in development terms in Africa than their autocratic alternatives, in part because of their self-corrective capacity and competitive nature.

There are three scenarios: One is where the regime muddles on, keeping a security lid on things, and maintaining support largely out of fear of another Arab Spring rather than the promise of delivery. A second scenario is where El-Sisi, or his replacement, most likely drawn from the military, moves rapidly to reform the economy, putting technocrats in place and curtailing the expansion of military companies. A third scenario is one of chaos.

This is a difficult path for El-Sisi to tread. He has to deliver, ensure structural change and keep the military – the key base but also a threat to his power – onside. He has to simultaneously keep the Islamists and the modernisers happy, hence the impression of the devout leader. It is not dissimilar to the tensions embodied by King Farouk, the monarch who was toppled by the coup of 1952: 'Torn between East and West, the mosque and the nightclub.'[20] But El-Sisi also has to 'manage the Nile', as some put it, a metaphor for shrewd economics.

By continuing on the same economic reform path, spending more on the hardware of infrastructure than the software of education, El-Sisi is essentially discounting Egypt's opportunities. These lie in its geostrategic location, youthful population and position as a low-cost base for exports. He also risks turning the population – 'who are looking for employment, control of inflation and better treatment by the state, especially the police,' says one former minister – against the military.[21] The extent of this 'discount', and the fear of failure to reform to stay ahead of political and social expectations and pressures, can be seen in the relative cost of a three-year bond issuance in 2023 with an interest rate of 10.875 per cent, highlighting both the weakness of global markets and investors' concerns about Egypt's risks and solvency. In contrast, Morocco issued a $2.5-billion bond around the same time, attracting an interest rate of just 5.95 per cent.

The benefits of 'authoritarian stability' are a constant reference in this process. While the debt volume and the lack of returns have made international supporters twitchy, the need to maintain balance between reform and stability also poses a conundrum for external actors. For Arab states, fearing both democracy and Islamist radicalisation (and perhaps the two together, as with Morsi), there is an imperative for stability at any cost, including that of reform and the observation of human rights. For Western donors, it presents a dilemma between continuing support regardless of the regime's democratic record (there were, by 2023, at least 60 000 political prisoners in Egypt) and the absence of democracy, and the fear of the consequences of chaos, not least as to how unrest would affect Egypt's relationship with Israel.

Egypt's rich history – it is often referred to as *Umm al-Dunya*, which translates to 'Mother of the World') – as well as its geostrategic location, its default as a melting pot of different social groups and the size of its population have made it a regional anchor. It is sometimes forgotten that, until 1948, Palestinians – Christians, Muslims and Jews – travelled to Europe regularly through the port of Alexandria. The contemporary limitations of borders in the Middle East are only seventy-five years old, peace with Israel itself reminding us how quickly things can change. Shifting from autocratic to democratic stability won't be easy. 'You need a formula for political inclusion beyond the army, just like we had peace with Israel, despite years of hate speech,' says Sadat of his uncle's era. 'We should not throw into jail or exile those who refrain from violence and respect the constitution. Rather we should allow them to practise their rights.' After all, you can't run a country on fear alone.

Egypt's elite will have to be wise to the need for this change, including the leadership in knowing when to go.

The southern end of the western Cairo suburb of Manshiyat Naser is better known to outsiders as Garbage City. Located just across the highway from the twelfth-century Citadel of Saladin, its 30 000 inhabitants, known as the Zabbaleen or 'garbage people', service Cairo's residents and businesses by collecting their rubbish and transporting it back to Garbage City, where it is carefully sorted into resaleable, recyclable material.[22]

At first glance, it's a place of desperation and extreme poverty. Beneath the winding, narrow, unpaved streets and piles of garbage, however, exists a sophisticated and lucrative economy. One person's rubbish has become another's treasure through dint of hard work and few options.

Similar places exist in other African metropoles, including Johannesburg, where the 'recycling men' drag mounds of plastics and metals on makeshift trollies to the Robinson landfill site on Turffontein Road, among others. In Nairobi's Dandora, 3 000 families live off recycling from the 2 000 tonnes of waste dumped each day by the city's 4.5 million residents.

What makes Manshiyat Naser unusual is that it's entirely dedicated to the garbage industry and is both door-to-door and superefficient, despite its crude methods including donkey carts for transportation and manual sorting. An estimated 90 per cent of the garbage is recycled, around four times the percentage in the mechanised West. In a social twist, its inhabitants are mostly Coptic Christians who moved to Manshiyat Naser in the late 1960s from Upper Egypt in search of work. The community is grouped around the Monastery of Saint Simon the Tanner, containing Saint Sama'ans Church, also referred to as the Cave Cathedral, considered the largest church in the Middle East with seating for 20 000 worshippers. Chiselled into the side of Mokattam Mountain and completed in 1986, the church features religious images etched into the walls.

The job of the Zabbaleen was made more difficult in the first decade of the twenty-first century with two decisions by the government. The first, in 2003, was to hire private companies for garbage disposal. Then, in 2009, the Cairo municipal government ordered the culling of 350 000 pigs as a preventive measure against the threat of an outbreak of swine flu. Pigs complemented the efforts of the Zabbaleen by weeding out organic waste. They were also a source of income – they would later be sold to restaurants catering to non-Muslim clients in another form of 'recycling'. The residents saw these as punitive acts by the Mubarak government against the Coptic community. Nevertheless, despite the government's best efforts, the Zabbaleen have weathered these man-made threats because of their relative efficiency.

Two decades on, more than 14 000 tonnes of mixed garbage pass through the neighbourhood daily, about 85 per cent of all the waste produced by Cairo's twenty-two million residents. A tonne of aluminium fetches $190 and cardboard $65, in a country where the minimum monthly wage is $90. Around 3 000 families process the rubbish in a carefully worked-out system: from sorting to washing, crushing, processing and converting as it heads towards reuse. There are eight different jobs in every tonne of recycled plastic, the lowest earning $6 per day.

There is an effort to rebrand Garbage City to Recycling City, with guided tours around its streets. Yet its existence is a source of shame to many Cairenes. Most taxi drivers don't know where to go when you get there, while mention of a visit to the middle class is met with upturned noses. 'It's a bad place, many thieves,' they will tell you.

Just fifteen minutes away on Cairo's concrete confusion of motorways, along which cars, trucks and motorbikes drift with scant cognisance of the fading white lines, is Tahrir Square, the epicentre of the 2011 revolution. Queues of tourists wait to enter the Egyptian Museum, overlooked by the modernist steel-and-glass Nile Ritz-Carlton, where the charge for breakfast is 850 Egyptian pounds, nearly US$30, three times what an Uber driver makes in a ten-hour day.

Twenty-five minutes from Manshiyat Naser is the suburb of Heliopolis, where the rich party the evenings away, their cars parked for them in giant elevator stacks. Such relative dearth and excess, one a world of sweat and the other of privilege. Connecting the two worlds is part of a planned $2.5-billion, ninety-six-kilometre overhead railway. Billboards on the construction site proudly declare it will be the longest driverless monorail anywhere.

Yet bringing these worlds together will require more than building infrastructure and banking on trickle-down growth. It will need a complex set of measures, including improving education and healthcare, making things easier for small businesses, ensuring macroeconomic stability and investing in transport. It's as much a meeting of minds as geography, and it demands changing the political economy in Egypt as in many countries across Africa: from a system of entrenched rents holding back reforms, an outsized civil service and antagonism to business, to one that releases the power of entrepreneurship.

Herein lies a consistent paradox for reformers. Making difficult choices is in the interests of Africa's people, even if it is not always in the immediate interests of African governments and their leaders. The answer to Egypt's diversification conundrum lies in empowering individual entrepreneurs, which in turn demands relaxing the barriers to entry to the economy, in part by getting the military out of business. Ironically, some of the answers to doing so lie next door in Israel.

For many years, Israel's defining economic characteristic was a lack of oil or any other natural resource. To mitigate this, it has grown an entrepreneurial class that has driven new, dramatic economic activity. While the education of Israel's human talent base differs from African countries, it does offer lessons on how people can drive economic change.

It all started in agriculture. Just 20 per cent of Israel is arable, yet since independence in May 1948, the country's agricultural output has increased sixteen-fold, many times the rate of population growth. This is down to a lot of perspiration and, more importantly, a large dollop of innovation and cooperation. Israel produces over two-thirds of its food requirements. Agricultural exports, more than half of which were fresh produce, including flowers, vegetables and exotic fruits, were worth $1.2 billion in 2020.[23]

While Israel's external image is dominated by conflict and perceptions of injustice, such progress is down to smart development. In agriculture, for example, Israelis have utilised technology to reduce water usage and increase output, and higher-yield crops to increase both volumes and financial sales values. Drip- and direct-feed computerised irrigation systems are the norm, saving water, increasing yields and improving returns. Just 40 per cent of the fresh water used for agriculture sixty years ago is used today, and half of that is recycled.

It's a far cry from 1948, when the Jewish state seemingly had little going for it. Not only was it a piece of dry, rocky, and theologically and militarily contested countryside, but it also had neighbours who wanted to wipe it off the map, enemies within and without the domestic population, and a citizenry of just 800 000, many of them traumatised from their war experiences.

Despite rapid population growth (now over 9.3 million), Israelis enjoy a per capita income of $40 800, putting them in the top fifty worldwide, between the United Arab Emirates (UAE) and New Zealand.[24] Their direct neighbours, Egypt, Jordan, Syria, Lebanon and the embryonic Palestinian state, have incomes of $3 900, $3 800, $725, $6 100 and $3 100 respectively.[25]

Although Israel depends on imports for nearly all its raw materials, from oil to diamonds, it has become a global industrial hub. It is a world leader in diamond polishing and cutting, food processing, electronic and medical equipment, and, more recently, software, semiconductors and telecommunications, where the concentration of high-tech start-up industries has given it the monikers 'Silicon Wadi' and 'Start-Up Nation'.

Israel boasts the highest density of start-up ventures by population in the world. After the US, Canada and China – three countries whose combined GDP exceeds $38 trillion – Israel has more companies listed on the NASDAQ than any other country.[26] Put differently, by 2008, per capita venture capital investment in Israel (some $250 per person per year) was two and a half times greater than in the US, thirty times than in Europe, eighty times than in China and 350 times than in India. It's a long way from grainy images of *kibbutzim* farmers as the pioneering, rural ideal of happy socialist cooperation in the Jewish homeland.

The easy shorthand to explain Israel's success is that there is a concentration of educated, motivated, brighter-than-average people facing an existential threat in a small geographic space – at 400 people per square kilometre, it has a similar density to Rwanda, the Netherlands and India.

Being performance-driven through adversity is significant, though Israel is not unique in this regard. US assistance, some $3 billion annually, is another oft-cited reason. Much of this is spent on military kit, but Egypt gets the same chunk under the 1977 Camp David Accords, and their tranche is seldom used to positively define that country's circumstances. Moreover, this figure amounts to 1.5 per cent of Israel's and Egypt's GDP, even though the latter has more than ten times as many people as the former.

The explanation for Israel's recent success in the high-tech field lies in a combination of human and other factors, such as the very high levels of civilian and military research and development (R&D) expenditure. Israel's civilian R&D is 5.4 per cent of GDP, while the United States' is 3.5 per cent, Japan's 3.3 per cent, China's 2.4 per cent and the United Kingdom's 1.7 per cent.[27] To this must be added military R&D.

More important perhaps than money from the military is the culture it has engendered of accountability no matter the rank, agility, questioning and problem-solving flexibility, as well as a can-do, risk-taking attitude. Funding through government schemes has been part of the success, as has the creation of a dynamic venture capital market. Translating such technology into business ventures relies, additionally, on the availability of skills in the supportive 'cluster' of talent, capital and markets.

It is important not to overstress the cultural aspect. While culture is an important unifying element, it does not explain why certain countries have done well and others badly. As Lee Kuan Yew reminds us, the value of culture in development is only determined by history, not by argument.

It is possible to learn lessons from Israel, and not only from the bits that are palatable. The whole innovation package includes embracing immigration (and the diversity of skills that results) and not just limited work permits (as in Dubai); ensuring government sponsorship is agreed to and managed on a strictly commercial basis and not on the basis of friendships, patronage or identity (including race); letting the market select projects and not picking winners (Malaysia); educating to challenge norms and not learning by rote (the Arab world); empowering women and not excluding them (again, the bulk of the Arab world); and operating government with maximum flexibility and minimum bureaucracy and hierarchy (which is apparently largely antithetical to much of Asia and Africa).

The chances of Israel's lessons being positively identified, learnt and applied until now have been lost in the swirl of politics. The bottom line is that the Jewish state's progress is down to having a system that encourages and caters for entrepreneurship. Yet it's much easier – and self-satisfying – to bash rather than emulate Israel.

Further afield, Dubai and Qatar, among others, offer examples in diversifying, though their relevance is questionable outside of oil-rich countries with small populations. True, this money has been well spent in some areas, but there has been a lot of it to go around. There is little need to create employment. The expat (foreign) population of the whole of the UAE totals 88.5 per cent, or nine million, while the nationals only amount to 11.5 per cent, or 1.2 million.[28] The Dubai model has done best in creating jobs for foreigners.

Two other examples, with complex political and social make-ups, contain lessons closer to the regional norm.

Between Iraq and a Hard Place

'We are Kurds. We never lose, but we never win. We get just to the finish line, and then we stop.'
– Qubad Talabani, deputy prime minister, Kurdistan Regional Government

Az Zubayr, an Iraqi town of around 250 000 people, sits just south of the city of Basra. At the time of the invasion to remove Saddam Hussein from power in 2003, Basra had grown to more than three million people, most of them Shia and many so-called Marsh Arabs (or Ma'dān) who had been forcibly relocated when the Iraqi dictator drained their wetlands and removed their livelihoods in retribution for the failed 1991 Shia uprisings, converting the area into a desert.[29]

In August 2004, I asked a government official in Az Zubayr how he identified himself. 'Muslim,' he answered. I gingerly probed further. 'Shia,' he responded, then 'Ma'dān', 'Zubayr', 'Arab' and, finally, 'Iraqi'.

It was a personal *ah-ha* moment regarding the Iraq War, a fast-changing puzzle of identity and self that has played out in the following two decades. Identity is a complex issue, as are the domestic and regional relationships that lie behind it. Changing one dimension inevitably creates problems and challenges in other areas.

That's not to say the world is not a better place for the passing of Saddam, a man responsible for hundreds of thousands of Iraqi deaths, and perhaps as much as a million more in the eight-year Iran–Iraq War, which he kicked off in September 1980. From the start, he was the prototype strongman, monstrously brutal yet politically cunning, a master of the politics of redistribution.

Having taken over formally as Iraq's leader in July 1979, just six days later he staged an internal party purge, a psycho-drama carried out on live television, its black-and-white images complete with public admissions of guilt, scenes of the denounced (and soon to be executed) being forcibly led out of the hall, and Saddam's own flamboyant cigar-puffing theatre.[30] His feared secret police, or Mukhabarat (literally, 'communications'), carried out much of his dirty work, assassinating dissidents at home and abroad. No one knows how many people were killed under Saddam's regime but estimates on domestic deaths and disappearances run as high as half a million, with another three million Iraqis (among a nation of seventeen million by 1990) forced to emigrate.

'Saddam was a monster and it is better for all of us that he was removed,' says Daban Shadala, the deputy foreign minister of the Kurdistan Regional Government (KRG) in Iraq's north. The Kurdish population of northern Iraq suffered disproportionately under Saddam, an estimated 182 000 losing their lives during the 1988 Anfal alone. By the time the genocidal campaign ended in the autumn of 1988, 4 500 Kurdish towns and villages had been destroyed. Sulaymaniyah's Amna Suraka ('lest we forget') museum, housed in the former Mukhabarat headquarters, details the atrocities committed by Saddam's regime. There was no presumption of innocence, no stone left unturned if Saddam thought he saw a threat, and women and children were not immune to a machine that had no bounds in its ruthless, imaginative methods. A separate section details the war with Islamic State (IS) between 2014 and 2017, in which 8 000 Kurds lost their lives in stopping IS from reaching Baghdad. The museum illustrates a proud, stubborn and bloody Kurdish history in a rough neighbourhood.

Ottoman collapse, Iraqi opportunity

The Kurdish minority had long been a thorn in Saddam's Sunni side, as had the Iraqi majority Shia. Kurdish resistance to Baghdad's rule and the desire for autonomy were rooted in a combination of their distinct cultural identity and the collapse of the Ottoman empire at the end of the First World War.

The British response was to create Iraq – a seventh-century name meaning 'well-rooted country' – whose boundaries largely mimicked the territories of three Ottoman provinces. The selection of this land was partly to keep Turkey to the north and Iran to the east in check, and partly to maintain British interests over Iraq's burgeoning oil production. A Hashemite royal, Faisal, was installed as king on 23 August 1921.

'It was an amazing thing to see all Iraq, from North to South, gathered together,' wrote Gertrude Bell, the British colonial official who had recommended Faisal to her government and would remain his advisor. 'It is the first time it has happened in history.'[31]

It was the last time, too, despite tremendous resources. With the world's fifth-largest proved crude oil reserves at 145 billion barrels, Iraq today produces around 3.3 million barrels per day. At an average production and transport cost of around $12 per barrel, at current prices this endowment should offer a huge development windfall. But so far it has failed to do so, the reason centring on politics, both domestic and international.

And it's been like this for the better part of a century.

On 14 July 1958, Iraq's constitutional monarchy came to a brutal end when troops led by Colonel Abd al-Karim Qasim stormed the palace in Baghdad and killed King Faisal II, the twenty-three-year-old grandson of the first monarch, and several of his relatives. The Ramadan Revolution in February 1963, led by the Ba'ath Party under General Ahmed Hassan al-Bakr, killed the now prime minister Qasim, while a palace coup in November 1963 saw pro-Nasserist Iraqi officers take over from the Ba'athists. By then, the Kurds were at war with Baghdad in a struggle for greater autonomy in the north, that phase ending with a decisive Kurdish victory at the Battle of Mount Handrin in 1966.

In April 1966, President Abdul Salam Arif was killed in a helicopter crash and succeeded by his brother, General Abdul Rahman Arif. The Ba'ath Party retook power two years later when Ahmed Hassan al-Bakr returned to become president and chairman of the Revolutionary Command Council, the ultimate decision-making body in Iraq. A peace deal ending the First Iraqi–Kurdish War was reached in March 1970, providing for a measure of Kurdish autonomy. The relationship once more deteriorated, however, with the Arabisation of the rich oilfields in the north, especially around Kirkuk, leading to the Second Iraqi–Kurdish War between 1974 and 1975. This phase ended in Kurdish collapse and the exile of the Kurdistan Democratic Party (KDP).

Then, following Saddam's takeover from his Tikriti kinsman al-Bakr in 1979, the country descended into an even more turbulent period with the Iran–Iraq War and the Anfal phase of the war against the Patriotic Union of Kurdistan (PUK), which had split from the KDP in 1975.

Resonance of cruelty

Ba'athist Saddam's brutality touched the moral bottom when his cousin General Ali Hassan al-Majid ordered an attack using gas on the Kurdish town of Halabja in March 1988 in the final months of the war with Iran. The previous day, PUK fighters, allied with Iran, whose border was just eleven kilometres away, had taken the town. There is a recording of al-Majid – who acquired the moniker 'Chemical Ali' as a result – boasting: 'I will kill them all with chemical weapons. Who is going to say anything? The international community? Fuck the international community and those who listen to them!'[32]

After Saddam's forces attacked the occupying Peshmerga (Kurdish guerrillas; literally, 'those who face death') with artillery and air strikes, the Kurdish fighters withdrew from Halabja to the surrounding hills, leaving behind women, children and the elderly. The following day, 16 March, the town was bombed by Iraqi jets with a cocktail of VX, sarin and mustard gas, many of the ingredients for which had been supplied by Western companies. The horror is captured below:

16 March 1988

Groaning flags
Memorising death
Flapping hearts
Choking breath

Proud Peshmerga
At his feet
A woman's shield
Gathering clouds, shimmering heat

In the backdrop
Sukhoi, merchant of death
Saddam, monster in life
Chemical Ali, lieutenant to Macbeth

5 000 about
So rounded, moral bankruptcy
Impersonal, left out
Resonance of cruelty

Narrow interests
Pull up the ladder
Thieves of the living
Blistering reminder

Layers on the skin
Poaching opportunity
Pricking our conscience
Not in their memory

More than 5 000 civilians lost their lives at Halabja, and at least twice this number suffered long-term health effects, from blindness to miscarriages. Al-Majid, the chief of the Mukhabarat, among other roles, was tried and executed in January 2010 for his part in this crime.

The cultivated flatlands on the drive to Halabja hint at its history as a market town. Today, however, it is better known for the 1988 atrocity and its politics. Inside the town is a memorial to the attack, the roof of the building constructed to resemble blisters. Nearby is a gravesite containing the fallen, sometimes with three names per stone, sometimes whole families in a row. To put these numbers into context, the US-led invasion to topple Saddam cost 4 825 coalition lives over an eight-year period between 2003 and 2011. It is little wonder a fading sign outside the cemetery reads: 'Not allowed for bathesm to enter.'

No sooner had peace been made by Iraq and Iran in 1988 than Saddam invaded Kuwait on 2 August 1990, motivated partly by reasons of territory and debt. The ensuing Gulf War and Iraq's inevitable defeat at the hands of an international coalition in February 1991 was the beginning of Saddam's end.

Encouraged by the defeat of Saddam's forces and by the rhetoric of President George H.W. Bush, the Kurds again rose in hopeful rebellion a month later, as did the Shia in the south. Once again, however, they were crushed by the might of Saddam's artillery and air power. By April 1991, when no-fly zones were imposed by the American, British and French governments over southern and northern Iraq, between 100 000 and 180 000 people were dead, an estimated 800 000 Shia had fled to the southern marshes on the border with Iran and nearly two million Kurds had sought shelter in the northern mountains. Along with widespread sanctions against Saddam, the no-fly zones eventually led to the establishment of a de facto Kurdish state, the Green Line running roughly from the Turkish border near Zakho down to the Iranian border near Khanaqin, forming the 'border' between Iraq and Iraqi Kurdistan. Erbil, the largest city in Iraqi Kurdistan, lies just north of the line, while Kirkuk, a city with a mixed Kurdish and Arab population, is just below it in the area once under Saddam's control. While on the map the territory is still Iraq, on the ground it is governed as the Kurdistan Region of the Republic of Iraq (KRI). 'The existence of the KRI is not a by-product of the Iraqi constitution, but a reality faced on the ground since 1991,' Dr Rewaz Fayeq, speaker of the Iraqi Kurdistan parliament, reminds us.

This was not without its internal frictions, including a civil war between the two Kurdish factions – the KDP and the PUK – during the mid-1990s, which divided Iraqi Kurdistan into two roughly equal areas, the KDP in the north and the PUK in the south. Despite signing a formal peace treaty in 1998, tensions between the two have worsened in recent years.

While the Kurds welcomed Saddam's demise following the March 2003 invasion and worked closely with American forces to accomplish it, many are scathing about the chaotic and incoherent post-war plan and administration of Iraq, not least the Coalition Provisional Authority (CPA), the transitional government established by the United States.

Legacy of bad decisions

'From one day to the next, two million Ba'athists lost their jobs, in the government and the army, and with it their means of income, prestige, power and manhood,' says Daban Shadala, reflecting on CPA administrator Paul Bremer's issue of Order

Number 2 on 23 May 2003, which effectively dissolved the entire former Iraqi army and put 400 000 Iraqi soldiers out of work. Such plans were complicated by differences in the approach of the Pentagon and the US State Department, notes Shadala. The chaos following Saddam's removal was the product of either a naive world view or sloppy thinking and went hand in hand with dollops of incompetence, arrogance and ignorance. A cursory reading of Iraqi history should have told them that this was not going to be easy and that hoping it would all turn out right in the end wouldn't suffice. Iraq after 2003 proved the adage that aspiration is not a strategy and hope is not a plan.

A failure to think through the consequences of Saddam's removal, a lack of understanding of the complexity and thus the need to manage regional politics, as well as the extent of Iraq's domestic divisions combined to create a cycle of national disorder, resurfacing divisions that had remained restive since the country's creation in 1921. As a result of the CPA's bad decisions, America's legacy was civil war.

For instance, in the regional arena, the invasion and its aftermath effectively 'gave' Iraq to Iran through its Shia majority, particularly since the Islamic republic felt increasingly trapped between US forces on either side with the earlier invasion and occupation of Afghanistan. Saudi Arabia was unlikely to allow this, while both it and Iran were hardly domestically aligned on the United States' democratic ambition for Iraq. To the north, Turkey had its own interests, not least in keeping the Kurds in check and in exploiting the trade on offer.

The origins of the Kurds are not completely clear, but they have inhabited the area for a very long time. The Kurdish minority in Turkey, Syria, Iran and Iraq today totals more than forty million, the largest ethnic group worldwide to lack a formal state of its own. None of the host countries has an interest in the establishment of an independent Kurdish state.

Domestically, Saddam maintained his rule over a disparate and fractious country through patronage and fear, handing out contracts through especially the Sunni tribal sheikhs while hammering his opponents among the communists, Shia and Kurds. The Iraqi Kurds, spread over an area the size of Denmark, are themselves made up of more than fifty tribes. While the two main parties, the KDP and the PUK, are dynastic, led by the Barzani and Talabani families respectively, there are complex cross-cutting religious, ideological and regional geographic affiliations. Although Sunni in character, the community is divided between the Naqshbandi and Qadiriyya orders. 'An onion with many layers,' says one Kurdish analyst describing the make-up of this relatively homogenous people.

Qubad Talabani, the deputy prime minister of the KRG and a member of the PUK, says that, on reflection, three key mistakes were made in the post-conflict peace strategy with regard to Iraq. First, there was little attempt to align regional powers, with the consequence that each sought to pursue their own interests at the expense of the Iraqis. Second, there was little calibration of financing to governance priorities and metrics. Third, and perhaps most importantly, aid was given to fix all the problem areas, rather than trying to consolidate the areas that worked. 'The coalition should have expanded their operations out from the areas that functioned – like Kurdistan – and made them more of a model, than trying to fix areas that didn't work,' he says.[33]

The outcome was a cycle of extraordinary violence resulting in the loss of over 100 000 Iraqi lives, the rise of IS and a significant loss of resources. For instance, it is estimated that while the operation to remove Saddam and its decade-long aftermath cost the United States $2 trillion, the cost of four decades of war to hard infrastructure alone has been as much as a backlog of $300 billion. To put this into perspective, in 2022, Iraq's GDP was $193 billion according to the World Bank. Even if this money is forthcoming, it requires soft infrastructure – technical, managerial and organisational skills and discipline – to manage its delivery and usage. Such systemic thinking and skills are apparently in short supply. 'The chief limiting factor to the success of development in Iraq may prove to be neither the amount of money for investment, nor even the limits of skilled labour and materials available, but the efficiency of the administrative machine,' observed Lord Salter in 1955.[34] A 2018 World Bank study titled 'Connecting to Compete', for instance, found that businesses in Iraq face one of the worst logistical systems in the world, the country ranking 147th out of the 160 nations evaluated.[35]

Comparatively, the Kurdish region, having benefitted from a longer period of self-governance and stability since the introduction of the no-fly zone in 1991, has prospered, seeing a twofold increase in per capita GDP to $7 000 in the ten years to 2017 and a steady improvement in logistics. By the time the US troops left in 2011, Kurdistan was considered a safe and modernising region amid the chaos of post-Saddam Iraq.

The KRI finds itself in a different and far more affluent situation compared to just twenty years ago, reminding us that recovery from the trauma of Saddam's rule takes time. Iraqi Kurdistan had a twelve-year head start on the rest of Iraq. Regardless, the Kurds have indubitably made it more difficult for themselves. The compact between the KDP and the PUK has become increasingly frayed with tensions over the wisdom of greater autonomy from Baghdad and closer ties with Ankara especially. 'It is the difference between a more tribal, centralised vision and [the PUK] vision of a decentralised state,' says Talabani.

This has led to several blind alleys, notably the referendum on KRI independence in 2017. While supported by nearly 93 per cent of Kurds, it was rejected by the region and internationally as a bad idea, or at best as a reasonable idea at a bad time, despite what some of the KRG's notable international advisors were saying. The costs were immediate. The referendum led to conflict with the Iraqi central government, in which the KRI lost 40 per cent of its territory and revenue from the Kirkuk oilfields, while Masoud Barzani resigned as president. Perhaps more importantly, it was a strategic disjuncture in developmental terms, erroneously attempting to shift the focus towards a chimera of quick wins and away from a longer and tougher road to governance and diversification.

Independence is never going to work when Kurdistan has to go through a region that does not favour this goal. 'If we had this geography in Europe, it would be very beneficial,' says Dr Fayeq. 'Our definition of the state and non-state elements around us is that they are a threat to us.'

This highlights the overall challenge: the Kurds have great potential, but they live in a bad neighbourhood and sometimes they don't help themselves. Choosing short-term gain rarely helps long-term progress. Perhaps this is a product of a national liberation struggle; you don't stay alive in the mountains by thinking about strategies for peace, love and development. You also have the financial payback for its participants and the entitlement that surrounds it, a feature that has echoes elsewhere.

Such choices in the oil industry, for example, are about who earns and keeps what. Previously the KRG received a share (initially 17 per cent) of total oil revenue from Baghdad, less the value of the oil it sold directly (450 000 barrels per day) from fields under KRG control. This formula was suspended in 2014 when the then prime minister of Iraq, Nouri al-Maliki, withheld the KRG's share of the federal budget. The same year, the Peshmerga (now formally under the command of the KRG) took control of the disputed territory of Kirkuk, allowing the KRG to seize the province's northern oilfields, or some 250 000 barrels per day, much of which was smuggled to Turkey until Iraqi forces retook the area in October 2017. Since 2014, the KRG has kept all the oil produced in its territory. From the start of 2023, however, all oil proceeds were circuited through Baghdad, reducing KRI autonomy.

Not all of it allegedly goes through the government's books, however. There are concerns about the legality, transparency and commercial implications of this arrangement, not least given the ongoing disagreement with Baghdad, especially regarding the oil pumped from the so-called disputed (or Article 140) territories in the border areas between Iraq and the KRI. This creates contractual uncertainty and possible future legal vulnerabilities for international operators, and illustrates a further generational disjuncture, one familiar to Africa.

Conclusion: Escaping the nostalgia and independence trap

The pattern of Iraqi Kurdistan's politics is familiar: a liberation elite holding the reins of power largely living on nostalgia without a post-liberation agenda, and a youth increasingly disconnected from politics. One anecdotal measure is in the ambition for emigration in search of a better life. This is not entirely about jobs, as there are around 50 000 mostly South and Southeast Asian contract labourers working in the KRI. 'Younger people don't see equality of opportunity. They see corruption and patronage' is a common refrain.

Much of the current focus in government seems to be on the division of spoils based on the past. That past is synonymous with struggle, suffering, and the fight for self-government and freedom. Now that this has to a great extent been achieved, Iraqi Kurds will have to turn their attention to what they want the KRI to become, and how. To do this, government requires a strategy and the resources and plans to achieve it.

Escaping the nostalgia trap requires changing the mindset of the parties, away from the mullahs and sheikhs who gained disproportionate political leverage through having men under their authority to supply into the martial struggles that have defined the Kurds for generations, to a more liberal order, based on issue rather than identity politics. There is also a need for government to view criticism as constructive and not simply as a threat to power. Of course, a balance must be maintained: the Peshmerga remain essential to Kurdish security in such a tricky neighbourhood, yet it is becoming increasingly necessary to judge that security in economic rather than purely military terms.

As a country without formal recognition, absent a central bank and its own currency, Erbil has few policy levers to pull. It is already heavily indebted, its stock growing from zero in 2014 to an estimated $35 billion by 2022. It is severely affected by climate change. The underground water table on which the growing urban areas are dependent is falling fast and it experiences routine power blackouts, ironic for a country that exports oil in such volumes. The relations with its key neighbours are fraught, the Kurds seldom being viewed as equal partners and certainly not sovereign agents. Bilateral matters are usually subordinated to a wider strategy that includes the Kurdish minorities and the economic interests of their neighbours. Until now, Iraqi Kurdistan has survived and prospered despite its neighbourhood.

Nevertheless, there is a considerable upside to being in this region.

Kurdistan is rich in natural and other resources. Its direct neighbours, including Iraq, offer a $1.6-trillion, 230-million-person market. A million-strong overseas diaspora provides conduits for skills, tech and capital. It has massive agricultural potential, untapped water resources from its winter snow and remarkable solar opportunities (summer temperatures can reach over fifty degrees Celsius). Its cement and steel industries, among others, ensure Kurdistan makes up nearly one-third of Iraq's industrial output. There are also untapped gas opportunities, particularly around Sulaymaniyah, in a world moving away from oil and from dependency on Russian gas.

Contrary to the Manichean nature of the political discourse – achieve independence or face national failure – Iraqi Kurdistan should look towards interdependence with both Baghdad and the region. Rather than upholding Kurdish as the language of national pride, the focus should shift to speaking Arabic, Turkish, Farsi and English in addition to Kurdish, in line with becoming a 'land-linked' service centre. The independence debate is too often a licence for rent-seeking, protectionism and other anti-competitive practices.

Bruce Ferguson has been president of the American University of Iraq, Sulaimani in Sulaymaniyah since 2016. A key challenge he identifies is to create independent institutions in an environment where affiliation – to clan, party or personality – pervades. Steeped in a tradition of unquestioning rote memorisation, this will require highlighting experiential learning, the acceptance of responsibility for one's actions and the centrality of soft skills.

There are some green shoots in this regard. Dr Fayeq says she is an 'Iraqi Kurd', the one 'permanent feature' of her identity. Whatever their complex make-up, Kurds are proud of the history that delivered a different world for them, even with its challenges.

And there are other positive aspects. The citizens of Sulaymaniyah, the largest Kurdish city in Iraq, have a reputation for forthrightness. In identifying the three major constraints – the size of the pool of clientele, the (un)availability of local skills and the cost of imported goods – which dominate his business, Shad, the manager of a hip restaurant popular with eighteen to thirty-five-year-olds, is critical of government. 'They don't do anything for us,' he says, with a government minister at our table, 'but rather make our lives more difficult with their permits.' Presuming he does not know the minister, I anticipate a tough retort. But it turns out they know each other. The minister simply shrugs and smiles.

If this attitude and advice is welcomed and acted on, Iraqi Kurdistan will change and prosper. If not, the world will look back on the KRI's legacy of relative freedom, stability and bountiful oil and say: 'They blew it.'

Have a Good Crisis

'You never want a serious crisis to go to waste. And what I mean by that is an opportunity to do things that you think you could not do before.'
— Rahm Emanuel, American politician and diplomat

THE opening scene of Orson Welles's acclaimed 1951 film of Shakespeare's *Othello* pans the length of the Skala de la Ville, the eighteenth-century rampart protecting the medina of the Moroccan city of Essaouira from the crashing waves of the Atlantic.

Now, as seventy years ago, the harbour is packed with blue boats, tourists sidestepping piles of drying nets, a confusion of swooping gulls and coveting cats, and open trays of skate, prawns and sardines destined for the seafood restaurants inside the city's walls. The alleyways of the medina exude a surprising calm despite the usual pungent Moroccan scents of sandalwood, lemonwood, leather and spices and the clash of colours of clothes, carpets and ceramics.

Welles used the bastion's walkways in his production, which earned him a Palme d'Or despite early financial difficulties and the disappearance of several Desdemonas and at least one Iago. While he directed and starred in the titular role, Welles recruited locals as extras, the town's tailors making up suits of armour from sardine cans. One of these extras was a young Jewish schoolboy named André Azoulay, who would later become counsellor to two kings of Morocco.

Just as Welles was able to turn around his great production, Azoulay, too, has stood at the helm of a turnaround in the fortunes of Essaouira. As sub-Saharan Africa struggles to find a formula to better access investment from 98 per cent of the global economy, which lies outside the sub-continent, it might do well to look at what has been achieved in the ancient and modern versions of this Atlantic city.

In 1506, the Portuguese built a fortress in what was then known as Mogador. Called the Castelo Real de Mogador, its construction was strongly opposed by local Berbers, who eventually successfully routed the Portuguese garrison stationed there in 1510. The castle was demolished in the eighteenth century, as part of Moroccan king Mohammed III's plans to build and develop the fortress and city of present-day Essaouira. The result was an early version of a special economic zone. By implementing a zero per cent tax – business or personal – the king drew in skills and the finance to turn Mogador into a trading hub between Europe and

Africa. A French engineer, Théodore Cournut, was among those tasked with building the fortress and city along modern lines. Originally called Souira (the small fortress), the port city eventually became Es-Saouira (the beautifully designed).

Things were done differently in Essaouira. Even as the schism between the Muslim and Jewish faiths deepened, Mohammed III encouraged Moroccan Jews to settle in the city and handle the trade with Europe. Jews who took up the offer were given the protection of the king's personal *tughra*, or seal, and made the king's leaders. As a result, Essaouira became the only Muslim city with a majority Jewish population, totalling some 18 000 around 1950. Muslims and Jews lived side by side, with thirty-seven synagogues intermingled with the city's mosques. Essaouira was a thriving global centre of trade, hosting twenty-seven foreign embassies from as far afield as Brazil.

This integration – domestically, regionally and globally – was the recipe for Morocco's success then as now. As other countries in the region collapsed in the wake of the Arab Spring, Morocco accelerated its reforms.

It's not the first time in recent memory that Morocco has successfully avoided troubles at home to emerge as a reformer, from a low-grade insurgency in Mauritania, cyclical political instability in Tunisia, violent and dysfunctional government in Libya, the enduring failure of politics to deliver social and economic change in Algeria, and the 'volatility, polarization, and stereotyping' that now define Egyptian politics,[36] to the divisions and violence that continue to afflict politics in the Middle East.

The reasons for these troubles are well known. Since winning its independence from France in 1962, after an eight-year war, power in Algeria has consistently emerged from the barrel of a gun and remains solidly in the hands of the military-civilian elite that took charge on independence.[37] Libya has not recovered since the NATO-led operation that removed Gaddafi from power in 2011. Egypt's troubles reside in the political divisions and the socio-economic circumstances that reinforce them: liberals versus conservatives, Muslims versus Christians. And the Middle East has its own, related issues, centring on Islam, Israel, pressures of population increase and the role of external powers. In 1960, the population of the Middle East and North Africa region was 105 million, in 2000 it was 321 million, and twenty years later it was 486 million.[38] Projections for 2050 have it almost doubling to 784 million.[39]

Morocco is not entirely alone in bucking the regional trend and becoming a face that modern Africa needs, as Iraqi Kurdistan shows, despite deeper historical enmities, tribal divisions, weak governance, a ready resort to violence and lacking formal recognition. Both are, comparatively, in the success column of the ledger of reform.

Morocco has gradually liberalised, rolling out big infrastructure projects, including Africa's only high-speed rail network and the continent's largest port complex. Where others have deliberated, Morocco has delivered. It has also turned its minimal natural resources into a national asset, contrary to others in the oil-rich region.

A focus on infrastructure

Two hundred kilometres inland from Essaouira is the city of Marrakesh. Surrounded by mountains and desert landscapes, it has been likened to 'a rose among palm trees' and 'an oasis in the desert'. Winston Churchill said of Marrakesh that it was 'simply the nicest place on earth to spend an afternoon'. The British statesman spent a little longer than that in Morocco, painting a winter holiday away in the North African country in 1935, during his political 'wilderness years', frustrated by the Baldwin government's refusal to give him a cabinet position. It was his first of six trips to Morocco in twenty-three years. In Tangier, Churchill stayed in the Hotel Continental, whose guests included the likes of artist Edgar Degas and author Paul Bowles, and in Marrakesh at the La Mamounia, a tranquil and enchanting hotel oasis, rich in history as well as tiles and tapestries.[40]

Almost ninety years later, eleven million foreign tourists seemingly agree that Morocco is a nice place to spend an afternoon or three. But it's so much more than just medieval medinas, bustling souks, sun-baked gingerbread houses and spectacular sunsets.

Al Boraq, Morocco's high-speed rail network linking Tangier with Casablanca, is the first of its kind on the African continent. Named after the Buraq, a mythical winged creature, and inaugurated in November 2018 by King Mohammed VI, the train line is an impressive piece of hardware, with trains reaching over 300 kilometres an hour and cutting the passenger time to Casablanca to just two hours. As part of a scheme to upgrade cities and infrastructure started by Mohammed VI on his inauguration on 30 July 1999, Al Boraq has boosted downtown Tangier.

Roughly forty-five kilometres northeast of Tangier is the Tanger Med industrial port complex, the second phase of which opened in June 2019. The port, like Tangier, is situated on the Strait of Gibraltar and is capable of handling nine million containers annually, three times more than Egypt's Port Said, the next largest in Africa. Tanger Med is concessioned between several operators on thirty-year leases, split roughly between containers, car transporters and ferries, and has pushed Morocco up the connectivity rankings. In the 2021 World Bank Container Port Performance Index, Tanger Med is ranked sixth overall (out of 370) in terms of efficiency.[41] Port Said is in fifteenth position and Djibouti in nineteenth. Tema in Ghana is down at 354; Nouakchott in Mauritania at 356; Lagos at 358; Abidjan at 360; Dar es Salaam at 361; Pointe-Noire in Congo at 362; and South Africa's

Ngqura (formerly Port Elizabeth), Durban and Cape Town at 363, 364 and 365 respectively, just above Luanda at 366. Right at the top is Saudi Arabia's King Abdullah Port; at the bottom are Long Beach (369) and Los Angeles (370), both in California.

Between Tangier and the port is the Renault car plant, which fills six 200-car trains per day to Tanger Med with vehicles destined for export. The plant, which employs 11500 workers and is the company's third-largest worldwide, produced 402 000 cars in 2018, of which nearly 360 000 were sold abroad, mostly in Europe. Renault is just one of 900 companies in various SEZs countrywide.

Inaugurated in 2007, Tanger Med is the result of $4 billion of public investment concentrated on the port, the purchase of land and the construction of fifty kilometres of expressway. The private sector added 'everything on top', says Rachid Houari, director of the port, including cranes, factories and warehousing. There are three private container port operators with twenty-five-year concessions, and one each for hydrocarbon and car operations.

Although most of the traffic is transhipment, the concept of Tanger Med was unlike any other major port. 'We had ambitions to be the most modern port in Africa but also to make best use of our excellent geographic position to attract big factories,' Houari says, the Rock of Gibraltar clearly visible over his shoulder on a clear day. 'The Dubai model is mostly about logistics, not manufacturing. I suppose we would like to look like Rotterdam in terms of container handling, Dubai in terms of logistics, and Singapore in terms of industry.'

Vision is important, but political stability and predictability play a key part too. 'We were able to leverage Morocco's reputation as a safe, stable country where you can do business in a predictable way,' notes Houari, who received his post-graduate education at the University of Southampton, famed for its naval engineering excellence.

There is one additional, related and crucial advantage. Morocco has free-trade agreements with the EU, the US and Gulf countries, among others, representing 1.6 billion people and 60 per cent of global GDP. In an era where globalisation seems to be on the retreat, Morocco has made access to richer markets a core foreign policy ambition.

Openness is nothing new to Tangier. In some respects, it's a case of back to the future, just as with Essaouira to the southwest. As an international protectorate from 1923 until Morocco's independence in 1956, Tangier was always open to trade, the free use of currencies and as a countercultural icon. It became a nub for hedonistic experimentation, in writing as in drugs and in living openly gay, the setting for William S. Burroughs' *Naked Lunch* and long-time resident Paul Bowles' *The Sheltering Sky*. As Burroughs put it: 'Tangier is one of the few places left in the world where, so long as you don't proceed to robbery, violence, or some form of crude, antisocial behaviour, you can do exactly what you want.' He certainly did, indulging in heroin, morphine, majoun and various other opioids.

Opposite the French mission, the corrugated facade of the Gran Café de Paris, supposedly the haunt of Burroughs, Bowles, Jack Kerouac, Allen Ginsberg and other disciples of the Beat Generation, offers a clear 180-degree vantage of the passing traffic through its floor-length windows. Sad-faced, moustachioed, red-jacketed waiters mill their way through the heavy brown leather chairs, serving coffee and the occasional croissant, just as they might have done sixty years ago. A kilometre away, the Gran Café Central on the old medina's Petit Socco, with its fin-de-siècle frontage, offers similar people-watching opportunities, with shop vendors hassling tourists in hustling all manner of tat from fezzes to fridge magnets.

From the ubiquitous felines to the fetid smells, one can imagine the effect on Burroughs in the spaced-out writing style of his disturbing if seminal *Naked Lunch* as he traversed his dreamlike Interzone.

Bowles described Tangier as 'rich in prototypal dream scenes: covered streets like corridors with doors opening into rooms on each side, hidden terraces high above the sea, streets consisting only of steps, dark impasses, small squares built on sloping terrain so that they looked like ballet sets designed in false perspective, with alleys leading off in several directions; as well as the classical dream equipment of tunnels, ramparts, ruins, dungeons and cliffs.'

That's the Tangier portrayed more recently in *The Bourne Ultimatum*, in the gripping fight to the death between the eponymous hero and itinerant hitman Desh Bouksani. It's a cameo of high-speed chases through cobbled medina lanes, up stairwells, along narrow streets and ramparts, over flat-topped roofs dodging satellite dishes, through windows and, finally, into a small bathroom where the grim fight is concluded.

Powering up

A thirty-minute flight from Marrakesh over the High Atlas mountains is the sweltering city of Ouarzazate. Known as Little Hollywood on account of its role in the global film industry (it was a location for *Game of Thrones*, *Prison Break*, *Gladiator*, *The Mummy* and Timothy Dalton's James Bond in *The Living Daylights*, among other hits), today it is the centre of Morocco's drive for renewable energy. The concentrated solar power (CSP) tower and the 3 000 hectares of solar panels of the Ouarzazate Solar Power Station can be seen blinking from a long way out on the flight approach, hardly surprising since the Inconel-plated tower of the 160-megawatt Noor I facility heats up to 560 degrees Celsius. Noor I alone has half a million solar mirrors.

When completed, Noor's four stages will produce 580 megawatts of power from a combination of mostly CSP and some (70 megawatts) photovoltaic cells. It's expensive (at $2.2 billion) and faces long-term technological challenges, including the storage of heat for peak usage, but costs are coming down fast to the point that, at $0.08 per kilowatt-hour, the plant currently makes money.

Like Al Boraq and Tanger Med, Noor is a calculated gamble. Again, it is funded by a combination of government and concessional loans. But Morocco had little option given its dependency on imported coal for most of its energy. It aims to shift the energy mix to mostly renewables by 2030, from a combination of hydro, wind and solar.

The lesson of Morocco's contemporary success at delivering and then efficiently using big infrastructure assets is down to a combination of leadership, vision and delivery – of the need, simply, for both software and hardware. Just providing infrastructure is not enough. You need skills and systems too, and a supportive policy environment.

'When His Majesty took over on the death of his father, King Hassan II, he had a plan,' explains Mohcine Jazouli, Morocco's delegate minister of investment, convergence and the evaluation of public policies. 'Like a good commander, he has led his troops in a clear direction.' This has included moves to better balance gender rights, modernise and devolve government, deepen its limited democracy, and improve the country's foreign relations, not least through a big diplomatic and economic push into Africa. Morocco now enjoys preferential trade relations with fifty-five countries. The state-owned Royal Air Maroc has been part of this push, especially in expanding its operations to include thirty-four African destinations in twenty-five countries.

The share of government financing has come from two sources: an increase in borrowing, pushing the fiscal deficit to over 3 per cent of GDP in the process, and an increase in tax revenue. There has been a threefold real increase in the tax take in the last twenty years, which depends on improved and sustained growth. As the spending catalyst for growth kicked in, so revenue expanded.

The positive cycle does not end there. The Renault plant has a government-funded training facility alongside it, which has produced more than 10 000 graduates since the factory opened in 2012. With more growth has come greater demand for talent.

Likewise, the aerospace hub clustered around Casablanca employs 16 700 people in 140 companies, making everything from wings to wiring harnesses for the likes of Boeing, Airbus and Bombardier. Workers are trained at a government-funded facility, IMA Casablanca (Institut des Métiers de l'Aéronautique), inside the free zone, which has produced 7 000 graduates since 2011. Aviation has become a

$1.7-billion industry for Morocco and there are plans to get an even bigger manufacturing slice of the 35 000 aircraft to be constructed worldwide in the next two decades. The sector is targeting the doubling of its employment and output, in part by increasing the proportion of locally produced components in its assemblies to 35 per cent.

The development path is not open to all, perhaps even most, other African countries. Firms are no doubt attracted to Morocco by labour rates, which, at $350 per worker per month, are a fraction of European costs with virtually identical geography and logistics. But as the IMA's president, Hamid Benbrahim El Andaloussi, explains, the 'best incentives are those for long-term activity, not those which governments might provide. In aerospace, the critical drivers are innovation, cost and talent. We are not able to compete in the first area, but we can do so in the latter two respects. We say Morocco is the place to be if you want to be competitive in Europe.'

Champions of change

All this required a champion.

King Hassan II took over power in 1961 aged just thirty-one. A target of two failed coups in 1971 and 1972, his rule was characterised by authoritarianism and civil rights abuses. Growing military spending in the Western Sahara along with widening inequality led to resentment and unrest during the 1980s among unusual bedfellows, including journalists, trade unionists, Marxists, Islamists, Berber nationalists, women's groups and the working poor. This erupted into public protests after the government removed basic food subsidies in 1981 under IMF pressure. Government reprisals were swift and brutal, with hundreds killed and several thousand detained, during a period later described as the 'Years of Lead'. Pressure continued regardless, with Hassan II founding in response an Equity and Reconciliation Commission in 1991 to investigate human rights abuses during his own reign.

In his very first public statement as king upon his father's death in 1999, Mohammed VI said he would right the wrongs of the past, awarding reparations to nearly 10 000 victims of the Years of Lead. Then came 9/11, followed by the 2003 Casablanca bombings and the Arab Spring seven years later. Despite an initial tendency to resort to the same security tactics of the 1980s, Morocco emerged stronger from these crises. Mohammed VI has been central in driving economic and political change since his accession. And when there has been a crisis, he has used it well. Where others have deliberated, Morocco has delivered.

While Casablanca is just a four-hour flight from Lagos, Nigeria, it's a world away in nearly all other respects.

Instead of paralysing traffic, we move quickly on a multilane highway towards the capital Rabat, not a pothole in sight. Instead of sprawling tin and timber slums, the expressway is dotted with cranes atop new multistorey housing settlements stretching out to the horizon. Instead of yellow Lagosian *danfo* minibus taxis clustered at informal stops hindering the flow, Morocco's roadside amenities and its *péages* (tolls) would not be out of place in Europe, nor would Casablanca's surly immigration officers. Yet traditions remain. Women in *djellaba* and men in Obi-Wan Kenobi-style pointy-hatted *burnoose* tend sheep on the verges of the motorway.

Tangier is at the epicentre of this merging of European modernity and Berber tradition, which has so far worked to Morocco's advantage, the economy touching 5 per cent growth for nearly fifteen years. This has been driven by foreign investors and they, in turn, by a carefully sweated combination of policy, stability and infrastructure.

When Ridley Scott was looking for a location for his 2001 film *Black Hawk Down*, which depicts the 1993 US mission to capture a Somali warlord that went disastrously wrong, the original site of the event, Mogadishu, was deemed to be far too dangerous. Instead, he shot the film in Morocco, transforming Salé's Sidi Moussa district into the Somali capital and the seventeenth-century Rabat medina into Mogadishu's Bakaara Market.

Today, Scott would have to go elsewhere. Morocco's slum removal initiative, the *Programme national d'action pour l'urbaine fabric*, launched in 2001, and the subsequent *Villes sans bidonvilles* ('cities without slums') programme, launched in 2004, combined with an aggressive industrialisation and job creation strategy are dramatically changing the face of cities across the country.

Morocco is not without its challenges. At independence the population was 10.5 million. Sixty years later it had more than tripled, to thirty-five million in 2016. By 2021, it had reached thirty-seven million. But this trend is flattening, with population growth falling from a high of 3.3 per cent per annum in the late 1950s to 1.4 per cent in 2016. Tangier's population has swelled sixfold to over 1.5 million in the last thirty-five years. With a need to create jobs for 200 000 graduates every year, the pressure is on not just to plan but also to do. Urbanisation has been similarly rapid. At independence, 29 per cent of the population lived in cities; now it's close to 60 per cent. And yet poverty levels remain high. Four million today live near or in poverty, three-quarters of them in rural areas.

Such challenges are nothing new. The focus following independence in 1956 was to deliver political stability and territorial consolidation along with basic infrastructure. In the process, the government, led by the monarchy, had to confront huge social challenges. By 1981, as much as 60 per cent of the population lived below the poverty line, unemployment was at 20 per cent (perhaps twice as high among the youth), and around one-fifth of those in the cities lived in shanties. There were significant bread riots in 1981 and 1984, as well as other popular protests.

With a young, sometimes restive population, Morocco has to work hard to create the opportunities needed for social stability. There is little alternative but to forge ahead on job creation, a lesson that the rest of Africa would be wise to heed as it faces a doubling of its population over the next generation. 'Africa needs to average 7 per cent economic growth each year until 2050 if it is to keep pace with population growth and achieve income growth,' observes Mohcine Jazouli.

Bottom of form

And then there is the issue of Western Sahara, a harsh place of desert flatlands and searing temperatures, of a nomadic people – the Sahrawis – legendary for their toughness as much as for the colourful flowing *melhfa* robes with built-in air-conditioning worn by their women. It is one of the world's most sparsely populated areas with just 2.13 people to each of its 266 000 square kilometres, ranking it just above the likes of Mongolia (2.04), the Falklands (0.28) and Greenland (0.03).[42]

Half the population (around 218 000) lives in Laayoune on the Atlantic coast, 106 000 and 43 000 live in the coastal cities of Dakhla and Boujdour respectively, 57 000 reside in the inland town of Smara, and perhaps as many as 90 000 survive in the refugee camps in Tindouf, Algeria. The desert is virtually unpopulated, divided down its length by a giant sand berm demarcating the territory under the control of the Kingdom of Morocco to the west and that controlled by the Polisario Front to the east.

It is divided since there is a difference of opinion about what to do about it. In the summer of 1975, Spain began negotiations to cede administrative control of the territory known as Spanish Sahara to Morocco and Mauritania, both of whom had laid claim to it. In October, however, the International Court of Justice (ICJ) ruled that the indigenous population (the Sahrawis) owned the land, and thus possessed the right of self-determination. Since 1973, a Sahrawi guerrilla war led by the Polisario Front (armed and financed by Algeria) had been challenging Spanish control, and by 1974 it seemed their wish for independence would be granted. That August, Spain served formal notice of its intention to hold a referendum in the colony in the first half of 1975. But then Morocco and Mauritania intervened. King Hassan II deployed military forces along Morocco's southern border and 'prevailed upon the UN General Assembly to postpone the referendum in order to provide time for the International Court of Justice at The Hague to give a consultative assessment of Moroccan and Mauritanian claims to the territory'.[43]

Within three weeks of the unfavourable ICJ ruling, on 6 November 1975,

Hassan II launched 350 000 unarmed Moroccans on the Green March across the border into Spanish Sahara. He had already quietly moved troops into remote parts of the colony during the preceding month, and as the marchers crossed into Spanish territory, more units of the Moroccan military moved towards the towns of Bir Lehlou, Farsiya, Tifariti, Haouza and Id Ben Irya. With General Franco on his deathbed and with the Spanish population 'in no mood for war', Spain conceded.[44] On 14 November, a tripartite agreement – the Madrid Accords – was signed by which Spain agreed to withdraw from the territory and transfer administrative authority to a joint Moroccan–Mauritanian administration.

Three months later, in February 1976, the pro-independence Polisario proclaimed the establishment of the Sahrawi Arab Democratic Republic, establishing a government in exile based in the Algerian town of Tindouf. And so began the fifteen-year Western Sahara War, which saw between 10 000 and 20 000 deaths and displaced anywhere between 165 000 and 200 000 Sahrawis. 'During the first half of 1976, between 75 000 and 150 000 civilian refugees fled from Moroccan military operations designed to pacify the local population. About half of these fled across the Algerian border to the area south of Tindouf,' writes Simon Baynham, then of the Africa Institute.[45]

By 1979, Mauritania had signed a peace accord with the Polisario and relinquished its territorial claims. The vacuum, however, was quickly filled by Hassan II, who immediately occupied Mauritania's southern portion and declared it a Moroccan province. Rabat eventually secured de facto control of two-thirds of Western Sahara, with the territory divided along the lines of a ceasefire administered by a UN peacekeeping mission in 1991.

In the court of international opinion, Western Sahara remains a territory in limbo. Various plans to determine its future status through a referendum have fallen foul of the impasse between Algeria and the Polisario on the one hand, and Morocco on the other. The former wants a list of 74 000, based on the original Spanish census, to contest the vote; Morocco wants a figure closer to one million, including all the thirty-two tribes of the territory and those who have decamped to other areas in Morocco and Mauritania.

It seems that, to parody Kipling, Algeria is East and Morocco is West, and never the twain shall meet. In the interim, Western Sahara ploughs on, and at an impressive rate of development and growth.

The port town of El Marsa is an example of this progress. From a few fishing boats and no paved roads at the time of independence from Spain, today there are forty fish factories, four of which process and package nearly 200 million cans of sardines and mackerel mostly for the European market. The remainder focus on fishmeal, fish oils and frozen fish. Down the road is a fully fledged $30-million reverse osmosis desalination plant capable of producing 26 000 cubic metres of fresh water daily, 'which has turned our water from a salty trickle from boreholes to something we can at last drink,' says Mansour Lamina of the office of the local *wali* (governor). She should know, having spent her childhood in the remote southwestern Moroccan oasis town of Assa, 550 kilometres away, where her father was a goat and camel trader.

A short distance south is the port through which two million tonnes of phosphate are exported annually along a 100-kilometre conveyor belt. This totals about 8 per cent of Morocco's annual production, the kingdom possessing 70 per cent of the world's phosphate reserves. Formed in 1920, the Moroccan state-owned OCP Group is the world's largest fertiliser producer, holding a one-third share of the global phosphate market, employing 23 000 people in Morocco alone, and enjoying revenues of over $8 billion in 2021. The company has rapidly expanded globally, with more than 160 customers on five continents, and operates in sixteen African nations through twelve subsidiaries.

Faced with accusations of exploiting Western Sahara for its own gain, Rabat has put substantially more into the region than it is taking out, a net inflow of several hundred million dollars into parks, schools, hospitals, sports facilities, highways, waste management and potable water, library and cultural centres, renewable energy generation, ports and airports.

This is in part down to King Mohammed VI's more liberal attitude compared to his father, Hassan II, who, in the words of one contemporary report, was 'obsessed with the preservation of his power rather than with its application toward the resolution of Morocco's multiplying domestic problems'.[46] Mohammed VI embarked on widespread social and political reforms, freeing political prisoners, improving the position of women under the law, improving social conditions, and stimulating the economy.

Today Morocco is a modernising social and economic standout nation in what is, admittedly, a troubled region. And Algeria is the Polisario's benefactor for reasons that have less to do with questions of principle and practices of human rights, where it has an uncertain record at best, than its rivalry with Morocco.

Conclusion: The premium of policy and leadership

Until the mid-nineteenth century, Essaouira's trade thrived with volumes about double those of Rabat, the port servicing West Africa and the Sahel, as well as Marrakesh, 200 kilometres inland. Known as Timbuktu's port, Essaouira linked the Sahel hinterland with Europe and served as a centre of diplomatic activity. Banking links with Europe made doing business easy.

Then the politics changed, and with it, the city's fortunes. To force Morocco to withdraw its support for Algeria against France, the French bombarded and occupied Essaouira in August 1844. France maintained an administrative and military presence from that time. From 1912 to 1956, Essaouira was part of the French protectorate of Morocco.

The founding of Israel in 1948, the resulting wars with Arab states and Moroccan independence led to most Sephardic Jews leaving the kingdom. Today, Morocco has approximately 2 500 Jewish inhabitants.

By the late 1950s, the city had become run-down.

In 1991, King Hassan II rekindled the old relationship between Jews and Muslims when he made André Azoulay, a Jewish banker from Essaouira, his economic advisor. Azoulay set about restoring Essaouira's ancient fortifications and revived the city's history of religious tolerance and economic innovation. In 2001, UNESCO designated the medina a World Heritage Site, describing Essaouira as 'an exceptional example of a late-18th-century fortified town, built according to the principles of contemporary European military architecture in a North African context'. Azoulay is known locally as 'the man who speaks to stones' for his efforts to rebuild the old city.

Bayt Dakira, or the House of Memory, is a Jewish museum located in the Jewish quarter of the medina and situated in a former nineteenth-century family home of wealthy traders, who had added a small synagogue. Restored at Azoulay's instigation to honour the historical role of Jews in Morocco, it is the only museum of its kind in the Muslim world. It is a rich historical reservoir. Inside the heritage house are portraits of the life of a dynamic community, drawn from old photographs, archive footage, musical recordings, traditional dress and religious objects. Among the city's notables are Azoulay himself; Israeli actress Ronit Elkabetz, whose Moroccan Jewish family were originally from Essaouira; Chief Rabbi David Pinto; Israeli politician Jacques Amir; and Victor Elmaleh, a Moroccan-born American businessman who became one of the first to import Volkswagens to the United States before turning to real estate.

Inaugurated in only January 2020 by King Mohammed VI, Bayt Dakira had attracted nearly one million tourists before the Covid-19 pandemic shut down the world. It continues to attract visitors, and not by chance. They are drawn by a carefully thought-out plan putting culture at the centre of Essaouira's offerings.

Essaouira has also been recognised as a centre of innovation. At a virtual meeting on investment organised by the French Chamber of Commerce and Industry of Morocco in 2021, Azoulay highlighted 'the double rendezvous that history can give to Essaouira with, on the one hand, the radical change that will experience the economic, industrial and commercial landscape for the post-Covid days and, on the other hand, the accentuated focus of tomorrow's investors in the direction of clean industries, bioproducts and the optimization of various sectors of renewable energy'.[47]

Among Essaouira's economic advantages are its fisheries and its unique argan trees, which produce an oil used in cosmetics. The Beni Antar Cooperative outside Essaouira employs 200 women to extract the seed from the argan nut. The industry survived the Covid-19 lockdowns by allowing women to crack the nuts at home. Morocco produces 100 000 litres of argan oil annually, with Israel and Korea among its largest customers in a $2-billion annual market.

Essaouira has also become a trendsetter in the arts. During the 1960s, as the city struggled to rebuild its identity, it went through a hippie phase, playing host to Frank Zappa and Jimi Hendrix, among others, the latter supposedly writing 'Castles Made of Sand' about Essaouira. Then, in 1996, the city held its first Gnaoua World Music Festival for mainly Gnawa artists. Organisers were taken by surprise when tens of thousands of music lovers showed up, draining the city's supply of bread and milk. Numbers would grow to 600 000 before a new plan was adopted to split into more, smaller festivals. These days Essaouira hosts eleven annual music festivals that celebrate chamber music and opera, jazz, trance and, for the younger set, techno.

The revival of Essaouira and Morocco's economic resurgence are evidence of how, then as now, policy and leadership matter. It has taken three decades of concerted effort to embed Essaouira's new economic narrative and for Azoulay to be able to state: 'It is known as a happy city, a place which shows we are all humanity finding a way to live together without frontiers, without barriers. There are not many places where Judaism and Islam are in such proximity and intimacy.'

A bas-relief of Orson Welles in a small square near the medina remembers the actor-director who once strode Essaouira's walls in his search for a different perspective. As Azoulay reminds us: 'We are not spectators in someone else's play. We have to change things ourselves, with leadership, but from the bottom-up.'

Conclusion
From Poor State to Rich State

> 'You can't change people's minds with technical reforms; you need to change their mindset to change the scope of reforms.'
> – Artis Pabriks, Latvian deputy prime minister

ROBERT Kiyosaki's bestselling financial advice book *Rich Dad, Poor Dad* makes a critical distinction between those who become wealthier and those who struggle on in relative poverty. 'Rich dads' take charge of their money – however small it might be to start with – and acquire assets that compound their wealth, while 'poor dads' are buffeted by circumstances and spend their money on liabilities that keep them forever behind the curve.[1]

So too with states, although there are added complexities.

The difference between rich and poor states lies in the way in which leaders go about their task, in how their people respond, and in how the outside world engages. And yet one notable difference between Africa and the class of performers is in the learnt helplessness of decision-makers. Hopefully the next generation of African leaders can put this right before the development hole gets even deeper. This book aims to help these leaders make the difficult decisions and implement them.

The challenges in freeing up the system to enable fresh investment into Zambia has taught me that political will and even the right public noises are not enough. The mindset of government has to change from that of simply a regulator to a facilitator. A president who wants to do the right thing, such as Zambia's Hakainde Hichilema, is a good and necessary element but insufficient if the reforms are to survive contact with the ground and continue beyond his or her term(s) of office. 'Africa needs strong institutions and it needs strong leaders,' says former Nigerian president Olusegun Obasanjo. But creating those institutions, matching rhetoric with delivery, and maintaining discipline and predictability is no easy task, requiring external and internal alignment on their focus, operations and composition, at the very least. And it requires managing an elite that is constantly manoeuvring and hindering progress to maintain their position and flow of rents.

Africa's patronage networks, where contracts are fed to political allies, are a product of kinship and politics. They are designed to reward and, in the process, strengthen any grip on power. The security forces are employed primarily to maintain rule, not to ensure the rule of law. In this environment, power is only dangerously challengeable. Leaders rely on a small circle of trusted advisors.

Foreigners are tolerated only insofar as they provide goods or a measure of diplomatic protection, but they are seldom popular, not least because of the envy that comes with their role.

Identifying and moving quickly against such vested interests is an essential part of successful reform. Latvians, for instance, acknowledge that they should have dismantled the Soviet system much faster, as the Russians were able to 'ingrain certain habits and practices culturally and institutionally,' says Pabriks.[2] South Africa moved quickly to change the system after the end of apartheid but only to the extent that it replaced one set of (racial) elites with another. And the attempts to reform the system after the political demise of Jacob Zuma were a failure, not least because the same problems of integrity and veracity permeated the entire ANC. Sudden reforms – and prosecutions – were required, but this did not happen on a sufficient scale as it went against the ANC's constituents and sense of justice.

Indeed, the problem in many African countries is that the political and administrative class is completely rotten, acting according to their own entrenched interests. Without fundamental institutional change to transform decision-making into action – to turn opacity, arbitrariness, incompetence and corruption into transparency, predictability, competence and accountability – there is likely no end in sight to the failure of African (and some other) regimes to deliver against their promises, and therefore to the suffering of ordinary people.[3]

The management of such entrenched interests is precisely what threatened to trip up Hichilema's early attempts at reform in Zambia. The critical public response to action and inaction on such difficult policy choices illustrates that public approval should guide only to an extent, and that using the mandate given to leaders at elections is what separates the performers from the failures. The Zambian case also highlights the importance of there being consequences for bureaucratic mismanagement.

Leadership is one component, the purpose of which is not primarily to separate an elite from the misery whence they came but to get them to determine a sound path, display attention to detail, and inspire and lead others. When the cavalcades, blue lights and perks become how others see the job, then the wrong expectations and incentives follow.

While much is written about what is wrong, much less is written about how to fix things. Describing how we have found ourselves in this or that situation has become an art form, in South Africa at least, with writers producing a whole library of books on state capture, for instance, detailing its various personalities, intrigues and consequences. Outlining the choices that must be made in taking a different way involves some scrutiny of failure but also, more importantly, a clear understanding of success.

Points of success

How can one create a positive cycle of opportunity, investment, growth, stability, trade, skills, health, governance and inclusion, and in the process encourage a compounding continuum of better choices? What is the political economy of change – what political choices enable the economy to develop faster and in a more inclusive fashion?

Key to answering this economic growth–development puzzle is to ensure that the politics enables leaders to make the changes to policy that are required.

There follows the need to encourage the spontaneous, individual problem-solvers, rather than those who simply identify the problems and preach about the solutions. Someone has to actually make things happen. This includes understanding where and how government must *not* act. It requires answering the formula for better governance, whether this lies in a highly centralised state or, in larger countries, in a devolution of authority to local government agencies – cities, municipalities and/or provinces – and in which areas, from taxation to policing.

How government devises and pursues a realistic revenue model to fund itself and its agenda is crucial to long-term development. A failure to invest sufficiently in people's welfare, education and health, or in physical assets, including electricity and transport, is going to shape the long-term growth trajectory. Too much expenditure on infrastructure and political stability is likely to suffer; similarly, too much on bureaucracy and consumption, and the failings of infrastructure will undermine the economy. And someone must pay for the things on which the government chooses to spend money. Usually, privatisation – or at least a concessioning of state assets, if not an outright sale – offers a relatively easy technical solution to a lack of efficiencies, but governments can be reluctant to pursue this for several reasons: it can backfire politically due to the perception of the loss of control of national assets; the market pricing of services can amplify wealth divides and worsen difficulties of access to a modern economy; and, most relevant for most governments, the loss of exclusive control of such assets removes an opportunity for rent extraction, including the placement of politically connected individuals in jobs, and creates rival centres of power and privilege in the private sector.

Another solution is to allow the private sector to build, own and operate new assets for a stipulated period, allowing the market to decide by permitting citizens to exercise the power of competitive choice. To make this model work, government has to allow relatively generous (and stable) fiscal and policy terms, without which the private sector won't invest. Attempts by South Africa, for instance, to attract private sector investment in public utilities won't work as long as government dictates the terms of employment, investment and tariffs, and as long as rent-seeking remains the principal motivation of government action and inaction.

South Africa is one of several recalcitrant reformers, which poses the question: Why do some governments not reform when the problems are clear? Is this because they lack the ability to problem-solve and to execute solutions or does it go deeper than that? Even when clear policy decisions are made, we often find an apparent reluctance in the bureaucracy and within SOEs to execute these decisions and to bring in private partners. Is this because vested financial interests are threatened with dilution?

Reform also involves changing more than one aspect of governance. As Singapore demonstrates, it starts by not being a prisoner of the past, no matter how traumatic that past may have been, and continues along a spectrum through the commercialisation of public companies and making it easier for business to operate, to citizen empowerment by improving choices in the provision of healthcare and education.

Finding a formula for better governance therefore asks what the appropriate role for the state should be in licensing and regulating business. It asks whether and how the state should be involved in the provision of public goods, including transport, power and housing. It asks where the line should be drawn on fiscal sustainability, how to reduce debt while maintaining welfare expenditure to the most vulnerable, and how to promote capital investment over consumption. It asks whether politicians can become agents of change, rather than the source of the problem. It is never going to be easy to let go of the vested interests that ensure power but prevent change. This explains why the vicious cycle of poverty, high costs, low skills, limited investment, weak and expensive logistics, poor market access, low growth, violence, and social exclusion persists in many African contexts.

This process also asks how to make things happen – how to garner human and financial resources to tackle problems and fix things. This, however, is as much a political as a governance question.

Perhaps more than any other African state, Rwanda has enabled this focus but at a cost – it is questionable how many Rwandans, in particular how many of the Hutu majority, support President Paul Kagame and his government. Of course, this is an accusation that Kagame and other members of the minority Tutsi dismiss on the basis that they are all Rwandans (true), even though one group has benefitted disproportionately since the 1994 genocide (also true). It is questionable to what extent minority and undemocratic regimes can develop buy-in beyond authoritarianism. Absent such inclusivity, governance driven by the 'Big Man' invariably crumbles and fails.

Getting the politics right is critical. The answer as to exactly what type of political system is needed is dependent on the individual country's circumstances, but the African record is generally that the more democratic, the better the governance and developmental outcome.[4] In political terms, this amounts to a contest between two rival systems: one underpinned by constitutionalism, the rule of law, non-racialism, a market economy and a separation between party and state, with an independent, meritocratic public service; and the other an alternative, autocratic extreme[5] in which the leader controls the party, the party controls the state, the state controls the economy and society, and racial, religious or ethnic nationalism is employed to blame minorities and outsiders for the country's problems and governance failures.

The political and other conditions necessary for reform to deliver are summarised as follows:

What makes reforms happen and stick?	
When they won't	When they might
Retribution and redistribution, including ideological and populist solutions	As Deng Xiaoping put it, don't worry about the colour of the cats.
Play to social, racial or ethnic divides or past national liberation struggles	Look forwards, take the best out of the past, and move on no matter how hard and unfair this seems. A difference between success and failure is how socio-economic and political inheritance is managed, and how much it determines the future.
Externally driven development answers, including new and 'just' world orders	Local ownership of the problems, failures and thus solutions is required. External tools of discipline can help – such as trade and integration through NAFTA and the EU, as Mexico and Spain illustrate, and the market opportunities that grew in East Asia and assisted different countries on their development path.
Authoritarian, 'Big Man' rule – aimed at producing a combination of benevolence and delivery	Democratic competition is a powerful force for positive change in getting the basic ideas and principles right. This checks the temptation for self-referentialism by governments in offering such solutions and helps to guard against networks of authoritarians. Even in the cases of authoritarian growth, including Morocco and Singapore, legitimacy has depended on other efforts at social and political inclusion, from improving women's rights to greater political competition.
Aid for development	Aid that unlocks obstacles to progress is better. This could be humanitarian assistance, or peacekeeping, or aid that improves the flow of trade and investment by improving infrastructure or calibrates assistance based on conditions of domestic governance. Seldom, however, does development aid deliver.

A single cure, a magic solution	Understand the political economy of action and inaction – things happen for a reason but also don't happen for a reason. The growth story is complex and is a marathon without a finish line.
Protectionism and nationalism	Seek closer integration, not liberation, from foreign investment. Prioritise these efforts, integrating first with richer markets that offer complementarity in their partnership. Guard against protectionism and nationalism as means of institutionalising inefficiencies and rent-seeking.
Put the state at the centre	Liberate and empower people – through less state; fewer frictions; and market access to capital, technology, trade and skills. An appetite for instilling change is key.
Pick winners	Botswana's endless challenges with diversification illustrate just how imperfect a science this can be, and how subsidies and incentives can create unsustainable businesses while obscuring the need for deeper policy change.
Crack down on criticism and opposition, and employ divide-and-rule tactics using identity politics	National cohesion and common purpose reflect in the way in which institutions work and are respected, including especially the judiciary and parliament.
Sweeping visions, summits and state visits	Theatre is no alternative to policy substance and a clear plan. This involves reinventing the growth story, developing narratives, planning the next stage and attaching resources and time. It also includes aligning diplomacy with economic needs and building trust in democracy and its institutions.
Consensual and gradualist leadership – leading from behind	Leadership should be bold and move quickly, as there is a limited window for action. This is particularly true in a crisis. But watch the timing: don't, for example, try to do a Liz Truss and embark on ambitious but ill-timed reforms. Inspirational leadership, a narrative to match, decisiveness and attention to detail are all necessary in every reform instance.
Bring in Tony Blair or McKinsey & Company: drive change through technical, topical answers	Technical problems of the poor are a symptom and not a cause of poverty. Governance goes hand in hand with liberty, equality, values and rights, putting the battle of political ideas and logic at the centre of development.
Stability trumps all other needs	Stability helps but not at the price of slowing down reforms. Political instability is a risk that reformers take, as the Baltics and Poland demonstrate.

Bigger is always better	Small countries have done well in part because it's easier to extend governance over their territories. The response to Ukraine reminds us that smaller European countries possess powerful agency.
Geography, culture, climate, religion or war to explain low growth	Governments – and their ability to make better choices and implement them – set state performance apart, as the difference between Comoros and Mauritius and the success of Singapore and Vietnam illustrate.

Very often the answer provided to the question as to what separates high-performing countries from the rest is simplified down to 'good leadership'. This argument is often followed by some bluster about 'benign dictators', which is best ignored, if only because in Africa there has been no such thing, and dictators have in almost every instance been even worse at governance and development than their democratically elected counterparts. While people might want a Lee Kuan Yew, they're more likely to get a Jean-Bédel Bokassa, Idi Amin or some other unspeakably brutal and incompetent thug. While today they might get a different, less violent version – the medieval tyrant eclipsed by the 'spin dictator', as Sergei Guriev and Daniel Treisman have coined the new brand of authoritarian ruler – only a pretence of (electoral, not liberal) democracy and free choice will be tolerated.

The fact is most Africans overwhelmingly reject autocratic rule. Nearly three-quarters of Africans surveyed prefer democracy, even though – or perhaps because – more than 90 per cent of them today live under a shade of authoritarianism.[6] The absence of institutional accountability and public debate in such autocratic situations tells its own story about why development success has eluded much of Africa.

But then what are the qualities that define a 'good' leader?

Can leaders be made or at least tutored and shaped into a model of efficiency and compassion? Are there useful role models that cut across geography, history, race and religion? What mixture of attention to detail and micromanagement is required and to what extent should leaders delegate authority? Good leaders are supposed to prioritise, but what factors shape a 'priority' and what might assist a leader best in its resolution?

The premium of leadership

The cost of poor leadership can be massive and long-lasting. Former Zambian president Edgar Lungu's apparently dazed mode of presidential detachment, for instance, paralleled Zambia's economic slide at a time when the country should have boomed, as prices for copper, its principal export, rose and money was cheap to borrow in international markets. Instead, the windfall was squandered and borrowed money stolen as patronage and sycophancy became the operating system of government. President Hichilema's subsequent hands-on style stands out in contrast, but the bureaucracy presents its own challenges in an environment where selfish, personal interests habitually trump everything else.

The cost of poor leadership is perhaps best illustrated by comparing the actions of Afghanistan's former president Ashraf Ghani with those of Ukraine's Volodymyr Zelenskyy.

While Ghani fled his country when the heat was turned up, Zelenskyy, the comedian 'television President'[7] who had a 40 per cent approval rating before the war on account of his (lack of) governance, became a Churchillian figure. His ability to transmit leadership proved a key element in his early success, pushing his approval rating to 91 per cent by the end of the second week of the conflict. Zelenskyy appeared perfectly skilled and trained for this role. His appearance, actions and words were all carefully calibrated for maximum public effect, from his combat fatigues and the unshaven look of a man working round the clock to his courting of foreign dignitaries and snappy soundbites – who can forget his 'I need ammunition, not a ride' remark?

Zelenskyy's version of leadership instantly reinforced Ukraine's sense of agency in the war, despite the overwhelming comparative size of its foe – Russia has nearly four times the population and ten times the economy. By comparison, the Afghans never owned the problem and thus the solution. The Ukrainians certainly do. They have agency of a type that former presidents Hamid Karzai and Ghani could only ever dream of. Policy and direction stem from leadership, from the way it is presented and how it engages with the public through the media and other institutions of state. Zelenskyy has put his life on the line to fight an autocratic invader. Going into combat, military or otherwise, to fight for democracy no doubt builds a proper appreciation of the difference between freedom and its absence.

Perhaps for this reason, a lot of time is spent studying great military leaders in pursuit of a model for leadership. They operate in an environment where their decisions have life and death consequences, and where they have to display qualities that will encourage extraordinary things from ordinary people.

Al Murray's *Command* examines the characteristics of ten soldiers of the Second World War, from the marquee names (Bernard Montgomery, George Patton, William Slim and Omar Bradley) to the lesser-known like Bernard Freyberg and Percy Hobart.[8] Noting that 'quantity does not guarantee quality' and without command 'mass counts for nothing', he identifies two tendencies between the contrasting personal styles: those who were single-minded and uncompromisingly unsympathetic to anyone else's ideas, and those who sought to convey a 'consensus in command'.

Good leaders can be autocratic (Montgomery and Patton) or modest (Bradley and Slim). In today's world of media scrutiny, however, it is difficult to imagine General Patton surviving his profane outbursts as he did in the Second World War. Equally, it's difficult to envisage an eccentric such as Major General Orde Wingate holding on, both for his personal habits (which included eating raw onions and garlic from a string around his neck, wearing an alarm clock on his wrist that would go off at odd times and greeting visitors stark naked) and the exposure of the failings of his approach, despite his obvious courage and leadership. Sincerity is not a vindication of failure.

For all the differences in style and the divide between autocratic over more democratic leadership, there are several enduring traits of good leaders. These generally value delegation, professional understanding, innovation and the use of technology, self-discipline, moral integrity, intellectual curiosity and the ability to work with others, both within their own country and without. While some put more store in ruthlessness, iron will, political allegiance and discipline, good leaders are able to build a powerful team of minds and competencies that complements their own skills rather than satisfies their insecurities. This requires enough humility to listen and learn so that leadership is capable of constantly adapting and adjusting in a very dynamic era.

Field Marshal Sir Harold Alexander is often cited as a model for leadership. In the world of high command, where ego and personal ambition often go hand in hand, he had very little of the former and almost none of the latter. He was a man of 'unflinchingly calm demeanour', writes historian James Holland. When Alexander visited Aïn Beïda in Algeria as commander-in-chief of Middle East Command in 1942/43, British resident minister in Algiers and future prime minister Harold Macmillan wrote in his diary: 'The whole atmosphere of the camp is dominated by his personality – modest, calm, confident.'[9]

Character matters, as does politeness and manners in gathering others around you. 'You lose nothing by being polite,' noted Lee Kuan Yew in 1965. Alexander was brought up to respect honour and duty and to always display impeccable manners. He possessed an 'unflappable ability' to make the best of a bad situation and was, through brilliant diplomacy, able to persuade others – especially his American allies – to accept his ideas as their own, making them think that they had thought of it all themselves. Such a skill is as enduring as it is endearing to those leaders worried by their image. And such a command style is particularly suited to coalition operations of the sort that every country faces in today's hyper-globalised world. There was less coercion than suggestion in his way of dealing with others.

'Alexander proved all that I had heard, a patient, wise, fair-minded, shrewd, utterly charming professional soldier with a firm strategic grasp,' wrote General of the Army Omar Bradley. Alexander led by example, getting out there, touring the front and making the necessary decisions. He was not averse to being tough, however. Rudyard Kipling, in his history of the Irish Guards, in which Alexander served and in which his own son, John Kipling, fought and was killed in action in 1915, noted, 'it is undeniable that Colonel Alexander had the gift of handling the men on the lines to which they most readily responded... His subordinates loved him, even when he fell upon them blisteringly for their shortcomings; and his men were all his own.'[10]

Leaders such as Alexander do not usually seek fame and do not always find fortune. Field Marshal Alan Francis Brooke, later the 1st Viscount Alanbrooke, was Chief of the Imperial General Staff (the title of the professional head of the British Army) during the Second World War and principal military advisor to Prime Minister Winston Churchill. After the war, Brooke's financial situation dictated the appointments he was able to take up and forced him and his wife to move into the gardener's cottage of their former home, where they lived for the rest of their lives.

In contrast to Alexander, Field Marshal Bernard Montgomery was characterised by 'his total inability to show any sensitivity to others'.[11] He assiduously worked to put himself at the centre. As Churchill famously observed of him: 'In defeat, unbeatable: in victory, unbearable.' Although his overconfidence had its advantages, it also had massive drawbacks in working with allies. 'He cared not a jot about rubbing people up the wrong way, and seemed to have no awareness of his appalling rudeness,' writes Holland of the man who led the Allies to victory at El Alamein.[12] Almost all the senior commanders reportedly 'loathed' Montgomery; while 'that didn't make him a bad commander ... it did complicate matters, especially when there was quite enough pressure and tension to deal with as it was.'[13]

The human dimension of leadership is therefore critical, since the challenge for outsiders especially is not to tell people what to do and, more importantly, what they are doing wrong. This is inevitably seen as patronising and counterproductive. Rather, the secret is to build relationships that enable change. This requires showing genuine care for those under one's leadership. It also depends on what phase of government one is in: whether you are looking to stop and turn around failure, or initiate and carry through reforms, or build off a base of pre-existing solid growth. Some are not so lucky with the nature of their inheritance.

The ability to work with others, to maintain collegiality but also to decide on a course of action and then ruthlessly pursue it is more difficult but particularly necessary in those countries beset by division and an absence of trust across races, religions, tribes and geographies, and between the public and private sectors.

The image of the showy individual cultivated by the likes of Montgomery and Patton, or Mobutu Sese Seko and Donald Trump in a political context, can funnel authority in a positive way, but the peacocking has to be purposeful rather than driven by ego alone. Headlines are necessary, as Zelenskyy shows, but only in tuning in the public and turning the debate in the interests of the mission.

There is no need to openly play the autocrat; believing that getting the best results demands autocratic methods may in fact demonstrate weakness. Rather, as Alexander demonstrated, it is better to get people to reach the same conclusion through explanation and instigation, rather than coercion. Leaders must be firm but not rude. An inner self-discipline is required to keep ego in check.

General David Petraeus, who commanded multinational forces in Iraq and Afghanistan, and who served briefly as director of the CIA, identifies four tasks of 'strategic' leadership. The first 'is to get the big ideas right'. The second 'is to communicate them effectively throughout the breadth and depth of the organization'. The third is to oversee their implementation. 'And the fourth is to determine how the big ideas need to be refined, changed, augmented, and then repeating the process over again and again and again.'[14]

As Petraeus notes, ideas are not enough. Execution is critical. As General Bradley observed to the US Army War College on the subject of leadership in 1971: 'While it takes a good staff officer to initiate an effective plan, it requires a leader to ensure that the plan is properly executed. That is why the work of collecting information, studying it, drawing a plan, and making a decision is only a small part of the total endeavor; seeing the plan through is the major part.'[15] In practical terms, there is the danger of announcing a project and then expecting it to be delivered. It takes a lot of hustling and sweat to ensure the job gets done, infinitely more perspiration than inspiration.

There is a constant imperative 'to think things through to the finish', agrees Nick Carter, former Chief of the Defence Staff, the professional head of the British Armed Forces. Besides dollops of political will, this usually requires tempering ambition, reducing the number of tasks, dedicating sufficient resources to tasks and allocating tasks to key people. This approach avoids overstretch and failure. 'No leader knows it all,' continues Bradley. 'A leader should encourage the members of his staff to speak up if they think the commander is wrong. He should invite constructive criticism. It is a grave error for the leader to surround himself with "Yes" men.' General George C. Marshall was an exponent of his subordinates speaking up. According to Bradley, General Marshall once told him, 'Unless I hear all the arguments concerning an action, I am not sure whether I have made the right decision or not.'

Another critical quality of leadership is accepting responsibility for defeat. If a mission or plan fails and if people have done their jobs, then the ultimate responsibility rests with the person at the top. As Field Marshal William Slim reflected on the early Second World War defeats in Malaya and Burma: 'Defeat is bitter. Bitter to the common soldier, but trebly bitter to his general. The soldier may compensate himself with the thought that, whatever the results, he has done his duty faithfully and steadfastly, but the commander has failed in his duty if he has not won victory – for that is his duty. He has no other comparable to it.'[16]

Few political leaders are willing to take responsibility for defeat – most prefer passing the buck, their egos preventing them from even identifying their mistakes, let alone learning from them.

There is no denying the personal pressures of leadership. '[A]t the end of the day this is a seven-day-a-week, twenty-four-hour-a-day exercise,' said Petraeus of his own role as a strategic commander in Iraq. 'And the challenges of it should not be minimized, they can't be, and you have to be ready for that, you have to be equal to that, and you have to stay strong in the face of all the pressures that are brought to bear.'[17]

No one knows this better than President Zelenskyy. But while he is probably crucial to Ukrainian success, especially in gathering support and in turning the conflict from a losing to a worthy and winnable cause, his leadership alone is insufficient to win the struggle. Good leaders recognise the need to build strong institutions to carry forward their work, and not just make it about themselves. This means guarding, too, against institutional self-deception. This, in turn, requires not only the brightest people but also those present and engaged, whose courage will prevent the institutionalisation and conspiracy of optimism, where facts and feedback to leaders can commonly be tilted to suit the narrative and to define loyalty.

A careful selection of priorities and the application of resources to them can create another reinforcing leadership attribute: a tradition of success. This requires a can-do spirit, but more than that, an ability to learn to identify and admit what worked and what failed, and thus what is required to win.

In *The Best and the Brightest*, David Halberstam examines what went wrong in Vietnam, how obviously able and dedicated men propelled the United States into an unwinnable war. Halberstam takes his readers through the flawed decision-making process that allowed a group of talented individuals to misunderstand key aspects of the conflict. By recounting the perils of groupthink and painting detailed profiles of the personalities involved, from the US Secretary of Defense,

Robert McNamara, to a young Tony Lake (later Bill Clinton's national security advisor) and Richard Holbrooke (later Clinton's UN ambassador), the book outlines several key reasons why America got sucked into a war it could not win.[18] 'What was it about the men, their attitudes, the country, its institutions and above all the era which had allowed this tragedy to take place?' Halberstam asks. They were, after all, 'the best and the brightest'.[19]

It happened, he concludes, because 'they had, for all their brilliance and hubris and sense of themselves, been unwilling to look and learn from the past'. They ignored the history of Hanoi, failed to understand the country and its leadership, and were 'swept forward by their belief in the importance of anti-Communism (and the dangers of not paying sufficient homage to it)'. What more vivid way to convey the ingrained Cold War suspicions and assumptions than Lyndon B. Johnson's immediate thoughts on that November day in Dallas when Kennedy was assassinated 'that the Communists had done it'?

This reflected not only their ideological prejudice, however, but also their lack of experience in dealing with that part of the world. As a result, while the individuals might have been brilliant in their fields, they lacked common sense. In this environment, too, anyone who bucked the prevalent groupthink or who questioned policy and the results that escalating the war would have, or who tried to make accurate projections about what level of resources a war in Vietnam would require, was deprived of power and influence. Even though the original plans to win the war had called for the deployment of a million American troops, this was deemed politically impossible and a lower figure was fabricated that would be more palatable. Politically, also, inertia set in; rather than admitting failure or changing strategy, more and more resources were committed.

Being brutally honest to political leaders – speaking truth to power – is precisely what the senior leadership of the US military failed to do regarding Vietnam. While situations like this require a political leadership willing to recognise their own limits (which is, admittedly, unusual), they also demand outsiders who possess the courage of their convictions, as well as the personal and institutional means to encourage political change. In echoes of the excesses of a woke world, Halberstam captures the stultifying atmosphere by showing Frederick Nolting, the American ambassador to South Vietnam from 1961 to 1963, replacing a portrait of Thomas Jefferson with one of George Washington in anticipation of a television interview because Jefferson was deemed too controversial. Given this environment, it made little difference to hire 'the best and the brightest'.

Despite these lessons, political leaders continue to ignore history.

Papers released in 2022 by the UK National Archives show that, back in 2002, Tony Blair believed that Vladimir Putin was a 'Russian patriot' at heart, worthy of a seat at the international 'top table'. Despite the reservations of senior British civil servants about the former KGB agent's trustworthiness, Blair thought that this would encourage the then new Russian president to adopt Western values and would thus ensure stability among NATO allies.[20] Blair also thought that a Russian proposal for a gas pipeline supplying the Netherlands, Sweden and the UK via Belarus would 'ensure stable supplies for decades to come', even though officials were warning as to the levels of Russian espionage amid the rhetoric. The document lists a string of assurances given by Putin to Blair, including that Moscow would cease supplying Iran's nuclear programme and would support the West's approach to dealing with Saddam Hussein, all of which turned out to be false.

Egoism and idealism are two sides of the coin of leadership. But there are immense dangers when these two driving forces get out of kilter, allowing charismatic and bright neophytes at the top to believe that they know better and that they alone know how to read people, gain their confidence and swing their opinions, that experts 'just read books', that history is bunk, and that if leaders get on, countries will.[21] Politicians will always interfere, since self-belief is how they rose to power in the first instance. Such personalities are not wired to listen, and this is not helped by groupthink and the weakness of leaders to see obeisance as loyalty.

Leadership for Africa

Translating this into an African context, where capacity is thin, the politics fractious and institutions threadbare, there is a need for closer integration between the components of strategy: the goals, ways and means. While big vision is important, there is an imperative to focus on small deliverables, but ones that are key enough to get the ball rolling. The lesson of the reset in the Zambian mining sector is one example. And from there, these changes can be consolidated and reinforced, and as reforms gain momentum, gradually expanded to other areas. 'We did a few things right and well, and continued to do them right and well, widening and deepening them all the time,' Lee Kuan Yew told Nigerian president Olusegun Obasanjo of the reasons for Singapore's reform success.[22] In other words, there are no miracles.

Africa needs leaders who can carefully prioritise their actions and marshal their resources, who have a firm grip on the detail as well as the ability to see the sweep of the bigger picture, who trust enough people around them to get things done without losing control, who do not mind contrarian argument (at least in private) and see loyalty not just through the prism of agreement, who act, like Thatcher, to achieve their mandate rather than attempt to maintain consensus, and who have a laser-like focus on implementation.

Better politics produces better leaders. But this is no small challenge in the media age, when politics seldom seems to attract the best and the brightest, to use Halberstam's phrase. The danger is then a reversion to crude contests of identity over ideas, where the narratives are formed less around what is to be done and how than the personalities. Perhaps the answer lies in the lessons from Peru and Argentina, in the need for an 'integral' rather than simply an 'institutional' response, preparing political leaders adequately for their role and enabling them to develop long-term solutions to the complex problems faced by modern society.

The leadership solution lies also in the creation of agency beyond government, both through policy (permitting private competition to correct state inefficiency and more easily allowing business to operate) and in the way in which private citizens engage with the political class and system, with business and in society at large. 'Active citizens within a political system,' says Thabo Makgoba, the archbishop of Cape Town, are key to building what he terms 'communities of change'.[23]

Malawi is stuck. Among the five poorest countries at independence, in 2021 it ranked second from the bottom globally.[24]

Its per capita income is $390, a quarter of the sub-Saharan African average, itself seven times less than the global average. Malawians were very poor at independence in 1964, their average income just 5 per cent of the global average; today they have unimaginably slipped further backwards to a paltry 3.5 per cent. Put differently, Malawians are nearly thirty times poorer than the average global citizen, an astonishing statistic when one contemplates its development advantages (rich agricultural land and a lake covering a quarter of the country's total area) and how well we now understand development choices, challenges and options.

Following independence, Malawi's growth patterns initially tracked those of sub-Saharan Africa, increasing at 3.7 per cent annually. Since 1980, however, it started to fall behind the rest of the continent, by then hardly a stellar performer. Malawi's real per capita GDP grew at an average of just 1.5 per cent between 1995 and 2015, for example, well below the 2.7 per cent average in non-resource-rich African economies.

There are few countries as poor that are not at war. At least Malawi has that going for it. Yet, to add insult to injury, it has remained vulnerable to episodic financial crises, characterised by balance-of-payment issues, forex unavailability, rising inflation, high debt levels and a collapse in growth rates.

Why is Malawi so poor, and why the recurrent tendency to crisis and constant slippage?

The answer is multifaceted, of course.

Many Malawians point to a combination of their poor colonial inheritance, being landlocked, poverty and unfavourable terms of trade. Others single out the harsh regime of Hastings Kamuzu Banda, the Scottish-educated authoritarian who ran the country with an iron fist from 1964 until the advent of multipartyism in 1994 – though Malawians are divided in their loyalty over the legacy of a man who referred to his own people as 'children in politics'.

Even though things started to fall apart during Banda's rule, especially by the late 1980s, and growth was low, forcing the arrival of the World Bank and the imposition of a series of pro-market reforms, he was feared and consequently remains revered. 'If I am a dictator, it is because my people want me to be,' Banda said in 1966. 'I am a dictator of the people, by the people and for the people.'[25]

The last three decades have been shaped by Banda's brand of 'Big Man' politics, manifest in the poor choices made by subsequent leaders and the corrosive nature of government. It's not that Malawi lacks governance, but rather that the purpose of government has been to enrich an elite at the expense of the poor. The political pact among the elite to extract rents – even to the extent of driving macro-instability – means there is no will to grow the pie for all. Instead, what there is, is shared among the few. This is borne out by the resistance to securing a proper rail network (acting in the interests of a transport mafia), the resistance to land reform (keeping the people poor and elite interests secured), the resistance to reforming fertiliser subsidies (for those who sell and distribute) and in the variety of state intermediaries in almost every area of the economy, from tobacco auction houses to buying-agents for maize. In each of these areas, there are rents to be protected and constituencies to be maintained.

It explains why government has retained the middleman style of state intervention in the economy that had proved unwieldy even by the end of the supposedly relatively prosperous 1980s, to the point that assistance had to be sought from the World Bank. It also explains why Malawi keeps going with agricultural input subsidy schemes and bucking regional market opportunities, and why the civil service is comparatively large (at 180 000), guided less by performance than by loyalty and a pernicious 'per diem' culture of allowances to augment low salaries.

For Malawi to progress so that its growing number of citizens can lift themselves out of poverty, this system must be broken. Is this likely and could outsiders perhaps help?

There are several schools of thought, dotted on a spectrum of optimism.

One says that it will never happen and that donors are simply compounding the problem. Certainly, the $26 billion in donor funding since 1964 has failed to change the system of governance and the locked-in, cyclical poverty (low income, weak public finances, poor education and healthcare, limited infrastructure, low investment, and low growth). To the contrary, it has encouraged rent-seeking behaviour and disincentivised reforms by providing a safety net. While the donors argue against this – in part because turkeys seldom vote for Christmas and because there are valid humanitarian concerns about cutting off aid – the evidence suggests that, at best, donor spending has made things 'less bad'.

A second school of thought advocates 'development through aid'. This argument is that more donor money is needed – that the current $1 billion annually to Malawi is too little to make a difference, simply offering a Band-Aid for what is a sucking chest wound in developmental terms. The dangers in this approach can be seen in the catastrophic failure of schemes such as Professor Jeffrey Sachs's Millennium Villages Project, which operated at two sites in Malawi.

A third view is that change is possible if one looks for green shoots in Malawians themselves, in the judiciary (which held the line against President Peter Mutharika in upholding an election rerun), in NGOs and in the private sector. A version of this answer can be found in a bottom-up initiative on Lake Malawi, designed to prevent overfishing and create a virtuous cycle of management by locals.

Ripple Africa began as a reforestation initiative in 2003 and within ten years had expanded its focus to include sustainable fishing. In the twenty years leading up to 2011, fish stocks in Lake Malawi had decreased by 90 per cent due to overfishing and especially the uncontrolled fishing of breeding grounds with mosquito nets. Nothing better illustrates the folly of careless development aid than the distribution of mosquito nets. The nets, provided to stem malaria, were repurposed to catch fish. The tiny holes in the nets ensure that every small, immature fish in their path is harvested, with devastating consequences for future stocks.

'It was chaos. Fishing was an open access activity,' says Bernard Gula, a boat owner and chairman of the local Beach Village Committee (BVC) in Cape Maclear, a neglected tourist favourite in the southern region of Lake Malawi. 'Anyone who wanted could go fishing. The community were not empowered to conserve; rather, the power was with government, not the people.'

The fishing communities were locked in a vicious downwards spiral. Government 'control' removed local ownership. As human population numbers increased – from four million at independence to twenty million today, and a projected forty million by 2050 – the pressure on fish stocks grew, leading to lower catches, worsening frictions between communities and government, and more poverty in a microcosm of what has occurred nationally. Such declines have an especially big impact in very poor communities such as those in Malawi, where 83 per cent are rural based and just 10 per cent have access to electricity. In the case of Lake Malawi, the impact has been compounded by the virtual collapse of foreign tourism, largely on account of South Africa's diplomatic opening to the rest of the world post-apartheid.

Arresting this cycle had to involve a mindset change, a seemingly impossible task. The solution, thought Ripple Africa's British founders, Geoff and Liz Furber, was not to be found in a stronger state or centralised control, but rather in local communities getting together and getting better organised. It was not going to be a short-term solution either, and therefore unlikely to appeal to the limited electoral mindset of politicians, both local and foreign.

Force Ngwira was a curio carver when he met Geoff Furber at Nkhata Bay in Lake Malawi's northern region. He has worked with Ripple Africa since its founding in 2003. 'Malawians believe in today; we don't really care for tomorrow,' he says. 'This includes our view of natural resources. So, we had to change this mindset.'

With the help of the district fisheries offices, Ripple Africa set up Beach Village Committees, local voluntary groups that represent the interests of the fishing communities. Working (so far) with five of the eight lakeside districts in building 474 BVCs from the bottom up, Ripple has used a combination of carrots, transition periods and clear messaging to convince more than 35 000 'fishers' – fishermen and -women – to move to bigger nets and away from breeding areas. Every evening, fleets of home-built boats row past the shore of Lake Malawi to hunt for usipa (a small freshwater sardine-like fish) under lights and with nets. The beaches are policed by some 5 000 BVC members – a political and governance force to be reckoned with, which has confiscated the gear of over 1 600 fishers to date.

With Ripple's measures in place, catch yields have steadily improved. Monthly sales of chambo (another type of freshwater fish endemic to Lake Malawi), for example, increased sixfold in value between 2016 and 2022, with 133 breeding areas under protection by 2023. While there has been a 60 per cent drop in the volume (in litres) of usipa caught, the number of larger fish has increased from 46 per cent to 70 per cent per litre, and income by 20 per cent.

Ripple's operation is less about threats than the incentives of change.

Agnes Mpinganjira is a BVC member in Nsumbi, a lakeside village near Monkey Bay in the south. 'We had to look after our farm, our land,' she says, pointing to the lake, 'just like we would look after our forests and our trees.'

And the Furbers have stayed true to their vision of local lead. Ripple Africa is run entirely by Malawians (more than 450 to date), albeit on foreign donations totalling $900 000 annually (a tiny fraction of the more than $1-billion annual national aid tranche) for their 'Fish for Tomorrow' programme.

Ngwira describes the positive ecological cycle that they have managed to create and sustain, where local ownership is cemented from the bottom up, rather than attempted from the top down. It is driven by the education of local stakeholders (in this case, the fishers); the involvement of local policing; the construction of local institutions with a monitoring and policing capacity; partnerships with government departments, including fisheries and wildlife; and integration with other sustainability measures, such as reforestation and eco-friendly cooking methods.

In other areas, externally driven efforts to reform have created incentives for local governments to establish the form but not the function of institutions. External pressure has created a Newtonian reaction, moving domestic reformers in a contrarian, regressive direction, a trend often fuelled by populist instincts and easy answers. Managed badly, too much pressure can cut off dialogue and upset relationships – and without a trusted messenger, there can be no message.

The Ripple experience highlights the importance of getting the incentives right, of the need for local buy-in and of the complementary role that can, in the right conditions, be played by outsiders. Ripple shows that by starting small, strengthening local voices in the places where change is needed and sticking with it no matter how long it takes, the most desperate and seemingly impossible of circumstances can be changed.

If outsiders can do this and avoid amplifying their own voices to advance their own careers and interests, trust can be enhanced and progress made. In Malawi, this also requires a leadership capable of not only pinpointing the problems, but also prioritising and executing the solutions, avoiding self-defeating populist economic choices (such as the maize export ban and the latest land reforms, which effectively prohibit foreigners from owning land and give the government sweeping powers to seize foreign-owned land), and being willing to relinquish control or at least share in the benefits of change.

'Let go to get going' is the message for governments, local and foreign, a message contained in the following song (written with Robin Auld):

Take, Take, Take

Take take take
Another slice of power
Take take take
Another piece of cake
Take take take
Rich State or Poor State
Take take take
It's not a matter of fate

Blink of the tin
Sand in the toes
Small lives in the bin
Big people, who knows

Looking ahead
People who care
Marie Antoinette
Never learnt to share

Living the Lokasi
Houses on the hill
Down in Makasi
Dreams to fulfil
If they don't eat
Leaders shouldn't sleep
At night, the heat
No peace on the cheap

Can we ever find
The chiefs we trust
Corruption of the mind
Change but not adjust
Eternal struggle
Crocodiles eat the sun
Dreams turn to rubble
Where's that liberation?

Perhaps the last word on leadership should be left to General Omar Bradley, who was aware of the immutable value of practicality over theory in war. 'Amateurs talk about strategy, professionals talk about logistics,' he once said. According to Bradley, a leader needs to be an all-rounder and must possess a plan. Leadership, he concludes, centres on confidence, 'creating it, radiating it, and inspiring it'.[26]

Creating a coincidence of global interests

In June 1947, in a speech at Harvard University, US Secretary of State George C. Marshall proposed that European nations create a plan for their economic reconstruction to which the United States would provide financial assistance. Ten months later, President Harry Truman signed the Economic Recovery Act, which became known as the Marshall Plan, under the terms of which the US would transfer over $13 billion – approximately $150 billion in today's terms – to sixteen European nations by the time the programme concluded in 1952.

Such was the immediate and positive impact of the Marshall Plan that Truman proposed an international development assistance programme in 1949, which morphed into the United States Agency for International Development, founded in 1961. Today, official development assistance – aid from developed to developing countries – totals $185 billion annually. This figure excludes private flows and money from non-traditional donors, including China, Turkey and the Middle East.

The Marshall Plan was very successful in terms of its objectives. The European countries involved experienced a 35 per cent increase in output by 1952, becoming a bulwark against communist expansion in the process. In a virtuous cycle, this created growing and reliable markets for American goods (where much of the funding was spent), improving European social and political stability and enabling economic recovery.

The Marshall Plan worked because it built on existing human capacity and the European partners were willing – indeed, desperate in the wake of the Second World War – to play their part. The establishment of counterpart funds in local currency provided a crucial source for industrial investment, especially in West Germany.

The success was such that the Marshall Plan has become a metaphor for dramatic, transformative, large-scale development assistance projects, especially in Africa. 'We need a Marshall Plan' has become a rhetorical default setting for unimaginative politicians looking for a radical answer to a difficult development situation.

But herein lie three problems.

First, the Marshall Plan was built on pre-existing skills. For all the damage that the war did, there were still many highly qualified and technically proficient Germans able to pick up the pieces. The Marshall Plan provided, initially, liquidity to buy essential food, fuel and other consumables, and then capital goods along with access to markets for local production. That access already exists for Africa, but what does not exist are technical and technocratic skills and a governance environment able to use them.

The relative absence of skills, governance and capacity can be seen in the peak ratio of aid to GDP to Europe under the Marshall Plan (2.5 per cent) compared to Africa (less the two largest economies of South Africa and Nigeria) circa 2020 (5 per cent).[27] More money will not address these productive shortages on its own, especially the shortage of institutional capacity and skills.

Second, the Europeans were willing partners, intent on playing their part in recovery. By comparison, aid to Africa has failed where Africans have seen it less as an incentive for reform and an investment in change than a form of reparations. It has also failed given that external attempts to impose conditions (which was a key aspect in the Marshall Plan) have proven impossible in Africa, in part because local politicians are especially adept in playing this off against colonial and racial guilt, and because foreign governments have lacked the spine to apply the principles of 'take it or leave it'. The bipolar nature of the Cold War weakened such conditionalities, where partnerships were determined by support for one side or another and not any adherence to governance norms. A return to this world order would be detrimental to African reformers.

Third, besides funding (which is helpful, if spent on well-priced capital rather than consumer goods), international actors can play a useful role in development by providing cheaper market access (since more trade equals greater growth) and by being a tool of external incentivisation and discipline, as the EU has done in Europe and NAFTA in, especially, Mexico. The challenge for outsiders working with Africa is to imagine a system of reciprocal advantage beyond trade preferences based on foreign guilt and local desperation, a system that knits together wider aspects of growth and development.

As one Spanish diplomat observed about Brussels' role in Spain's domestic fiscal policy in the context of the spendthrift ways of Prime Minister José Luis Rodríguez Zapatero's administration (2004–11): 'The EU is a vaccine against irresponsible national politicians.'

As with Europe and Mexico, the overall aim of integration processes in Africa must be to tap into richer markets. That is how Asia developed – by supplying cheap goods to richer markets, initially using its labour cost differential. As 97.2 per cent of the global economy lies outside Africa, and nearly 40 per cent in the US and the EU alone,[28] African countries must aim to reduce the barriers to trade with the outside world – as Morocco has managed – at least as much as with one another.

Historically, during the colonial era, external interests in Africa were driven by the intersection of interests of politicians, civil servants and businessmen. Policy was geared towards the maintenance of law and order, the raising of taxes to pay for the administration of the colony, the stimulation of the production of raw materials for export to the colonial power, and the establishment of a consumer market to purchase manufactured goods in return. As Frederick Forsyth reminds us in his treatment of the callousness of the British in the Nigerian Civil War, Africa represented 'not a land with a population of real people, but a market'. Any threats to the market were to be discouraged, even if that involved ignoring democratic process and human rights.[29]

Such indifference has been perpetuated in the post-colonial period. Policy is usually based not on support for local populations and their needs, but on the maintenance of outside interests through the local regime in power. This should not surprise Africa; it is not the responsibility of outsiders to be more interested in the fortunes and welfare of Africans than in maintaining their own strategic and commercial interests. This attitude is perhaps at its most cynical when outsiders hold forth on the need to maintain stability over democracy during contested African elections, a guide that Western countries would wholesale reject as their own formula.

Added to this is a realisation on the part of outsiders that you can get away with dealing with a small elite, that if you control (or influence) the capital, you control the country. Hence there is little interest in promoting governance, especially representative governance, and administration (including tax collection) in areas outside of the capital.

In the contemporary era, optimism about Africa and externally driven schemes for development are therefore seldom informed by what's best for African people. After all, they are not the principal constituents of outside powers. Instead, the focus is on securing the interests of the outside powers. That Africans don't get screwed in the process is up to their own governments, and when that safeguard fails, as it routinely does, to African civil society. The same is true for the role of business; business seldom finds a government it does not like. It's up to Africans to hold business to account, not least through the institutions established for this purpose: the courts, parliament and the media included.

Colonialism, which had its own routine of extraction and local disempowerment, has undoubtedly contributed to the way in which locals see the benefits of change and the role of outsiders, and to the extent to which they are prepared to take leadership responsibility themselves. Actions by outsiders that contribute to the lack of trust and perceptions of a lack of respect are unlikely to assist. The fault also lies in the tendency of local elites to see the world through a lens of suspicion and conspiracy, a neo-mercantilist outlook that is antithetical to the functioning of the global economy. Vested interests and views contrary to reform must be managed into relative political irrelevance. The way to do this is to deliver on promises.

The failure to take local responsibility and to develop organic responses to problems is hardly helped by the habit of outsiders to serially prepare plans for assistance and recovery based on rote solutions, and highlighting generalised points in politically inclusive (and correct) language, as per the following:

> We are proud to announce the launch of a comprehensive five-point plan [or three- or ten-, take your pick] aimed at tackling governance, demographic, and economic challenges in sub-Saharan Africa. With a strong commitment to fostering progress and sustainable development, we will be taking proactive measures to address these critical issues and create a brighter future for the region. Our five-point plan has been carefully designed to ensure a holistic approach, combining targeted interventions and collaborative efforts. By

addressing governance, demographics, and economic development simultaneously, we aim to make substantial progress towards building resilient societies and empowering local communities, fostering progress and sustainable development, and combatting climate change.

As part of the plan, we will focus on the following key areas:

1. Strengthening governance: Recognising the importance of transparent and accountable governance, we will support efforts to enhance institutional capacities, promote the rule of law, and combat corruption. Through partnerships and capacity-building initiatives, the plan aims to foster good governance practices that will lay the foundation for sustainable development.
2. Investing in education and healthcare: Recognising the transformative power of education and healthcare, we will work closely with local stakeholders to improve access to quality education and healthcare services. By supporting the development of educational infrastructure, training programmes, and healthcare facilities, we seek to empower individuals and communities, ensuring they have the necessary tools to thrive.
3. Promoting women's empowerment: We firmly believe in gender equality and women's empowerment as key drivers of development. We will launch initiatives to promote women's rights, ensure equal opportunities, and combat gender-based violence. By empowering women and promoting their active participation in decision-making processes, the plan seeks to build inclusive societies and foster sustainable development.
4. Enhancing economic opportunities: Economic development plays a crucial role in addressing the challenges faced by sub-Saharan Africa. We will support initiatives that promote entrepreneurship, job creation, and sustainable economic growth. By fostering innovation and providing technical assistance, we aim to unlock the region's economic potential and create opportunities for all.
5. Strengthening regional cooperation: Recognising the importance of collaboration, we will actively engage with regional organisations, governments, civil society, and other stakeholders. Through partnerships and knowledge sharing, the plan aims to foster regional cooperation and amplify the impact of interventions, ensuring long-term sustainability and positive change.

We aim to create an environment where progress and sustainable growth can thrive. We believe that through collaboration and targeted interventions, we can make a tangible difference in the lives of people in the region. This is an important and shared journey in which we invite all stakeholders to join hands in the pursuit of positive change, progress and prosperity in sub-Saharan Africa.[30]

Those that produce such templatic responses to poverty, as unimaginative as they are generalised and unworkable, make it difficult not to be as pessimistic about their role as cynical.

More importantly, those who believe that salvation is going to come from outside, or that the problem lies outside the continent, are similarly off the mark. Africa expends too much energy (and diplomacy) on this area of policy, but for good reason. Externalising the solution (as the problem) assists in deflecting attention away from the failures of domestic actors. Hence the disproportionate expenditure of time on tax evasion, and conspiracy narratives about the role of multinational companies and the externalisation of profits, instead of focusing on the things more easily changed domestically, not least improving productivity and reducing business frictions.

The latter requires aligning policy and its implementation with an economic growth agenda. Underperformance due to incompetence and a lack of accountability has nothing (or very little) to do with external practices and actors. And squeezing outside actors for a greater share is not the way to greater prosperity; to the contrary, it will ensure greater penury. Even if corporate taxes are raised to 100 per cent, tax compliance is universal and the externalisation of any profits is zero, productivity and economic growth will not improve, as 'an economy doesn't grow by taxes, it grows by production of goods and services'.[31] In this way, the political constraints and costs of making better choices, improving the incentives, and moving away from excuses towards a growth agenda remain significant impediments to development.

There are other limits to the role of outsiders. Their interests in fixing failure cannot be greater than the interests of locals if any reform process is to be sustainable. Africa must learn to rely less on the charity of external actors than on their interests in making money.

Conclusion: The imperative to let go

There are unforeseen dangers ahead if Africa cannot quickly deliver on the reforms necessary to encourage private citizens, at home and abroad, to invest their savings in local businesses.

Without providing a platform for investment today, in twenty to thirty years we could come full circle in Africa: with failing and highly frictional governance systems, investment in infrastructure will be insufficient to maintain port cities, which will be controlled by foreign syndicates to ensure raw materials keep flowing no matter what. Beyond the borders of these African city-states, there will be very little functional infrastructure. The development of autonomous drones for transport, of both critical goods and people, could accelerate the collapse of road networks and all that entails, while 3D printing and developments in AI could be bad news for dreams of developing a manufacturing base, since even the first rung on that development ladder, the creation of a cheap textile production and clothing manufacturing base, will move back to the northern hemisphere. This will close off traditional development avenues to Africa, ending any hopes of large-scale employment.

Regardless of the impact of new technologies, there are other challenges to the creation of African manufacturing. From Singapore to Vietnam, East Asia's export-led growth has pulled hundreds of millions of people out of poverty over the past sixty years. The region is consequently embedded in the global tech supply chain. Continued growth has required constant changes to regulatory and labour software, and, increasingly, infrastructure hardware, from energy to logistics. For these reasons, it is unclear whether this manufacturing development option is available to many African countries, given the high levels of bureaucratic friction, low standards of infrastructure development and efficiency, and comparatively low labour productivity when measured against the abundant and cheap labour supply of Asia. While average monthly wages in the manufacturing sector in China had risen to $1 000 by 2023, those in Malaysia were $600, in Vietnam just $300, and even less in the Philippines, India and Indonesia.[32] Africa will have to radically improve its productivity in manufacturing to pursue an export-led growth strategy, or find another high-growth, high-employment development path.

The dystopian future outlined above could be offset by another, utopian alternative, where the growth in African populations drives consumption and consumerism, where digitisation improves access to banking and markets and reduces the frictions inherent in government systems, and where the combination of changing demographics and improving governance drives foreign investment.

The only way developing countries can achieve convergence with their developed counterparts is by growing at a faster pace.[33] This demands investment from savings, either from abroad or from home, where domestic investors are usually the better judges of market health. This requires a rate of return that competes with alternative investment destinations and that is, in turn, easier to determine when there is policy predictability, if not certainty, on a medium- to long-term horizon, regardless of the government in power. Spend more than the state gathers in revenue – or can sustainably finance – and there is a risk of inflation. Spend disproportionately on salaries over capital and operational expenses, and infrastructure will suffer. The cost of protecting domestic inefficiencies and low productivity is invariably borne by the local consumer and taxpayer. Maintain high levels of bureaucratic friction, and investors will keep their distance. A failure to provide basic services – from security to healthcare and education – not only adds a premium to the cost of trying to do business, but also invariably serves to drive a wedge between those who can access private services and those who can't – in other words, between rich and poor – undermining the long-term health of society. And even subjectively weaken the rule of law, such as around special interests, and you discount your country's prospects of success.

For a system of government to be inclusive rather than extractive requires using politics to economic advantage and not allowing elites or history or entrenched interests to dictate the range of choices. This has to be driven from inside, although it can be assisted by integrating external tools and institutions.

The distinction between rich states and poor states is stark. Rich states grow their economies and drive development by taking the key decisions – however unpopular they might be with the entrenched elite – needed to unlock their potential. They then act, empowering those with the technical know-how to drive implementation. They create powerful institutions capable of managing complex activities and withstanding political pressure and the fight-back from those who lose access to rents. The progress of the country is always placed ahead of elite enrichment.

Poor states are good at identifying the problems but seldom pinpoint the causes when these highlight their own political dysfunction. Outsiders, history or discrimination are always to blame. This cauterises them against making the tough decisions unless these – such as wealth taxes or land nationalisation – are aimed at those outside the rent-seeking elite. Technocrats are not valued because they have the temerity to question political decisions and to propose solutions that will shake the rent tree. The progress of the country plays second fiddle to elite enrichment.

The difference between rich states and poor states, between success and failure, depends on the extent of external economic integration and the exercise of leadership in acting quickly, identifying and setting priorities, and seeing them through to the finish. This highlights the nub of the problem: Where there is an absence of political will and a willingness to alienate some constituencies to produce better overall economic outcomes, expect extractive, elitist economies and frustrated attempts at reform.

Development that leads to growth in a competitive global economy requires a great deal of planning and the right technocrats to implement complex policies.

CONCLUSION

There are countless examples of local and global experts focusing on this task, yet producing dismal outcomes. This is because there is no avoiding the core challenge for reformers: Without a conducive political context, nothing can be achieved.

Notes

INTRODUCTION

1. The interview with Professor Landsbergis was conducted in Vilnius during a research trip to Lithuania in October–November 2022.
2. Jonathan Steele, 'Why Gorbachev failed', *New Left Review*, 216, 1996, pp. 141–152.
3. This has been made into a feature-length documentary titled *The Other Dream Team* (Sorrento Productions, 2012), Marius A. Markevicius (dir.).
4. Martin Creamer, 'Mine nationalisation lost Zambia $45bn, Eunomix study finds', *Engineering News*, 22 March 2013, available at https://www.engineeringnews.co.za/print-version/mine-nationalisation-lost-zambia-45bn-eunomix-study-finds-2013-03-22 (last accessed 7 July 2023).
5. Daron Acemoglu and James A. Robinson, *Why Nations Fail: The Origins of Power, Prosperity and Poverty* (New York: Crown, 2012).
6. Estonia GDP per capita data from the World Bank, available at https://data.worldbank.org/indicator/NY.GDP.PCAP.KD?locations=EE (last accessed 7 July 2023).
7. For details, see Adalbert Knöbl, Andres Sutt and Basil Zavoico, 'The Estonian Currency Board: Its introduction and role in the early success of Estonia's transition to a market economy', IMF Working Paper WP/02/96, May 2002, available at https://www.imf.org/external/pubs/ft/wp/2002/wp0296.pdf (last accessed 7 July 2023).
8. Between 2009 and 2019, the number of civil servants in South Africa grew from 1 780 553 to 2 108 125 – an increase of 327 572. To this number should be added the South African Police Service and the South African National Defence Force, some 200 000 and 75 000 respectively, and the employees of the 108 parastatals, some 100 000. Statistics South Africa's Non-Financial Census of Municipalities for the year ended 30 June 2020 showed that there were 311 364 funded posts across all municipalities in South Africa. There were also 447 123 teaching staff in South Africa in 2021. The public sector wage bill trebled between 2006 and 2019. See 'Factsheet: South Africa's civil service in numbers', Africa Check, 2 June 2002, available at https://africacheck.org/fact-checks/factsheets/factsheet-south-africas-civil-service-numbers; and 'Here's how many police officers there are in South Africa – and what they earn', *BusinessTech*, 24 April 2022, available at https://businesstech.co.za/news/government/579116/heres-how-many-police-officers-there-are-in-south-africa-and-what-they-earn/ (both last accessed 7 July 2023).
9. South African demographic data from Statista, available at https://www.statista.com/statistics/1116081/population-receiving-social-grants-in-south-africa-by-province/ (last accessed 7 July 2023).
10. Ciaran Ryan, 'State capture scorecard: R500bn looted, zero assets recovered',

Moneyweb, 5 July 2022, available at https://www.moneyweb.co.za/news/south-africa/state-capture-scorecard-r500bn-looted-zero-assets-recovered/ (last accessed 7 July 2023).

11. Rudi Louw and Victoria O'Regan, 'The good, the bad and the shocking: A visual gauge of the financial state of South Africa's municipalities', *Daily Maverick*, 26 June 2022, available at https://www.dailymaverick.co.za/article/2022-06-26-the-good-the-bad-and-the-shocking-a-visual-gauge-of-the-financial-state-of-south-africas-municipalities/ (last accessed 7 July 2023).

12. South Africa murder/homicide rate data from Macrotrends, available at https://www.macrotrends.net/countries/ZAF/south-africa/murder-homicide-rate (last accessed 7 July 2023).

13. For a discussion on this topic, see Charles Kenny, 'Economic growth is necessary to reduce global poverty', Center for Global Development, 20 March 2023, available at https://www.cgdev.org/blog/economic-growth-necessary-reduce-global-poverty?utm_source=20230328&utm_medium=cgd_email&utm_campaign=cgd_weekly (last accessed 7 July 2023).

14. 'South Africa's "real" matric pass rate is far lower than government's figures: DA', *BusinessTech*, 21 January 2022, available at https://businesstech.co.za/news/government/552394/south-africas-real-matric-pass-rate-is-far-lower-than-governments-figures-da/ (last accessed 7 July 2023).

15. 'South Africa's education system in crisis', *BusinessTech*, 15 October 2022, available at https://businesstech.co.za/news/business/634271/south-africas-education-system-in-crisis/ (last accessed 7 July 2023).

16. Government expenditure on education data from the World Bank, available at https://data.worldbank.org/indicator/SE.XPD.TOTL.GD.ZS (last accessed 7 July 2023).

17. Sergei Guriev and Daniel Treisman, *Spin Dictators: The Changing Face of Tyranny in the 21st Century* (Princeton: Princeton University Press, 2022).

18. See, for instance, David Halberstam, *The Making of a Quagmire: America and Vietnam During the Kennedy Era*, rev. ed. with an introduction by Daniel J. Singal (Lanham, MD: Rowman & Littlefield, 2008).

19. 'African Youth Survey 2022', Ichikowitz Family Foundation White Paper, June 2022, available at https://biz-file.com/f/2206/AfricanYouthSurvey2022_Final_08June2022.pdf (last accessed 7 July 2023).

20. By 2060, one in five of the world's oldest countries will be in East Asia, compared with just one in twenty-five in 2010, according to the World Bank. See 'Rapid aging in East Asia and Pacific will shrink workforce and increase public spending', World Bank, 9 December 2015, available at https://www.worldbank.org/en/region/eap/brief/rapid-aging-in-east-asia-and-pacific-will-shrink-workforce-increase-public-spending (last accessed 7 July 2023). In Europe, as the post–Second World War baby-boom generation retires, the ratio of over-sixty-five-year-olds to the working-age population is set to rise dramatically, while the number of under-fifteens will decline by nearly 15 per cent by 2060. The age dependency ratio in the EU in 2015 was, on average, 27.5 per cent. It is projected to rise to 49.4 per cent by 2050, when there will be only two people of working age for every retiree. See Paul Taylor, 'Aging Europe needs the migrants it doesn't want', *Reuters*, 1 December 2014, available at https://www.reuters.com/article/us-europe-demographics-idUSKCN0JF1KA20141201 (last accessed 7 July 2023).

21. Tilman Altenburg, 'Migration of Chinese manufacturing jobs to Africa: Myth or reality?' Brookings Institution, 5 March 2019, available at https://www.brookings.edu/blog/africa-in-focus/2019/03/05/migration-of-chinese-manufacturing-jobs-to-africa-myth-or-reality/ (last accessed 7 July 2023).
22. John Lewis Gaddis, *On Grand Strategy* (London: Penguin, 2018), p. 100.
23. For a discussion on this point, see Walter Russell Mead, *God and Gold: Britain, America and the Making of the Modern World* (New York: Random House, 2007), esp. pp. 42–45.
24. For these arguments and the detailed empirical correlation between democracy and growth, see Greg Mills, Olusegun Obasanjo, Jeffrey Herbst and Tendai Biti, *Democracy Works: Rewiring Politics to Africa's Advantage* (Johannesburg: Picador, 2019).
25. E. Gyimah-Boadi and Joseph Asunka, 'Do Africans want democracy – and do they think they're getting it?' Afrobarometer, 2 November 2021, available at https://www.afrobarometer.org/articles/do-africans-want-democracy-and-do-they-think-theyre-getting-it/ (last accessed 7 July 2023).
26. Economist Intelligence Unit, 'Democracy Index 2022: Frontline Democracy and the Battle for Ukraine', 2023.
27. 'Freedom in the World 2022: The Global Expansion of Authoritarian Rule', Freedom House, February 2022, available at https://freedomhouse.org/sites/default/files/2022-02/FIW_2022_PDF_Booklet_Digital_Final_Web.pdf (last accessed 7 July 2023).
28. I am grateful to Jeremy Gordin for this point.
29. 'Malawi Systematic Country Diagnostic: Breaking the cycle of low growth and slow poverty reduction', World Bank Report No. 132785, December 2018, available at https://documents1.worldbank.org/curated/en/723781545072859945/pdf/malawi-scd-final-board-12-7-2018-12122018-636804216425880639.pdf (last accessed 7 July 2023).
30. Douglas Yates, 'The rise and fall of oil-rentier states in Africa', in J.A. Grant, W.R.N. Compaoré and M.I. Mitchell (eds), *New Approaches to the Governance of Natural Resources* (London: Palgrave Macmillan, 2015).
31. Tax revenue data from the World Bank, available at https://data.worldbank.org/indicator/GC.TAX.TOTL.GD.ZS (last accessed 7 July 2023).
32. 'Deep structural reforms guided by evidence are urgently needed to lift millions of Nigerians out of poverty, says new World Bank report', World Bank Press Release No. 2022/052/AFW, 22 March 2022, available at https://www.worldbank.org/en/news/press-release/2022/03/21/afw-deep-structural-reforms-guided-by-evidence-are-urgently-needed-to-lift-millions-of-nigerians-out-of-poverty (last accessed 7 July 2023).
33. Discussion with Iyorchia Ayu in Abuja, Nigeria, 21 February 2023.
34. Discussion with Samson Itodo in Abuja, Nigeria, 21 February 2023.

PART I: AFRICA

1. 'Togolese box hub maintains top 100 standing with another year of double-digit volume growth', Lloyd's List, 15 August 2022, available at https://lloydslist.maritimeintelligence.informa.com/LL1141343/96-Lom-Togo (last accessed 7 July 2023).
2. World Bank, 'The Container Port Performance Index 2021: A Comparable Assessment of Container Port Performance', 2022, available at https://thedocs.worldbank.org/en/doc/66e3aa5c3be4647addd01845ce353992-0190062022/original/Container-Port-Performance-Index-2021.pdf (last accessed 7 July 2023).

3. Ayi Renaud Dossavi, 'In 2020–2021, the average waiting time of ships at the port of Lomé was down five hours', *Togo First*, 30 April 2022, available at https://www.togofirst.com/en/logistics/3004-9872-in-2020-2021-the-average-waiting-time-of-ships-at-the-port-of-lome-was-down-five-hours#:~:text=News-,In%202020-2021%2C%20the%20average%20waiting%20time%20of%20ships%20at,Lomé%20was%20down%20five%20hours (last accessed 7 July 2023).
4. Anha Osei, 'Like father, like son? Power and influence across two Gnassingbé presidencies in Togo', *Democratization*, 25 (8), 2018.
5. These interviews were conducted during a visit to Togo in February 2023.
6. Michael Davenport, Adrian Hewitt and Antonique Koning, *Europe's Preferred Partners? The Lomé Countries in World Trade* (London: Overseas Development Institute, 1995), available at https://cdn.odi.org/media/documents/7983.pdf (last accessed 7 July 2023).
7. 'Togo promises development, not democracy', *Economist*, 26 January 2023, available at https://www.economist.com/middle-east-and-africa/2023/01/26/togo-promises-development-not-democracy (last accessed 7 July 2023).
8. Cited in 'Obituary: Gnassingbe Eyadema', *BBC News*, 5 February 2005, available at http://news.bbc.co.uk/2/hi/africa/830774.stm (last accessed 7 July 2023).
9. Fredline M'Cormack-Hale and Mavis Zupork Dome, 'Support for elections weakens among Africans; many see them as ineffective in holding leaders accountable', Afrobarometer Dispatch No. 551, 16 September 2022, available at https://www.afrobarometer.org/wp-content/uploads/2022/09/AD549-PAP15-Support-for-elections-weakens-in-Africa-Afrobarometer-Pan-Africa-Profile-6sept22.pdf (last accessed 7 July 2023).
10. Arvind Subramanian and Devesh Roy, 'Who can explain the Mauritian miracle: Meade, Romer, Sachs, or Rodrik?' IMF Working Paper WP/01/116, August 2001, available at https://www.imf.org/external/pubs/ft/wp/2001/wp01116.pdf (last accessed 7 July 2023).
11. Discussion with Sam Matekane in Maseru, Lesotho, 5 December 2022.
12. Enoch Randy Aikins and Jacobus du Toit McLachlan, 'Africa is losing the battle against extreme poverty', *ISS Today*, 13 July 2022, available at https://issafrica.org/iss-today/africa-is-losing-the-battle-against-extreme-poverty#:~:text=Central%20Africa%20has%20the%20highest,36.8%25%20and%2033.8%25%20respectively (last accessed 7 July 2023).
13. WhatsApp exchange with Mayor Geordin Hill-Lewis, 5 December 2022.
14. See the UN Department of Economic and Social Affairs, Statistics Division's 'National Accounts – Analysis of Main Aggregates (AMA)', available at https://unstats.un.org/unsd/snaama/ (last accessed 7 July 2023).
15. Margaret Keitheile and Masego Mokubung, *The SACMEQ II Project in Botswana: A Study of the Conditions of Schooling and the Quality of Education* (Harare: SACMEQ, 2005).
16. GDP per capita data from the World Bank, available at https://data.worldbank.org/indicator/NY.GDP.PCAP.KD?locations=ZG-ZA-BW (last accessed 7 July 2023).
17. Botswana adult literacy data from the World Bank, available at https://data.worldbank.org/indicator/SE.ADT.LITR.ZS?locations=BW (last accessed 7 July 2023).
18. 'CPI 2021 for sub-Saharan Africa: Amid democratic turbulence, deep-seated corruption exacerbates threats to freedoms', Transparency International, 25 January 2022,

available at https://www.transparency.org/en/news/cpi-2021-sub-saharan-africa-amid-democratic-turbulence-deep-seated-corruption (last accessed 8 July 2023).
19. Botswana overview in 'Freedom in the World 2023', Freedom House, available at https://freedomhouse.org/country/botswana/freedom-world/2023 (last accessed 8 July 2023).
20. Daron Acemoglu, Simon Johnson and James Robinson, 'An African success story: Botswana', MIT Department of Economics Working Paper 01-37, 11 July 2001, available at https://tinyurl.com/4umvffwr (last accessed 8 July 2023).
21. Lesego Sekwati, 'Economic diversification: The case of Botswana', Revenue Watch Institute, available at https://resourcegovernance.org/sites/default/files/RWI_Econ_Diversification_Botswana.pdf (last accessed 8 July 2023).
22. Discussion with Gary Ralfe, 12 October 2022.
23. An economic term for the negative consequences that can arise from a spike in the value of a nation's currency.
24. 'Hyundai, a case of overreaching', IOL, 16 January 2000, available at https://www.iol.co.za/business-report/companies/hyundai-a-case-of-overreaching-791510 (last accessed 8 July 2023).
25. Sekwati, 'Economic diversification: The case of Botswana'.
26. Interview with Ian Khama, Gaborone, Botswana, June 2016.
27. Martin Creamer, 'South Africa takes 354 days to issue prospecting right, Botswana does it in 40', Mining Weekly, 10 October 2022, available at https://www.miningweekly.com/article/south-africa-takes-354-days-to-issue-a-prospecting-right-botswana-does-in-40-days-2022-10-10 (last accessed 8 July 2023).
28. Botswana tourist arrival data from the World Bank, available at https://data.worldbank.org/indicator/ST.INT.ARVL?locations=BW (last accessed 8 July 2023).
29. Botswana tourism statistics 1995–2023 from Macrotrends, available at https://www.macrotrends.net/countries/BWA/botswana/tourism-statistics (last accessed 8 July 2023).
30. 'Failure to diversify is the bane of our economy', Botswana Guardian, 13 May 2022, available at https://www.pressreader.com/botswana/botswana-guardian/20220513/281694028372541 (last accessed 8 July 2023).
31. Ntando Thukwana, 'Botswana banned SA fruit and veg. Now traders there are demanding a U-turn', News24, 13 October 2022, available at https://www.businessinsider.co.za/botswana-traders-want-goverment-to-uturn-on-its-vegetable-import-ban-policy-2022-10 (last accessed 8 July 2023).
32. Interview with Ian Khama, Gaborone, Botswana, June 2016.
33. J. Corkery, T.O. Daddah, C. O'Nuallain and T. Land, 'Management of Public Service Reform: A Comparative Review of Experiences in the Management of Programmes of Reform of the Administrative Arm of Central Government', International Institute of Administrative Sciences, 1998.
34. Botswana public sector data from Statista, available at https://www.statista.com/outlook/co/public-sector/Botswana (last accessed 8 July 2023).
35. Gabby Arenge and Jenny Perlman Robinson, 'Taking education "back-to-the-basics" at scale in Botswana', Brookings Institution, 31 October 2019, available at https://www.brookings.edu/blog/education-plus-development/2019/10/31/taking-education-back-to-the-basics-at-scale-in-botswana/ (last accessed 8 July 2023).

36. Air transport data from the World Bank, available at https://data.worldbank.org/indicator/IS.AIR.GOOD.MT.K1?locations=ZA-BW (last accessed 8 July 2023).
37. Mqondisi Dube, 'Botswana's longtime diamond deal with De Beers under threat', *VOA News*, 14 February 2023, available at https://www.voanews.com/a/botswana-s-longtime-diamond-deal-with-de-beers-under-threat-/6962872.html (last accessed 8 July 2023).
38. This chapter is based, in part, on a research trip to Mauritius in 2017 and Comoros in January 2023. Grateful appreciation is expressed to South Africa's ambassador to Comoros, Anesh Maistry, for his role and help in setting up meetings in Moroni. Additionally, see Jeffrey Frankel, 'Mauritius: African Success Story', M-RCBG Faculty Working Paper No. 2012-06, Harvard Kennedy School, 2012, available at https://www.hks.harvard.edu/sites/default/files/centers/mrcbg/files/MRCBG_FWP_2012_06-Frankel_Mauritius.pdf (last accessed 10 July 2023). See also Ali Zafar, 'Mauritius: An economic success story', World Bank, 2011, available at https://documents1.worldbank.org/curated/en/304221468001788072/930107812_2014082530900808/additional/634310PUB0Yes0061512B09780821387450.pdf (last accessed 10 July 2023).
39. Frankel, 'Mauritius: African Success Story'.
40. See the Heritage Foundation's '2023 Index of Economic Freedom', available at https://www.heritage.org/index/country/mauritius (last accessed 10 July 2023).
41. Murder rate data from the UN Office on Drugs and Crime's International Homicide Statistics database, available at https://data.worldbank.org/indicator/VC.IHR.PSRC.P5?locations=MU-LS-ZA (last accessed 10 July 2023).
42. Daron Acemoglu, Simon Johnson and James Robinson, 'Colonial origins of comparative development: An empirical investigation', *American Economic Review*, 91, 2001, pp. 1369–1401.
43. D. Brautigam, 'The "Mauritius Miracle": Democracy, Institutions, and Economic Policy', in Richard Joseph (ed.), *State, Conflict, and Democracy in Africa* (Boulder, CO: Lynne Rienner, 1999).
44. Own calculations.
45. Frankel, 'Mauritius: African Success Story'.
46. Discussion with Fouday Gouilame, Moroni, Comoros, 16 January 2023. Unless otherwise indicated or referenced, the quotes in this section were obtained from a series of interviews conducted in Comoros during this visit.
47. Marlise Simons, 'Bob Denard, hired gun for coups, is dead at 78', *New York Times*, 16 October 2007, available at https://www.nytimes.com/2007/10/16/world/europe/16denard.html (last accessed 10 July 2023).
48. Sophie Nicholson, 'Obituary: Bob Denard', *Guardian*, 16 October 2007, available at https://www.theguardian.com/news/2007/oct/16/guardianobituaries.france (last accessed 10 July 2023).
49. Telephonic discussion with Glenn Babb, 16 October 2022. See also his memoir, *In One Era and Out of the Other* (Hermanus: Footprint Press, 2022).
50. UNDP, 'UNDP Human Development Report 2021–22: Uncertain Times, Unsettled Lives: Shaping our Future in a Transforming World', 2022, available at https://hdr.undp.org/system/files/documents/global-report-document/hdr2021-22pdf_1.pdf (last accessed 10 July 2023).
51. Gemma Pitcher, 'Destination report Comoros', Siyabonga Africa, available at https://

www.islandsofafrica.co.za/tanzania-safari-destination-comoros.html (last accessed 10 July 2023).
52. Information from 'Sun International Hotels Limited' on Reference for Business, available at https://www.referenceforbusiness.com/history2/4/Sun-International-Hotels-Limited.html (last accessed 10 July 2023).
53. WhatsApp correspondence with David Coutts-Trotter, 13 October 2022.
54. International tourism data from the World Bank, available at https://data.worldbank.org/indicator/ST.INT.ARVL?locations=KM-MG; Zanzibar figures from the Office of the Chief Government Statistician, Zanzibar, available at https://www.ocgs.go.tz/infigure (both last accessed 10 July 2023).
55. Net enrolment data from UNICEF's 'Education Budget Brief 2019/2020, Zanzibar', available at https://www.unicef.org/esa/media/8446/file/UNICEF-Tanzania-Zanzibar-2020-Education-Budget-Brief-revised.pdf (last accessed 10 July 2023).
56. Data from the World Bank, available at https://data.worldbank.org/country/KM and https://data.worldbank.org/indicator/SE.PRM.CMPT.ZS (both last accessed 10 July 2023).
57. 'Poverty in Comoros: Instability, investment and improvement', *Borgen Magazine*, 22 October 2017, available at https://www.borgenmagazine.com/poverty-in-comoros/ (last accessed 10 July 2023).
58. World Bank, 'The Container Port Performance Index 2021'.
59. 'Comoros seeks $4.6bn in investment to climb out of poverty', *Al Jazeera*, 1 December 2019, available at https://www.aljazeera.com/economy/2019/12/1/comoros-seeks-4-6bn-in-investment-to-climb-out-of-poverty (last accessed 10 July 2023).
60. I am grateful to Glenn Babb for these reminisces.
61. Research for this chapter included a road trip in November 2022 from Johannesburg to Cape Town with interview stops at Hartswater, Jan Kempdorp, Vaalspan, Kimberley, De Aar, Graaff-Reinet, Somerset East, Cookhouse, Bedford, Adelaide, Fort Beaufort, Alice, Dimbaza, Peddie, Makhanda, Gqeberha, Plettenberg Bay and George.
62. Louw and O'Regan, 'The good, the bad and the shocking'.
63. Rod Amner, 'The lowlights of Makana's auditor-general report', *Grocott's Mail*, 15 June 2022, available at https://grocotts.ru.ac.za/2022/06/15/the-lowlights-of-makanas-auditor-general-report/ (last accessed 10 July 2023).
64. Where captives develop positive feelings towards their captors or abusers over time as a coping mechanism.
65. World Inequality Lab's 'World Inequality Report 2022', available at https://wir2022.wid.world (last accessed 10 July 2023).
66. World Bank Poverty & Equity Brief, Sub-Saharan Africa, South Africa, April 2018, available at https://databankfiles.worldbank.org/public/ddpext_download/poverty/33EF03BB-9722-4AE2-ABC7-AA2972D68AFE/Archives-2018/Global_POVEQ_ZAF.pdf (last accessed 10 July 2023).
67. Prinesha Naidoo, 'South African welfare recipients surpass number of taxpayers', *Bloomberg*, 16 February 2022, available at https://www.bloomberg.com/news/articles/2022-02-16/south-african-welfare-recipients-surpass-number-of-taxpayers (last accessed 10 July 2023).
68. Ibid.

69. South Africa central government debt data from the World Bank, available at https://data.worldbank.org/indicator/GC.DOD.TOTL.GD.ZS?locations=ZA (last accessed 10 July 2023).
70. IMF data on forty-six countries for 2017 shows public sector compensation for national government, provincial government and state entities was an average of 9.4 per cent of GDP. See Sizwe Dlamini, 'SA wage bill at R630bn is higher than the global norm as a percentage of GDP', *IOL*, 10 November 2020, available at https://www.iol.co.za/business-report/economy/sa-wage-bill-at-r630bn-is-higher-than-the-global-norm-as-a-percentage-of-gdp-463ab0b6-97c4-4c6a-84fd-2885a4eef729 (last accessed 10 July 2023).
71. Data gathered by Anine Kriegler and Mark Shaw for the Global Initiative Against Transnational Organized Crime (GI-TOC).
72. See GI-TOC's 'Strategic Organized Crime Risk Assessment for South Africa', September 2022, available at https://globalinitiative.net/wp-content/uploads/2022/09/GI-TOC-Strategic-Organized-Crime-Risk-Assessment-South-Africa.pdf (last accessed 10 July 2023).
73. Jolene Marriah-Maharaj, 'Bheki Cele "hell-bent" on reducing crime as murder rate increases by 10 percent', *IOL*, 17 February 2023, available at https://www.iol.co.za/news/crime-and-courts/bheki-cele-hell-bent-on-reducing-crime-as-murder-rate-increases-by-10-percent-64264d5e-6409-4ca9-81dc-276712050ff6 (last accessed 11 July 2023).
74. Daniel Brown and Azmi Haroun, 'The wars in Iraq and Afghanistan have killed at least 500,000 people, according to a report that breaks down the toll', *Business Insider*, 27 August 2022, available at https://www.businessinsider.com/how-many-people-have-been-killed-in-iraq-and-afghanistan (last accessed 11 July 2023).
75. John Nieuwenhuysen, 'Social economics and political change in South Africa', *International Journal of Social Economics*, 5 (3), 1978, pp. 148–157.
76. Eskom 1994 Annual Report, available at https://www.eskom.co.za/heritage/wp-content/uploads/2021/09/1994-Annual-Report.pdf (last accessed 11 July 2023).
77. Kyle Cowan, 'Eskom staff running SA's power stations have major gaps in technical skills, knowledge', *News24*, 9 August 2022, available at https://www.news24.com/news24/investigations/exclusive-eskom-staff-running-sas-power-stations-have-major-gaps-in-technical-skills-knowledge-20220809 (last accessed 11 July 2023).
78. Antony Sguazzin, Prinesha Naidoo and Paul Burkhardt, 'Eskom turns 100 next year – here's how it went from world best to SA's biggest economic risk', *News24*, 27 September 2022, available at https://www.news24.com/fin24/economy/eskom-turns-100-next-year-heres-how-it-went-from-world-best-to-sas-biggest-economic-risk-20220927 (last accessed 11 July 2023). See also a list of Eskom's previous leadership at https://www.eskom.co.za/heritage/museum/gallery/previous-eskom-leadership/ (last accessed 11 July 2023).
79. For details on Eskom's power stations, see https://www.eskom.co.za/eskom-divisions/gx/coal-fired-power-stations/ (last accessed 11 July 2023).
80. Zoom call with Busisiwe Mavuso, 21 November 2022.
81. Michelle Banda, 'Eastern Cape's ailing municipalities rack up R3.1bn in irregular expenditure', *Daily Maverick*, 23 August 2022, available at https://www.dailymaverick

.co.za/article/2022-08-23-eastern-capes-ailing-municipalities-rack-up-r3-1bn-in-irreg ular-expenditure/ (last accessed 11 July 2023).
82. Pedro Mzileni, 'Buhlungu's mission is to fix Fort Hare but it comes at a high cost', *Mail & Guardian*, 23 January 2023, available at https://mg.co.za/opinion/2023-01 -23-buhlungus-mission-is-to-fix-fort-hare-but-it-comes-at-a-high-cost/ (last accessed 11 July 2023). For the price of toilet rolls, go to: https://robotindustrial.co .za/RIS-CLEANING-Nova-Toilet-Paper-2ply-48-Pk-NOVA-12213?search=toilet%20 paper.
83. Statistics South Africa, Quarterly Labour Force Survey, Quarter 4: 2022, available at https://www.statssa.gov.za/publications/P0211/P02114thQuarter2022.pdf (last accessed 11 July 2023).
84. Statistics South Africa, Mid-year population estimates, 2021, available at https://www .statssa.gov.za/publications/P0302/P03022021.pdf (last accessed 11 July 2023).
85. These figures were obtained in correspondence with Western Cape premier Alan Winde and Cape Town mayor Geordin Hill-Lewis, 21 November 2022.
86. Information from the Grahamstown Railway Station thread on the Heritage Portal, available at https://www.theheritageportal.co.za/thread/grahamstown-railway-station (last accessed 11 July 2023).
87. 'Lockdown looting ruins South Africa's railway network', *AfricaNews*, 30 March 2021, available at https://www.africanews.com/2021/03/30/lockdown-looting-ruins-south -africa-s-railway-network/ (last accessed 11 July 2023).
88. David Williams, 'Why there are so many trucks on the road and so few trains on the tracks', Brenthurst Foundation, 13 April 2021, available at https://www.thebrenthurst foundation.org/publications/why-there-are-so-many-trucks-on-the-road-and-so-few -trains-on-the-tracks/ (last accessed 11 July 2023).
89. Figures taken from Statistics South Africa's archived land transport surveys available at https://www.statssa.gov.za/?page_id=1866&PPN=P7162&SCH=7553 (last accessed 11 July 2023).
90. Transnet Freight Rail 2021 Annual Report, available at https://www.transnet.net/Inves torRelations/AR2021/Transnet%20Freight%20Rail.pdf (last accessed 11 July 2023).
91. Discussion with Gladwell Nkumbi, De Aar, 16 November 2022.
92. Foreword to *The South African Railways: History, Scope and Organisation* (Union of South Africa: Railways and Harbours Board, 1947), available at https://ia600207.us .archive.org/18/items/TheSouthAfricanRailways/06.ForewardByTheHon.F.c.Sturrock M.p.MinisterOfTransport.jpg (last accessed 11 July 2023).
93. Williams, 'Why there are so many trucks on the road and so few trains on the tracks'.
94. Ibid.
95. Emsie Ferreira, 'Gama "had no idea" Essa had a finger in most parts of the irregular locomotive deal', *Mail & Guardian*, 20 April 2021, available at https://mg.co.za/news/ 2021-04-30-gama-had-no-idea-essa-had-a-finger-in-most-parts-of-the-irregular-loco motive-deal/ (last accessed 11 July 2023).
96. World Bank, 'The Container Port Performance Index 2021'.
97. Ibid.
98. R.A. Janse van Rensburg, 'The history of the rail transport regulatory environment in South Africa', Department of Transport Economics of the University of Stellenbosch,

Stellenbosch, 1996, available at https://scholar.sun.ac.za/bitstream/handle/10019.1/85556/jansevanrensburg_history_1996.pdf?sequence=3 (last accessed 11 July 2023).

99. GI-TOC, 'Strategic Organized Crime Risk Assessment for South Africa'.
100. 'Did 34% of households have access to electricity in 1994?', *Mail & Guardian*, 14 May 2015, available at https://mg.co.za/article/2015-05-14-did-only-32-of-households-have-access-to-electricity-in-1994/ (last accessed 11 July 2023).
101. 'Basic water services in South Africa are in decay after years of progress', *The Conversation*, 1 August 2022, available at https://theconversation.com/basic-water-services-in-south-africa-are-in-decay-after-years-of-progress-185616#:~:text=The%20country%20has%20made%20clear,to%20obasic%20water%20supply%20services (last accessed 11 July 2023).
102. 'Housing delivery in South Africa', Fuller Housing Centre Report, 2014, available at https://fullercenter.org/wp-content/uploads/sites/default/files/Housing%20delivery%20-%20South%20Africa.pdf (last accessed 11 July 2023).
103. Sipho Masondo, 'Joburg's crippling water cuts: R61 billion needed to fix collapsing infrastructure', *News24*, 22 October 2022, at https://www.news24.com/news24/investigations/exclusive-joburgs-crippling-water-cuts-r61-billion-needed-to-fix-collapsing-infrastructure-20221022 (last accessed 11 July 2023).
104. Clip available at https://web.facebook.com/watch/?v=10153146604816107 (last accessed 11 July 2023).
105. South Africa datasets from the IMF, available at https://www.imf.org/external/datamapper/profile/ZAF (last accessed 11 July 2023).
106. Zoom call with Busisiwe Mavuso, 21 November 2022.
107. 'South Africa passes 200 days of load shedding in 2022', *TechCentral*, 27 December 2022, available at https://techcentral.co.za/south-africa-passes-record-200-days-of-load-shedding-in-2022/218888/ (last accessed 11 July 2023).
108. 'SA sun and wind, unlike Eskom's coal, can't be stolen by "sophisticated" crooks, says De Ruyter', *Polity*, 24 November 2022, available at https://www.polity.org.za/article/sa-sun-and-wind-unlike-eskoms-coal-cant-be-stolen-by-sophisticated-crooks-says-de-ruyter-2022-11-24 (last accessed 11 July 2023).
109. Hajra Omarjee and Denene Erasmus, 'De Ruyter assassination attempt shows the "battle for SA", says Gordhan', *Business Day*, 8 January 2023, available at https://www.businesslive.co.za/bd/national/2023-01-08-de-ruyter-assassination-attempt-shows-the-battle-for-sa-says-gordhan/?__vfz=medium%3Dconversations_top_pages (last accessed 11 July 2023).
110. William Easterly, *The Tyranny of Experts: Economists, Dictators, and the Forgotten Rights of the Poor* (New York: Basic Books, 2013). These factors and the interplay between outsiders and aid are more completely examined in Greg Mills, *Expensive Poverty: Why Aid Fails and How It Can Work* (Johannesburg: Picador, 2021).
111. According to ANC internal polling; discussion with Thabo Mbeki, 21 February 2023.
112. 'Provincial Economic Review and Outlook 2022/23', Western Cape Government Provincial Treasury, September 2022, available at https://www.westerncape.gov.za/provincial-treasury/files/atoms/files/2022%20PERO%20Final%20for%20WEB.pdf (last accessed 11 July 2023).
113. '2021 National Senior Certificate Examination Report', Republic of South Africa

Department of Basic Education, available at https://www.education.gov.za/Portals/0/Documents/Reports/2021NSCReports/DBE%20Matric%20Exam%20Results%20Report%202021.pdf?ver=2022-01-21-170016-397#:~:text=The%20overall%20pass%20rate%20in,career%20interests%20at%20a%20University (last accessed 11 July 2023).
114. Statistics South Africa, General Household Survey, 2021, available at https://www.statssa.gov.za/publications/P0318/P03182021.pdf; Statistics South Africa, Quarterly Labour Force Survey, Quarter 2: 2022, available at https://www.statssa.gov.za/publications/P0211/P02112ndQuarter2022.pdf (both last accessed 11 July 2022).
115. WhatsApp correspondence with Alan Winde, 12 December 2022.

PART II: ASIA

1. Based on an interview with Justin Lin in Beijing, China, 30 July 2019.
2. In this chapter, I use East Asia as a catch-all for those countries comprising East and Southeast Asia. The countries of East Asia are China, Japan, Mongolia, North Korea, South Korea and Taiwan. Southeast Asia comprises Brunei, Cambodia, Indonesia, Laos, Malaysia, Myanmar (formerly Burma), Philippines, Singapore, Thailand, Timor-Leste (East Timor) and Vietnam.
3. I am grateful to Ray Hartley for pointing this out. *Financial Times*, 28 June 1993.
4. Justin Lin and Célestin Monga, *Beating the Odds: Jump-starting Developing Countries* (Princeton: Princeton University Press, 2017).
5. Discussion with Goh Chok Tong, the Istana presidential palace, Singapore, 13 February 2018.
6. Edward Miguel and Gérard Roland, 'The long-run impact of bombing Vietnam', *Journal of Development Economics*, 96 (1), September 2011, pp. 1–15. Draft available at https://eml.berkeley.edu/~groland/pubs/vietnamoct09.pdf (last accessed 11 July 2023).
7. Vietnam GDP growth data from the World Bank, available at https://data.worldbank.org/indicator/NY.GDP.MKTP.KD.ZG?locations=VN (last accessed 11 July 2023).
8. These and other quotes from Lee Kuan Yew in this chapter are taken from Lee Kuan Yew, *From Third World to First: The Singapore Story, 1965–2000* (Singapore: Marshall Cavendish, 2012).
9. Interview with S.R. Nathan, Singapore Management University, Singapore, December 2013.
10. See, for example, Skytrax World Airport Awards, 'Airport of the Year Winners', available at https://www.worldairportawards.com/airport-of-the-year-winners/ (last accessed 11 July 2023).
11. In an interview with Liu Thai Ker on 31 August 2012, published in *Urban Solutions*, issue 2, 2013.
12. Lijie Huang and Joyce Fang, *Front Page: Stories of Singapore Since 1845* (Singapore: Strait Times Press, 2015).
13. Iain Manley, *Tales of Old Singapore* (Hong Kong: Earnshaw Books, 2010), p. 9.
14. In 2015, declassified cabinet papers, kept in a file codenamed Albatross, were put on display at the National Museum. Personally compiled by Dr Goh Keng Swee, the file included documents discussing proposed 'constitutional rearrangements' between Malaysia and Singapore, highlighting that the separation was a negotiated process between the two parties from Malaysia and Singapore, rather than a straightforward

expulsion by Malaysia. See Edmund Lim, 'Secret documents reveal extent of negotiations for Separation', *Straits Times*, 22 December 2015, available at https://www.straitstimes.com/opinion/secret-documents-reveal-extent-of-negotiations-for-separation (last accessed 11 July 2023).
15. Cited in *Founding Fathers* (Singapore: Straits Times Press, 2015), p. 123.
16. This chapter is based on several trips to Singapore over the last fifteen years, an earlier version of which appeared in Greg Mills, Olusegun Obasanjo, Haliemariam Desalegn and Emily van der Merwe, *The Asian Aspiration: Why and How Africa Should Emulate Asisa* (Johannesburg: Picador, 2020). This quote was taken from a discussion with Raila Odinga, Nairobi, Kenya, 1 February 2016.
17. Commonly held to be Lee Kuan Yew, David Marshall, Devan Nair, Eddie Barker, Goh Keng Swee, Lim Kim San, Ong Pang Boon, Othman Wok, S. Rajaratnam and Toh Chin Chye.
18. Chua Beng Huat, *Liberalism Disavowed: Communitarianism and State Capitalism in Singapore* (Singapore: NUS, 2017), p. 1.
19. Gaël Raballand, Salim Refas, Monica Beuran and Gözde Isik, 'Why Does Cargo Spend Weeks in Sub-Saharan African Ports? Lessons from Six Countries', World Bank, 2012, available at https://unctad.org/meetings/en/Contribution/dtltlbts-AhEM 2018d3_WorldBank_en.pdf (last accessed 11 July 2023).
20. See Temasek Holdings' portfolio, available at https://www.temasek.com.sg/en/our-investments/our-portfolio (last accessed 11 July 2023).
21. Discussion with Goh Chok Tong, Singapore, 15 July 2008.
22. I.M. Pei, who inter alia designed the pyramid at the Louvre in Paris, and Kenzo Tange were roped in to improve the cityscape of Singapore in the 1970s. Lee had met Tange when receiving an honorary degree at the University of Hong Kong in 1970, and the following year invited him to the Istana. Tange redesigned the United Overseas Bank Plaza, while Pei designed the Raffles City complex and rebuilt the Oversea-Chinese Banking Corporation headquarters.
23. From the Chairman's Statement in the HDB 2020/21 Annual Report, available at https://assets.hdb.gov.sg/about-us/news-and-publications/annual-report/2021/chairman-statement.html (last accessed 11 July 2023).
24. Discussion with Sng Cheng Keh, HDB, Singapore, 5 December 2013.
25. *UNDP and the Making of Singapore's Public Service: Lessons from Albert Winsemius* (Singapore: UNDP Global Centre for Public Service Excellence, 2015).
26. Thanks to Professor Barry Desker for this insight.
27. Cited in Manley, *Tales of Old Singapore*, p. 132.
28. Interview with Tharman Shanmugaratnam, Singapore, 23 May 2018.
29. Yew, *From Third World to First*.
30. Email correspondence with Barry Desker, 27 June 2019. See also Huat, *Liberalism Disavowed*.
31. See tweet by Mike Abel, last edited 21 May 2023, available at https://twitter.com/abelmike/status/1660249132814983168?t=ja9NfKihovISiwHODsdqyg&s=08 (last accessed 11 July 2023).
32. Email correspondence with Barry Desker, 27 June 2019; and teleconference, 1 July 2019.
33. Cited in 'The man who worked an economic miracle', *The Times*, 20 December 1984.

34. Cited in David Halberstam, *The Best and the Brightest* (New York: Random House, 2002).
35. Vietnam GDP per capita data from the World Bank, available at https://data.worldbank.org/indicator/NY.GDP.PCAP.CD?locations=VN (last accessed 11 July 2023).
36. Ibid.
37. 'Saigon's annual per capita income to reach $9,800 by 2020: official', *Saigoneer*, 20 October 2017, available at https://saigoneer.com/saigon-news/11578-saigon-s-per-capita-income-to-reach-$9,800-by-2010-official (last accessed 11 July 2023).
38. Unless otherwise cited, the interviews in this chapter were conducted by the author during several visits to Vietnam, starting in 1995 and including more recently to Saigon in March 2016 and Hanoi in November 2018 and July 2019.
39. Figures from the United States Census Bureau, 'Trade in goods with Vietnam', available at https://www.census.gov/foreign-trade/balance/c5520.html#1995 (last accessed 11 July 2023).
40. Figures from the United States Department of Commerce, International Trade Administration, 'Vietnam country commercial guide', available at https://www.export.gov/article?id=Vietnam-Market-Overview (last accessed 11 July 2023).
41. Figures from the United States Department of State, '2021 investment climate statements: Vietnam', available at https://www.state.gov/reports/2021-investment-climate-statements/vietnam/ (last accessed 11 July 2023).
42. Anthea Jeffery, *People's War: New Light on the Struggle for South Africa* (Johannesburg: Johnathan Ball, 2009).
43. Quoted in Herbert N. Foerstel, *From Watergate to Monicagate: Ten Controversies in Modern Journalism and Media* (Connecticut: Greenwood Press, 2001).
44. Jeffery, *People's War*.
45. Govan Mbeki, *Sunset at Midday: Latshon 'ilang 'emini!* (Braamfontein: Nolwazi, 1996).
46. Howard Barrell, 'The turn to the masses: The African National Congress' strategic review of 1978–79', *Journal of Southern African Studies*, 18 (1), 1992, pp. 64–92.
47. Martin Legassick, 'Myth and reality in the struggle against apartheid', *Journal of Southern African Studies*, 24 (2), 1998, pp. 443–458.
48. Mbeki, *Sunset at Midday*.
49. David Lamb, *Vietnam, Now: A Reporter Returns* (New York: PublicAffairs, 2003).
50. Yoshino Takeyama, 'Reform of state owned enterprises: A big challenge to the Vietnamese economy', Institute for International Monetary Affairs Newsletter, 12, 2018, available at https://www.iima.or.jp/en/docs/newsletter/2018/NL2018No_12_e.pdf (last accessed 11 July 2023).
51. Figures from the Ministry of Planning and Investment of Vietnam, at https://www.mpi.gov.vn/portal/Pages/default.aspx.
52. The visit to the Giap house and the events and individuals cited here were, unless otherwise indicated, part of the findings of a research trip to Hanoi and Ho Chi Minh City in May 2019.
53. Related by Vu Khoan during a roundtable event organised by the Vietnam Academy of Social Sciences and the Institute of Asian, African and Middle Eastern Studies, 2 May 2019.

NOTES

54. World Bank and Ministry of Planning and Investment of Vietnam, 'Vietnam 2035: Toward Prosperity, Creativity, Equity, and Democracy', 2016, p. 82, available at https://documents1.worldbank.org/curated/en/996421479825859721/pdf/103435-v2-PUBLIC.pdf (last accessed 11 July 2023).
55. 'Vietnam's coffee high could be in jeopardy', *Gro Intelligence*, 14 December 2016, available at https://gro-intelligence.com/insights/vietnamese-coffee-production (last accessed 11 July 2023).
56. United Nations Conference on Trade and Development, 'World Investment Report 2021: Investing in Sustainable Recovery', 2021, available at https://unctad.org/system/files/official-document/wir2021_en.pdf (last accessed 11 July 2023).
57. Unless otherwise stated, all data (including for graphs) was sourced from the World Bank DataBank, at https://databank.worldbank.org.
58. Keegan Elmer, '"Don't give our land away": the clash of interests in Vietnam's anti-China protests', *South China Morning Post*, 23 June 2018, available at https://www.scmp.com/news/china/diplomacy-defence/article/2152150/dont-give-our-land-away-clash-interests-vietnams-anti (last accessed 11 July 2023).
59. Takeyama, 'Reform of state owned enterprises: A big challenge to the Vietnamese economy'.
60. K12 Academics, 'Education in Vietnam: Teaching quality issues', available at https://www.k12academics.com/Education%20Worldwide/Education%20in%20Vietnam/teaching-quality-issues (last accessed 11 July 2023).
61. Vietnam school enrolment figures from IndexMundi, available at https://www.indexmundi.com/facts/vietnam/school-enrollment (last accessed 11 July 2023).
62. Figure from the United States Department of State, '2019 investment climate statements: Vietnam', available at https://www.state.gov/reports/2019-investment-climate-statements/vietnam/ (last accessed 12 July 2023).
63. Ha Phuong, 'What the future holds for Vietnam's ubiquitous street vendors', *VNExpress*, 5 April 2017, available at https://e.vnexpress.net/projects/sidewalk-economics-what-the-future-holds-for-vietnam-s-ubiquitous-street-vendors-3565620/index.html (last accessed 12 July 2023).
64. Duy Tran, 'Saigon's Captain Sidewalk steps down after cleanup campaign fails', *VNExpress*, 8 January 2018, available at https://e.vnexpress.net/news/news/saigon-s-captain-sidewalk-steps-down-after-cleanup-campaign-fails-3695873.html (last accessed 12 July 2023).
65. For Vietnam's ranking, see Transparency International Corruption Perceptions Index, available at https://www.transparency.org/en/countries/vietnam; Vietnam overview in 'Freedom in the World 2023', Freedom House, available at https://freedomhouse.org/country/vietnam/freedom-world/2023 (both last accessed 12 July 2023).
66. Peter Church, *A Short History of South-East Asia* (Singapore: Wiley, 2017), pp. 218–19.
67. 'Viet Nam: Prisoners of conscience in Viet Nam', Amnesty International, 4 April 2018, available at https://www.amnesty.org/download/Documents/ASA4181622018ENGLISH.PDF (last accessed 12 July 2023).
68. Vietnam international tourism arrivals data from the World Bank, available at https://data.worldbank.org/indicator/ST.INT.ARVL?locations=VN (last accessed 12 July 2023).

69. Vietnam life expectancy data from the World Bank, available at https://data.worldbank.org/indicator/SP.DYN.LE00.IN?locations=VN (last accessed 12 July 2023).
70. Finn Tarp, 'Vietnam: The dragon that rose from the ashes', WIDER Working Paper No. 2018/126 (Helsinki: United Nations University World Institute for Development Economic Research (UNU-WIDER), 2018).
71. Kate Hodal, 'Hanoi is choking on the fumes of 5m motorbikes, but can ban break its habit?', *Guardian*, 23 July 2017, available at https://www.theguardian.com/global-development/2017/jul/22/hanoi-motorcycles-ban-2030-pollution-transport (last accessed 12 July 2023).
72. 'Up to 8.5 million motorbikes flood Saigon's streets each day', *Saigoneer*, 8 January 2016, available at https://saigoneer.com/saigon-news/6089-up-to-8-5-million-motorbikes-flood-saigon%E2%80%99s-streets-each-day (last accessed 12 July 2023).
73. World Bank, 'Doing Business 2020: Economy Profile of Vietnam', available at http://www.doingbusiness.org/content/dam/doingBusiness/country/v/vietnam/VNM.pdf; see also 'Vietnam drops one place in ease of doing business ranking', *VNExpress*, 1 November 2018, available at https://e.vnexpress.net/news/business/data-speaks/vietnam-drops-one-place-in-ease-of-doing-business-ranking-3832750.html (both last accessed 12 July 2023).
74. 'The guide to Vietnam industrial zone', Savills Industrial Property, 21 January 2022, available at https://industrial.savills.com.vn/2022/01/vietnam-industrial-zone/#:~:text=With%20investors%20relocating%20manufacturing%20to,hectares%20as%20of%20May%202021 (last accessed 12 July 2023).
75. Susan Dunn, 'Jefferson and Vietnam', *New York Times*, 20 September 2016, available at https://www.nytimes.com/2016/09/21/opinion/jefferson-and-vietnam.html (last accessed 12 July 2023).
76. Cited in Lamb, *Vietnam, Now*.

PART III: EUROPE
1. Followed by Poland and Slovakia at 4 per cent during this period, with the remainder of the EU states being between 2 per cent and 3 per cent.
2. This chapter is partly based on a visit to Estonia in June 2022, and Latvia and Lithuania in October/November 2022. All quotes are taken from interviews conducted during these visits unless otherwise indicated.
3. United States Department of State, 'The JUST Act Report: Latvia', available at https://www.state.gov/reports/just-act-report-to-congress/latvia/ (last accessed 12 July 2023).
4. *Encyclopaedia Britannica Online*, s.v. 'Baltic States: Soviet republics', available at https://www.britannica.com/place/Baltic-states/Soviet-republics (last accessed 12 July 2023).
5. The word *blat* refers to the system of informal contacts and personal networks used to obtain goods and services under the rationing that characterised Soviet Russia.
6. Taken from the Museum of the Occupation of Latvia, Riga, Latvia, October 2022.
7. 'The Three Occupations of Latvia 1940–1991: Soviet and Nazi Take-Overs and Their Consequences', Occupation Museum Foundation, Riga, 2005, available at https://www.mfa.gov.lv/lv/media/2001/download (last accessed 12 July 2023).
8. Latvia and South Africa homicide data from the World Bank, available at https://data

.worldbank.org/country/LV and https://data.worldbank.org/country/ZA (both last accessed 12 July 2023).
9. Anders Åslund, 'The Baltic Tigers: Past, present and future', CESifo Forum 4/2015 (December), available at https://www.cesifo.org/DocDL/forum-2015-4-aslund-baltic-tiger-december.pdf (last accessed 12 July 2023).
10. Andrew Roth, 'Putin compares himself to Peter the Great in quest to take back Russian lands', *Guardian*, 10 June 2022, available at https://www.theguardian.com/world/2022/jun/10/putin-compares-himself-to-peter-the-great-in-quest-to-take-back-russian-lands (last accessed 12 July 2023).
11. For an excellent summary of the Estonian economy, see Heido Vitsur, 'A hundred years of the Estonian economy', *Estonian World*, 19 August 2021, available at https://estonianworld.com/business/a-hundred-years-of-the-estonian-economy/ (last accessed 12 July 2023).
12. 'Estonia among top 3 in the UN e-Government Survey 2020', e-Estonia, 24 July 2020, available at https://e-estonia.com/estonia-top-3-in-un-e-government-survey-2020/ (last accessed 12 July 2023).
13. See the Heritage Foundation's '2023 Index of Economic Freedom', available at https://www.heritage.org/index/country/estonia (last accessed 12 July 2023).
14. Estonia GDP per capita, 1855 to 1994, data from Maddison Project Database 2020, via Our World in Data, available at https://ourworldindata.org/grapher/gdp-per-capita-maddison?tab=chart&time=earliest..1994&country=~EST (last accessed 13 July 2023).
15. Estonia unemployment data from the World Bank, available at https://data.worldbank.org/indicator/SL.UEM.TOTL.ZS?locations=EE (last accessed 12 July 2023).
16. Cited in James Crisp, 'Europe's new "Iron Lady" Kaja Kallas says the West mustn't negotiate with Putin', *Telegraph*, 8 October 2022, available at https://www.telegraph.co.uk/world-news/2022/10/08/europes-new-iron-lady-kaja-kallas-says-west-mustnt-negotiate/ (last accessed 13 July 2023).
17. Sub-Saharan Africa internet penetration data from the World Bank, available at https://data.worldbank.org/indicator/IT.NET.USER.ZS?locations=ZG (last accessed 13 July 2023).
18. Åslund, 'The Baltic Tigers: Past, present and future'.
19. Latvia's top exports in 2021 were broadcasting equipment ($794 million), sawn wood ($787 million), wheat ($695 million), fuel wood ($557 million) and packaged medicaments ($488 million), exporting mostly to Lithuania ($2.47 billion), Estonia ($1.59 billion), Russia ($1.26 billion), Germany ($1.1 billion) and the UK ($892 billion). Data from the Observatory of Economic Complexity, available at https://oec.world/en/profile/country/lva (last accessed 13 July 2023).
20. Åslund, 'The Baltic Tigers: Past, present and future'.
21. Samuel P. Huntington, *The Third Wave: Democratization in the Late Twentieth Century* (Oklahoma: University of Oklahoma Press, 1991).
22. See, for example, Guillermo O'Donnell, Laurence Whitehead and Philippe Schmitter (eds), *Transitions from Authoritarian Rule: Tentative Conclusions About Uncertain Democracies* (Baltimore: Johns Hopkins University Press, 1986).
23. Matthew Karnitschnig, 'The most dangerous place on earth', *Politico*, 20 June 2022,

available at https://www.politico.eu/article/suwalki-gap-russia-war-nato-lithuania-poland-border/ (last accessed 13 July 2023).
24. Tweet by journalist Lucian Kim, 2 May 2016, available at https://twitter.com/lucian_kim/status/727215539823742980 (last accessed 13 July 2023).
25. This chapter is based on several research trips to Poland in 2018 and 2022. The interviews were conducted during these trips, unless otherwise indicated.
26. Inhabitants of Warsaw.
27. This was penned at Auschwitz-Birkenau, 27 February 2022.
28. The purpose of the ghettos was to eliminate smaller concentrations of Jews scattered throughout the city. This also occurred in other major cities, including Kraków and Łódź.
29. Nadezhda Teffi on Lenin, cited in Antony Beevor, *Russia: Revolution and Civil War, 1917–1921* (London: Penguin, 2022).
30. Radosław Trębiński and Piotr Zalewski, 'Polish aviation engineering: Past, present and future', *Flight Test – Sharing Knowledge and Experience*, Meeting Proceedings RTO-MP-SCI-162, Paper KN1 (Neuilly-sur-Seine, France: RTO, 2005).
31. Data from the Polish Investment & Trade Agency, available at https://www.paih.gov.pl/sectors/aerospace (last accessed 13 July 2023).
32. For a discussion of this process, see Mikołaj Gliński, 'How Warsaw came close to never being rebuilt', *Culture.pl*, 3 February 2015, available at https://culture.pl/en/article/how-warsaw-came-close-to-never-being-rebuilt (last accessed 13 July 2023).
33. Information from the Museum of Life under Communism, Warsaw, September 2022.
34. Ewelina Krajczyńska, 'Meat was a symbol of security in the communist Poland', *Science in Poland*, 30 July 2016, available at https://scienceinpoland.pap.pl/en/news/news%2C410613%2Cmeat-was-a-symbol-of-security-in-the-communist-poland.html (last accessed 13 July 2023).
35. See the register of the Leopold Tyrmand papers, at https://oac.cdlib.org/findaid/ark:/13030/tf5c60044n/entire_text/ (last accessed 13 July 2023).
36. See, for example, Stanisław Gomułka, 'Poland's economic and social transformation 1989–2014 and contemporary challenges', *Central Bank Review*, 16 (1), March 2016, pp. 19–23, available at https://www.sciencedirect.com/science/article/pii/S1303070116000068 (last accessed 13 July 2023).
37. Ibid.
38. Aleks Szczerbiak, 'Can Civic Platform recover?' *The Polish Politics Blog*, 1 July 2015, available at https://polishpoliticsblog.wordpress.com/2015/07/01/can-civic-platform-recover/ (last accessed 13 July 2023).
39. 'Rule of law: European Commission acts to defend judicial independence in Poland', European Commission Press Release, 20 December 2017, available at https://ec.europa.eu/commission/presscorner/detail/en/IP_17_5367 (last accessed 13 July 2023).
40. See reports of the Social Diagnosis Project: Objective and Subjective Quality of Life in Poland, available at http://www.diagnoza.com/index-en.html (last accessed 13 July 2023).
41. 'Putin: Soviet collapse a "genuine tragedy"', *NBC News*, 25 April 2005, available at https://www.nbcnews.com/id/wbna7632057 (last accessed 13 July 2023).
42. This chapter is based on a research trip to Spain in August/September 2022, including

visits to Irun, Pamplona, Bilbao, Guernica, Santander, Oviedo, Vitoria-Gasteiz, El Escorial, Jarama, Mingorrubio and Urnieta.
43. John Simkin, 'Soviet Union and the Spanish Civil War', Spartacus Educational Publishers, September 1997 (updated January 2020), available at https://spartacus-educational.com/SPrussia.htm (last accessed 13 July 2023).
44. Giles Tremlett, *The International Brigades: Fascism, Freedom and the Spanish Civil War* (London: Bloomsbury, 2020). See also Paul Mason's review at https://www.theguardian.com/books/2020/oct/06/the-international-brigades-by-giles-tremlett-review-lost-voices-from-the-spanish-civil-war (last accessed 13 July 2023).
45. Walter Janka, a fellow German communist and member of the International Brigades, said that he was interrogated by Mielke in 1936, who demanded to know why he had travelled to Spain rather than being assigned there by the party. When he told Mielke to get lost, Janka was demoted and then expelled from the Brigades. Janka recalled, 'While I was fighting at the front, shooting at the Fascists, Mielke served in the rear, shooting Trotskyites and Anarchists.' See Ludwig Niethammer, 'Obituary: Erich Mielke – the career of a German Stalinist', World Socialist Web Site, 24 August 2000, available at https://www.wsws.org/en/articles/2000/08/miel-a24.html (last accessed 13 July 2023); Tremlett, *The International Brigades*; and 'The tragic idealism of the International Brigades', *Economist*, 22 October 2020, available at https://www.economist.com/books-and-arts/2020/10/22/the-tragic-idealism-of-the-international-brigades (last accessed 13 July 2023).
46. Hugh Thomas, *The Spanish Civil War* (London: Penguin, 1965).
47. Cited in Peter Day, *Franco's Friends: How British Intelligence Helped Bring Franco to Power in Spain* (London: Biteback, 2011).
48. Spain life expectancy figures from Statista, available at https://www.statista.com/statistics/1041108/life-expectancy-spain-all-time/ (last accessed 13 July 2023).
49. Antony Beevor, *The Battle for Spain: The Spanish Civil War, 1936–1939* (London: Penguin, 2006).
50. Thomas, *The Spanish Civil War*.
51. Day, *Franco's Friends*.
52. I am grateful to Ricardo Rico for this point. Zweig refers to the 'the world of yesterday' in describing his return to Vienna after the end of the First World War; he couldn't imagine that 'after war' could be at least as terrible as the war period itself.
53. Enrique Moradiellos, 'Franco's Spain and the European integration process (1945–1975)', *Bulletin for Spanish and Portuguese Historical Studies*, 41 (1), 2016, available at https://asphs.net/wp-content/uploads/2020/02/Francos-Spain-and-the-European-Integration-Process.pdf (last accessed 13 July 2023).
54. Speech broadcast on 31 December 1956.
55. Leandro Prados de la Escosura, Joan Rosés and Isabel Sanz-Villarroya, 'Economic reforms and growth in Franco's Spain', *Revista de Historia Económica*, 30 (1), 2011.
56. Beevor, *The Battle for Spain*.
57. Zoom interview with Román Escolano, 2 September 2022.
58. Beevor, *The Battle for Spain*.
59. Spain population ages data from the World Bank, available at https://data.worldbank.org/indicator/SP.POP.0014.TO.ZS?locations=ES (last accessed 13 July 2023).

60. Spain population data from PopulationPyramid.net, available at https://www.populationpyramid.net/spain/1950/ (last accessed 13 July 2023).
61. WhatsApp correspondence with Alfonso Guerra, 6 September 2022.
62. Interview with Pablo Hernández, Madrid, Spain, 7 September 2022.
63. Interview with Ricardo Martínez Rico, Madrid, Spain, 31 August 2022.
64. Interview with Josep Piqué, Madrid, Spain, 30 August 2022.
65. Interview with Giles Tremlett, Madrid, Spain, 4 September 2022.
66. All values are constant 2011. See Maddison Project Database, version 2020. Jutta Bolt and Jan Luiten van Zanden, 'Maddison style estimates of the evolution of the world economy. A new 2020 update', Maddison-Project Working Paper WP-15, available at https://www.rug.nl/ggdc/historicaldevelopment/maddison/publications/wp15.pdf (last accessed 13 July 2023).
67. Argentina GDP per capita data from the World Bank, available at https://data.worldbank.org/indicator/NY.GDP.PCAP.KD?locations=AR (last accessed 13 July 2023).
68. Zoom interview with Román Escolano, 2 September 2022.
69. Baher Kamal, 'To be a Latin-American migrant in Madrid', *The Wire*, 25 December 2015, available at https://thewire.in/external-affairs/latin-american-migrant-madrid (last accessed 13 July 2023).
70. Graham Keeley, 'Spain ponders US plan to accept Latin American immigrants', *VOA*, 9 June 2022, available at https://www.voanews.com/a/spain-ponders-us-plan-to-accept-latin-american-immigrants-/6610605.html#:~:text=Spain%20hosts%20about%205.3%20million,move%20for%20work%20to%20Spain (last accessed 13 July 2023).
71. For details on Latin American migrants, see Gonzalo Fanjul and Ismael Gálvez-Iniesta, 'Extranjeros, sin papeles, e imprescindibles: Una fotografía de la inmigración irregular en España', porCausa Foundation, June 2020, available at https://porcausa.org/wp-content/uploads/2020/07/RetratodelairregularidadporCausa.pdf (last accessed 13 July 2023).
72. Spain population data from PopulationPyramid.net.
73. On this history, see Jaume Marti Romero, 'The remarkable case of Spanish immigration', Bruegel, 8 December 2015, available at https://www.bruegel.org/blog-post/remarkable-case-spanish-immigration (last accessed 13 July 2023).
74. Interview with Gabriel Elorriaga, Madrid, Spain, 6 September 2022.
75. Day, *Franco's Friends*.
76. Danny Bird, 'Eight decades after Spain's civil war, a controversial monument still haunts the country', *TIME*, 1 April 2019, available at https://time.com/5560387/spain-civil-war-monument/ (last accessed 13 July 2023).
77. Beevor, *The Battle for Spain*.
78. Discussions with Dr Hryhoriy Nemyria and Yulia Tymoshenko, Kyiv, Ukraine, September 2022.
79. Vladimir Putin, 'On the historical unity of Russians and Ukrainians', Office of the President of Russia, 12 July 2021, available at http://en.kremlin.ru/events/president/news/66181 (last accessed 13 July 2023).
80. Speech by Vladimir Putin, 24 February 2022, full transcript available at https://www.news24.com/fin24/opinion/they-have-deceived-us-they-have-played-us-read-putins-full-televised-speech-on-ukraine-20220224 (last accessed 13 July 2023).

81. John Kane-Berman, 'Ukraine: The country they loathe, fear, and covet', *politicsweb*, 31 January 2022, available at https://www.politicsweb.co.za/opinion/ukraine-the-country-they-loathe-fear-and-covet (last accessed 13 July 2023).
82. Matthew Palmer, 'Privatisation in Ukraine: Economics, law, and politics', *Yale Journal of International Law*, 16 (2), Summer 1991, pp. 453–517, available at https://core.ac.uk/download/pdf/72837413.pdf (last accessed 13 July 2023).
83. 'Timothy Snyder: Germany's historical responsibility for Ukraine', *Tyzhden*, 7 May 2022, available at https://tyzhden.ua/timothy-snyder-germany-s-historical-responsibility-for-ukraine/ (last accessed 13 July 2023).
84. Anne Applebaum, 'The reason Putin would risk war', *The Atlantic*, 3 February 2022, available at https://www.theatlantic.com/ideas/archive/2022/02/putin-ukraine-democracy/621465/ (last accessed 13 July 2023).
85. Gideon Rachman, 'Russia and China's plans for a new world order', *Financial Times*, 23 January 2022, available at https://www.ft.com/content/d307ab6e-57b3-4007-9188-ec9717c60023 (last accessed 13 July 2023).
86. 'IRI Ukraine poll shows overwhelming support for Zelensky, confidence in winning the war, desire for EU membership', International Republican Institute, 9 May 2022, available at https://www.iri.org/news/iri-ukraine-poll-shows-overwhelming-support-for-zelensky-confidence-in-winning-the-war-desire-for-eu-membership/ (last accessed 13 July 2023).
87. Yuriy Gorodnichenko, 'Ukraine's economy went from Soviet chaos to oligarch domination to vital global trader of wheat and neon – and now Russian devastation', *The Conversation*, 21 March 2022, available at https://theconversation.com/ukraines-economy-went-from-soviet-chaos-to-oligarch-domination-to-vital-global-trader-of-wheat-and-neon-and-now-russian-devastation-178971 (last accessed 13 July 2023).
88. 'Achieving Ukraine's agricultural potential: Stimulating agricultural growth and improving rural life', a joint World Bank and OECD working paper, June 2004, available at https://documents1.worldbank.org/curated/zh/917841468778476570/pdf/299190UA0White1riculturaloPotential.pdf (last accessed 13 July 2023).
89. Pekka Sutela, 'The underachiever: Ukraine's economy since 1991', Carnegie Endowment for International Peace, 9 March 2012, available at https://carnegieendowment.org/2012/03/09/underachiever-ukraine-s-economy-since-1991-pub-47451 (last accessed 13 July 2023).
90. Francis Fukuyama, *The Origins of Political Order: From Prehuman Times to the French Revolution* (London: Profile Books, 2011).
91. John Lough, 'Ukraine's system of crony capitalism: The challenge of dismantling "systema"', Chatham House Research Paper, 1 July 2021, available at https://www.chathamhouse.org/2021/07/ukraines-system-crony-capitalism (last accessed 13 July 2023).
92. See 'Ukraine Executive Summary' as part of Freedom House's 'Nations in Transit 2022', available at https://freedomhouse.org/country/ukraine/nations-transit/2022 (last accessed 13 July 2023).
93. For Ukraine's ranking, see Transparency International Corruption Perceptions Index, available at https://www.transparency.org/en/countries/ukraine (last accessed 13 July 2023).

94. For Ukraine's profile, see the Heritage Foundation's '2022 Index of Economic Freedom', available at https://www.heritage.org/index/pdf/2022/countries/2022_Index ofEconomicFreedom-Ukraine.pdf (last accessed 13 July 2023).
95. For detail, see the World Economic Forum's Global Competitiveness Index 2017–2018 edition, available at https://www3.weforum.org/docs/GCR2017-2018/03CountryProfiles/Standalone2-pagerprofiles/WEF_GCI_2017_2018_Profile_Ukraine.pdf (last accessed 13 July 2023).
96. For information on the World Bank's Worldwide Governance Indicators, see https://info.worldbank.org/governance/wgi/ (last accessed 13 July 2023).
97. Discussion with Pavlo Sheremeta, Lviv, Ukraine, May 2022.
98. 'Ukraine agricultural production and trade', Foreign Agricultural Service, US Department of Agriculture, April 2022, available at https://www.fas.usda.gov/sites/default/files/2022-04/Ukraine-Factsheet-April2022.pdf (last accessed 13 July 2023).
99. Ukraine cereal production data from the World Bank, available at https://data.worldbank.org/indicator/AG.PRD.CREL.MT?locations=UA (last accessed 13 July 2023).
100. 'Ukraine agricultural production and trade', Foreign Agricultural Service.
101. Food and Agricultural Organization of the United Nations, 'Chapter 2: Crop production systems', in *Fertilizer Use by Crop in Ukraine* (Rome: FAO, 2005), available at https://www.academia.edu/8004193/Fertilizer_use_by_crop_in_Ukraine; for wheat, see 'Ukraine harvests 3.6 mln T grain with low yield so far, farm ministry says', *Hellenic Shipping News*, 18 July 2022, available at https://www.hellenicshippingnews.com/ukraine-harvests-3-6-mln-t-grain-with-low-yield-so-far-farm-ministry-says/; for maize, see USDA International Production Assessment Division, 'Crop explorer – World agricultural production (WAP) briefs – Ukraine, Moldova and Belarus', available at https://ipad.fas.usda.gov/cropexplorer/pecad_stories.aspx?regionid=umb&ftype=prodbriefs (all last accessed 14 July 2023). Dry ground yields may be at least twice as great according to figures supplied by Gideon Schreuder, managing director at Equalizer, via WhatsApp correspondence, 29 September 2022.
102. Arkadiusz Sarna, 'The transformation of agriculture in Ukraine: From collective farms to agroholdings', Centre for Eastern Studies, 7 February 2014, available at https://www.osw.waw.pl/en/publikacje/osw-commentary/2014-02-07/transformation-agriculture-ukraine-collective-farms-to (last accessed 14 July 2023).
103. Interview with Mykhailo Podolyak, Kyiv, Ukraine, 2 June 2023.
104. See, for example, Jamie Dettmer, 'The strengths and weaknesses of Volodymyr Zelenskyy', *Politico*, 27 February 2023, available at https://www.politico.eu/article/strength-weaknesse-ukraine-president-volodymyr-zelenskyy/ (last accessed 14 July 2023).
105. Zoya Sheftalovich, '"Go fuck yourself," Ukrainian soldiers on Snake Island tell Russian ship before being killed', *Politico*, 25 February 2022, available at https://www.politico.eu/article/go-fuck-yourself-ukraine-soldiers-snake-island-russia-war-ship-killed/ (last accessed 14 July 2023).
106. World Bank, 'Ukraine Growth Study final document: Faster, lasting and kinder', 2019, available at https://documents1.worldbank.org/curated/en/543041554211825812/pdf/Ukraine-Growth-Study-Final-Document-Faster-Lasting-and-Kinder.pdf (last accessed 14 July 2023).

107. World Bank, 'Ukraine country economic memorandum: Strategic choices to accelerate and sustain growth in Ukraine', no. 55895-UA, August 2010.

PART IV: LATIN AMERICA

1. Discussion with Mahamadou Issoufou, Niamey, Niger, 9 February 2023.
2. Fabrice Lehoucq and Aníbal Pérez-Liñán, 'Regimes, competition, and military coups in Latin America', *Comparative Political Studies*, 47 (8), 2014.
3. Information from *Wikipedia*, s.v. 'List of coups and coup attempts by country', available at https://en.wikipedia.org/wiki/List_of_coups_and_coup_attempts_by_country (last accessed 14 July 2023).
4. Robert Dix, 'Military coups and military rule in Latin America', *Armed Forces & Society*, 20 (3), Spring 1994.
5. Economist Intelligence Unit, 'Democracy Index 2022: Frontline democracy and the battle for Ukraine', 2023.
6. See, for example, Francisco Ferreira and Marta Schoch, 'Inequality and social unrest in Latin America: The Tocqueville Paradox revisited', World Bank Blogs, 24 February 2020, available at https://blogs.worldbank.org/developmenttalk/inequality-and-social-unrest-latin-america-tocqueville-paradox-revisited; and Leonardo Gasparini and Guillermo Cruces, 'The changing picture of inequality in Latin America: Evidence for three decades', UNDP, 9 August 2022, available at https://www.undp.org/latin-america/blog/changing-picture-inequality-latin-america-evidence-three-decades (both last accessed 14 July 2023).
7. Léo Rodrigues, 'Brazilian whites earn 75.7% more than blacks: 2021 survey', Agência Brasil, 15 November 2022, available at https://agenciabrasil.ebc.com.br/en/economia/noticia/2022-11/ibge-average-income-white-workers-757-higher-blacks; Alicia Bárcena and Winnie Byanyima, 'Latin America is the world's most unequal region. Here's how to fix it', ECLAC, 15 January 2016, available at https://www.cepal.org/en/articulos/2016-america-latina-caribe-es-la-region-mas-desigual-mundo-como-solucionarlo#:~:text=In%202014%20the%20richest%2010,wealth%20than%20the%20remaining%2099%25 (both last accessed 18 July 2023).
8. Cristina Moreno, 'Mexico ranks as fourth most crime-ridden country in the world', *Atalayar*, 11 May 2022, available at https://atalayar.com/en/content/mexico-ranks-fourth-most-crime-ridden-country-world (last accessed 18 July 2023).
9. Nathaniel Parish Flannery, 'Mexico's president does not know how to fight crime', *Forbes*, 29 September 2022, available at https://www.forbes.com/sites/nathanielparishflannery/2022/09/29/mexicos-president-does-not-know-how-to-fight-crime/?sh=54848e3e772c (last accessed 18 July 2023).
10. This section is based on a research trip to Mexico with Lyal White during October/November 2015. Note all figures denoted by $ are US dollars. A further research trip to Mexico followed in 2018, while several Zoom interviews were conducted in 2022, as cited in the text.
11. Office of the United States Trade Representative, 'US–Mexico trade facts', available at https://ustr.gov/countries-regions/americas/Mexico (last accessed 18 July 2023).
12. Information supplied by Manuel Zambrano, Honorary Consul of South Africa in Monterrey, Mexico.

13. And behind China (25.7 million), the US (10.8 million), Japan (9.7 million), Germany (4.6 million) and India (4.5 million).
14. Data from the International Organization of Motor Vehicle Manufacturers, at https://www.oica.net (accessed 11 October 2022).
15. This chapter is based on two trips to Argentina, in March 2018 and April 2023. Unless otherwise indicated, the interviews cited were conducted during these trips. Special thanks go to Matt Pascall, Richard Harper, John Dean and Domingo Cavallo for their assistance in organising these meetings.
16. Domingo Felipe Cavallo and Sonia Cavallo Runde, *Argentina's Economic Reforms of the 1990s in Contemporary and Historical Perspective* (Oxford: Routledge, 2017), p. 4.
17. 'UCA report puts Argentina's poverty rate at 43.1%', *Buenos Aires Times*, 6 June 2022, available at https://www.batimes.com.ar/news/argentina/uca-report-puts-argentinas-poverty-rate-at-431.phtml.
18. Private correspondence with Domingo Cavallo, April 2023.
19. Cited in Michael Stott and Benedict Mander, 'Argentina: How IMF's biggest ever bailout crumbled under Macri', *Financial Times*, 2 September 2019, available at https://www.ft.com/content/5cfe7c34-ca48-11e9-a1f4-3669401ba76f (last accessed 18 July 2023).
20. Jill Hedges, *Argentina: A Modern History* (London: I.B. Tauris, 2015).
21. Ibid.
22. Ibid.
23. Interview with Rosendo Fraga, Buenos Aires, Argentina, 2018.
24. Zoom interview with Franco Moccia, 10 May 2023.
25. Discussion with Miguel Pertino, La Plata, Argentina, 14 April 2023.
26. Fiona Ortiz, 'Raul Alfonsin, hero of Argentine democracy', *Reuters*, 1 April 2009, available at https://www.reuters.com/article/us-argentina-alfonsin-idUSTRE5300DH20090401 (last accessed 18 July 2023).
27. Domingo and Sonia Cavallo, *Argentina's Economic Reforms of the 1990s in Contemporary and Historical Perspective*.
28. Carlos Menem was interviewed in March 2018 at his residence in Palermo, Buenos Aires.
29. Martin Redrado, *No Reserve: The Limit of Absolute Power* (New York: Amazon, 2011).
30. Domingo and Sonia Cavallo, *Argentina's Economic Reforms of the 1990s in Contemporary and Historical Perspective*, p. 238.
31. 'President Macri and his failed experiment', Agora Economics, 25 June 2016, previously available at https://agoraeconomics.com/2016/06/25/president-macri-and-his-failed-experiment/ (page no longer available).
32. Domingo and Sonia Cavallo, *Argentina's Economic Reforms of the 1990s in Contemporary and Historical Perspective*, p. 238.
33. Interview with Sergio Berensztein, Buenos Aires, Argentina, March 2018.
34. South African Government media statement, 'Employment and labour on falling trade union membership in South Africa', 22 February 2023, available at https://www.gov.za/speeches/employment-and-labouron-falling-trade-union-membership-south-africa-22-feb-2023-0000#:~:text=Trade%20union%20membership%20in%20South%20Africa%20was%20declining%20at%20an,Muldersdrift%2C%20near%20Johannesburg%20on%20Wednesday (last accessed 18 July 2023).

35. James Francis Whitehead, 'Argentine transport unions show their strength during a month of scattered strikes', Courthouse News Service, 29 April 2022, https://www.courthousenews.com/argentine-transport-unions-show-their-strength-during-a-month-of-scattered-strikes/ (last accessed 18 July 2023).
36. For Argentina's ranking, see Transparency International Corruption Perceptions Index, available at https://www.transparency.org/en/countries/argentina (last accessed 18 July 2023).
37. Discussion with Hendrik Jordaan, Buenos Aires, Argentina, 17 April 2023.
38. With thanks to Domingo Cavallo for this point.
39. For a discussion on this point, see, for example, Ferreira and Schoch, 'Inequality and social unrest in Latin America: The Tocqueville Paradox revisited'.
40. Interview with Alfonso Prat-Gay, Tswalu Dialogue, November 2019.
41. Zoom conversation with Alfonso Prat-Gay, 2022.
42. Zoom interview with Franco Moccia, 10 May 2023.
43. James Sturcke, 'The art of the possible', *Guardian*, 29 October 2007, available at https://www.theguardian.com/world/2007/oct/29/argentina.jamessturcke (last accessed 18 July 2023).
44. Cited in Tendai Biti, Nic Cheeseman, Christopher Clapham, Ray Hartley, Greg Mills, Juan Carlos Pinzón and Lyal White, *In the Name of the People: How Populism is Rewiring the World* (Johannesburg: Picador, 2022).
45. Ferreira and Schoch, 'Inequality and social unrest in Latin America: The Tocqueville Paradox revisited'.
46. This chapter is based on a research trip to Peru in April 2023. Unless otherwise indicated, the interviews cited were conducted during this time. Thanks are expressed to Ambassador Jorge Félix Rubio Correa, Guillermo van Oordt and Jorge Benavides for their kind assistance during this research visit.
47. Peru poverty data from the World Bank, available at https://data.worldbank.org/indicator/SI.POV.NAHC?locations=PE (last accessed 18 July 2023).
48. Alessandra Marini and Claudia Rokx, 'Standing tall: Peru's success in overcoming its stunting crisis', World Bank, 2017, available at https://documents1.worldbank.org/curated/en/815411500045862444/pdf/FINAL-Peru-Nutrition-Book-in-English-with-Cover-October-12.pdf (last accessed 18 July 2023).
49. *Perú: La despensa del mundo* (Lima: Planeta, 2018).
50. Cristina Marcano and Alberto Barrera Tyszka, *Hugo Chávez: The Definitive Biography of Venezuela's Controversial President* (New York: Random House, 2017).
51. Scott Malcomson, 'Alan Garcia & the crisis of populist rule in Peru', *Against the Current*, 11, November/December 1987, available at https://againstthecurrent.org/atc011/alan-garcia-the-crisis-of-populist-rule-in-peru/ (last accessed 18 July 2023).
52. Carol Graham, 'Peru: The prison of poverty is the problem', Brookings Institution, 11 January 1997, available at https://www.brookings.edu/opinions/peru-the-prison-of-poverty-is-the-problem/ (last accessed 18 July 2023).
53. Cited in 'The world; Fujimori in the time of cholera', *New York Times*, 24 February 1991, available at https://www.nytimes.com/1991/02/24/weekinreview/the-world-fujimori-in-the-time-of-cholera.html (last accessed 18 July 2023).
54. See, for example, 'Peru foreign direct investment 1970–2023', Macrotrends, available

at https://www.macrotrends.net/countries/PER/peru/foreign-direct-investment (last accessed 18 July 2023).
55. Roque Benavides, 'Responsible Mining and its Contribution to the Development of Peru', 3rd edition, 2018, available at https://www.buenaventura.com/assets/responsible-mining/index.html#p=1 (last accessed 18 July 2023).
56. 'Peru: Over 500 years of mining and counting', *Resource World*, n.d., available at https://resourceworld.com/peru-over-500-years-of-mining-and-counting/ (last accessed 18 July 2023).
57. Javier Herrera, 'Poverty and economic inequalities in Peru during the boom in growth: 2004–14', in *Alternative Pathways to Sustainable Development: Lessons from Latin America*, International Development Policy Series No. 9 (Geneva, Boston: Graduate Institute Publications, Brill-Nijhoff, 2017), pp. 138–173, available at https://journals.openedition.org/poldev/2363 (last accessed 18 July 2023).
58. Technically, on the coastal strip the maximum land holding permitted under the new law was 150 hectares, or 200 if the owner undertook local infrastructure works, paid their taxes and offered their employees 10 per cent of the profits. In the Sierra, the maximum holding was between 15 and 55 hectares depending on the land's location, or double that in dry areas. On forest and pastureland, this figure could rise to 1500 hectares, or enough to graze 1500 sheep. Profitable large estates and indigenous areas could be formed into co-operatives. See Immigration and Refugee Board of Canada, 'Peru: Agrarian reform under the military régime of Juan Velasco Alvarado, including what the program entailed and its impact on Peruvian society (1968–1975)', 14 September 1999, PER32785.E, available at https://www.refworld.org/docid/3ae6ad7228.html (last accessed 18 July 2023).
59. International Trade Administration, 'Peru – Country Commercial Guide', 17 August 2022, available at https://www.trade.gov/country-commercial-guides/peru-agriculture-sectors (last accessed 18 July 2023).
60. Ibid.
61. Rory Carroll, 'Maria Vargas Llosa under fire for Peru election endorsement', *Guardian*, 28 April 2011, available at https://www.theguardian.com/books/2011/apr/28/mario-vargas-llosa-peru-election (last accessed 18 July 2023).

PART V: NORTH AFRICA AND THE MIDDLE EAST

1. Mohamed ElBaradei, 'The eternal promise of the Arab Spring', *Project Syndicate*, 14 January 2021, available at https://www.project-syndicate.org/commentary/arab-spring-democratic-transition-four-lessons-by-mohamed-elbaradei-2021-01?barrier=accesspaylog (last accessed 18 July 2023). This section is based on several research trips to Egypt, most recently in June 2019 and March 2023.
2. Josh Halliday, 'Arab spring: Google's Wael Ghonim on the fall of Mubarak', *Guardian*, 18 May 2011, available at http://www.theguardian.com/media/pda/2011/may/18/google-wael-ghonim-mubarak (last accessed 18 July 2023).
3. Wael Ghonim, *Revolution 2.0: The Power of the People Is Greater Than the People in Power* (New York: Houghton Mifflin Harcourt, 2012).
4. Discussions, February 2011.

5. Tarek Osman, *Egypt on the Brink: From the Rise of Nasser to the Fall of Mubarak* (New Haven: Yale University Press, 2011), pp. 242–3.
6. Omar Ashour, 'Egypt: Return to a generals' republic?', *BBC News*, 21 August 2013, available at http://www.bbc.com/news/world-middle-east-23780839 (last accessed 18 July 2023).
7. Ibid.
8. Discussion, Cairo, Egypt, 26 March 2014.
9. Phebe Marr (ed.), *Egypt at the Crossroads: Domestic Stability and Regional Role* (London: Create Space, 2012), pp. 39–40.
10. Interview, Cairo, Egypt, 28 March 2014.
11. 'World Bank Group to extend current strategy in Egypt to maintain momentum on reforms', World Bank Press Release, 30 April 2019, available at https://www.worldbank.org/en/news/press-release/2019/04/30/world-bank-group-to-extend-current-strategy-in-egypt-to-maintain-momentum-on-reforms (last accessed 18 July 2023).
12. '"Egypt's new Pharaoh" assumes sweeping powers', *Financial Review*, 23 November 2012, available at https://www.afr.com/policy/foreign-affairs/egypt-s-new-pharaoh-assumes-sweeping-powers-20121123-j1fl9 (last accessed 18 July 2023).
13. George T. Abed, 'The Egyptian economy: In the clutches of the deep state', Carnegie Middle East Center, 26 October 2020, available at https://carnegie-mec.org/2020/10/26/egyptian-economy-in-clutches-of-deep-state-pub-83027 (last accessed 18 July 2023).
14. Ibid.
15. Discussion, Cairo, Egypt, 4 March 2023.
16. 'How the Arab world's most populous country became addicted to debt', *CNN*, 16 December 2022, available at https://edition.cnn.com/2022/12/16/business/egypt-debt-crisis-mime-intl/index.html (last accessed 18 July 2023).
17. Zoom discussion with Hafsa Halawa, 7 March 2023.
18. Yezid Sayigh, 'Egypt's military now controls much of its economy. Is this wise?', Carnegie Middle East Center, 25 November 2019, available at https://carnegie-mec.org/2019/11/25/egypt-s-military-now-controls-much-of-its-economy.-is-this-wise-pub-80281 (last accessed 18 July 2023).
19. 'Egypt is the "most attractive reform story" among EEMEA countries: Renaissance Capital', *Enterprise*, 4 April 2019, available at https://enterprise.press/stories/2019/04/04/egypt-is-the-most-attractive-reform-story-among-eemea-countries-renaissance-capital/ (last accessed 18 July 2023).
20. Philip Mansel, *Sultans in Splendour: The Last Years of the Ottoman World* (London: André Deutsch, 1988), p. 173, cited in Toby Wilkinson, *The Nile: Downriver through Egypt's Past and Present* (London: Bloomsbury, 2015).
21. Discussion, Cairo, Egypt, 4 March 2023.
22. This section is based on a personal visit to Manshiyat Naser in March 2023.
23. 'Agriculture in Israel: Price indices of output and input', Israel Central Bureau of Statistics, No. 1849, January 2022, previously available at https://www.cbs.gov.il/he/publications/DocLib/2022/1849/e_print.pdf (page no longer available).
24. GDP per capita (constant 2015 US$) data from the World Bank, as accessed in February 2023.
25. Ibid.

26. Author's calculations using NASDAQ market activity data, as accessed in February 2023.
27. R&D expenditure (% of GDP) data from the World Bank, as accessed in February 2023.
28. 'United Arab Emirates population statistics 2023', Global Media Insight, 28 June 2023, available at https://www.globalmediainsight.com/blog/uae-population-statistics/#:~:text=The%20Total%20Expat%20Population%20of,to%20official%20Dubai%20Government%20website (last accessed 18 July 2023).
29. This chapter is based on a research trip to Iraq in August 2022, and on three prior visits to the country in 2003 and 2004.
30. Watch 'Saddam Hussein's Very Public Purge', American Heroes Channel, YouTube, available at https://www.youtube.com/watch?v=kLUktJbp2Ug (last accessed 18 July 2023).
31. Jonathan Kandell, 'Iraq's unruly century', *Smithsonian Magazine*, May 2003, available at https://www.smithsonianmag.com/history/iraqs-unruly-century-82706606/ (last accessed 18 July 2023).
32. 'Chemical Ali in his own words: The Ali Hassan Al-Majid Tapes', Human Rights Watch, 7 April 2003, available at https://www.hrw.org/legacy/campaigns/iraq/chemicalali.htm (last accessed 18 July 2023).
33. Interview with Qubad Talabani at the Delphi Forum VIII in Delphi, Greece, 28 April 2023.
34. 'Lord Salter, The Development of Iraq; A plan of Action issued by the Iraq Development Board (1955)', Mss Eur F203/76, British Library: Asian and African Studies.
35. Jean-François Arvis et al., 'Connecting to Compete 2018: Trade Logistics in the Global Economy', World Bank, 2018, available at https://openknowledge.worldbank.org/bitstream/handle/10986/29971/LPI2018.pdf (last accessed 18 July 2023).
36. Ambassador Mahmoud Karem at a meeting, 'Egypt: A U.S. Dilemma', hosted on 10 April 2013 by the Middle East Program at the Woodrow Wilson Center, available at https://www.wilsoncenter.org/event/egypt-us-dilemma (last accessed 18 July 2023).
37. See Marina Ottaway's comments in 'Algeria: The enduring failure of politics', Middle East Program, Wilson Center, 13 October 2013, available at https://www.wilsoncenter.org/article/algeria-enduring-failure-politics (last accessed 18 July 2023).
38. Middle East and North Africa population data from the World Bank, available at https://data.worldbank.org/indicator/SP.POP.TOTL?locations=ZQ (last accessed 18 July 2023).
39. 'Total population across the Middle East and North Africa from 1990 to 2050', Statista, available at https://www.statista.com/statistics/978535/mena-total-population/ (last accessed 18 July 2023).
40. This chapter is based on several trips to Morocco, most recently in July 2019 and October 2021. The interviews cited here were conducted during these visits.
41. World Bank, 'The Container Port Performance Index 2021'.
42. 'The 10 least densely populated places in the world', *World Atlas*, available at https://www.worldatlas.com/articles/the-10-least-densely-populated-places-in-the-world-2015.html (last accessed 18 July 2023).
43. Simon Baynham, 'The war in Western Sahara', *Africa Insight*, 21 (1), 1991, pp. 48–56, available at https://journals.co.za/doi/pdf/10.10520/AJA02562804_1231 (last accessed 18 July 2023).

44. Ibid.
45. Ibid.
46. Cited in Piero Gleijeses, 'Cuba's first venture in Africa: Algeria, 1961–1965', *Journal of Latin American Studies*, 28 (1), February 1996, pp. 159–195.
47. 'Azoulay: Essaouira, valuable asset for future economy', Kingdom of Morocco News, 1 April 2021, available at https://www.maroc.ma/en/news/azoulay-essaouira-valuable-asset-future-economy (last accessed 18 July 2023).

CONCLUSION

1. Robert T. Kiyosaki, *Rich Dad, Poor Dad* (New York: Warner Books, 2000).
2. Interview with Artis Pabriks, Riga, Latvia, October 2022.
3. I am grateful to Tommy Koh for this point.
4. This relationship is discussed in detail in Mills et al., *Democracy Works*.
5. This juxtaposition is outlined by the Multi-Party Coalition Advocacy Group at twitter.com/MultiCoalition.
6. Gyimah-Boadi and Asunka, 'Do Africans want democracy – and do they think they're getting it?'
7. David Remnick, 'The weakness of the despot: An expert on Stalin discusses Putin, Russia, and the West', *New Yorker*, 11 March 2022, available at https://www.newyorker.com/news/q-and-a/stephen-kotkin-putin-russia-ukraine-stalin (last accessed 19 July 2023).
8. Al Murray, *Command: How the Allies Learned to Win the Second World War* (London: Headline, 2022).
9. Cited in James Holland, *Together We Stand: North Africa 1942–1943: Turning the Tide in the West* (London: HarperCollins, 2005), esp. pp. 674–6.
10. Rudyard Kipling, *The Irish Guards in the Great War, Volume 2: The Second Battalion* (New York: Doubleday, 1923).
11. James Holland, *Sicily '43: The First Assault on Fortress Europe* (London: Atlantic Monthly, 2020).
12. Ibid.
13. Holland, *Together We Stand*.
14. Emile Simpson, 'David Petraeus on Strategic Leadership', Belfer Center for Science and International Affairs, Harvard Kennedy School, 8 February 2016; see the full transcript of the interview at https://www.belfercenter.org/sites/default/files/files/publication/DavidPetraeusTranscript.pdf (last accessed 19 July 2023).
15. Omar N. Bradley, 'On leadership', *Parameters*, 11 (3), 1981, pp. 2–7, available at https://press.armywarcollege.edu/cgi/viewcontent.cgi?article=1240&context=parameters (last accessed 19 July 2023).
16. Cited in John Terraine, 'British military leadership in the First World War', *Leadership & War*, 1998, available at https://www.westernfrontassociation.com/world-war-i-articles/british-military-leadership-in-the-first-world-war-by-john-terraine/ (last accessed 19 July 2023).
17. Simpson, 'David Petraeus on Strategic Leadership'.
18. Halberstam, *The Best and the Brightest*; see also Wesley Clark's review in the *Naval War College Review*, 26 (1), July/August 1973, pp. 42–53; and Victor S. Navasky, 'How we

got into the messiest war in our history', *New York Times*, 12 November 1972, available at https://archive.nytimes.com/www.nytimes.com/books/98/03/15/home/halberstam-best.html (last accessed 19 July 2023).
19. Halberstam, *The Best and the Brightest*.
20. William Wallis and Arjun Neil Alim, 'Blair argued Putin deserves a seat at the "top table"', *Financial Times*, 30 December 2022, available at https://www.ft.com/content/9d0937c4-7e75-417e-8128-604ca2d7d3bc (last accessed 19 July 2023).
21. With thanks to Dr James Sherr for his insights here.
22. This was relayed by President Olusegun Obasanjo and was said by the former prime minister during a visit by the African Leadership Forum to Singapore in November 1993.
23. WhatsApp exchange with Archbishop Thabo Makgoba, 18 June 2023.
24. This section is based on a research trip to Malawi in January 2023, during which time the interviews were conducted.
25. Cited in Alec Russell, *Big Men, Little People: The Leaders Who Defined Africa* (London: Macmillan, 1999).
26. Murray, *Command*, p. 163.
27. This comparison is highlighted in Mills, *Expensive Poverty*.
28. GDP data from the World Bank, available at https://data.worldbank.org/indicator/NY.GDP.MKTP.CD (last accessed 19 July 2023).
29. Frederick Forsyth, *The Biafra Story: The Making of an African Legend* (London: Penguin Books, 1969).
30. With thanks to Johan Borgstam for his guidance here!
31. I am grateful to Sydney Matamwandi for this point.
32. For a discussion of comparative wage rates and other advantages, see Orla Ryan, 'Vietnam becomes vital link in supply chain as business pivots from China', *Financial Times*, 3 July 2023, available at https://www.ft.com/content/29070eda-3a0c-4034-827e-0b31a0f3ef11 (last accessed 19 July 2023).
33. In this regard, see the comments of the Greek prime minister Kyriakos Mitsotakis at the Delphi Economic Forum VIII in Delphi, Greece, 28 April 2023.

Index

Page numbers in *italics* indicate graphs and tables.

7 Independent Company 59
Abacha, Sani 26
Abdallah Abderemane, Ahmed 59–60, 65
Abel, Mike 113
Aboudou, Assoumany 64
accountability 21–22, 57, 201, 252, 272, 303, 321
Acemoglu, Daron 9, 40–41, 54–55
ACP states 34
Act on the Re-Establishment of the State of Lithuania 4–5
aerospace industry 289–290
Afghanistan 304
Africa
  economic growth 35–37, 321–322
  elites 35, 37
  labour costs 19–20
  leadership for 310–311
  population size 19
  ports 104
  poverty 36
African, Caribbean and Pacific (ACP) group of countries *see* ACP states
African Growth and Opportunity Act (US) 53
African National Congress *see* ANC
African Youth Survey (2022) 19

Afrobarometer 21, 34
Agent Orange 95, 117, 124
Agrarian Reform Law (Peru) 249
agriculture sector
  Argentina 221, 224–225, 228–229
  Botswana 43–44
  Comoros 61
  Estonia 137, 142–143, 153
  Israel 271
  Latvia 137
  Lithuania 137
  Peru 237–240, 246, 249–250
  Ukraine 15, 202–204
  Vietnam 115, 122
aid 16, 39, 95–96, 105, 122, 263, 301, 312–321
aircraft industry *see* aviation industry
airports 31, 46–47, 84, 98, 156
Alanbrooke, 1st Viscount *see* Brooke, Alan Francis
Al Boraq high-speed rail network 286
Alexander II, Tsar 133
Alexander, Sir Harold 305–307
Alfonsín, Raúl 225
Alfonso XII, King 175
Alfonso XIII, King 175–176
Algeria 259, 285, 292–294
Alice's Adventures in Wonderland 65
Alice, South Africa 79–80

American Popular Revolutionary Alliance *see* APRA
Amir, Jacques 295
amnesty 180
ANC 16–17, 59–60, 67, 70, 73, 77–80, 83–90, 117–120, 298
Andropov, Yuri 3
Anglo American 41, 77
Angola 12, 212–213, 287
Antapaccay copper mine 247
Anušauskas, Arvydas 5
Aoki, Morihisa 236
apartheid 12, 41, 54, 59–60, 79, 86–87, 298
apathy among citizens 44
APOYO Consultoria 247–248
Applebaum, Anne 195
APRA 240–241, 243
aquaculture 64
Arab Spring 18, 259–263, 267
Arafat, Yasser 86
Arendt, Hannah 150
argan oil 296
Argentina 217–235
  agriculture sector 221, 224–225, 228–229
  coups d'état 221–222, 234
  economic growth 184–185, *184*, 218–220, 223, 225–226
  elections 230–232
  elites 220–221, 223–224, 232, 234

355

INDEX

history of 221–223
Kirchners 217, 227–229,
  233–234
leadership 211–212, 232, 311
Macri, Mauricio 217,
  219–220, 224, 229–234
Menem, Carlos 211, 217,
  219, 225–226, 233
Peronism 22, 217–224,
  231–234
poverty 218, 222–224, 228,
  231, 233, 235
reforms 17, 218–220,
  225–227, 230–232, 235
Spain and 178
unemployment 219, 228
YPF 232–233
Arif, Abdul Rahman 276
Arif, Abdul Salam 276
armed struggle 118–119
armies *see* militaries
arts 296
ASEAN 96
Asian community in
  Kenya 48
Asian countries 96, 223
ASKY 31
Åslund, Anders 140, 148
Association of Southeast
  Asian Nations
  see ASEAN
Assoumani, Azali 64–65
Auden, W.H. 189
audit assessments 67–69, 80
Auld, Robin 315–316
austerity measures 180, 264
authoritarianism
  Argentina 232
  Egypt 268
  Latin America 211–212
  Poland 171
  Russia 195–196
  Singapore 101, 111–114
  South Africa 12
  Spain 177, 190
  system of 21–22, 300–301
autocratic rule 18, 303, 307

aviation industry 161–162,
  289–290
Ayacucho, Peru 240
Aylwin, Patricio 13
Ayu, Iyorchia 25
Azali, Nour El Fath 64
Aznar, José María 182
Azoulay, André 284, 295–296
Az Zubayr, Iraq 274

Ba'ath Party 276
Babb, Glenn 59–60
Babi Yar massacre 135
Bad Child's Book of Beasts
  65–66
Bahrain 8
al-Bakr, Ahmed Hassan 276
Balcerowicz, Leszek 14,
  165–167, 169–170
Baltic states 2–6, 22, 133–134,
  136–142, *141*, 147–150,
  153–154, 302
  see also Estonia; Latvia;
  Lithuania
Bamangwato Concessions
  Ltd 41
Banda, Hastings Kamuzu 312
Barrell, Howard 118
barriers to trade 52, 318
Barzani, Masoud 281
basic services 323
basketball 6
Basra, Iraq 274
Batkivshchyna (political
  party) 197
Baynham, Simon 293
Bayt Dakira museum 295
BEAC 42, 49
Beach Village Committees
  see BVCs
beef 41, 220, 224–225
Beevor, Antony 176, 179
Belarus 133, 171
Belaúnde, Fernando
  239–240
Bell, Gertrude 275
Belloc, Hilaire 65–66

Ben Ali, Zine El Abidine 259
Benavides, Ismael 245
Benavides, Roque 245, 247
Benbrahim El Andaloussi,
  Hamid 290
Beni Antar Cooperative 296
'benign dictatorship' 9, 101,
  113, 186, 303
Berbera, port of 84
Bérenger, Paul 51, 56–57
Berensztein, Sergio 227
Berlin Wall, fall of 195
Best and the Brightest, The
  308–309
Bien Hoa, Vietnam 123
'Big Man' phenomenon
  32–33, 48, 110, 252,
  300–301, 312
Binh Duong, Vietnam 123
biometric voting 26–27
black economic
  empowerment 78
Black Hawk Down (film) 291
black markets 163
Blair, Tony 309–310
blueberries 250
Blue Ribbon Commission
  208
Boko Haram 24
Bolívar, Simón 239–240
Bolivia 212, 252
Bolsonaro, Jair 211, 212
bonds 268
Bonfoh, Abiratou 31, 34
books published 139
Botswana 38–49
  challenges 42–49, 302
  economic growth 35,
    38–39, *40*, 49, 51
  education 39, 45
  elites 40–41, 47–49
  poverty 44
  Southern African Customs
    Union 54
  successes 18, 38–42
Botswana Bureau of
  Standards 43

Botswana Development
    Corporation 43
Botswana Excellence
    Strategy 43
Botswana Export
    Development and
    Investment Authority 43
Botswana National
    Productivity Centre 43
Bouazizi, Mohamed 259
Bourhane, Nourdine 61–62,
    65
Bourne Ultimatum, The
    (film) 288
Bowles, Paul 287–288
Bradley, Omar 304–308, 316
Brandt, Willy 173, 190
Bräutigam, Deborah 55
Brazil 211–213, 215, 228
bread riots, Egypt 263
Bremer, Paul 278–279
Brenthurst Foundation 42,
    70, 79, 88
Brezhnev, Leonid 3
Britain 39, 50, 94, 97–99, 102,
    186, 275, 318
Brooke, Alan Francis (later
    1st Viscount
    Alanbrooke) 306
BSS 156
Buenaventura mining firm
    245
Buenos Aires, Argentina
    220–221
Buhlungu, Sakhela 80
Bukele, Nayib 211
bureaucracy 1, 37, 129
Burkina Faso 34, 211
Burma *see* Myanmar
Burroughs, William S.
    287–288
Bush, George H.W. 278
Business and Economic
    Advisory Council
    see BEAC
business community
    see private sector

business services sector
    see BSS
BVCs 313–314

cable theft 81, 83
Cabo Verde 51, 55
cadre deployment 73, 78,
    86, 88
Cambiemos (Let's Change)
    229
Camp David Accords 272
Cámpora, Héctor 217
Canada 213
can-do attitude 204–205,
    272, 308
Capa, Robert 174
Cape Town, South Africa 81
'capture' 68, 104
Cárdenas, Emilio 218
Carlos IV, King 174
Carrero Blanco, Luis 189
cars *see* motor industry
Carter, Nick 307
Castillo, Pedro 238, 240, 247,
    251–254
Castro, Fidel 86
Catholic Church 169, 174, 177
Catholic University of
    Argentina 218
Cavallo, Domingo 218–219,
    225–227
Cave Cathedral (Saint
    Sama'ans Church) 269
Cele, Bheki 76
*Celebrated Travels and
    Travellers* 99
Central Kalahari Park 38
Central Provident Fund
    see CPF
Central Reserve Bank (Peru)
    252–253, 255
Cerrón, Vladimir 251
CFK *see* Kirchner, Cristina
    Fernández de
Chad 59, 211
champions 290–291
Chancellor House 78

Change 90 (political party)
    241
Changi Airport 98
Chatham House report 200
Chávez, Hugo 211, 227, 240
Cheng Tong Fatt 106
Chernenko, Konstantin 3
Chiang Kai-shek 94
Chief Administration of
    Corrective Labour
    Camps *see* Gulag
child mortality 116, 128
Chile 8, 13, 212, 228
China 18–19, 93–94, 99,
    115–116, 121–122, 203,
    254, 322
Chin, Bobby 107
Chirac, Jacques 32
choices, making difficult
    46–49, 102, 114, 197
Churchill, Clementine 173
Churchill, Winston 57, 206,
    286, 306
Chyzhykov, Gennadiy 204,
    208
Citizen Entrepreneurial
    Development Agency 42
Čiurlionis, M.K. 2
civil service
    Argentina 228
    Baltic states 148
    Botswana 45
    Egypt 263
    Estonia 146, 148, 152
    Singapore 13
    South Africa 10–11,
        72–73, 80
    Spain 182
Clausewitz, Carl von 21
Clegg, Johnny 67
climate change 128, 282
clothing and textiles
    industries 36, 53–54, 322
coal 78, 83
Coalition Provisional
    Authority *see* CPA
Cold War 37, 150–151, 178, 318

Collor de Mello, Fernando 211
Colombia 212, 213
colonialism
  Africa 37, 317–319
  Botswana 41
  Comoros 62
  Latin America 212–213
  Mauritius 55–56
  Peru 238–239, 245
  Singapore 97, 101–102, 113–114
  Ukraine 194, 197
  Vietnam 116–117
Command 304–305
command economy 198
commodities 36–37, 230–231
communism 127, 165, 309
Communist Party (Lithuania) 139
Communist Party of Vietnam 127, 129
Communist Party (Soviet Union) 3, 6
Comoros 18, 57–65, 303
competitiveness 13, 32, 46–49, 126, 140
Congo 35, 95, 212–213, 286
Congress of People's Deputies of the Soviet Union 3–4
Congress of Peru 243–244, 252
Connected Development 25
constitution
  of Comoros 64
  of Mauritius 57
  of Peru 244–245, 254–255
  of Spain 174, 180
consumption culture 61–62
Container Port Performance Index 84
Convertibility Law (Argentina) 226
Copenhagen criteria 141
copper industry 8, 41, 245–248

corn 202–203
Correa, Rafael 212
corruption
  Argentina 228, 233
  Baltic states 148
  Botswana 40
  Egypt 261
  Iraq 282
  Latin America 212
  Mexico 213
  Nigeria 24–25
  Peru 238, 248, 251–254
  South Africa 70, 78, 80, 86–87
  Spain 175–176, 180
  Ukraine 201, 206
  Vietnam 127
Corruption Perceptions Index 126–127, 201, 228
Costa Rica 212
Côte d'Ivoire 35
Cotonou Agreement 34
coups d'état
  Africa 211
  Argentina 221–222, 234
  Comoros 57–59, 61, 64–65
  Egypt 262, 268
  Iraq 276
  Latin America 211
  Lesotho 54
  Madagascar 57
  Morocco 290
  Nigeria 26
  Peru 239–240
  Spain 174–176
  Togo 32–33
Cournut, Théodore 285
Coutts-Trotter, David 50, 63
Covid-19 pandemic 11, 46, 72, 81, 83, 233, 296
CPA 278–279
CPF 102, 106–107, 111
crime 11, 54, 75–76, 75, 139, 213, 219, 253–254
Crimean Peninsula 191
crises 290
criticism 302, 307–308

crony capitalism 37, 198, 200–201
Crook, David 173
CRRC Corporation 83
Cuba 175
cultural aspects 61–62, 64, 69, 122, 272, 297, 303
currencies 10, 49, 145–147, 219, 244, 264

DA 67, 89
De Aar, South Africa 82
Death of a Loyalist Soldier (photograph) 174
De Beers 18, 39, 41–42, 47, 77
De Beers Global Sightholder Sales 47
Debswana joint venture 41, 45
debt 72, 152, 162, 227, 233, 264, 267–268, 282
decentralisation 248
deception 174
decolonisation 35
deforestation 61
De Klerk, F.W. 188
De la Calle, Luis 215
De la Rúa, Fernando 224, 226
democracy
  Africa 21–22, 37, 303
  Arab Spring 259–261
  Botswana 40, 43–44
  economic growth and 21–22, 301
  Egypt 268
  Latin America 212
  Mauritius 18, 55, 57
  Nigeria 24–25
  Poland 164, 169–170
  Singapore 111
  South Africa 69, 88
  Ukraine 195–197, 206–207
Democracy Index 212, 260
Democratic Alliance *see* DA
Democratic Centre Union 180
Democratic Front 243

Democratic Republic
  of Congo (DRC)
  see Congo
Denard, Bob 58–61
Deng Xiaoping 94, 301
dependency 44–45, 105, 297
deregulation 147
De Ruyter, André 87
desalination plants 294
Desker, Barry 13, 112
DGSE 59
diamond industry 39, 41–42, 44–47
Diamond Processing Zone 38
Diamond Trading Company (DTC) *see* De Beers Global Sightholder Sales
dictatorship 9, 101, 113, 186–187, 303
Dien Bien Phu, Battle of 120–121
digitisation 140, 143–144, 146–147
dioxin 117, 197
diplomacy 305
Directorate-General for External Security *see* DGSE
diversification 36, 42–49, 52, 55, 113, 273, 302
Doan Ngoc Hai 126
dodos 50, 65–66
Dogs of War, The 59
Doi Moi 122–123, 126–128
Doing Business index (2007) 93
donor funding *see* aid
DRC *see* Congo
drones 150, 205
drug abuse 72, 99
Dubai 273
Dubai Ports World 84, 250
Duda, Andrzej 168
Duhalde, Eduardo 217, 226–227, 229
Duong Van Minh 115, 129

Ease of Doing Business index 51
East Asia 94–95, 322
Easterly, William 88
Eastern Cape, South Africa 67, 79–81
Economic Development Board, Singapore 103
economic freedom 144, 201–202
economic growth
  Africa 35–37
  Argentina 218–220, 223, 225–226
  Baltic states 140
  Botswana 38–39, *40*, 49
  Comoros 60
  Egypt 263
  Estonia 145, 152–153
  Latvia 141–142
  Malawi 311
  Mauritius 18, 35, 52
  Morocco 35, 291
  Peru 237–239, 243, 251
  Poland 156–157, 164, *199*
  South Africa 11, 35, 51, 70, 74, 77, 87, 183–184, *184*
  Spain 178–181, 183–184, *184*
  sub-Saharan African 15
  Ukraine 199–200, *199*
  Vietnam 115–116, 122–123, 127–128
economic policies 9, 13–14, 40, 70, 122–123, 147, 170, 302
Economic Recovery Act *see* Marshall Plan
Economist Intelligence Unit 21, 212, 260
Ecuador 211–212, 244
education
  Arab world 272
  Baltic states 150
  Botswana 39, 45
  Mauritius 55
  Poland 161, 170

Singapore 108–109, *109*
South Africa 11–12, 85
Spain 182
Vietnam 126
Zanzibar 63
see also training
EEC 34, 181, 187
egoism 305, 307–308, 310
e-government 9–10, 142, 143–147, 152
E-Government Development Index 144
E-Government Survey 143–144
Egypt
  Arab Spring 259–260
  challenges 285
  economic growth 263, 271
  elites 261, 269
  history of 260–269
  investment 265, 267
  poverty 261–262
  reforms 263–265, 267–270
  unemployment 261–262
  wheat 203
El Alamein, Egypt 265–267
ElBaradei, Mohamed 260, 263
El dos de mayo de 1808 (painting) 174
elections
  Argentina 230–232
  Mauritius 57
  Nigeria 25–28
  Peru 254–255
  Poland 164, 169
  Singapore 110
  Spain 180
  Togo 34
  Ukraine 197
electricity 12, 63, 67, 69–70, 76–78, 85–87, 93
elites
  Africa 35, 37
  Argentina 220–221, 223–224, 232, 234
  Botswana 40–41, 47–49

Comoros 58
Egypt 261, 269
impact of 1, 21, 23–24, 297–298, 319, 323
Iraq 282
Malawi 312
Mauritius 54
Peru 238
Poland 168
South Africa 70–71, 90
Togo 32, 34
Ukraine 196
Elkabetz, Ronit 295
Elmaleh, Victor 295
Elorriaga, Gabriel 181, 186, 188
El Salvador 211
El-Sisi, Abdel Fattah 260, 262–265, 267–268
El tres de mayo de 1808 (painting) 174
Emanuel, Rahm 284
emigration *see* immigration
empathy 234–235
employment 45, 70, 82–83, 107–108, 125, 245, 291–292
see also unemployment
energy sector 143
entrepreneurship 43, 45, 56, 148, 153, 271–273
environmentalism 128
E-Participation Index 144
EPZs 18, 52–53, 56, 93–94
Eritrea 55
Escolano, Román 179, 185, 187
Eskom 12, 77–78, 86–88
Essaouira, Morocco 284–285, 294–296
Estonia
economic growth 142, 145, 152–153
e-government 9–10, 142, 143–147, 152
independence of 139–142, 144

past, break with 148–153
reforms 145–148, 152
rural areas 137
Second World War 137
Soviet Union and 2–3, 9–10, 136, 138–139, 142–144, 148–153
successes 16, 153–154
Estonian War of Independence 143
Eswatini 54
Ethiopia 23, 35, 203
ethnic diversity 40, 52–53, 57–58, 95, 110, 140, 251, 301
EU
Comoros 64
GDP per capita *199*
impact of 134, 301
Latvia 139, 141, 153
Lithuania 6, 133, 149, 153
Morocco 287
Poland 164, 169
Spain 13, 185
Togo 33–34
Ukraine 15, 197, 200, 208
euro 185
Euromaidan protests 15
European Economic Community *see* EEC
European identity 185
European Solidarity Centre 155, 170–171
European Union *see* EU
eurozone 152
Evita (film) 217
exceptionalism, Spain 179–180
exchange rates 23, 55, 226
export processing zones *see* EPZs
exports 41, 123, 237, *246*
externalising of solutions 301, 318–319, 321
extraction 9, 37, 166
Eyadéma, Étienne Gnassingbé 32–34

Faisal, King 275
Faisal II, King 276
Falklands 292
family planning 108
famines 192–194
see also hunger
Fangio, Juan Manuel 232
farming *see* agriculture sector
Farouk, King 268
Farquhar, William 98
fascism 177, 189
Fayeq, Rewaz 278, 281, 283
FDI 52, 117, 119, 122, 213, 244
Feldman, Oleksandr 192
Ferdinand VII, King 174
Ferguson, Bruce 283
Fernández, Alberto 217, 230
Fernández de Kirchner, Cristina *see* Kirchner, Cristina Fernández de
fertility rate 108
Fighting Solidarity 168
film industry 288, 291
Financial Assistance Policy 42
financial crisis of 2008 87, 182, 231
Finland 143, 147
First Carlist War 174
First Indochina War 120–121
First Iraqi–Kurdish War 276
First Opium War 94
First World War 136–137, 221
fisheries 64
fishing 313–314
fishmeal 254
Flores Nano, Lourdes 242–243
Fomboni Accords 65
Forbes 201
foreign direct investment *see* FDI
foreigners, attitudes towards 53, 117, 298, 319
foreign investment *see* investment

INDEX

foreign policy 86–87, 186–188, 206
Foreshores Act (Singapore) 106
Formula One World Championship 232
Forsyth, Frederick 318
forthrightness 283
For Whom the Bell Tolls 174
FOZ *see* Ortiz de Zevallos, Felipe (FOZ)
Fraga, Rosendo 222
France 32–34, 50, 59–62, 116, 120–121, 174, 295
Franco, Francisco 12–13, 21, 172, 177–180, 186–190, 293
Frankel, Jeffrey 58
Fraser Institute 144
freedom 2, 6, 21, 40, 55, 139–142, 186, 201–202
Freedom House 21, 40, 55
free-trade agreements 125, 249, 287
French Chamber of Commerce and Industry of Morocco 295
Freyberg, Bernard 304–305
Fujimori, Alberto 211, 236–238, 241–246, 249–252
Fujimori, Keiko 251, 254
Fukuyama, Francis 196, 200
funding for political parties 25, 253
Furber, Geoff and Liz 314

Gabon 35
Gaborone, Botswana 38–39
Gaddafi, Muammar 34, 86, 259, 285
garbage 269–270
Garbage City, Egypt 269–270
García, Alan 240–244, 251–253, 255
gas from Russia 200

Gdańsk, Poland 155–157
Gdańsk Science and Technology Park 156
Gdańsk Shipyard 155–156, 171
Gdańsk's Museum of the Second World War 157
GDP 11, 133, 152, 199, 219, 241, 280
GDP per capita
  Argentina 184, 223
  Baltic states 141
  Botswana 40
  Egypt 263
  Estonia 9–10, 144
  Mauritius 51, *51*
  Nigeria 24
  Peru 237, *237*
  Poland *164*
  Singapore 100
  South Africa 183–184, *184*
  Spain 183–184, *184*
  sub-Saharan African *184*
  Ukraine 199
  Vietnam 115, *116*, 123
General Household Survey (2021) 89
geography, benefits of 98, 105, 157, 170, 255, 303
Germany 2–3, 136, 143, 157, 159, 172–173, 317
Ghana 55, 286
Ghani, Ashraf 304
Ghonim, Wael 260
Gierek, Edward 162
Gini coefficient 70
  see also inequality
glasnost 3
Glencore 247
Global Competitiveness Index 40, 201
global financial crisis of 2008 87, 182, 231
Global Initiative Against Transnational Organized Crime 75, 213
globalisation 50, 98, 103, 125, 185–186

global support, for Ukraine 198
Gnaoua World Music Festival 296
Gnassingbé, Faure 33
Goh Chok Tong 95, 104–105, 110–112
Goh Keng Swee 100, 107, 111
gold 173, 245
Golden Tulip hotel 63
Gomułka, Władysław 162
Gonchar, Viktor 171
González, Felipe 13, 180–181, 190
Google 260
Gorbachev, Mikhail 3–6, 138–139, 194
Gordhan, Pravin 87
Górzyński, Józef 155–156
Gotland Communiqué 2
Gouilame, Fouday 58
governance 67, 70, 86, 89, 201, 299–300, 302, 317, 319
government spending 95, 225–226, 299
Goya, Francisco 174
Gqabi, Joe 118
Graduate Mothers' Scheme 111–112
Graham, John 68
Gran Café de Paris, Morocco 288
grants *see* welfare payments
Great Depression 176–177, 221
Greece 134
'Green Book' 118–119
Greenland 292
Grocott's Mail 68
gross domestic product *see* GDP
growth *see* economic growth
Grunitzky, Nicolas 32
Guam 175
Guatemala 252
Guernica (painting) 174, 188
Guernica, Spain 188
Guerra, Alfonso 181

INDEX

Guinea 211–213
Gukurahundi genocide 75–76
Gula, Bernard 313
Gulag 137
Gulf War 278
Gupta family 83
Guriev, Sergei 303
Guzmán, Abimael 236–237

Halabja, Iraq 276–278
Halawa, Hafsa 264
Halberstam, David 308–309
Hani, Chris 69, 118, 167
Hassan II, King 290, 292–295
HDB 106–107
Hedges, Jill 220
helplessness 297
Hemingway, Ernest 174, 190
Heritage Foundation 40, 53, 144, 201
Hernández, Pablo 181
'heterodox' trade policy 53
Hichilema, Hakainde 7–8, 297–298, 304
Hill-Lewis, Geordin 37
Historical Memory Law (Spain) 190
history, impact of 97, 170, 309
Hitachi 78
Hitler, Adolf 2–3, 159–160, 173, 194
Hobart, Percy 304–305
Ho Chi Minh 116–117, 120, 129–130
Ho Chi Minh City 124, 129
Ho Chi Minh Stock Exchange 119
Holbrooke, Richard 309
Holland, James 305–306
Holocaust 135, 154
Holodomor 192–194
Homage to Catalonia 174, 190
Hong Kong 96
Ho, Peter 106
Houari, Rachid 287

housing 85, 106–107, 109, 144
Housing and Development Board *see* HDB
Howard, Sir Esmé 175–176
Humala, Ollanta 247, 251–252
Human Development Index 61
Human Rights Watch 127
hunger 163, 193–194
Huntington, Samuel 149, 154
Hurtado Miller, Juan Carlos 241–242
Hussein, Saddam 19, 274–280, 310
hyperinflation 199, 241
see also inflation
Hyundai plant 43

Ibrahim Index of African Governance 51
ICJ 292
identity 69, 274
identity politics 1, 16, 85, 254, 302
ideology 128–129
IDZs 123–125
Ilves, Ieva 148
IMA Casablanca (Institut des Métiers de l'Aéronautique) 289
IMF
  Argentina 218, 231, 233
  Egypt 263–264
  Estonia 145
  Morocco 290
  Peru 241–243
  Spain 12, 178–179
  Ukraine 203
immigration 81, 103, 185–188, 221, 238, 272, 282
immunity 180
import substitution 23
Inca empire 212, 238–239, 249
incentives 13–14
indentured workers 50

independence 139–142, 147, 152, 197–198, 240, 252–253
Index of Economic Freedom 40, 53, 144, 201
India 45, 50, 203, 224, 322
Indonesia 95, 99–100, 203, 322
industrial development zones *see* IDZs
industrialisation 42–43, 291
industrial parks 127, 129, 214–215
inequality
  Argentina 230–231
  basic services and 323
  Egypt 261–262, 270
  Latin America 212
  Mauritius 18, 52
  Morocco 290
  Peru 248
  Singapore 99–100
  South Africa 70, 72
  Spain 175–176, 182
inflation
  Argentina 219, 225–226, 229, 233, 235
  Egypt 264
  Estonia 145
  Peru 241
  Ukraine 199
  Vietnam 116, 122
informal sector 126, 234, 238, 254
infrastructure
  Botswana 46–47
  Comoros 64
  Egypt 264
  importance of 95, 322–323
  Iraq 280
  Morocco 285–290
  Singapore 104
  South Africa 67
  Spain 182
  Vietnam 95
innovation 295–296
  see also technology

362

INDEX

instability *see* stability
Institut des Métiers de l'Aéronautique (IMA Casablanca) 289
institutions, importance of 1, 7–19, 297, 308
  Argentina 228, 232
  Botswana 40–41
  Egypt 265
  Iraq 283
  Mauritius 54–56
  Peru 252–253, 255
  Singapore 95, 102–103
  South Africa 11, 77, 85
  Spain 183–184, 186–187
  Ukraine 200, 206
intelligence services 161
International Court of Justice *see* ICJ
International Monetary Fund *see* IMF
international relations *see* foreign policy
international support, for Ukraine 198
International Trade Administration 250
internet 147
investment
  Egypt 265, 267
  impact of 302, 322–323
  Israel 271–272
  Mauritius 52, 55
  Mexico 213
  Morocco 291
  Peru 244, 254–255
  Singapore 103–104, 107–108
  Spain 178–179, 185–186
  Ukraine 200, 208
  Vietnam 117, 119, 122–126
  Zambia 7–9
Iran 279
Iran–Iraq War 274, 276
Iraq 274–283
  challenges 19
  history of 274–276

Hussein, Saddam 274–280
Iraq War 274
Kurdish population 275–276, 278–283
oil industry 275, 281–282
Shia group 275, 278–279
violence 276–278, 280
IS 275, 280
Isabella II, Queen 174
Iscor 77
Islam 261–262, 268, 285
Islamic State *see* IS
Israel 45, 260, 268, 271–273
Issoufou, Mahamadou 211
Italy 172–173
Itodo, Samson 27

Jabir, Shaikh 262
Jaffar, Said Mohamed 60
Jansons, Raimonds 138
Japan 94, 116, 251
Jarama, Battle of 189
Jaruzelski, Wojciech 156
Jasina, Łukasz 169
Jazouli, Mohcine 289, 292
Jefferson, Thomas 130, 309
Jewish community 94, 133, 135–137, 157–160, 170, 173, 285, 295
Jiménez, Juan 247, 255
job creation *see* employment
Johannesburg, South Africa 85–86, 269
John Paul II, Pope 169, 170
Johnson, Lyndon B. 309
Johnson, Simon 40–41, 54–55
Jordaan, Hendrik 229, 231
Jordan 271
Joseph Bonaparte 174
Juan Carlos I, King 13, 180
Judicial Commission of Inquiry into Allegations of State Capture, Corruption and Fraud in the Public Sector *see* Zondo Commission

Jurong Town Corporation complex 107
Juršėnas, Česlovas 4–5
Justicialist Party 222
Jwaneng diamond mine 42, 45–47

Kabye ethnic group 32
Kagame, Paul 300
Kalahari 38
Kaliningrad 150
Kallas, Kaja 146
Kallas, Siim 145–146
Kano, Nigeria 26
Kant, Immanuel 150
Kazungula Bridge 46
KDP 276, 278–280
Kehris, Ojārs 149, 154
Kennedy, John F. 115, 309
Kenya 48, 51, 55, 100, 269
Kerzner, Sol 60
key man risk 110
KGB 3, 4, 137, 152
Khama, Ian 43–44, 47
Khama, Sir Seretse 38–39, 41
Kharkiv, Ukraine 204
Khoan, Vu 122, 127
Kicillof, Axel 227
Kionka, Riina 146, 152
Kipling, John 306
Kipling, Rudyard 306
Kirchner, Cristina Fernández de 212, 217–219, 227–230, 232–234
Kirchnerism 227
Kirchner, Néstor 217, 227–229, 233
Kiyosaki, Robert 297
Kléber, Emilio (aka Manfred Stern) 173
Klympush-Tsintsadze, Ivanna 195
knowledge economy 45
knowledge process outsourcing *see* KPO
Kojala, Linas 141
Kombinat No. 7 151–152

363

KPO 156
Kraków, Poland 170
Krasovsky, Anatoly 171
KrAZ 199
KRG 275, 279, 281
KRI 278, 280–283
Kross, Eerik-Niiles 152
Kubilius, Andrius 6, 140–141, 146, 149
Kuczynski, Pedro Pablo 252
Kukliansky, Faina 154
Kurdish population 275–276, 278–283
Kurdistan Democratic Party see KDP
Kurdistan Regional Government see KRG
Kurdistan Region of the Republic of Iraq see KRI
Kuwait 8, 278

Laar, Mart 10, 144–147, 149
labour costs 93, *93*, 124–125, 214–215, 250, 290, 322
La Bourdonnais, Bertrand-François Mahé de 56
labour flexibility 249
Labour Party (Mauritius) 50–51, 56
labour relations 104–105
labour shortage 186
Ladybrand, South Africa 84
Lagos, Nigeria 286
Lake Malawi 313–314
Lake, Tony 309
Lamb, David 119, 129
Lamina, Mansour 294
Lanata, Claudio 237–238
Land Acquisition Act (Singapore) 106
Land Law (Peru) 246
land reform 102, 106–107, 162, 221
Landsbergis, Gabrielius 5
Landsbergis, Vytautas 2–7
language groups 95, 140
Las Bambas copper mine 247

Lase, Ieva 138
Laspina, Luciano 235
Latin America 185–188, 211–212, 223
Latvia 135–154
 economic growth 141–142
 First World War 137
 governance 139
 independence of 139–142
 oligarchs 147–148
 past, break with 148–150
 rural areas 137
 Second World War 137
 Soviet Union and 2–3, 138–139, 148–150, 153, 298
 successes 153–154
 violence 135–138
Lavagna, Roberto 228
Law and Justice see PiS
laws 145
leadership
 Africa 297, 310–311
 Estonia 144–147
 importance of 298, 302–303, 323
 institutions, importance of 7–19
 Mauritius 55
 qualities of good 303–310
 Singapore 110
 South Africa 17, 88
 strategy 19–28
 Ukraine 192–195, 204–206
 Vietnam 129–130
Lebanon 203, 259, 271
Le Duan 121–122, 129
Lee Hsien Loong 13, 112–113
Lee Kuan Yew 13, 95, 97–98, 100–107, 110–114, 272, 305, 310
Le Galawa hotel 62–63
Lenin, Vladimir 160
Le Phuoc Minh 120
Leshchenko, Serhiy 195
Lesotho 35–36, 53–54, 84
lessons 112–114

liberation struggles 70, 282, 301
Libya 34, 203, 259, 285
Lietuvos Persitvarkymo Sąjūdis see Sąjūdis
life expectancy 52, *116*, 128, 176, 178, 199
Lima, Peru 239, 254
Lim Boon Keng 99
Linh Trung industrial park 124–125
Lin, Justin 93–94
listening post in Comoros 59–60
literacy 39, 55, 63, 100, *116*, 126, 139, 176
Lithuania 2–7, 133, 136–142, 147–150, 153–154
Lithuanian Congress of People's Deputies 4
Liu Thai Ker 106
Lloyd's List of top 100 busiest ports (2021) 31
loadshedding 12, 67, 70, 76–78, 87
 see also electricity
local communities, relations with 247–248
Local Enterprise Authority 43
local governance 67, 70
local ownership of problems 301, 318–319, 321
Local Procurement Programme 43
logistical systems 280
lokasie see townships
Lomé Convention 34
Lomé, Togo 31–32
López Murphy, Ricardo 217, 223, 228
Lovedale see Alice, South Africa
Luanda, Angola 287
LuAZ 199
Lukács, Pál (aka Máté Zalka aka Béla Frankl) 173
Lukashenko, Alexander 171

Łukasiewicz, Piotr 170
Lukiškės Square, Lithuania 3
Lungu, Edgar 7, 303–304
Łupina, Andrzej 169
Lutheran Church 152
Luthuli House 87

Mabhida, Moses 118
Macera, Diego 243, 245
Macmillan, Harold 305
Macri, Mauricio 217, 219–220, 224, 229–234
Madagascar 18, 51, 57, 63
Madrid Accords 293
'magic solutions' 302
Maidan Revolution 191, 197, 208
maize 203
al-Majid, Ali Hassan 276–277
Make, Cassius 118
Makgoba, Thabo 311
Makhanda ka Nxele 68
Makhanda, South Africa 67–70, 81
malaria 313–314
Malawi 22–23, 311–315
Malaysia 95, 99–100, 322
Mali 34, 211
al-Maliki, Nouri 281
Malloch, Jack 59
malnutrition 163, 238
Mandela, Nelson 20, 69, 79, 86
Manshiyat Naser, Egypt 269–270
manufacturing sector 107, 143, 213–215, 322
Mao Zedong 94
maquiladoras 214–215
maritime trade 64
market access 317–318
Marrakesh, Morocco 286
Marshall, George C. 307–308, 316
Marshall Plan 177, 316–317
Martínez Rico, Ricardo 185

Masisi, Mokgweetsi 47
Mass Rapid Transit system see MRT
Matekane, Sam 36
mathematics 109, 160–161
matric results 11, 89
Mauritania 286, 292–293
Mauritian Militant Movement see MMM
Mauritian Social Democratic Party 51, 56
Mauritius 50–66
 crime 54
 economic growth 18, 35, 52
 education 55
 history of 50–51
 Human Development Index 61
 institutions, importance of 54–56
 investment 52, 55
 successes 51–58, 65–66, 303
 tourism 52, 63
Mavuso, Busisiwe 79, 86–87
'May God help us' speech 242
Mbeki, Govan 118
Mbeki, Thabo 118
McNamara, Robert 309
Meade, James 52, 65
meat 41, 162–163, 220, 224–225
media 118–119, 127, 253, 305
megaprojects 264
Mein Kampf 194
memorials 32–33, 133, 142, 148–149, 155, 159–161, 172, 189, 234, 277
Mendès-France, Pierre 58
Menem, Carlos 211, 217, 219, 225–226, 233
Menem, Eduardo 226, 229–230
mercenaries 58–59, 60, 65
Mercosur (Southern Common Market) 187
Merriman, Robert Hale 173, 189

Mexico 14, 212–215, 228, 301
México Evalúa 14
Mhlaba, Raymond 69
middle class 183, 260
Middle East and North Africa region 8, 285
Mielke, Erich 173
migration see immigration
militaries
 Argentina 221, 224
 Egypt 260–265, 267–268, 270
 Latin America 211
 Mauritius 57–58
 Peru 239–240
 Spain 175, 182
 Ukraine 150, 191–192
Millennium Villages Project 313
Mines and Minerals Act (Botswana) 41
mining sector 7–9, 44, 76, 245–248, 310
MiSUMi 125
MMG 247
MMM 51, 56
Mobutu Sese Seko 48, 307
Moccia, Franco 218, 220, 222, 232
Modise, Joe 117–118
Mohammed III, King 284–285
Mohammed VI, King 286, 290, 294–295
Molefe, Brian 83
Molotov–Ribbentrop Pact 136, 157
Monastery of Saint Simon the Tanner 269
Mongolia 292
Montesinos, Vladimiro 251
Montgomery, Bernard 304–307
monuments 32–33, 133, 142, 148–149, 155, 159–161, 172, 189, 234, 277
Morales, Evo 212, 252

INDEX

Morawiecki, Kornel 168–169
Morocco 284–296
  bonds 268
  challenges 291–292
  champions 290–291
  colonialism 175
  economic growth 35, 291, 301
  Essaouira 284–285, 294–296
  history of 284–286, 290, 294–295
  infrastructure 285–290
  reforms 18, 285–286
  renewable energy 288–289
  Tangier 286–288, 291
  Western Sahara and 292–294
Morsi, Mohamed 260, 262–263
mosquito nets 313–314
motor industry 163, 178, 198–199, 215
Mount Handrin, Battle of 276
Mount Karthala, Comoros 62
Mozambique 12, 212–213
Mpinganjira, Agnes 314
MRT 111
MRTA 236–237, 242
Msaidie, Houmed 64
Mubarak, Gamal 261
Mubarak, Hosni 259–264
Mugabe, Robert 75–76
Muhammad Ali Pasha 260
Muhammed, Murtala 26
municipalities, in South Africa 67, 80
Munira, Egypt 262
Munyama, Killion 169
murder rate 54, 139
Murray, Al 304–305
Museveni, Yoweri 206
music festivals 296
Muslim Brotherhood 260, 262
Mussolini, Benito 173, 222–223

Mutharika, Peter 313
Myanmar (Burma) 95, 213

NAFTA 14, 213–215, 301
Naguib, Mohamed 261–262
Naked Lunch 287–288
Namibia 12, 54, 76
Nano, Flores 244
Napoleon Bonaparte 150, 174
Narva, Estonia 142–144, 151
Nasser, Gamal Abdel 261–263
Nathan, S.R. 97–98
National Democratic Party 260
nationalisation 8, 56–57, 103, 162, 182
nationalism 116, 140, 194, 232–233, 302
National Museum of the Holodomor-Genocide 193–194
NATO
  Baltic states 139, 149–150, 153
  Lithuania 6
  Spain 13, 181
  Togo 34
  Ukraine 15, 197, 200
natural resources 38–39, 224, 282
Nazi Germany 136, 157
Nehru, Jawaharlal 173
Nemyria, Hryhoriy 193, 198
Netherlands 50, 162
nets 313–314
New Alamein, Egypt 265–267
New York Times 118
Ngiam Tong Dow 107
Ngwira, Force 314
Nicaragua 211
Niger 211
Nigeria 23–28, 35, 48, 55, 95, 286, 318
Njoku, Emmanuel 25
Nkrumah, Kwame 105

Nkumbi, Gladwell 82
NKVD 3, 173
Nolting, Frederick 309
Noor I facility 288–289
North American Free Trade Agreement *see* NAFTA
North Atlantic Treaty Organization *see* NATO
nostalgia 282
nyaope 72
Nzo, Alfred 118

Obasanjo, Olusegun 24, 297
OCP Group 294
Odessa File, The (film) 135
Odinga, Raila 100
O'Donnell, Guillermo 149
OECD 178, 200
oil industry 8, 23, 180, 214, 275, 281–282
oligarchs 147–148, 198, 201–202, 234
Olympics (1992) 6
Olympio, Gilchrist 33
Olympio, Sylvanus 32
opium 99
opposition voices 2, 111, 302
Orange Revolution 15, 197, 208
Orapa mine 41, 47
Organisation for Economic Co-operation and Development *see* OECD
Organized Crime Index 75
Ortega, Daniel 211
Ortiz de Zevallos, Felipe (FOZ) 241–243, 248
Orwell, George 174, 190
Othello (film) 284
Ottoman empire 275
Ouarzazate, Morocco 288

Pabriks, Artis 139–140, 150, 297–298
Pact of Forgetting 189–190
Pact of Madrid 178

366

Pakistan 203
Palace of Culture and Science 161
Palestine 271
Palmer, Matthew 194
PAP 100, 109–110
parastatals *see* SOEs
Passenger Rail Agency of South Africa *see* PRASA
past, break with 96–97, 116–117, 148–153, 188, 190, 300–301, 309
Patriotic Union of Kurdistan *see* PUK
patronage 68–69, 78, 86, 221, 297–298, 304
Patton, George 304–305, 307
Pavilionis, Žygimantas 149
Pei, I.M. 106
Peña, Marcos 231, 235
pension schemes 166, 219
People's Action Party *see* PAP
People's Commissariat for Internal Affairs *see* NKVD
People's Democratic Party 25
People's Party *see* PP
'people's war' 117–119, 121
per capita consumption 241
per capita income
 Africa 35
 Argentina 184–185, 218
 Botswana 38–39, *40*
 Comoros 58
 Israel 271
 Latvia 141–142
 Poland 164
 South Africa 74–75, *74*
 Spain 182
 Vietnam 123
 Zanzibar 63
per capita wealth 145
perestroika 3, 138–139, 144, 194
performance 13–14, 108–109, 112
Perón, Eva 217, 222, 233

Peronism 217–224, 231–234
Perón, Juan Domingo 22, 178, 211, 217, 220, 222–224, 232–234
Pertino, Miguel 224
Peru 236–255
 agriculture sector 237–240, 246, 249–250
 crime 253–254
 economic growth 237–239, 243, 251
 Fujimori, Alberto 211, 236–238, 241–246, 249–252
 history of 236–237, 238–241
 Inca empire 212, 238–239, 249
 institutions, importance of 252–253, 255
 investment 244, 254–255
 leadership 311
 mining sector 245–248
 poverty 238, 241, 250–251
 reforms 241–245, 250–251, 253, 255
Peruvian Armed Forces 236, 240
Peshmerga 281, 282
Peter the Great 142
Petraeus, David 307–308
Philby, Kim 173
Philippines 94–95, 175, 322
phosphate 294
Picasso, Pablo 174, 188
pigs 269
Piliso, Mzwai 118
Piłsudski Square, Poland 160–161
Pinochet, Augusto 13
Pinto, David 295
Piqué, Josep 182–183, 190
PiS 166, 167
Pizarro, Francisco 239
planning 302, 319–321
Plettenberg Bay, South Africa 71

Podolyak, Mykhailo 205
Poland 155–171
 economic growth 156–157, 164, *199*
 immigration 208
 reforms 14, 165–167
 Second World War 155, 157–161, 163, 170
 Solidarity trade union movement 14, 155–156, 164–165, 167–169
 Soviet Union and 160–164
 successes 18, 169–171, 302
 Wałęsa, Lech 14, 155–156, 164–165, 169–170
Polisario Front 292–294
Polish United Workers' Party *see* PZPR
politeness 305
political economy 22
political parties, funding for 25, 253
political stability *see* stability
politics, impact of 1, 8, 15, 21–22, 32, 54, 69, 109–112, 252, 299–301, 323–324
population size
 Africa 19
 Argentina 224
 Egypt 261
 Israel 271
 Lesotho 54
 Malawi 313
 Middle East and North Africa region 285
 Morocco 291–292
 Peru 239
 Poland 160
 South Africa 85
 Spain 186
 Vietnam *116*
populism 1, 20, 88, 206, 211–212, 222, 224, 232, 253
Poroshenko, Petro 197

ports 31, 63–64, 84, 88, 98–99, 104, 250, 286–287, 293–294
POUM 173, 190
poverty
  Africa 36
  Argentina 218, 222–224, 228, 231, 233, 235
  Botswana 44
  Comoros 58, 61
  Egypt 261–262
  Latvia 139
  Lesotho 54
  Malawi 313
  Morocco 291–292
  Peru 238, 241, 250–251
  Singapore 100
  South Africa 72, 88
  Vietnam 116, 128
power 1, 13, 109–112
PP 181–182
pragmatism 129–130
PRASA 81–82
Prat-Gay, Alfonso 17, 230–232
Primo de Rivera, José Antonio 174
Primo de Rivera, Miguel 176
private sector
  Argentina 17
  Botswana 48–49
  China 93
  Comoros 63–64
  impact of 7–8, 299–300, 319
  Mauritius 56–57
  Peru 240, 253
  Singapore 102, 104, 113
  South Africa 51, 73, 78–79, 88, 299–300
  Vietnam 126–127
privatisation
  Argentina 219, 226
  Baltic states 147, 149
  Egypt 263
  Estonia 144–145
  impact of 299

Peru 244–245
Poland 165–166
South Africa 77
Ukraine 201–202
Vietnam 119, 126
productivity 13–14, 72, 87, 321–323
Programme for International Student Assessment 152
Prometheus, statue of 151
propaganda 174
PRO party 229
property rights 50, 58
protectionism 223, 302
protests 104–105, 126, 212, 230–231, 292
  see also Arab Spring
PSOE 180–181
Public Enterprises Evaluation and Privatisation Agency 43
public expenditure
  see government spending
public listings 119
Puerto Rico 175
PUK 276, 278–280
punteros 227
Putin, Vladimir 142, 145–146, 170–171, 191–193, 195–197, 206–207, 309–310
PZL 161
PZPR 155, 160, 163

Qasim, Abd al-Karim 275–276
Qatar 8, 273
Quayle, Dan 242

R&D 272
race issues 20, 56, 70, 74, 212–213, 251, 317–318
Rachman, Gideon 196
Radical Civic Union see UCR
Raffles, Sir Thomas Stamford 97–98

Raik, Katri 145, 151–152
rail network 77, 80–84, 156, 255
Railways Police, South Africa 82–83
Rajoy, Mariano 182
Ralfe, Gary 42
Ramadan Revolution 276
Ramaphosa, Cyril 112–113
Ramgoolam, Sir Seewoosagur 51, 55–57
Ramírez, Óscar 237
rationing 162–163
Raymond Mhlaba Local Municipality 80
Reagan, Ronald 215
real gross domestic product 76–77
real per capita GDP 311
recycling 269–270
redistribution 10, 85, 167, 222, 224, 251, 301
Redrado, Martín 228
red tape see bureaucracy
Reform and Development Party 262
reforms
  Argentina 17, 218–220, 225–227, 230–232, 235
  Baltic states 147–149, 153–154
  Egypt 263–265, 267–270
  Estonia 145–148, 152
  Israel 271
  Morocco 18, 285–286
  Peru 241–245, 250–251, 253, 255
  Poland 14, 165–167
  reasons for success of 298, 300–303
  Singapore 110, 113–114, 310
  South Africa 73–74, 77, 83, 298
  Spain 181–182, 185
  Ukraine 195–198, 202–204, 208, 303
  Vietnam 119–120, 122–123

regional integration, Spain 187
Rejewski, Marian 161
remittances 61–62
Renault car plant 287, 289
renewable energy 288–289
rent-seeking
   Africa 22–24
   Egypt 263
   impact of 297–300, 302, 323
   Latvia 147
   Lesotho 54
   Malawi 312
   South Africa 16–17, 70, 72, 78–79, 85, 88–90
   Ukraine 200–201
Repsol 232–233
Republican Proposal (PRO) party *see* PRO party
research and development *see* R&D
Reserve Bank, Botswana 49
Revolutionary Command Council 276
Rhodesian Bush War 75–76
   see also Zimbabwe
Rhodes University College 68
Rich Dad, Poor Dad 297
Rico, Ricardo Martínez 181–182
Riga Autobus Factory 140
Riga, Latvia 135, 137–138, 140
right-wing politics 166–168
Ripple Africa 313–315
road network and transportation 78, 82–84, 156, 255
Robben Island 68, 69
Robinson, James 9, 40–41, 54–55
rocket launchers 204
Rodrigo, Luis Carlos 248
Rodríguez Zapatero, José Luis 318
Rogoff, Kenneth 219–220
Rolling Stones 161

Romaszewska, Zofia 168–169
Romejko, Wojciech 160
Romilly, Esmond 173
Roschmann, Eduard 135
rote solutions 319–321
Royal Air Maroc 289
Różycki, Jerzy 161
Rúa, Fernando de la 219, 224
rubbish *see* garbage
Rubio, Luis 14
Rumba, Aldis 137–138
Rumba, Rudolfus 137
Rumbula forest 135–136
rural areas 67, 115, 137, 166
Russia
   Baltic states 134, 139–140, 149–150
   Estonia 10, 145
   GDP per capita 199
   Togo 34
   Ukraine 14–15, 146, 150, 191–193, 195–196, 198, 206–208, 304
   see also Soviet Union
Rwanda 51, 300

Saavedra, José Carlos 247–248
Sachs, Jeffrey 313
Sadat, Anwar 261–265, 268
Sadat, Mohamed Anwar Esmat 262
Sahrawi Arab Democratic Republic 293
Sahrawis 292–293
Saied, Kais 259
Saint-Exupéry, Antoine de 172
Saint Sama'ans Church (Cave Cathedral) 269
Sąjūdis 2, 4, 140
Saleh, Ali Abdullah 259
Salter, Lord 280
sanitation 89
Sanjurjo, José 176
San Martín, José de 239
San people 38

São Tomé and Príncipe 55
Saudi Arabia 8, 279, 287
savings 102, 106–107
Saxon Palace 160–161
Schindler, Oskar 170
Schindler's List (film) 170
Schmitter, Philippe 149
schooling *see* education
Scioli, Daniel 229
Scott, Ridley 291
Second Chimurenga 75–76
Second Iraqi–Kurdish War 276
Second World War
   China 94
   Egypt 265–267
   Estonia 137, 142–143
   Latvia 136–137
   leadership 304–305, 308
   Lithuania 133
   Marshall Plan 317
   Poland 155, 157–161, 163, 170
   Spain 172–173, 177, 179, 188
   Vietnam 116–117, 130
security forces 57–58, 297
Selebi-Phikwe copper-nickel deposits 41
'self-coup' 243–244, 252
Serrano Elías, Jorge 252
Serra Puche, Jaime 213
Servant of the People (television show) 205
services sector 10, 43, 127, 156
7 Independent Company 59
sewerage 72
Seychelles 51, 55, 63
SEZs 126, 156, 284, 287
Shadala, Daban 275, 278–279
Shanmugaratnam, Tharman 13–14, 108–109
Sheftalovich, Zoya 206
Sheltering Sky, The 287–288
Sheremeta, Pavlo 201–202, 208
Shia group 275, 278–279
Shining Path 236–237, 240, 242–243, 245

INDEX

Shubin, Vladimir 118
Sillamäe, port of 151–152
'Silmet' facility 152
silver 245
Šimašius, Remigijus 140, 153
Šimonytė, Ingrida 149
Singapore 98–114
   authoritarianism 21, 94–95
   competitiveness 13–14
   education 108–109, *109*
   employment 107–108
   history of 98–101
   housing 106–107, 109
   investment 103–104, 107–108
   land 102, 106–107
   lessons from 102–105, 112–114
   past, break with 96–97, 300
   politics 109–112
   reforms 110, 113–114, 310
   successes 101, 301, 303, 310
   unemployment 111
Sir Seretse Khama International Airport 38
Skaisgirytė, Asta 6
skills
   Asia 95
   Baltic states 150
   Botswana 45
   Comoros 64
   impact of 317
   Mauritius 53
   Singapore 103, 110–111
   South Africa 78, 85
   Vietnam 126
   Zanzibar 63
   see also training
Skujenieks, Knuts 135
Skype 147
slavery 50, 194, 212–213
Slim, William 304–305, 308
Slovo, Joe 69, 118
slums *see* townships
Small Business Act (Botswana) 43

SMMEs (small, medium and micro enterprises) 37, 43
Sng Cheng Keh 107
Snyder, Timothy 194
socialism 7–8, 44–45, 115, 119, 127
Socialist Front 107
social media 212, 234–235, 260
social unrest *see* protests
SOEs 104, 119, 126–127, 180, 240, 263
'softer' aspects of leadership 20
Soilih, Ali 59–60
solar power 288–289
Solidarity trade union movement 14, 155–156, 164–165, 167–169
Somaliland 84
Soto, Hernando de 241
South Africa 67–90
   agriculture sector 250
   Botswana and 41, 44–45
   challenges 16–17, 70–79, 85–90
   Comoros and 59–60, 63
   Eastern Cape 67, 79–81
   economic growth 11, 35, 51, 70, 74, 77, 87, 183–184, *184*
   education 11–12, 85
   elites 70–71, 90
   history of 67–70, 86–87, 188
   immigration 187–188
   leadership 112–113
   Lesotho and 54
   Mauritius and 55
   Poland and 167
   ports 84, 88, 286–287
   poverty 72, 88
   private sector 44, 51, 73, 78–79, 88, 299–300
   reforms 10–12, 73–74, 77, 83, 298
   successes 85–86

   trade unions 228
   unemployment 67, 75, 75, 80–81, 89, 139
   welfare payments 72–74, 73, 89
South African Border War 76
South African Police 76, 83
South African Post Office 80
Southern African Customs Union 54
Southern Common Market (Mercosur) 187
Southern Sun 60
South Korea 94, 96, 215
South Sudan 55
Soviet Committee for State Security *see* KGB
Soviet Union
   Baltic states 133, 136–143, 148–151, 153, 298
   Estonia 142–143, 151
   Latvia 137–138, 298
   Lithuania 2–7, 133
   Peru 240
   Poland 14, 155–157, 160–164
   South Africa 69
   Spain 173
   Supreme Soviet 4
   Ukraine 192–194, 197–198
   Vietnam 121–122
   see also Russia
Spain 172–190
   challenges 188–190
   economic growth 178–181, 183–184, *184*
   European orientation 185, 318
   exceptionalism 179–180
   foreign policy 186–188
   Franco, Francisco 12–13, 21, 172, 177–180, 186–190, 293
   González, Felipe 13, 180–181, 190
   history of 172–177

institutions, importance of 183–184, 186–187
investment 178–179, 185–186
Latin America and 212
lessons from 186–188
past, break with 188, 190
Peru and 239, 245
reforms 181–182, 185
Spanish Civil War 172–174, 177, 179, 188–190
successes 182–185, 301
unemployment 177, 180–182, 186
Western Sahara 292–293
Spanish Civil War, The 175
Spanish Socialist Workers' Party *see* PSOE
special economic zones *see* SEZs
'spin dictator' 303
stability
  Africa 35
  Baltic states 148
  Botswana 49
  Egypt 268
  impact of 21–22, 302
  Lesotho 54
  Mauritius 50, 58, 63
  Morocco 287
  Peru 238
  Singapore 103
  South Africa 76
  Togo 33
  Vietnam 124
Stabilization Plan 178
Staķis, Mārtiņš 148–149
Stalin, Joseph 2–4, 140, 155, 159, 162, 172, 192–194
State Aviation Works *see* PZL
state capture 11
state employees *see* civil service
state-owned enterprises *see* SOEs

states, differences between rich and poor 297–298, 323–324
Statistics South Africa 81
Steele, Jonathan 4
steps, taking deliberate 112–114
Strait of Gibraltar 286
Straits Times 98
strategy 19–28
strengths 105
strikes *see* protests
'strong man' 101, 211–212, 254
Suárez, Adolfo 180, 188
sub-Saharan Africa 15, 35, 184
subsidies 218–219, 224
subsistence agriculture 238
  see also agriculture sector
successes, reasons for 299–303
Sucre, José de 240
Sudan 211–213
Suez Canal 52, 99
sugarcane 50, 52, 58
Sulaymaniyah, Iraq 283
sunflower oil 202–203
Supreme Soviet 4
Sutela, Pekka 200
Suwałki Gap 150
Syria 259–260, 271, 279

Tahrir Square, Egypt 270
Taiwan 94, 96
Takaful and Karama social protection programme 264
Take, Take, Take (song) 315–316
Talabani, Qubad 274, 279–280
talent 103
  see also skills
Tambo, Oliver 117–118
Tanger Med industrial port complex 286–287

Tangier, Morocco 286–288, 291
Tanzania 12, 35
taxes 55, 73, 73, 228–229, 246, 249, 254, 289, 321
taxi monopolies 83
technology 53, 146–147, 220, 271–272, 322
television 108
Temasek Holdings Ltd 104, 123
templatic responses to poverty 319–321
terrorism 33–34
tertiary sector 153, 156
textiles and clothing industries 36, 53–54, 322
Thatcher, Margaret 10, 13, 145, 149, 310
Third Carlist War 175
Thomas, Hugh 175–176
TIME 107, 189, 233
Time of the Hero, The 238
Times, The 173
TIMSS 109
tin 245
Tinubu, Bola 27–28
Togo 31–34
Toledo, Alejandro 248, 252–253
totalitarianism 2–3, 189
tourism
  Botswana 44–45
  Comoros 61–64
  Malawi 313
  Mauritius 52, 63
  Morocco 286
  Peru 237
  Spain 178–179
  Vietnam 127–128
Townsend, Augusto 253–254
townships (slums) 71–72, 291
trade
  Africa 318
  Baltic states 147
  China 94
  Mauritius 53

Morocco 285
Singapore 98–99, 103
Vietnam 117, 122–123
trade unions *see* unions
training 107–108, 289–290
  see also education; skills
Transnet 82–83
Transparency International 40, 126–127, 201, 228
transportation costs 63–64, 204
Treaty of Lisbon 167
Treaty of Tartu 142–143
Treblinka extermination camp 159–160
Treisman, Daniel 303
Tremlett, Giles 182
Trends in International Mathematics and Science Study *see* TIMSS
Truman, Harry 316
Trump, Donald 213, 307
Truss, Liz 302
trust 112–113, 197
Tunisia 203, 259
Túpac Amaru II 239
Túpac Amaru Revolutionary Movement *see* MRTA
Turkey 203, 279
Tymoshenko, Yulia 193, 197–198
Tyrmand, Leopold 163

UCR 221
UK National Archives 309–310
Ukraine 191–208
  challenges 198–202, 208
  economic growth 199–200, *199*
  elites 196
  history of 194–195
  independence of 197–198
  investment 200, 208
  leadership 192–195
  oligarchs 198, 201–202
  reforms 195–198, 202–204, 208, 303
  Second World War 135
  Soviet Union and 193–194
  war in 5–6, 14–15, 133, 146, 148, 150, 191–193, 195, 197–198, 204–208
  Zelenskyy, Volodymyr 191–192, 196, 204–206, 304, 307–308
UN 6, 61, 143–144, 177–178, 208, 239, 292–293
UN Development Programme 208
UN Economic Commission for Latin America and the Caribbean 239
unemployment
  Argentina 219, 228
  Egypt 261–262
  Estonia 144–145
  Latvia 139
  Morocco 292
  Singapore 111
  South Africa 67, 75, *75*, 80–81, 89, 139
  Spain 177, 180–182, 186
  see also employment
UNESCO 295
Union of South Africa 77
unions 85, 104–105, 222, 227–228
United Arab Emirates 8, 271
United Democratic Movement 118
United Kingdom National Archives 309–310
United Nations *see* UN
United States *see* US
unity of purpose 102
Universal Child Allowance 228
University of Fort Hare 79–80
uranium processing plant 151–152
urban areas 90, 137, 221
urbanisation 239–240, 291
Uruguay 212
US
  Agency for International Development 316–317
  Geological Survey 245
  Iraq 278–280
  Israel 272
  Lesotho 53–54
  Marshall Plan 177, 316–317
  Mexico 213–215
  Morocco 287
  Peru 245
  ports 287
  Securities and Exchange Commission 78
  Singapore 103
  South Africa 78
  Spain 175, 178–179
  Ukraine 204
  Vietnam 15–16, 95, 117, 120, 123–124, 130

Vaalspan, South Africa 72
Valle de los Caídos 172, 189
vandalism 81–83
Van Oordt, Guillermo 249
Vargas, Getúlio 211
Vargas Llosa, Mario 236, 238, 241, 243, 251, 255
vehicle industry *see* motor industry
Velarde, Julio 252–253
Velasco Ibarra, José María 211
Velasco, Juan 239–240, 249
Venezuela 211, 227, 238
venture capital investment 271–272
Verne, Jules 99
Vietnam
  ANC and 117–120
  authoritarianism 21
  challenges 125–127

372

diamond industry 45
economic growth 115–116, 122–123, 127–128
foreign interference 15–16, 94–96
history of 115–117
IDZs 123–125
investment 117, 119, 122–126
leadership 129–130
poverty 116, 128
reforms 119–120, 122–123
success of 303
Vietnam War 15–16, 116–117, 123–124, 127–129, 308–309
Vo Nguyen Giap 117, 120–122, 128–129
wages 322
Vietnam National University 126
Vietnam Singapore Industrial Park *see* VSIP
Villiers, Gerald 176
Vilnius, Lithuania 133, 138
violence 26–27, 32–33, 37, 54, 76, 276–278, 280
violin, playing the 22, 181
visas 64–65
vision 17
Vision 2036 43
Vizcarra, Martín 252
Vo Hong Nam 120, 128
Vo Nguyen Giap 117, 120–122, 128–129
voucher privatisation 144, 147, 165
VSIP 123–125
Vu Dang Toan 115
Vyapoory, Barlen 57

wages 19, 53, 166, 250, 322
Wagner Group 34
Wałęsa, Lech 14, 155–156, 164–165, 169–170
Waluś, Janusz 167

War Remnants Museum 117
Warsaw Ghetto Uprising 159
Warsaw Institute of Aviation 161
Warsaw Pact 160
Warsaw, Poland 160–162
Warsaw Uprising 157, 159
Washington Consensus programmes 187
Washington, George 309
waste *see* garbage
water supply services 85–86, 89
wealth 58, 70, 157
welfare payments 11, 72–74, 73, 89, 218, 234, 264
Welles, Orson 284, 296
Western Cape, South Africa 81, 89
Western leaders 5, 140–141, 193
Western Munira, Egypt 262
Western Sahara 292–294
Western Sahara War 293
Westminster system 111
Westmoreland, William 118
wheat 202–203, 221
Whitehead, Laurence 149
whoonga 72
Wild Geese, The (film) 59
Wilson, Woodrow 195
Winde, Alan 89
Wine, Bobi 86
Wingate, Orde 305
winners, picking of 272, 302
Winsemius, Albert 97, 107
Wodehouse, P.G. 157
women 25–26, 273
Workers' Defence Committee 168
Workers' Party of Marxist Unification *see* POUM
World Bank
Argentina 225
Doing Business index (2007) 93

Ease of Doing Business index (2018) 51
Egypt 262
Iraq 280
Malawi 22, 312
port performance index 31, 64, 84, 104, 250, 286
South Africa 87
Spain 178
Ukraine 208
Worldwide Governance Indicators 201
World Economic Forum 40, 201
World Trade Organization *see* WTO
World War I *see* First World War
World War II *see* Second World War
Worldwide Governance Indicators 201
WTO 34, 125

Xhosa people 68
Xi Jinping 195–196
Xstrata 247

Yakubu, Mahmood 25
Yale Journal of International Law 194
Yamaha 129
Yang Kai Yong 124
Yanukovych, Viktor 191, 196–197, 208
Yates, Douglas 23
Yeltsin, Boris 5–6, 140, 144
Yemen 259–260
Yesufu, Aisha 25
Yiaga Africa 27
ylang-ylang essence 61
youth 24, 26, 127, 180, 235, 261–262, 282, 292
YPF 232–233
Yrigoyen, Hipólito 221
Yushchenko, Viktor 197

INDEX

Zabbaleen 269–270
Zakharenko, Yury 171
Zambia 7–9, 35, 46, 298, 303–304, 310
Zanzibar 63, 65
Zaporozhet cars 198–199

ZAZ 198–199
Zelenskyy, Volodymyr Oleksandrovych 191–192, 196, 204–206, 304, 307–308
Žeruolis, Darius 149
Zimbabwe 12, 35, 75–76

see also Rhodesian Bush War
zinc 245
Zondo Commission 11, 83
Zuma, Jacob 11, 87, 298
Zweig, Stefan 177
Zygalski, Henryk 161